LINES THAT DIVIDE

LINES THAT

DIVIDE

HISTORICAL ARCHAEOLOGIES
OF RACE, CLASS, AND GENDER

Edited by James A. Delle,
Stephen A. Mrozowski, and Robert Paynter

THE UNIVERSITY OF TENNESSEE PRESS / KNOXVILLE

The paper used in this book meets the minimum requirements of ANSI/NISO Z39.48-1992 (R 1997) (Permanence of Paper). The binding materials have been chosen for strength and durability. Printed on recycled paper.

Library of Congress Cataloging-in-Publication Data

Lines that divide : historical archaeologies of race, class, and gender / edited by James A. Delle, Stephen A. Mrozowski, and Robert Paynter. — 1st ed.

       p. cm.

Includes bibliographical references and index.

ISBN 1-57233-086-4 (cloth: alk. paper)

1. Social archaeology. 2. Archaeology and history. 3. Racism—History. 4. Social classes—History. 5. Sex role—History. 6. Eurocentrism—History. I. Delle, James A.

II. Mrozowski, Stephen A.

III. Paynter, Robert.

IV. Title.

CC72.4 .L56 2000

 907'.2—dc21   99-050986

CONTENTS

Part II.
Lines Defining Gender: The Material Worlds of Men and Women

Part III.
Lines Defining Class: Archaeologies of Ownership and Production

ILLUSTRATIONS

·FIGURES

MAPS

TABLES

INTRODUCTION

Stephen A. Mrozowski,
James A. Delle, & Robert Paynter

Over the past decade historical archaeology, like many of the social sciences, has felt the impact of postmodernism. The intellectual popularity of post-structuralism and deconstructionism, coupled with a growing disquiet with scientific positivism, has shaken the philosophical foundations of historical archaeology to the core. The beginnings of this dilemma were evident in the presentations made at the 1987 plenary session of the Society for Historical Archaeology in Savannah (Honerkamp 1988). Marking the twentieth anniversary of the society's founding, the plenary sought to take the pulse of the field at a time when the session's organizer, Nick Honerkamp, suggested it had entered a phase of normal science. His goal was to jump-start the discipline out of its complacency with the field's accepted epistemologies. These coalesced around four general paradigms: historical archaeology as a supplement to American history, a scientific positivism engaged with pattern recognition and explanation, a structuralist method for interpreting culture, and a vaguely populist concern with the general theme of the American experience. The overwhelming sense of inadequacy expressed by many of the session's participants confirmed Honerkamp's suspicions concerning these paradigms. More importantly, the session presaged a dissatisfaction among other archaeologists that resulted in their calling for a shift from scientific to more contextual epistemologies (for example, Hodder 1986; Shanks and Tilley 1987a, 1987b).

More than a decade removed from the 1987 plenary the field continues to feel the pains of disciplinary growth. Some practitioners in the early 21st century continue to adhere rather closely to one of the four research agendas discussed in 1987 and would probably disagree with our sense that these research strategies have run out their string. In part, this is because aspects of these paradigms fit well with the needs of cultural resource management reflecting the omnipresent division of labor within the discipline between CRM and the academy (see Patterson 1999). Indeed, and from a self-critical position, the restlessness with paradigms represented in this collection undoubtedly stems in part from the imperatives of career development within the academy.

Some of the pressures for paradigm change come from neighboring disciplines. For example, history has increasingly turned to anthropology for theoretical inspiration (for example, Isaac 1982; Hunt 1989; Kirch 1992; Revel 1995; Morgan 1998). Anthropology has itself experienced a period of self-examination that has revolved around an unease with the positivist program of social science. In its place, a number of authors have advocated a return to history (for example, Sahlins 1981, 1985, 1992; Comaroff and Comaroff 1991, 1997; Schneider 1995, Schneider and Rapp 1995). This concern for history has been joined with a continuing struggle to link global processes with practices at the local scale (for example, Wolf 1982; Marcus and Fisher 1986; Harvey 1996). The final and perhaps most important development in the social sciences as a whole has been the growing number of theoretical and empirical studies that focus on the role of race, class, and gender in structuring social practices and ideologies.

The chapters in this volume reflect these streams of change. Although we advance no singular research agenda, the authors in this volume accept as a given the importance of history to shaping cultural consciousness. Each recognizes the need to situate local experiences in contexts that illuminate global connections as well as the emergence of the central lines that divide the social formations of the modern and historical world: race, class, and gender. These papers confront, some explicitly, others implicitly, the abstract qualities of race, class, and gender as analytical constructs by examining particular histories and their material manifestations. In the process their aim is to recast one or more of these abstractions into the realities that shaped lives in the past and continue to influence our work in the present. A second, equally important goal is to advance the position that race, class, and gender are intertwined and inseparable. In order to situate the volume, this introduction will examine issues of history and global process, how the chapters confront the evidentiary quality of material culture, and how together they provide an essential commentary on race, class, and gender.

MATERIALITY, EVIDENCE, AND CONTEXT

Archaeology's place in the social sciences is defined by the discipline's focus on the relationship of material culture to other realms of human existence. One of the most important developments in archaeological method and theory has in fact been the investigation of the relationship between material culture and the social and ideological domains of culture. In 1962 Binford offered a critique of the then prevailing pessimism about archaeology's ability to read the past from objects. This pessimistic approach suggested that material culture worked best as evidence of energy-processing relations, such as subsistence, but less so as one climbed the ladder of inference through social relations toward ideology (for example, Hawkes 1954). Binford instead argued that artifacts functioned on a variety of levels, as technological aids, social instruments, and ideological symbols. To Binford (1962) archaeology suffered from a lack of theory rather than any deficiency in the evidence.

One of the success stories of the paradigmatic changes that took place after the appearance of Binford's 1962 article has been the ability of some archaeologists to link stylistic attributes of artifacts to various forms of social relations based on kin (Deetz 1965; Hill 1970; Longacre 1970; Tilley 1984), ethnicity (for example, Wobst 1977; Plog 1980), gender (Hodder 1984; Conkey and Spector 1984; Gero and Conkey 1991; Seifert 1991), and the state (Wright and Johnson 1975; Wright 1977; Renfrew and Cherry 1986; Patterson and Gailey 1987)—in sum demonstrating the relationship between the material and the social. With the growth of post-processual archaeologies, symbolic and ideological relations have received increasing attention in areas such as Paleolithic art (Conkey 1989) and state ideologies (Kus 1983, 1986; Conrad and Demarest 1984; Leone 1995). While processual and post-processual approaches may differ in their definitions of the appropriate metaphor for understanding the past, both agree that the central focus of archaeological practice is linking the material to the social.

Historical archaeology has emerged as a significant voice in such discussions especially those surrounding the importance of the material domain to the construction of social relations. Examples include examinations of exchange relations (Adams 1977; Schuyler 1980; Miller 1991), artifact patterning (South 1977), architectural style (Glassie 1975; Deetz 1977; Johnson 1993), status (Spencer-Wood 1987), senses of self (Shackel 1993; Leone 1995), class (Beaudry 1989; McGuire 1991; Wurst 1991), race (Singleton 1988, 1995; Orser 1990; Ferguson 1992; Hall 1992; Schrire 1995), and gender (Mrozowski 1984, 1988; Spencer-Wood 1987, 1996; Seifert 1991; Little 1994; Scott 1994). While earlier engagements with structuralism (Glassie 1975; Deetz 1977) and systematics (South 1977) have continued (see Yentsch 1991, 1994; Johnson 1993; Seifert 1991), an increasing number of scholars have begun to recognize and accept that historical archaeology, more than any other field of archaeological inquiry, is concerned with the construction of knowledge about ourselves, our social and historical contexts, and the material shape and direction of our world. As such, whether or not consensus is reached on defining the goals of historical archaeology, the field is concerned with understanding how capitalism has emerged and remains the driving force behind colonization and the growth of the modern world (for example, Delle 1998, Leone 1982, 1988, 1995; Shackel 1993, 1996; Beaudry 1989; McGuire 1991; Orser 1990, 1996). As a field concerned with understanding the material dimensions of capitalism, historical archaeology must examine how material culture relates to the social categories constructed within the capitalist system, particularly race, class, and gender.

The essays in this volume analyze the material construction of these capitalist social relations. Each of the authors accepts that capitalism is a dominating force in shaping cultural consciousness and practice; however, it is not our goal to advocate any singular view of capitalism or how it should be analyzed, but rather to explore its manifestations in a variety of cultural and temporal contexts. In so doing we hope to avoid the pitfalls of examining issues such as white supremacy or the exploitation of labor through the wage system in the abstract, choosing instead case studies that allow the reader to witness their impact in concrete form.

RACE, CLASS, AND GENDER AND THE ARCHAEOLOGY OF CAPITALISM

Any consideration of class, race, or gender in colonial and postcolonial societies must begin with the forces of capitalism, a political economy dominated by individuals skilled in the practice of accumulating capital. These capitalists came to eclipse the tributary or kin relations that governed exchange in most premodern economies (Wolf 1982, 73–100). In their place, new social relations developed between those whose wealth provided the means to control entire sectors of an economy and those whose labor or skill was their chief commodity. Played out on a global arena over centuries, studies of the origins and transformation of capitalism have been central points of debate in European historiography for close to a century (for example,

Pirenne 1925, 1936; Bloch 1939; Dobb 1946; Slicher van Bath 1963; Braudel 1981, 1984; Wallerstein 1974a, 1980; Weber 1970; Revel 1995). The view supported by many European historians since Pirenne (1925, 1936) has been that the unbridled cupidity of the merchant class, their fixation on accumulation, and their activities in money lending beginning in the twelfth century have all the essential earmarks of capitalism. This period of economic expansion also gave rise to what many conceive as the spirit of capitalism, a characteristic that Weber (1970) attributed to the Protestant Reformation and the work ethic it engendered (see also MacFarlane 1987, 135). Braudel (1984, 57) has championed this position as well. He states quite clearly that "I am therefore in agreement with Marx who wrote (though he later went back on this) that European capitalism—indeed he even says capitalist production—began in thirteenth-century Italy" (Braudel 1984, 57).[1]

For Immanuel Wallerstein (1974b) and earlier Maurice Dobb (1946) it is the sixteenth century and the emergence of a world economy (to use Wallerstein's term) that signals the debut of capitalism. For Wallerstein capitalist relations began to assert their dominance in the early sixteenth century, when plantations using slave labor were established at the same time that European military technology was providing the tools to plunder the New World of its treasures and raw materials (Wallerstein 1974a). Combined with the growth of commercial agriculture in northwest Europe and a burgeoning class of merchants realizing fortunes through an expanding world market, the essential elements were in place for capitalism's meteoric rise to global dominance (Wallerstein 1974a, 1974b, 67–129). Several labels have been attached to this period of economic change, *mercantile capitalism* and *agricultural capitalism* being the two most widely used.

Wolf raises some important questions concerning how we should define capitalism. Evoking Marx, Wolf argues that "the capitalist mode of production came into being when monetary wealth was enabled to buy labor power" (1982, 77). He further clarifies this view by stating the following:

> *Wealth in the hands of holders of wealth is not capital until it controls means of production, buys labor power, and puts it to work, continuously expanding surpluses by intensifying productivity through an ever-rising curve of technological inputs. To this end capitalism must lay hold of production, must invade the productive process and ceaselessly alter the conditions of production themselves .... Only where wealth has laid hold of the conditions of production in the ways specified can*

we speak of the existence or dominance of a capitalist mode. There is
no such thing as mercantile or merchant capitalism, therefore. There
is only mercantile wealth. Capitalism, to be capitalism, must be capi-
talism-in-production. *(emphasis added, 78–79)*

Historical archaeologists would appear to be well positioned to examine, if not answer, some of the central questions concerning the history and
growth of capitalism. Why then have their efforts been so limited until recently? Part of the reason may be in the lack of a historiographic tradition in
the United States that focuses on capitalism; historians in the United States
have only recently turned their attention to issues dealing explicitly with capitalist social relations (for example, Clark 1990; Kulikoff 1992). This may explain why early efforts in historical archaeology focused on cultural issues
pertaining to the growth of Anglo-American society (for example, Noël Hume
1963, 1969; Deetz 1977). Even now, historical archaeology has contributed little
to the debate concerning the emergence of capitalism in the New World.
Orser (1996, 76–81) is one of the few to explicitly focus on the transition from
a noncapitalist to a capitalist world and in the process argue that historical
archaeology has a unique perspective on the issue.

An archaeology of capitalism offers historical archaeology two major
analytical advantages over that provided by either structural or systemic approaches. The first concerns capitalism as context. The history of capitalism
has been punctuated by periods when social, economic, and political forces
have converged to create crisis. These crises result in cyclical waves of prosperity and depression during which social boundaries become more rigid, a
process often manifest in material distinctions. In a world of tense colonial
competition on a global scale, the periods of capitalist expansion and contraction provide some basis for examining changing social relations over time
(see Paynter 1988). The Long Sixteenth Century, for example, a period of
economic growth that lasted from the late fifteenth to the early seventeenth
century, was followed by an equally long period of prolonged crisis. This
period of depression and conflict, known as the Long Seventeenth Century,
was felt in Europe, the Western Hemisphere, and southeast Asia. It was the
beginning of the industrial revolution that kindled an unprecedented growth
in productive capacity that fueled a new cycle of capitalist expansion that
lasted until the later stages of the twentieth century.

This kind of periodicity can be used to frame or reframe explanations
put forward by historical archaeologists. It can also place the colonization

of the New World, Africa, and Asia in a broad global perspective. Leone (1982, 1988) has, for example, provided an alternative explanation for the spread of Glassie's (1975) and Deetz's (1977) Georgian order by suggesting it was a reaction to just such a crisis. He argues that between 1730 and 1765 Maryland's social elite adopted landscapes and material culture that reinforced their belief in natural law. Feeling the sting of alienation from both the working classes in the Chesapeake and what they perceived as their social brethren in England, they sought to convince people that a rational social order based on nature was possible and that those with such access to its laws were its natural leaders (Leone 1988, 250).

Examining the discursive use of material culture to mediate social tensions is but one example of the manner in which historical archaeology can contribute to a greater understanding of capitalism's changing face. Another is to explore the meaning of constructs like race, class, and gender in concrete contexts that involved real actors in politically charged social arenas like prerevolutionary colonial America. The essays in our volume attempt to move beyond the reification of constructs like race, class, and gender in an attempt to understand them as forces in the lives of those in the past. In doing so they seek to explore race, class, and gender building on new ideas being developed in the social sciences as a whole. Over the past decade the importance of race, class, and gender have occupied many in the social sciences. From a review of this work it soon becomes apparent that the precise meaning of each concept is open to interpretation, a discourse that can help frame the essays presented in this volume.

Class

E. P. Thompson's use of the word "making" in his famous *The Making of the English Working Class* (1963) attracted attention to the creative process involved in people's construction of their own identity. Members of the English working class came to view themselves as such through the ideological struggles that punctuated the transition to industrial capitalism during the late eighteenth to mid-nineteenth century. The rhetoric that characterized these struggles was central to the dialectic that shaped the formation of class lines in Britain (Thompson 1963, 55–76, 350–400). One of the lessons of Thompson's treatise is the fluid nature of class, its changing face and repeated recasting as part of the greater dialectic of social relations. It is a lesson that historical archaeology is just now learning (see for example the articles in Wurst and Fitts 1999).

As historical archaeologists began intensifying their efforts to understand the changing character of capitalism, notions of class served as the baseline for material comparisons. Leone (1982, 1984) was one of the first to expressly examine class relations and, more importantly, the issue of ideology (also see Paynter 1988). Using the dominant ideology thesis of Althusser (1971), Leone (1984) characterized social discourse in eighteenth-century Maryland from the perspective of the elite. Leone's study prompted several important questions concerning the need for archaeologists to recognize the existence of multiple materialities and multiple meanings (see Hodder 1986, 66–67; Beaudry et al. 1991, 156–67; Hall 1992, 382; Leone 1994, 223). Beaudry et al. (1991) explored the issue of multivocality in their study of Lowell mill workers. The interpretive approach they employed sought to give voice to the workers and their attempts to construct their own cultural identities. Orser (1996, 160–82) went on to criticize both the "inside-out" approach of Beaudry et al. (1991) as well as the "top-down" perspective employed by Leone (1984) in calling for a more dialectical approach that gives voice to all those involved in the discourse.

If historical archaeologists are to contribute to the intellectual discourse concerning the meaning of class, then we must emphasize our strength, the study of the material world in all its complexity. This is particularly true given the dialectical relationship that links the growth of class consciousness with the production of its material trappings. If we accept that class can seem contradictory (see Wright 1993, 29), this merely reinforces our understanding of its multivocality and the multifaceted character of its material expression. Architecture, dress, table settings, food, and landscapes all served as vehicles for class identity in the broader social arena. Indeed it is the rich texture of this material domain that affords us the opportunity to explore the labyrinth of class formation and its nexus with other social divides like race and gender. Developing a new appreciation for the convergence of class, race, and gender in configuring the colonial and postcolonial worlds is one of the central concerns of this volume.

Gender

The archaeological exploration of gender involves several theoretical and methodological questions. It is not enough to acknowledge gender as a fundamental social construct; archaeologists must also identify its material signature and understand its widespread variability over space and time (Gero and Conkey 1991). These methodological issues notwithstanding, there have been several advancements in the development of gender-related research in the social sciences. The first is the recognition that sex, gender and sexuality connote different things. As a result biological reproduction (sex), social production and reproduction along sexual lines (gender), and carnal relations between individuals (sexuality) are no longer viewed as biologically determined (Bleier 1984; Moore 1988; Ferguson 1989; Kryder-Reid 1994; Scott 1994). In its place is a much broader, more nuanced conceptualization of sex, gender, and sexuality that moves beyond the dichotomous view long so paramount in Western ideology (Moore 1988; Morgen 1989; Walby 1990; Wylie 1991; Wall 1994, this volume).

Another of the more interesting developments in gender-related research has been the growing examination of patriarchy as a social force. Born of the same cultural traditions that bred racism and a disdain for the working class, this patriarchy encompassed both the ideology and practices that saw men "dominate, oppress and exploit women" (Walby 1990, 20). Within a colonial context it helped justify the enslavement of Africans and Native Americans. In later form it set the tenor for the social relations of industrial production. One of its most central features is a belief in male superiority that was part of a larger perception that saw male/female–culture/nature dichotomies as the product of natural law. In the fullness of daily discourse this divide was omnipresent but not omnipotent in its influence. Indeed one of the most distinctive characteristics of the modern period was the collision of European notions of class and gender with the issue of race that erupted as a product of colonialism (see McClintock 1995). Another feature was a class-influenced notion of separate spheres in which women were to be the arbiters of the domestic domain while men were to deal with the political and economic dimensions of public life (Cott 1977; Mies 1986; Amott and Matthaei 1991; Kowaleski-Wallace 1997).

These notions of male superiority and separate spheres were also mainstays of much that has been written concerning gender and colonialism. More recently, however, these rather static perceptions of gender have been replaced by a new appreciation for the manner in which race, class, and gender are intertwined (J. Scott 1988; E. Scott 1994; McClintock 1995; Kowaleski-Wallace 1997). One of the goals of this new literature has been to broaden the notion of gender beyond that of merely women. This is the chief reason why notions of separate spheres has been rejected, because it perpetuates the idea of women living in isolation (see Scott 1988, 32). A second and perhaps larger goal has been to understand the very different experiences that colonial women (white women) had from the women of color who were being colonized. This acknowledgment has come in large measure as a response to women of color who have criticized white feminists and their notions of gender and inequality (hooks 1982; Amos and Parmer 1984; Mohanty 1988). It has also emerged as the product of studies conducted by anthropologists and historians who have examined colonization and its impact on the postcolonial world (for example, Callaway 1987; Comaroff 1997; Comaroff and Comaroff 1991, 1997; McClintock 1995). In *Imperial Leather* Anne McClintock provides a powerful examination of race, class, and sexuality during the nineteenth century (1995). She argues that "imperialism cannot be fully understood without a theory of gender power. Gender power was not a superficial patina of empire, an ephemeral gloss over the more decisive mechanics of class or race. Rather gender dynamics were, from the outset, fundamental to the securing and maintenance of the imperial enterprise" (1995, 7). McClintock does not, however, argue for the dominance of gender over class or race as the central force in imperialism. Instead she echoes the writing of other scholars who have advocated the view we advance in this book: race, class, and gender are intertwined realities that helped shape the modern world.

One way of highlighting this interconnectedness is to examine gender dynamics in a wide array of contexts that include looking as much at questions surrounding whiteness as those relating to women of color. Although this presents methodological challenges, it nevertheless points the way for a new direction in archaeological research. For example, it means examining women and men of various classes and races simultaneously and not in isolation. It also means reexamining our epistemological assumptions concerning processes such as colonization. Different histories, different geographies, and different cultures have resulted in a mosaiclike colonial landscape that requires a more nuanced reconsideration. The same is true for the various forms of capitalist production. As we noted at the outset, any consideration of race, class, and gender must begin with an understanding that capitalism and colonialism were not monolithic structures. The men and women who participated in the events of the past five hundred years were actors in an ever-changing drama that saw their identities forged through interactions with others. Race, class, and gender were three of the divides that intersected to shape those identities.

Stephen A. Mrozowski, James A. Delle, and Robert Paynter

❖   xx   ❖

Race

The concept of race is a particularly sensitive subject in any anthropological consideration. This is due in large measure to the concept's historical relationship to both anthropology and New World colonization. Indeed it is virtually impossible to separate the concept of race, the global expansion of European and Euro-American colonialism, and the development of anthropology as a discipline (Baker and Patterson 1994; Blakey 1994; Gregory and Sanjek 1994; Harrison 1995). Early in its history, the concept of race was viewed as a biological reality. This was particularly true of physical anthropology and its treatment of non-Europeans. In studies too numerous to mention, the physical characteristics of racial differences were subjected to rigorous measurement and dissection (Gregory 1994; Sanjek 1994; Harrison 1995). Today, anthropologists and historians view race as an ideological and political outgrowth of the post-Columbian world. From this perspective it reflects a broader ideology of racism that is part of the dialectic of colonization and white supremacy. Regardless of the context, racism was an integral component of the engine of capitalism.

Considerations of race and racism in historical archaeology share a similar dialectic. How do we separate histories that intersect at a variety of levels? How do we, for example, examine the period of Native American/European interaction without reference to concepts like culture contact, acculturation, or prehistory, which share a historical relationship with the political forces that shaped that interaction? The same is true of archaeologies of slavery. How is the African American past to be approached? From the detached perspective of positivist science that has itself been an instrument of racist ideology, or from a dialectical perspective that acknowledges the biases inherent in many of our research agendas? The answers to at least some of these questions rely upon an archaeology of race that has as its goal the exploration of race as a cultural-historical construction.

The legacies of the concept of race and the material and social manifestations of racism have long haunted the theories and practices of historical archaeology. As Ferguson (1992, 3–7), for example, has pointed out, historical archaeology began as a method to refine the collective memory of the Anglo-American past. Racist assumptions about the whiteness of history have deeply influenced the analysis of artifacts; one need only consider that it took nearly a generation for mainstream historical archaeologists to accept that Colono-Indian ware excavated from sites in Virginia could possibly have been made and used by African Americans. In practice, historical archaeologists have, until recently, been primarily concerned with excavating sites associated with whites. There have, of course, been notable exceptions (for example, Ascher and Fairbanks 1971; Baker 1978; Deetz 1977:138–54; Fairbanks 1974; Mullins 1999), but for a great deal of the history of the field, historical archaeologists, largely driven by professional interests and accepted conventions, failed to see the significance of African American or Native American sites to the metahistory of our continent. Some interpret this phenomenon as a further extension of white control not only over the present but also over the construction of the past (see Blakey 1997; Franklin 1997). Happily, in recent years an ever-increasing number of scholars have recognized the significance of sites associated with historically oppressed groups. However, while places like Fort Mosé and the African Burial Ground are now widely accepted as having archaeological "significance," historical archaeologists must continually struggle against historically constructed, racist barriers to our understanding of non-European pasts (McGuire 1992; Franklin 1997; Trigger 1989; see Leone and Potter 1992 for a deconstruction of the concept of *archaeological significance*).

As should be evident by the chapters in this volume, historical archaeologists have begun not only to recognize that the construction of racial identities was part of the wider process of establishing and rationalizing the inequalities inherent in capitalism, but also that our daily action, including the practice of archaeology, is embedded in the very system that created the structures of race and racism. Historical archaeologists confronting the issue of race must recognize the existence of twin phenomena: the racist construction of inequality in the past and the prevalence of racist thinking in the present.

THE CHAPTERS IN THIS VOLUME

Each of the essays in part 1 of this volume address the dynamics of the racial system that emerged from European colonialism. Chapters 1 and 3 address the racial dynamics of the preservation and interpretation of the archaeological record. In chapter 1 Theresa Singleton and Mark Bograd, by reflecting on a recent museum exhibit they curated, argue that certain archaeological methodologies, such as typologizing and correlating specific types of artifacts to specific ethnic groups, in fact contribute more to the artificial definition of ethnic groups than to our understanding of the complex social dynamics that existed between European colonists, enslaved Africans, and indigenous Native Americans. In chapter 3, Bill Fawcett and Walter Lewelling confront the issue of why, in northern Utah, homesteads that belonged to Shoshoni who converted to Mormonism have been destroyed and forgotten, while white Mormon homesteads have been preserved as monuments to the pioneer past. To them, the answer lies in the relationship between both implicitly and explicitly racist interpretations of history and the construction of what is "archaeologically significant" to the construction of the past. This relationship has resulted in a collective amnesia about the material history of Shoshoni who converted to Mormonism in the late nineteenth and early twentieth centuries.

Chapters 2 and 4 address the familiar theme of slavery in the North American Southeast. Paul Shackel and David Larsen explore how the racist practice of African slavery was manifested in the early industrial era in Harpers Ferry, Virginia, while Terry Epperson explores how landscapes were used to reinforce the racial hierarchy that existed on tobacco plantations owned by Thomas Jefferson and George Mason. The concluding chapter of this section, chapter 5 by Warren Perry, explores the archaeology of the color line in colonial southern Africa through a reconsideration of what is known as the Mfecane/Difaqane and its aftermath.

The global order that has emerged in the modern world is based not only on racial hierarchies, but also on institutionalized inequities between members of the two generally recognized genders. The dynamics of gender, as they were experienced in New York City, South America, and the Caribbean, are addressed in part 2 of the volume. In chapter 6 Diana Wall explores the relationships that existed among material culture—especially tablewares—domesticity, and gender negotiation in nineteenth-century New York City. In examining the archaeological records of two houses belonging to one woman, Ross Jamieson explores in chapter 7 the dynamics of elite definitions of gender in colonial Ecuador. In chapter 8, James Delle analyzes historic treatises, vital records, and architectural remains of coffee plantations to discuss how gender was negotiated among enslaved laborers on coffee plantations in nineteenth-century Jamaica.

Each of the essays in part 3 explores the Western world's transition to industrial capitalism, focusing particularly on the dynamics of class analysis. In the same manner that the chapters in parts 1 and 2 help refine notions of race and gender, so too do the essays in this part of the book examine the active role material culture has played in the cultural construction and expression of class differences. As each of the three essays demonstrates, class-consciousness was a powerful force in people's lives that sometimes took subtle form. In other instances, class differences were more overt, often the result of planning or resistance. In chapter 9, Patricia Mangan examines the manner in which the transition to capitalism can be read in the built environment of eighteenth-century Catalonia. Chapter 10 by Michael Nassaney and Marjorie Abel provides a compelling example of how factory workers resisted the strictures of industrial work by routinely discarding mistakes at the Russell Cutlery in western Massachusetts. In chapter 11, Stephen Mrozowski explores the subtle character of class differences in the company-controlled city of Lowell, Massachusetts. As the first planned industrial city in the United States, Lowell provides the perfect medium for comparing the public expressions of class differences embodied in company-supplied housing with the more fluid character of cultural identity readable in various classes of material culture.

This third section is followed by a summary essay by Tom Patterson in which he further contextualizes the case studies presented in this volume. In this essay Patterson once again stresses the importance of constructs like race, gender, and class for a global historical archaeology.

As historical archaeology has matured over the past two decades, the field's practitioners have begun to move from being consumers of social theory to producers. As the essays in this volume demonstrate, historical archaeologists continue to contribute to the theoretical development of archaeology as a whole by helping to enliven and reconfigure notions such as race, gender, and class. In considering that material culture—whether expressed as buildings, portable artifacts, or landscapes—is itself an active agent in the negotiation of social difference, historical archaeologists can contribute both to defining and dismantling the lines that divide.

NOTE

1. Braudel does not provide a citation for his reference to Marx; however, we assume he is referring to Marx's early positions concerning the history of capitalist production outlined in *The German Ideology* with those put forth in *Capital* (see Tucker 1978, 180).

REFERENCES CITED

Adams, William H. 1977. *Silcott, Washington: Ethnoarchaeology of a Rural American Community.* Reports of Investigation 54. Laboratory of Anthropology, Washington State University, Pullman, Wash.

Althusser, Louis. 1971. Ideology and Ideological State Apparatuses. In *Lenin and Philosophy and Other Essays,* ed. L. Althusser, 27–86. New York: Monthly Review Press.

Amos, Valerie, and Pratibha Parmer. 1984. Challenging Imperial Feminism. *Feminist Review* 17 (autumn): 3–19.

Amott, Teresa L., and Julie A. Matthaei. 1991. *Race, Gender, and Work.* Boston: South End Press.

Ascher, Robert, and Charles Fairbanks. 1971. Excavation of a Slave Cabin: Georgia, U.S.A. *Historical Archaeology* 5:3–17.

Baker, Lee D., and Thomas C. Patterson, eds. 1994. Race, Racism, and the History of U.S. Anthropology. *Transforming Anthropology* 5.

Baker, Vernon. 1978. Historical Archaeology at Black Lucy's Garden, Andover, Massachusetts: Ceramics from the Site of a Nineteenth-Century Afro-American. *Papers of the Robert S. Peabody Foundation for Archaeology.* Vol. 8. Andover, Mass.: Philips Academy.

Beaudry, Mary C. 1989. The Lowell Boott Mills Complex and Its Housing: Material Expressions of Corporate Ideology. *Historical Archaeology* 23 (1): 18–32.

Beaudry, Mary C., Laura J. Cook, and Stephen A. Mrozowski. 1991. Artifacts and Active Voices: Material Culture as Social Discourse. In *The Archaeology of Inequality,* ed. Randall H. McGuire and Robert Paynter, 150–91. Oxford: Basil Blackwell.

Beaudry, Mary C., and Stephen A. Mrozowski. 1989. The Archaeology of Work and Home Life in Lowell, Massachusetts: An Interdisciplinary Study of the Boott Cotton Mills Corporation. *IA, the Journal of the Society for Industrial Archaeology* 14 (2): 1–22.

Binford, Lewis. 1962. Archaeology as Anthropology. *American Antiquity* 28:217–25.

Blakey, Michael L. 1994. Passing the Buck: Naturalism and Individualism as Anthropological Expressions of Euro-American Denial. In *Race,* ed. S. Gregory and R. Sanjek, 270–84. New Brunswick, N.J.: Rutgers Univ. Press.

———. 1997. Past Is Present: Comments on "In the Realm of Politics: Prospects for Public Participation in African-American Plantation Archaeology." *Historical Archaeology* 31 (3): 140–45.

Bleier, Ruth. 1984. *Science and Gender: A Critique of Biology and Its Theories on Women.* New York: Pergamon.

Bloch, Marc. 1939. Economie-nature ou economie-argent: Un pseudo-dilemme. *Annals d'histoire sociale* 1:7–16.

Braudel, Fernand. 1981. *Civilization and Capitalism, 15th–18th Century.* Vol. 1, *The Structures of Everyday Life, the Limits of the Possible.* New York: Harper and Row.

———. 1984. *Civilization and Capitalism, 15th–18th Century.* Vol. 3, *The Perspective of the World.* New York: Harper and Row.

Callaway, Helen. 1987. *Gender, Culture, and Empire: European Women in Colonial Nigeria.* New York: Macmillan.

Clark, Christopher. 1990. *The Roots of Rural Capitalism.* Ithaca, N.Y.: Cornell Univ. Press.

Comaroff, Jean. 1997. The Empire's Old Clothes: Fashioning the Colonial Subject. In *Situated*

Lives: Gender and Culture in Everyday Life, ed. Louise Lamphere, Helena Ragon, and Patricia
  Zavella, 400–417. London: Routledge.

Comaroff, Jean, and John. L. Comaroff. 1991. *Of Revelation and Revolution*. Vol. 1, *Christianity,
  Colonialism, and Consciousness in South Africa.* Chicago: Univ. of Chicago Press.

————. 1997. *Of Revelation and Revolution.* Vol. 2, *The Dialectics of Modernity on a South African
  Frontier.* Chicago: Univ. of Chicago Press.

Conkey, Margaret W. 1989. The Structural Analysis of Paleolithic Art. In *Archaeological Thought
  in America*, ed. C. C. Lamberg-Karlovsky, 135–54. Cambridge: Cambridge Univ. Press.

Conkey, Margaret W., and Janet Spector. 1984. Archaeology and the Study of Gender. In *Advances
  in Archaeological Method and Theory* 7, ed. M. Schiffer, 1–38. New York: Academic Press.

Conrad, Geoffrey W., and Arthur A. Demarest. 1984. *Religion and Empire: The Dynamics of Aztec
  and Inca Expansionism.* Cambridge, Eng.: Cambridge Univ. Press.

Cott, Nancy F. 1977. *The Bonds of Womanhood.* New Haven: Yale Univ. Press.

Deetz, James. 1965. *The Dynamics of Stylistic Change in Arikara Ceramics.* Illinois Studies in Anthropology No. 4. Urbana: Univ. of Illinois Press.

————. 1977. In *Small Things Forgotten.* New York: Anchor Press.

Delle, James A. 1998. *An Archaeology of Social Space: Analyzing Coffee Plantations in Jamaica's
  Blue Mountains.* New York: Plenum.

Dobb, Maurice. 1946. *Studies in the Development of Capitalism.* London: Routledge and Kegan.

Fairbanks, Charles. 1974. The Kingsley Slave Cabins in Duval County, Florida, 1968. *Conference
  on Historic Site Archaeology Papers* 7:62–93.

Ferguson, Ann. 1989. *Blood at the Root: Motherhood, Sexuality, and Male Dominance.* London:
  Pandora.

Ferguson, Leland. 1992. *Uncommon Ground.* Washington, D.C.: Smithsonian Institution Press.

Franklin, Maria. 1997. "Power to the People": Sociopolitics and the Archaeology of Black Americans. *Historical Archaeology* 31 (3): 36–50.

Gero, Joan M., and Margaret W. Conkey. 1991. *Engendering Archaeology: Women and Prehistory.*
  Oxford: Basil Blackwell.

Glassie, Henry. 1975. *Folk Housing in Middle Virginia: A Structural Analysis of Historic Artifacts.*
  Knoxville: Univ. of Tennessee Press.

Gregory, Steven. 1994. We've Been Down This Road Already. In *Race*, ed. S. Gregory and R. Sanjek,
  18–58. New Brunswick, N.J.: Rutgers Univ. Press.

Gregory, Steven, and Roger Sanjek, eds. 1994. *Race.* New Brunswick, N.J.: Rutgers Univ. Press.

Hall, Martin. 1992. Small Things and the Mobile, Conflictual Fusion of Power, Fear, and Desire.
  In *The Art and Mystery of Historical Archaeology*, ed. A. E. Yentsch and M. C. Beaudry, 373–
  99. Boca Raton, Fla.: CRC Press.

Harrison, Fay V. 1995. The Persistent Power of "Race" in the Cultural and Political Economy of
  Racism. *Annual Review of Anthropology* 24:47–74.

Harvey, David. 1996. *Justice, Nature, and the Geography of Difference.* Malden, Mass.: Blackwell Publishers.

Hawkes, Christopher. 1954. Archaeological Theory and Method: Some Suggestions from the Old World. *American Anthropologist* 56:155–68.

Hill, James. 1970. *Broken K Pueblo: Prehistoric Social Organization in the American Southwest.* Anthropological Papers of the University of Arizona, No. 18. Tucson: Univ. of Arizona Press.

Hodder, Ian. 1984. Burial, Houses, Women, and Men in the European Neolithic. In *Ideology, Power, and Prehistory,* ed. D. Miller and C. Tilley, 51–68. Cambridge: Cambridge Univ. Press.

Hodder, Ian. 1986. *Reading the Past: Current Approaches to Interpretation in Archaeology.* New York: Cambridge Univ. Press.

Honerkamp, Nicholas. 1988. Questions That Count in Historical Archaeology. *Historical Archaeology* 22 (1): 5–6.

hooks, bell. 1982. *Ain't I a Woman? Black Women and Feminism.* London: Pluto Press.

Hunt, Lynn. 1989. Introduction: History, Culture, and Text. In *The New Cultural History,* ed. Lynn Hunt, 1–22. Berkeley: Univ. of California Press.

Isaac, Reis. 1982. *The Transformation of Virginia, 1740–1790.* Chapel Hill: Univ. of North Carolina Press.

Johnson, Matthew. 1993. *Housing Culture: Traditional Architecture in an English Landscape.* Washington, D.C.: Smithsonian Institution Press.

Kirch, Patrick V. 1992. *Anahulu: The Anthropology of History in the Kingdom of Hawaii.* Vol. 2, *The Archaeology of History.* Chicago: Univ. of Chicago.

Kowaleski-Wallace, Elizabeth. 1997. *Consuming Subjects: Women, Shopping, and Business in the Eighteenth Century.* New York: Columbia Univ. Press.

Kryder-Reid, Elizabeth. 1994. "With Manly Courage": Reading the Construction of Gender in a Nineteenth-Century Religious Community. In *Those of Little Note,* ed. E. M. Scott, 97–114. Tucson: Univ. of Arizona Press.

Kulikoff, Alan. 1992. *The Agrarian Origins of American Capitalism.* Charlottesville: Univ. Press of Virginia.

Kus, Susan. 1983. The Social Representation of Space. In *Archaeological Hammers and Theories,* ed. J. A. Moore and A. S. Keene, 277–98. New York: Academic Press.

———. 1986. Sensuous Human Activity and the State. In *Comparative Studies in the Development of Complex Societies,* ed. W. A. Congress. London: Allen and Unwin.

Leone, Mark P. 1982. Some Opinions about Recovering Mind. *American Antiquity* 47:742–60.

———. 1984. Interpreting Ideology in Historical Archeology: The William Paca Garden in Annapolis, Maryland. In *Ideology, Power, and Prehistory,* ed. Daniel Miller and Christopher Tilley, 25–35. Cambridge: Cambridge Univ. Press.

———. 1988. The Georgian Order as the Order of Merchant Capitalism in Annapolis, Maryland.

In *The Recovery of Meaning: Historical Archaeology in the Eastern United States,* ed. Mark P. Leone and Parker B. Potter Jr., 235–61. Washington, D.C.: Smithsonian Institution Press.

————. 1994. The Archaeology of Ideology: Archaeological Work in Annapolis since 1981. In *Historical Archaeology of the Chesapeake,* ed. Paul A. Shackel and Barbara J. Little, 215–29. Washington, D.C.: Smithsonian Institution Press.

————. 1995. A Historical Archaeology of Capitalism. *American Anthropologist* 97 (2): 251–68.

Leone, Mark P., and Parker B. Potter Jr. 1992. Legitimation and the Classification of Archaeological Sites. *American Antiquity* 57 (1): 137–45.

Little, Barbara. 1994. People with History: An Update on Historical Archaeology in the United States. *Journal of Archaeological Method and Theory* 1 (1): 5–40.

Longacre, William. 1970. *Archaeology as Anthropology: A Case Study.* Anthropological Papers of the University of Arizona, No. 17. Tucson: Univ. of Arizona Press.

MacFarlane, Alan. 1987. *The Culture of Capitalism.* Oxford: Basil Blackwell.

Marcus, George E., and Michael M. J. Fischer. 1986. *Anthropology as Cultural Critique.* Chicago: Univ. of Chicago Press.

McClintock, Anne. 1995. *Imperial Leather: Race, Gender, and Sexuality in the Colonial Contest.* London: Routledge.

McGuire, Randall H. 1991. Building Power in the Cultural Landscape of Broome County, New York, 1880 to 1940. In *The Archaeology of Inequality,* ed. Randall H. McGuire and Robert Paynter, 102–24. Oxford: Basil Blackwell.

————. 1992. Archaeology and the First Americans. *American Anthropologist* 94 (4): 816–36.

Mies, Maria. 1986. *Patriarchy and Accumulation on a World Scale: Women in the International Division of Labour.* London: Zed.

Miller, George L. 1991. A Revised Set of CC Index Values for Classification and Economic Scaling of English Ceramics from 1787 to 1880. *Historical Archaeology* 25 (1): 1–25.

Mohanty, Chandra T. 1988. Under Western Eyes: Feminist Scholarship and Colonial Discourse. *Feminist Review* 30 (autumn): 61–88.

Moore, Henrietta L. 1988. *Feminism and Anthropology.* Minneapolis: Univ. of Minnesota Press.

Morgan, Philip D. 1998. *Slave Counterpoint: Black Culture in the Eighteenth-Century Chesapeake and Low Country.* Chapel Hill: Univ. of North Carolina Press.

Morgen, Sandra, ed. 1989. *Gender and Anthropology: Critical Reviews for Research and Teaching.* Washington, D.C.: American Anthropological Association.

Mrozowski, Stephen A. 1984. Prospects and Perspectives on an Archaeology of the Household. *Man in the Northeast* 27:31–49.

————. 1988. For Gentlemen of Capacity and Leisure: The Archaeology of Colonial Newspapers. In *Documentary Archaeology in the New World,* ed. M. C. Beaudry, 184–91. New York: Cambridge Univ. Press.

Mullins, Paul R., 1999. *Race and Affluence: An Archaeology of African America and Consumer Culture*. New York: Kluwer/Plenum.

Noël Hume, Ivor. 1963. *Here Lies Virginia*. New York: Alfred Knopf.

———. 1969. *Historical Archaeology*. New York: Alfred Knopf.

Orser, Charles E., Jr. 1990. Historical Archaeology on Southern Plantations and Farms: Introduction. *Historical Archaeology* 24 (4): 1–6.

———. 1996. *A Historical Archaeology of the Modern World*. New York: Plenum.

Patterson, Thomas C. 1999. The Political Economy of Archaeology in the United States. *Annual Review of Anthropology* 26: 155–74.

Patterson, Thomas C., and Christine W. Gailey, eds. 1987. *Power Relations and State Formation*. Salem, Wis.: Sheffield.

Paynter, Robert. 1985. Surplus Flow between Frontiers and Homelands. In *The Archaeology of Frontiers and Boundaries*, ed. S. W. Green and S. Perlman, 163–211. Orlando: Academic Press.

———. 1988. Steps to an Archaeology of Capitalism. In *The Recovery of Meaning: Historical Archaeology of the Eastern United States*, ed. M. P. Leone and Parker B. Potter Jr., 407–33. Washington, D.C.: Smithsonian Institution Press.

Pirenne, Henri. [1925] 1974. *Medieval Cities, Their Origins, and the Revival of Trade*. Princeton: Princeton Univ. Press.

———. 1936. *Economic and Social History of Medieval Europe*. New York: Macmillan.

Plog, Stephen. 1980. *Stylistic Variation in Prehistoric Ceramics*. Cambridge: Cambridge Univ. Press.

Renfrew, A. Colin, and James Cherry, eds. 1986. *Peer Polity Interaction and Socio-Political Change*. Cambridge: Cambridge Univ. Press.

Revel, Jacques. 1995. Microanalysis and the Construction of the Social. In *Histories: French Constructions of the Past, Postwar French Thought*, ed. Jacques Revel and Lynn Hunt, 1:492–502. New York: New Press.

Sahlins, Marshall. 1981. *Historical Metaphors and Mythical Realties: Structure in the Early History of the Sandwich Islands Kingdom*. Association for the Study of Anthropology in Oceania, Special Publication No. 1. Ann Arbor: Univ. of Michigan Press.

———. 1985. *Islands of History*. Chicago: Univ. of Chicago Press.

———. 1992. *Anahulu: The Anthropology of History in the Kingdom of Hawaii*. Vol. 1, Historical Ethnography. Chicago: Univ. of Chicago Press.

Sanjek, Roger. 1994. The Enduring Inequalities of Race. In *Race*, ed. S. Gregory and R. Sanjek, 1–17. New Brunswick, N.J.: Rutgers Univ. Press.

Schneider, Jane, and Rayna Rapp, eds. 1995. *Articulating Hidden Histories: Exploring the Influence of Eric R. Wolf*. Berkeley: Univ. of California Press.

Schrire, Carmel. 1995. *Digging through Darkness: Chronicles of an Archaeologist*. Charlottesville: Univ. Press of Virginia.

Schuyler, Robert L. 1980. Sandy Ground: Archaeology of a Nineteenth-Century Oystering Village. In *Archaeological Perspectives on Ethnicity in America,* ed. R. L. Schuyler, 48–59. Farmingdale, N.Y.: Baywood Publishing.

Scott, Elizabeth M., ed. 1994. *Those of Little Note: Gender, Race, and Class in Historical Archaeology.* Tucson: Univ. of Arizona Press.

Scott, Joan. 1988. *Gender and the Politics of History.* New York: Columbia Univ. Press.

Schneider, J. 1995. Introduction: The Analytical Strategies of Eric R. Wolf. In *Articulating Hidden Histories: Exploring the Influence of Eric R. Wolf,* ed. J. Schneider and R. Rapp, 3–30. Berkeley: Univ. of California Press.

Seifert, Donna J., ed. 1991. *Gender in Historical Archaeology.* Historical Archaeology 25 (4).

Shackel, Paul A. 1993. *Personal Discipline and Material Culture: An Archaeology of Annapolis, Maryland, 1695–1870.* Knoxville: Univ. of Tennessee Press.

———. 1996. *Culture Change and the New Technology: An Archaeology of the Early American Industrial Era.* New York: Plenum.

Shanks, Michael, and Christopher Tilley. 1987a. *Re-Constructing Archaeology.* Cambridge: Cambridge Univ. Press.

———. 1987b. *Social Theory and Archaeology.* Albuquerque: Univ. of New Mexico Press.

Singleton, Theresa. 1988. An Archaeological Framework for Slavery and Emancipation, 1740–1880. In *The Recovery of Meaning: Historical Archaeology in the Eastern United States,* ed. M. P. Leone and Parker B. Potter Jr., 345–70. Washington, D.C.: Smithsonian Institution Press.

———. 1995. The Archaeology of Slavery in North America. *Annual Review of Anthropology* 24:119–40.

Slicher van Bath, B. H. 1963. *The Agrarian History of Western Europe, A.D. 500–1850.* New York: St. Martin's Press.

South, Stanley, ed. 1977. *Research Strategies in Historical Archeology.* New York: Academic Press.

Spencer-Wood, Suzanne M. 1991. Toward an Historical Archaeology of Materialistic Domestic Reform. In *The Archaeology of Inequality,* ed. R. H. McGuire and R. Paynter, 231–86. Cambridge, Mass.: Basil Blackwell.

———. 1996. Toward the Further Development of Feminist Historical Archaeology. *World Archaeology Bulletin* 7:118–36.

———, ed. 1987. *Consumer Choice in Historical Archaeology.* New York: Plenum.

Thompson, E. P. 1963. *The Making of the English Working Class.* New York: Vintage Books.

Tilley, Christopher. 1984. Ideology and the Legitimation of Power in the Middle Neolithic of Southern Sweden. In *Ideology, Power, and Prehistory,* ed. D. Miller and C. Tilley. Cambridge: Cambridge Univ. Press, 111–46.

Trigger, Bruce. 1989. *A History of Archaeological Thought.* Cambridge: Cambridge Univ. Press.

Tucker, Robert C. 1978. *The Marx-Engels Reader.* New York: W. W. Norton and Co.

Stephen A. Mrozowski, James A. Delle, and Robert Paynter

Walby, Sylvia. 1990. *Theorizing Patriarchy.* Oxford: Basil Blackwell.

Wall, Diana. 1994. *The Archaeology of Gender: Separating the Spheres in Urban America.* New York: Plenum.

Wallerstein, Immanuel. 1974a. The Rise and Future Demise of the World Capitalist System: Concepts for Comparative Analysis. *Comparative Studies in Society and History* 16 (4): 387–415.

————. 1974b. *The Modern World System I: Capitalist Agriculture and the Origins of the European World-Economy in the Sixteenth Century.* New York: Academic Press.

————. 1980. *The Modern World-System II: Mercantilism and the Consolidation of the European World-Economy, 1600–1750.* New York: Academic Press.

Weber, Max. 1970. *The Protestant Ethic and the Spirit of Capitalism.* London: Unwin.

Wobst, H. Martin. 1977. Stylistic Behavior and Information Exchange. In *For the Director,* ed. C. Cleland, 317–42. Anthropological Papers, Museum of Anthropology, University of Michigan, Ann Arbor.

Wolf, Eric. 1982. *Europe and the People without History.* Berkeley: Univ. of California Press.

————. 1994. Perilous Ideas: Race, Culture, People. *Current Anthropology* 35 (1): 1–12.

Wright, Eric O. 1993. Class Analysis, History, and Emancipation. *New Left Review* 202:15–35.

Wright, Henry. 1977. Recent Research on the Origin of the State. *Annual Review of Anthropology* 6:379–97.

Wright, Henry T., and Gregory Johnson. 1975. Population, Exchange, and Early State Formation in Southwestern Iran. *American Anthropologist* 77:267–89.

Wurst, LouAnn. 1991. "Employees Must Be of Moral and Temperate Habits": Rural and Urban Elite Ideologies. In *The Archaeology of Inequality,* ed. Randall H. McGuire and Robert Paynter, 125–49. Oxford: Basil Blackwell.

Wurst, LouAnn, and Robert K. Fitts, eds. *Confronting Class. Historical Archaeology* 33 (1).

Wylie, Alison. 1991. Gender Theory and the Archaeological Record: Why Is There No Archaeology of Gender? In *Engendering Archaeology: Women and Prehistory,* ed. J. M. Gero and M. W. Conkey, 31–54. Oxford: Basil Blackwell.

Yentsch, Anne E. 1991. The Symbolic Divisions of Pottery: Sex-Related Attributes of English and Anglo-American Household Pots. In *The Archaeology of Inequality,* ed. R. H. McGuire and R. Paynter, 192–230. Oxford: Basil Blackwell.

————. 1994. *A Chesapeake Family and Their Slaves.* Cambridge: Cambridge Univ. Press.

PART ONE

Lines Defining Race
Archaeologies of Eurocentric Conquest,
Domination, and Resistance

CHAPTER ONE

Breaking
Typological Barriers

LOOKING FOR THE COLONO
IN COLONOWARE

Theresa A. Singleton
Mark Bograd

Humans typologize the world in order to understand it (Dunnell 1971, 1986; Whallon and Brown 1982). Although dividing the world into categories is a natural process, it is by no means a neutral one. As Gibbon (1990, 9) notes, "If our categories are not simply reflections of categories that exist objectively in the world, what are they reflections of? Of cultural preferences? . . . of what?" The decision to place an object in a particular category is a cultural decision with certain ramifications. If we divide some given items by chronology or cost, it is because we believe that the date of an object or the price is its salient characteristic. Our decisions about how to sort the world have their own costs because our choices channel our thoughts, making us look at the world in particular ways, and neglecting more significant interpretations of the archaeological record.

Typology is an important concept for archaeologists that has figured prominently in archaeological inquiry. Proponents of the culture history school often saw typologies as an end product of archaeological research rather than as a means to characterize or organize large amounts of descriptive data.

Even today archaeologists routinely typologize the archaeological record, although they spend a lot more time doing it than thinking about it. We often divide up artifacts by chronology, type of good, source of manufacture, paste composition, decorative treatment, and so forth, but we fail to reflect on how our typologies influence our interpretations of the past. We need to keep our typologies in check to ensure that by typologizing we frame, rather than determine, our interpretations of the past.

This paper considers the problems of typologies by looking at a debate surrounding a particular kind of pottery known as colonoware. The debate initially developed around the question: Who made these artifacts? Enslaved African Americans? Native Americans? In recent years there has been a growing acceptance that both African Americans and Native Americans were most likely engaged in the production of these wares. Consequently, the question of who made these objects has shifted to what these objects represent (Mouer 1993, 125; Orser 1996, 116). Yet, despite this changing view, archaeologists are still in pursuit of typologies for these artifacts that would lead to the cultural identity of its makers (for example, Crane 1993; Mouer 1993; Heath 1996). We argue in this essay that a research focus on ethnicity of artifact makers is limiting and perhaps misses the point in the study of colonial or multicultural settings. Instead, we think of colonoware as an intercultural artifact—one that provides opportunities to raise questions and issues about its appropriation and transformative meanings and uses. We illustrate this point by discussing how colonoware was used as a vehicle to convey a variety of stories about slavery and plantation life in an exhibition we curated for the Smithsonian Institution.

BACKGROUND

Colonoware is a general term used to refer to numerous varieties of low-fired, often locally produced, hand-built earthenware recovered from sites dating from the late seventeenth to the mid-nineteenth centuries in the eastern United States. Similar wares have also been recovered from sites in the Caribbean. On some islands, local potters still produce comparable pottery today. Both colonoware and the Caribbean wares are often found on plantations associated with the areas in which enslaved African Americans lived and worked.

Ivor Noël Hume (1962a) initially identified the earthenware from sites in Virginia and defined them as Colono-Indian wares. In coining this term he was suggesting that they were Indian wares of the colonial period. Noël Hume was particularly intrigued by the fact that a small percentage of these vessels were fashioned into forms that resembled English vessels. He found bowls with foot rings, handled cups, porringers, pipkins, and chamber pots. None of these forms had been made by Native Americans prior to European contact. Noël Hume suggested that these pots were made by Native Americans, because the manufacturing techniques were unlike those of European-trained potters. He further suggested that Native Americans were trading these wares onto plantations. Since he considered these pots crude in comparison to even the least expensive European earthenware, he presumed that Colono-Indian wares were purchased by or for enslaved Africans.

This definition went unchallenged until the mid-1970s, when archaeologists in South Carolina, of whom Leland Ferguson was the most prominent and prolific, began to offer an alternative explanation for Colono-Indian ware (Ferguson 1977, 1980, 1992). Many sites in South Carolina were producing wares similar to those described by Noël Hume in Virginia. The majority of the South Carolina wares were not made into European forms, but were globular in shape, resembling cooking pots and serving bowls. Puzzled by the large percentages of Colono-Indian wares reported in these excavations—in some cases amounting to well over half of the total ceramic assemblage—Ferguson and others eventually suggested that perhaps some of the earthenware was made by enslaved Africans.

More than just numbers figured into their conclusions. At Drayton Hall and Hampton Plantations in South Carolina, the discovery of pottery fragments that appeared to have been fired on the plantation suggested on-site manufacture. These findings, coupled with the knowledge that African Americans were the predominant group on these plantation sites, strongly suggested to Ferguson that at least some of these Colono-Indian pots were made by African Americans. He offered the more general term, colonoware, as a replacement for Colono-Indian ware.

Ferguson's interpretations were initially derived from his examination of colonoware in South Carolina. He later studied collections of colonoware pottery from Virginia and observed evidence of on-site manufacture on sherds recovered from Pettus and Utopia, two Virginia plantation sites. He inferred that enslaved African Americans probably made the pottery at the two plantation sites and that it was likely that they made pottery at other places in rural Virginia as well. With the exception of the pottery from Pettus and Utopia, however, Ferguson concluded that most of the colonoware he examined in Virginia was probably made by free Indians. He based this insight partially on the fact that the vast majority of the Virginia collections were recovered from sites in Williamsburg or nearby plantations. Ferguson reasoned that these collections reflected situations where enslaved people could purchase or trade pottery from nearby towns, and therefore it was not necessary for them to make pottery. This inference led Ferguson to recommend that future archaeological investigations be undertaken at remote plantations where it may have been necessary for the enslaved to make their own pottery (1992, 46–50).

Inspired by Ferguson's work, several archaeologists working in Virginia have suggested that African Americans made colonoware at specific sites (for example, Deetz 1988; 1993, 80–93; Parker and Hernigle 1990, 230–35). Perhaps the most controversial of these assessments is James Deetz's claim that "most scholars working with colono ware now agree that it was made and used by slaves" (1988, 365). Interpretations like Deetz's—especially those of Matthew Emerson (1988, 1994), who suggested African sources for the inspiration of certain designs on seventeenth-century terra-cotta pipes found in the Virginia Tidewater—have produced one of the liveliest debates in Chesapeake archaeology (Deetz 1993, 78; Mouer 1993, 124–25).

The debate over the production of colonoware has been shaped by two different research trajectories in which different kinds of questions are being addressed. One group of scholars see colonoware as a Native American artifact arising out of pre-Columbian pottery traditions. These scholars are interested in questions concerning the impact of European contact upon Native American communities. Most of their studies have focused on colonoware recovered from Indian settlements. The other group of scholars are interested in plantation studies. They see the recovery of colonoware from plantations as an opportunity to study an artifact made and used by enslaved communities that can potentially provide insights into the construction of African American identity (Heath 1996, 154–55). Although the research questions are different for each, both are attempting to grapple with interrelated processes. As Charles Orser has argued, colonoware would have been impossible without the impulse of Europeans to colonize the world, the widespread capitalist use of slavery, and the condescending view that Europeans were superior to all non-Europeans (Orser 1996, 122). Thus, there is a growing consensus that colonoware represents a process of interaction and that both African and Native Americans most likely made it.

There are sound reasons for drawing this conclusion. Both African Americans and Native Americans were capable of making this ware, each group having longstanding pottery-making traditions. Colonoware vessels were hand built rather than wheel-thrown. They were constructed using potting techniques such as coiling, pinching, and segmental modeling, or slab building (fig. 1.1; also see Rice 1987, 125–28). Vessels were fired without kiln technology, presumably in open pits. These potting techniques were used in both pre-European-contact Africa and North America.

Documentary evidence, though fragmentary, also suggests the manufacture of pottery by both Native Americans and African Americans. Probate wills and ledgers document the production and trade of "Indian Pans" and "Indian Pots" (Henry 1980, 21, 22). Further, anthropologists working with the Pamunkey in Virginia in the early twentieth century commented on their pottery. One noted, "the grandmothers of the present generation . . . made and sold large quantities of the ware for domestic use to their white and negro neighbors" (Harrington 1908, 406).

The documentary evidence for African American manufacture is more scanty, but what exists is compelling. A few interviews with formerly enslaved African Americans conducted by researchers working for the Works

Fig. 1.1. M. J. Harris, a Catawba, fashioning a coiled clay vessel.

Truman Michelson's Photographs, National Anthropological Archives, Smithsonian Institution.

Progress Administration (WPA) in the 1930s indicate that African Americans were engaged in pottery making. For example, an interview with Henry Clay (his name alone is suggestive) describes how the pots were prepared: "Mistress had me help the children of the other slaves to make pots because I was good at it. We made good clay pots and I have made hominy in them like the Creeks made lots of times. We would make the pots and hang them in the chimney to bake, sometimes a whole week, then pick out the ones that I didn't crack" (Rawick 1977, 113). Other African American interviewees told WPA fieldworkers that they remembered their parents and grandparents making pots (Ferguson 1992, 1–3).

The recognition that both African and Native Americans made pottery supports the notion that colonoware is an intercultural artifact. At the same time, however, this changing view continues to fuel research directed toward establishing typologies for colonoware produced by African Americans and that produced by Native Americans. In our opinion, the search for the ethnicity of the makers of colonoware is misguided because, like all typologies, such research merely classifies or labels action but fails to analyze it. Additionally, these typologies encourage the search for ethnic objects—which we believe limits the interpretative power of African American archaeology.

WHY NOT SEARCH FOR ETHNIC OBJECTS?

Searching for the ethnic origins of a potter limits the potential of African American archaeology because it encourages the further search for "African" artifacts or "Africanisms," which undoubtedly were a small part of the archaeological record of African America. As McGuire (1982) and Paynter (1992) note, the search for "Africanisms" has been the major preoccupation of archaeologists studying African American ethnicity. Identifying Africanisms has distracted archaeologists and led to a search for artifacts, not contexts; a search for Africa, not for an understanding of African America.

Typologizing colonoware as either African or Native American segments a culturally plural society, drawing boundaries between groups that may not have existed (see Sobel 1987). This practice is common in plantation studies where artifacts and plantation contexts are defined as black or white when in fact they are both. The plantation is as much a black landscape as it is a white one (Upton 1988). Most studies of African Americans on plantations focus on the slave quarter. While this is a reasonable place to study the lives of enslaved African Americans, the focus on quarters as black spaces often leads us to neglect other parts of the plantation landscape as sources of information on African Americans.

When we divide the world we channel our thoughts in particular directions. Although most archaeologists have abandoned the acculturationist concept—adoption of European-introduced objects by non-Europeans equals cultural change—many archaeologists consider only objects crafted by its users as indicators of cultural identity. What often makes an object important in the shaping of cultural identity is the act of appropriating it (Turgeon 1997, 21; see also Thomas 1991). In African American archaeology, archaeologists often define black artifacts as those items that show African influences or those objects that might uniquely be identified with the African American community. The object comes to define the group rather than the group defining the significance of the artifact.

African Americans frequently appropriated European American practices and material culture. For example, the marriage practice of jumping over a broomstick had long been observed in Britain and much of western Europe before it was practiced by blacks and whites in the southern colonies. For enslaved blacks, it was the only type of marriage permitted, and it quickly acquired a special meaning in African American culture (Fischer 1989, 282). African Americans also appropriated mass-produced objects, such as creamware or pearlware dishes, making these ceramics African American objects. The Quanders—a family descended from the enslaved community at Mount Vernon—have attached special significance to the blue-on-white transfer-printed pearlware ceramics they have kept in the family for generations (Benjamin Quander, pers. comm.). Appropriated mass-produced items are as important as hand-crafted items in the study of African American life.

Just as pearlware can be an African American artifact, colonoware can be a European American one. European American appropriation of colonoware is regrettably an underexplored topic. This oversight may be a consequence of archaeologists' preoccupation with who made colonoware rather than who used it and thus transformed its meaning. We recommend that archaeologists redirect their study of colonoware to examine the *colono*. In other words, examine how this artifact was used, appropriated, and transformed by its makers and users. In this way, colonoware becomes the catalyst for understanding identity formation, cultural interaction, and change under colonialism.

REPRESENTING COLONOWARE AS AN INTERCULTURAL ARTIFACT

At the National Museum of Natural History of the Smithsonian Institution, we organized and curated a small exhibition entitled "Pitchers, Pots, and Pipkins: Clues to Plantation Life." The exhibit opened in early 1992 and was on view for fourteen months. Our purpose was to illustrate how everyday utilitarian objects can provide insights into understanding plantation life and southern society. Another goal of the exhibit was to introduce historical archaeology, specifically the archaeological study of plantations, to a general audience in a museum where North American archaeology has traditionally focused upon pre-Columbian peoples. Using colonoware vessels, photographic panels, text labels, video footage, and a brochure accompanying the exhibition, we were able to show how archaeology is used to interpret eighteenth- and nineteenth-century American life.

The exhibition consisted of one large display case containing eleven vessels of colonoware from Virginia and South Carolina (fig. 1.2). Eight vessels were recovered archaeologically: seven from terrestrial sites and one from an underwater site. The sites in Virginia were all former plantations: Mount Vernon (Pogue 1990, 1994; White 1995), Portici (Parker and Hernigle 1990), and Rosewell (Noël Hume 1962b). The sites in South Carolina included Lexington Plantation (Wayne

Fig. 1.2. Overall exhibition case for "Pitchers, Pots, and Pipkins: Clues to Plantation Life."
Courtesy Office of Printing and Photographic Services Smithsonian Institution.

Theresa A. Singleton and Mark Bograd

and Dickerson 1990); an underwater provenience associated with the Bluff Plantation (Ferguson 1992, 11–15); and the Heyward-Washington House (Crane 1993), an urban residence of a South Carolina planter located in Charleston. The remaining three vessels were from the ethnological collections of the Charleston Museum and the National Museum of Natural History.

The introductory label set the tone for visitors to think of colonoware as an intercultural artifact by establishing that the use of pots, not their production, is suggestive of exchanges between Native Americans, European Americans, and African Americans:

> *Archaeologists are unearthing evidence that 18th-century plantation life in Virginia and South Carolina was not drawn on traditional black-and-white stereotypes. Excavations of slave quarter sites and mansions are turning up many examples of African-American and Native American influences in plantation society.*

> *Some evidence of these influences comes from clay pitchers and pots. Archaeologists identify these finds as colonoware because these are non-European wares from the colonial period. Some of this pottery was made by local Indians to sell to plantations, some by the slaves. Colonoware was used to store, cook, and serve food both for slaves and slave owners.*

> *The foods prepared in these pots represented a blending of cultures. What could be more southern than hominy, an Indian food? Or okra, an African import? As one nineteenth-century commentator noted, "Okra soup was always inferior if cooked in anything, but an Indian pot."[1]*

As indicated in the above text, we left the debate over the origins of specific pots to our colleagues, noting that both Native Americans and African Americans made colonoware.

Using the specific contexts of the vessels we were able to tell several stories organized around three themes: "Virginia: Tobacco and Slaves"; "South Carolina: Rice Country"; "Indian Pots: Made for Trade." Beginning with the vessels from Virginia, the text informed the visitor that colonoware was first "discovered" on sites in Virginia and explained the development of Virginian plantation society. A major point emphasized in this discussion was that prior to 1700 the plantation workforce included blacks, whites, and occasionally Native Americans, but after that date enslaved Africans and African Americans dominated the workforce. This information established that the Virginian vessels on display were associated with slave-worked plantations because two vessels date to the last quarter of the eighteenth century, and the third dates after 1820.

The main interpretative point conveyed in the grouping of Virginian colonoware was the difference between large and small plantations (fig. 1.3). Virginian gentry owned Rosewell and Mount Vernon. Mann Page I, the son-in-law of King Carter—one of the wealthiest planters in colonial Virginia—established a plantation and built the mansion at Rosewell in 1726. Considered the "finest, largest American house of the colonial period" (Waterman 1965, 113), the Rosewell mansion reflected the conspicuous consumption of Virginia's planter elite.

The owners of Rosewell were engaged in tobacco cultivation. It is not known how many enslaved workers they owned, but in 1744, Mann Page II, the son of Page I, applied for ownership of 76 slaves left by his father to his deceased brother Ralph. Of those, 28 enslaved persons were residing at

Fig. 1.3. Grouping of Virginia colonoware vessels.
Courtesy Office of Printing and Photographic Services, Smithsonian Institution.

Rosewell, and the others were dispersed at four other plantations. Later, in 1786, Mann Page II's son, John was recorded as owning 160 slaves (Noël Hume 1962, 158). Little else is known of the plantation operation except that all of the owners were plagued with financial difficulties.

Like Rosewell, Mount Vernon—the plantation home of George Washington—epitomized a planter's efforts to emulate the tastes and desires of the wealthy (Pogue 1994, 101). Over a forty-five-year period, 1754–99, Washington more than tripled the size of Mount Vernon, adding four outlying farms. He also acquired large numbers of enslaved workers. By the time of his death in 1799, the total number of enslaved people had reached 316 (Pogue 1994, 110).

The colonoware recovered from both Rosewell and Mount Vernon came from contexts where enslaved people lived or worked. In the case of Rosewell, the vessel came from a trash pit located west of the plantation house on the edge of a gully, about seventy feet from the presumed site of the detached kitchen. The pit was filled with trash dating between 1763 and 1790 (Noël Hume 1962b, 162–65). The Mount Vernon vessel came from refuse excavated from the "House for Families," a communal slave dwelling which housed as many as seventy enslaved persons from 1760 to 1793 (Pogue 1990). The text for the exhibition stated: "Slaves on large, prosperous Virginia plantations like Mount Vernon and Rosewell had more opportunities to acquire personal possessions than slaves on smaller holdings. Slaves occasionally earned money off the plantation from their skilled labor and may have traded directly with local Indians for colonowares and other goods."

The reference to skilled labor refers directly to Mount Vernon, where a census taken in 1786 lists fourteen of the forty-one enslaved adults as craftspeople such as seamstresses, spinners, knitters, carpenters, and smiths (Pogue 1994, 107). Written sources also indicate that the enslaved community at Mount Vernon bought and sold items in the seaport town of Alexandria (Pogue, pers. comm.).

In contrast to Mount Vernon and Rosewell, Portici was considered a middling plantation. Located in the Virginia piedmont near Manassas, Portici averaged about twenty enslaved workers and operated as an independent plantation. Rosewell and Mount Vernon, in contrast, each were one of several operating plantations owned by a single planter family. During the late antebellum period, Portici was reduced to a small plantation when a new owner purchased it and worked the land with the aid of one free black and an average of twelve slaves (Parker and Hernigle 1990, 20). This information on the later history of Portici provided the opportunity to describe slave life at both small and middling plantations. In the exhibition text, we stated that most enslaved workers lived on small plantations where owners and laborers often worked and lived close to each other. We also suggested that both groups most likely shared similar food traditions, including one-pot meals consisting of soups and stews.

With the grouping of South Carolinian colonoware, we compared plantation and urban slavery (fig. 1.4). The introductory label to these vessels indicated that blacks formed a majority population in South Carolina by the mid-1700s and were engaged in every form of skilled labor. The text also established that the strongest evidence of pottery production by African Americans has been recovered on South Carolina plantations.

The vessels used to depict plantation slavery were recovered from Lexington Plantation, located twelve miles northeast of Charleston. Lexington was probably developed as a plantation beginning in the 1750s, when Arnoldus Vanderhorst inherited the tract of land known as Four Men's Ramble. It stayed in the Vanderhorst family until it was sold in 1828, becoming known after that date as Lexington Plantation (Wayne and Dickerson 1990, 3–20). At its peak development in the nineteenth century, Lexington had as many as 117 enslaved men and women (Wayne and Dickerson 1990, 7–14).

Like the other plantations along the South Carolina coast, Lexington was engaged in rice and cotton cultivation; unlike most, the production of bricks was Lexington's most lucrative enterprise. An abundant supply of clay along the banks of Wando Neck ideally situated Lexington for brick produc-

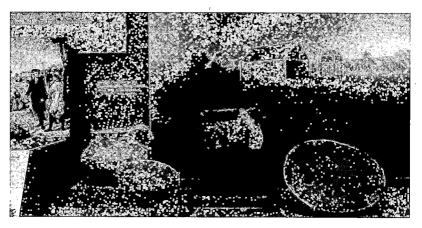

Fig. 1.4. Grouping of South Carolina colonoware vessels.
Courtesy Office of Printing and Photograph Services, Smithsonian Institution.

Theresa A. Singleton and Mark Bograd

tion. The production of brick quickly became the preferred industry of the plantation because the high salinity of the Wando River restricted the cultivation of rice and other crops to the upper reaches of the creeks (Wayne and Dickerson 1990, 6–4). Despite the abundance of clay and archaeological evidence of clay extraction, the colonoware recovered from the slave quarters associated with the brick kiln did not exhibit evidence of on-site manufacture. Rather than suggesting the possibility of plantation-made pottery, we focused on reasons why clay pots may have been preferable to other kinds of cooking equipment. We suggested that clay vessels "had many practical advantages over iron pots and other kinds of cookware. The clay vessels were inexpensive and easy to produce. Food cooked slowly in them, a necessity for soups, stews, spoon bread, and other popular dishes. This versatility may explain the presence of colonowares in the kitchens of planter families as well as in the cabins of slaves."

The archaeological context for the colonoware used to discuss urban slavery was recovered from the Heyward Washington House in Charleston. In the 1770s, Col. Daniel Heyward, a wealthy low-country rice planter, built the house. When the Heyward family sold the house in 1794, it was described as a "large house with twelve rooms, a fireplace in each, a cellar and loft, a kitchen for cooking and washing with a cellar of brick surrounded by brick walls" (Charleston Museum Brochure). Unfortunately, little is known of the enslaved population, as those records were lost in a fire.

The colonoware from the Heyward Washington House was recovered from the detached kitchen in a provenience associated with the Heyward occupation of 1772–94. We used this provenience to draw attention to slavery in urban settings, indicating that the Heywards were typical of many South Carolina planter families who were absentee owners, preferring to live in Charleston and other coastal cities. Enslaved people were part of these urban households, working both as domestics and as skilled artisans.

To interpret the Indian trade in colonoware, we selected vessels attributed to the Pamunkey and the Catawba (fig. 1.5). The role of both communities in the pottery trade is well documented (for example, Harrington 1908; Stern 1951). The two Pamunkey vessels in the display were collected by Dr. Dalrymple in 1861 and later donated to the Smithsonian. These vessels are now part of the ethnological collections of the National Museum of Natural History. The other trade vessel was a Catawba pitcher borrowed from the Charleston Museum in South Carolina. The pitcher was purchased in 1805 by a member of the Cordes family. The Cordeses were owners of Yaughan plantation in Berkeley County. Excavations at the slave settlements associated with Yaughan plantation yielded large quantities of colonoware, some of which was presumably made on the plantation (Wheaton, Friedlander, and Garrow 1983; Wheaton and Garrow 1985). This pitcher, however, has a definite Native American provenience.

We used the Indian-made vessels first to offer for consideration that the term *Indian pot* may refer to the maker or to the vessel shape (like its use in the quote about okra soup in the introductory label). We made this point because some colonial inventories specified the type of vessel purchased from Native Americans. This point was illustrated with a page from Lord Botetourt's account book, which had an entry "To the Indians for Earthen Pans." Lord Botetourt was the royal governor of Virginia from 1768 to 1770.

The second issue we raised with the trade vessels was that some colonoware vessels were made into forms that appealed to British colonial tastes. Some forms, like pipkins and porringers, were used to prepare and eat foods in the colonial period and are nearly unknown today. The practical pipkin, a cooking pot with three legs and a handle, could stand in the coals of the fireplace. The vessels not only allowed us to talk about trade between Native American communities and other groups, but, more importantly, they served to remind the audience that Native Americans played an important role in the formation of southern society.

The final vessel in the exhibition was one we identified as a "syncretic pot." The vessel's paddle-stamped surface decoration is associated with both

Fig. 1.5. Grouping of Native American colonoware vessels.
Courtesy Office of Printing and Photograph Services, Smithsonian Institution.

pre-Columbian and post-Columbian Native American pottery, but the form is unusual. It is the same vessel that inspired Leland Ferguson to begin his study of colonoware pottery with the hope of uncovering African influences in its manufacture (Ferguson 1992, 11–15).

Found in South Carolina's Combahee River, we used this vessel's unusual characteristics to suggest that it was perhaps the product of Native American and African interaction. We wanted visitors to understand that contacts between blacks and Indians sometimes involved more than trade relationships. In the early days of slavery, both Africans and Native Americans worked on plantations. On other occasions, enslaved Africans fled plantations to live with various Indian communities.

In retrospect, the syncretic vessel emphasized the difficulty of ascribing cultural affiliation to makers of pottery or to other artifacts in the absence of other forms of documentation. Interpretation of this vessel is further hampered because it was not recovered from a controlled excavation, which could have provided evidence of its association with other objects. Even when it is possible to assign cultural affiliations to the production of artifacts, this information still provides little insight into the meaning of the artifacts or their history of use. Thus, the syncretic vessel reinforces what we were trying to accomplish from the start—who made an artifact is less important than what it meant to the people who used it. In our opinion this is the proper goal of archaeological analysis.

AFTERTHOUGHTS ON THE EXHIBITION

Whether we were successful in conveying our ideas to museum visitors is unclear. Unfortunately, we were unable to conduct an evaluation of visitors' reactions to the exhibition. We did receive numerous comments and queries from visitors, usually asking for additional information. Copies of the videotape have been shown elsewhere and used in introductory courses in archaeology, American history, and even art history.

Two criticisms were directed toward the exhibition. The first was the use of the term *slave* in the text labels. Several African Americans commented that the term is depersonalizing and reduces human beings to things. We anticipated this problem, but exhibition editors insisted that the term *slave* is familiar and would be understood by most visitors. Terms such as *enslaved African Americans* or *people held in bondage* are not only wordy but also potentially confusing to visitors unfamiliar with American slavery.

The second criticism was our own observation that the oppressive nature of slavery was missing from the text. To correct this we made a conscious attempt to use language in the brochure and the video script (both of which accompanied the exhibition) that emphasized the oppressive conditions of slavery. However, most of this language did not make it through the editing process to the final copy.

We realize now that these issues are characteristic of museums in general. Unlike other scholarly products, exhibitions, particularly those at the Smithsonian Institution, are rarely the sole product of the content specialists who curate the show, but rather are team efforts. Despite its shortcomings, the exhibition was successful thanks to the professional input we received from specialists in exhibition design, fabrication, editing, illustration, object conservation, and video production. With their help we were able to introduce African American and historical archaeology to a broad audience, to suggest the complexity and diversity of plantation life, and to show the public how even simple objects can be used to make important observations about human experiences.

CONTEXT OVER TYPOLOGY

Regardless of who made colonoware vessels, we know that enslaved Africans used them and that excavations turn them up at large and small plantations, industrial plantation sites (for example, the Lexington brick kiln), and urban residences. We also know that enslaved African Americans used them to prepare food for themselves and for the slaveholding family. Finally, the foods prepared in them were suggestive of the interactions between African Americans, European Americans, and Native Americans.

Increasingly, archaeologists have shown that an artifact's context is what gives it meaning and value (for example, Hodder 1992). Therefore, merely labeling an artifact "African American," "European American," or "Native American" provides little insight into this value or meaning. By emphasizing the use of colonoware and not its possible manufacture by African Americans, the exhibit sent an important message concerning the active role African Americans played in the construction of southern society. Enslaved African Americans were not passive recipients of a planter dominated society but active participants in the construction of plantation lifeways. While the exhibit specifically examined southern food ways, this example has a broader application to southern life ways in general.

To achieve the goals of African American archaeology, archaeologists need to move beyond searching for African American artifacts and focus more upon understanding what these objects tell us about African American life. Archaeologists need to begin raising questions such as the following: How did African Americans transform the meanings of mass-produced objects? Why were certain objects valued over others? How were objects used in identity formation? Only when we begin to raise such questions will we be able to break away from the typological barriers that restrict us.

NOTES

We would like to acknowledge the members of the exhibition team—Marjorie Stoller, Thomas Thill, Nancy Brooks, Cissy Anklan, Maggi Jackson, Phil Anderson, and Eddy Bazemore—for their contributions to the exhibition project. A special appreciation goes to the institutions that loaned objects for the exhibition: the Charleston Museum; Department of Anthropology of the National Museum of Natural History, Smithsonian Institution; Dunes West and SouthArc, Inc., Florida; Institute of Archaeology and Anthropology University of South Carolina; Mount Vernon Ladies' Association, National Museum of American History, Smithsonian Institution. We are also gratefully appreciate the financial support we received from Smithsonian Women's committee and James Smithson Society to fabricate the exhibition and produce the brochure.

1. Quote taken from William Gilmore Simms, Loves of the Driver, *The Magnolia: Or Southern Monthly* 3 (1841): 122.

REFERENCES CITED

Crane, Brian. 1993. Colono Ware and Crillo Ware Pottery from Charleston, South Carolina and San Juan, Puerto Rico, in Comparative Perspective. Ph.D. diss., Dept. of American Civilization, Univ. of Pennsylvania, Philadelphia. Ann Arbor, Mich.: University Microfilms.

Deetz, James. 1988. American Historical Archaeology: Methods and Results. *Science* 239:362–67.

———. 1993. *Flowerdew Hundred: The Archaeology of a Virginia Plantation, 1619–1864.* Charlottesville: Univ. Press of Virginia.

Dunnell, Robert C. 1971. *Systematics in Prehistory.* New York: Free Press.

———. 1986. Five Decades of American Archaeology. In *American Archaeology, Past and Future,* ed. D. J. Melzer, D. D. Fowler, and J. A. Sabloff, 23–49. Washington, D.C.: Smithsonian Institution Press.

Emerson, Matthew. 1988. Decorated Clay Tobacco Pipes from the Chesapeake. Ph.D. diss., Dept. of Anthropology, Univ. of California, Berkeley. Ann Arbor, Mich.: University Microfilms.

———. 1994. Decorated Clay Pipes from the Chesapeake: An African Connection. In *Historical Archaeology of the Chesapeake,* ed. Paul Shackel and Barbara J. Little, 35–49. Washington, D.C.: Smithsonian Institution Press.

Ferguson, Leland G. 1977. Looking for the "Afro-" in Colono-Indian Pottery. *The Conference on Historic Site Archaeology Papers* 12:68–86.

———. 1980. Looking for the "Afro-" in Colono-Indian Pottery. In *Archaeological Perspectives on Ethnicity in America,* ed. Robert Schuyler, 14–28. Farmingdale, N.Y.: Baywood.

———. 1992. *Uncommon Ground: Archaeology and Early African America, 1650–1800.* Washington, D.C.: Smithsonian Institution Press.

Fischer, David H. 1989. *Albion's Seed: Four British Folkways in America.* New York: Oxford Univ. Press.

Gibbon, Guy. 1990. What Does an Observation Mean in Archaeology? In *Powers of Observation: Alternative Views in Archaeology,* ed. Sarah Nelson and Alice B. Kehoe, 5–10. Archaeology Papers of the American Anthropological Association No. 2, American Anthropological Association, Washington.

Harrington, M. R. 1908. Catawba Potters and Their Work. *American Anthropologist,* n.s., 10:399–407.

Heath, Barbara. 1996. Temper, Temper: Recent Scholarship on Colonoware in Eighteenth-Century Virginia. In *The Archaeology of Eighteenth-Century Virginia,* ed. Theodore Reinhart, 149–69. Special Publication No. 35. Richmond: Archaeological Society of Virginia.

Henry, Susan L. 1980. *Physical, Spatial, and the Temporal Dimensions of Colono Ware in the Chesapeake, 1600–1800.* Master's thesis, Dept. of Anthropology, Catholic Univ. of America, Washington, D.C.

Hodder, Ian. 1992. *Theory and Practice in Archaeology.* London: Routledge.

McGuire, Randall. 1982. The Study of Ethnicity in Historical Archaeology. *Journal of Anthropological Archaeology* 1 (2): 159–78.

Mouer, L. Daniel. 1993. Chesapeake Creoles: The Creation of Folk Culture in Colonial Virginia. In *The Archaeology of Seventeenth-Century Virginia,* ed. Theodore Reinhart and Dennis J. Pogue, 105–66. Special Publication No. 30. Richmond: Archaeological Society of Virginia.

Noël Hume, Ivor. 1962a. An Indian Ware of the Colonial Period. *Quarterly Bulletin of the Archaeological Society of Virginia* 17:2–14.

———. 1962b. Excavations in Rosewell in Gloucester, Virginia, 1957–1958. United States National Museum Bulletin 225. Contributions from the Museum of History and Technology, Paper 18. Washington, D.C.: Smithsonian Institution Press.

Orser, Charles E., Jr. 1996. *A Historical Archaeology of the Modern World.* New York: Plenum.

Parker, Kathleen A., and Jacqueline L. Hernigle. 1990. Portici: A Portrait of a Middling Plantation in Piedmont Virginia. Occasional Report No. 3. Regional Archaeology Program, National Capital Region, National Park Service, Washington, D.C.

Paynter, Robert. 1992. W. E. B. DuBois and the Material World of African Americans in Great Barrington, Massachusetts. *Critique of Anthropology* 12 (3): 277–91.

Pogue, Dennis. 1990. Slave Lifeways at Mount Vernon. In *Mount Vernon Ladies' Association of the Union: Annual Report 1989,* 35–40. Mount Vernon, Va.: Mount Vernon Ladies' Association of the Union.

————. 1994. Mount Vernon: Transformation on an Eighteenth-Century Plantation System. In *Historical Archaeology of the Chesapeake,* ed. Paul A. Shackel and Barbara Little, 101–14. Washington, D.C.: Smithsonian Institution Press.

Rawick, George, ed. 1977. *The American Slave: A Composite Autobiography.* Oklahoma Narratives Supplement, ser. 1, vol. 12. Contributions to Afro-American and African Studies 35. Westport, Conn.: Greenwood Publishers.

Rice, Prudence. 1987. *Pottery Analysis: A Sourcebook.* Chicago: Univ. of Chicago Press.

Simms, William G. 1841. Loves of the Driver. *The Magnolia: Or Southern Monthly* 3:122.

Sobel, Mechal. 1987. *The World They Made Together: Black and White Values in Eighteenth-Century Virginia.* Princeton: Princeton Univ. Press.

Stern, Theodore. 1951. Pamunkey Pottery Making. *Southern Indian Studies* 3:1–78.

Thomas, Nicholas. 1991. *Entangled Objects: Exchange, Material Culture, and Colonialism in the Pacific.* Cambridge, Mass.: Harvard Univ. Press.

Turgeon, Laurier. 1997. The Tale of the Kettle: Odyssey of an Intercultural Object. *Ethnohistory* 44 (1): 1–30.

Upton, Dell. 1988. White and Black Landscapes in Eighteenth-Century Virginia. In *Material Life in America, 1600–1860,* ed. Robert Blair St. George, 357–69. Boston: Northeastern Univ. Press.

Waterman, Thomas T. 1965. *The Mansions of Virginia, 1770–1776.* New York: Bonanza Books.

Wayne, Lucy R, and Martin F. Dickerson. 1990. Four Men's Ramble: Archaeology in the Wando Neck, Charleston County, South Carolina. Report on file, SouthArc, Inc., Gainesville, Fla.

Whallon, Robert, and James Brown. 1982. *Essays in Archaeological Typology.* Evanston, Ill.: Center for American Archaeology Press.

Wheaton, Thomas, Amy Friedlander, and Patrick H. Garrow. 1983. Yaughan and Curriboo Plantations: Studies in Afro-American Archaeology. Report on file, Archaeological Services Branch, National Park Service, Atlanta, Ga.

Wheaton, Thomas, and Patrick Garrow. 1985. Acculturation and the Archaeological Record in Carolina Low Country. In *The Archaeology of Slavery and Plantation Life,* ed. Theresa A. Singleton, 239–59. Orlando, Fla.: Academic Press.

White, Esther. 1995. Colonoware from Mount Vernon Plantation, Mount Vernon, Virginia: A Formal Description and Preliminary Analysis. Paper presented at the annual meeting of the Society for Historical Archaeology, Washington.

CHAPTER TWO

Labor, Racism, and the Built Environment in Early Industrial Harpers Ferry

Paul A. Shackel
David L. Larsen

The early stage of the industrial revolution in the United States was an era for experimentation with machines and labor. The introduction of industrial technology created new relations of production as manufacturing transformed society from a preindustrial to an industrial economy. The relationships of subordinate and dominant groups to new modes of production changed dramatically. Early industrial ideologies legitimated the use of women, children, and African Americans for industrial labor. By the middle of the nineteenth century new ideologies disfranchised these groups from direct participation in the industrial process (see Prude 1996, 237–55).

Examining Harpers Ferry, an early-nineteenth-century southern manufacturing town, provides us with an understanding of the disfranchisement of subordinate groups during this era. The excellent contextual information on the dynamics of group relations and the transformation of the built environment helps to identify changing historical social relationships. This work also allows us to focus on surveillance technologies, both social and material, that reinforced stratification. We examine issues of industrialization, social and work relations, and power and resistance between European Americans and African Americans who worked in and around the armory.

Understanding the town's development and built environment within the context of industrial slavery in the South enlightens us about the changing social relationships within the town. Harpers Ferry, we believe, is a valuable case study for understanding race in the context of labor, settlement pattern, and the built environment in a developing industrial community.

INDUSTRY AND SLAVERY IN THE URBAN AND RURAL SOUTH

Industrial slavery occurred in Harpers Ferry as well as elsewhere in the antebellum South. In fact, by the 1850s about 5 percent of the enslaved population in the country worked in industrial enterprises (National Bureau of Economic Research 1966, 30:117–210). Enslaved labor existed in most of the major southern industries. Industrial bonded labor in the form of artisans and mechanics was often in great demand in small towns or in rural areas (Foner and Lewis 1989, 1), while urban industry employed about 15–20 percent of the bonded population (Wade 1964, 30, app.). Workers were either owned by companies or hired from their owners. Throughout the nineteenth century about 80 percent of all industrial slaves were owned directly by industrialists, while employers rented the rest (Eaton 1961, 64–65). Plantation owners and farmers supplied most of the capital for industrial enterprises in the rural South. From the late eighteenth century, southerners invested in industrial slavery in an attempt to create a balanced economy that incorporated both agriculture and industry. Most southerners believed, however, that slave-based industry should be directed by slave owners rather than industrial entrepreneurs. This direction, they surmised, would ensure that existing class and race relationships would remain unchallenged (Starobin 1970, vii–viii).

The first southern cotton mill, established in 1789, hired slaves from nearby planters (Eaton 1961). Low cotton prices in the early nineteenth century and an ideology that established African Americans' suitability to perform the monotonous and repetitious functions of factory work allowed for an increasing number of free and bonded African Americans in the new industrial system (see Jones 1989 [1827], 77–82). Through the 1820s southern industrialists overwhelmingly believed that industrial slavery could be viable and profitable. One letter in 1827 in the *American Farmer* (Jones 1989 [1827]) noted that enslavement was particularly situated for industry and claimed: "In all extensive manufactories we meet with the veriest dolts, who become, as it were, from habit, adept in the business allotted to them, with a degree of dexterity and precision which appears almost miraculous ... their occupation would be those of mere routine and for this they are peculiarly fitted. . . . The negro possesses, in general, a degree of emulation, equal, at least to that of the white labourers . . . but in my estimation it is superior" (77–79). The author later justified that "The friends of emancipation must rejoice should one of the most serious obstacles to its accomplishments be removed, by training the slave to habits of industry, in a business which will tend to prepare him for a state of freedom" (81).

In 1828, before the North Carolina House of Commons, Charles Fisher further reinforced the need for African Americans in manufacturing: "What branch of mechanics have we in our country in which we do not find negroes often distinguished for their skill and ingenuity" (Fisher 1989 [1828], 85). He also pleaded that African Americans were intellectually qualified and possessed high moral principles for manufacturing. Fisher believed that to think otherwise would only reinforce the northerners' perception that African Americans' work discipline was substandard compared to whites. To think that African Americans were unqualified for factory labor would only justify the monopoly of growing industries in the North (85).

Generally, foreign capital could not be attracted to industrialize the South, except in New Orleans, and industrial growth severely lagged behind the industrial North (Egerton 1996, 215–16). Enslavement placed the South far "in the rear of our neighbors who are exempt for slavery," complained Henry Clay, "in the state of agriculture, the progress of manufacturers, the advance of improvement, and the general prosperity of society" (quoted in Egerton 1996, 215).

By the 1850s enslaved African Americans could be found in most major industries in the United States. For instance, antebellum southern ironworks employed about 10,000 slaves (Starobin 1970, 14–15; also see Christian 1972; Dew 1966, 1994a, 1994b; Lewis 1979). African Americans labored in tobacco factories and hemp processing. They were also found in secondary manufacturing industries and listed as mechanics, cobblers, and tanners. Sugar refining, rice milling, grist milling, and textile milling used more than 30,000 enslaved people (Starobin 1970, 16–20; Eaton 1961, 134–35; Miller 1981). Some southern industries employed both enslaved blacks and white freemen at the same factory. The extent of white and black frictions varied, although competition for jobs often created racial hostilities (Williamson 1965; Litwack 1961).

Industrial slavery existed until the Civil War, although various forms of resistance made southerners question this labor practice. Resistance took many forms, and "weapons of the weak" (Scott 1985, 29–39; 1990) were often reported by southern industrial entrepreneurs. The most subtle forms of protest included negligence, work slowdowns, feigned ignorance, pilferage, slander, arson, and sabotage. In slave society passive resistance proved more effective than the few fruitless and dangerous heroic acts. Slave resistance was effective "only to the extent that it hid behind the mask of public compliance" and never directly confronted the system of slavery (Scott 1985, 34; also see Paynter 1989; Paynter and McGuire 1991).

One writer provides insight into a master's response to this passive protest. Frederick Law Olmsted (1861, 104–5) wrote in 1861: "We have tried reward and punishment, but it makes no difference. It's his nature and you cannot change it. All men are indolent and have a disinclination to labor, but this is a great deal stronger in the African race than in any other."

Overt resistance and rebellion were most often led by artisans or industrial slaves rather than plantation slaves. In 1800, Gabriel Prosser, a blacksmith, designed a conspiracy in Henrico County, Virginia, and planned an uprising in Richmond's industrial community. Plantation field hands allied themselves with urban artisans, although planters detected the conspiracy before it could be executed. Denmark Vessey, a carpenter, organized the 1822 Charleston conspiracy. Many of his co-conspirators were also skilled artisans, including a "first-rate" ship carpenter, mechanics, and blacksmiths. In 1831, Nat Turner had been a carpenter and a wheelwright before he became a preacher. Turner and his followers moved from farm to farm, recruiting blacks and killing fifty-five whites. Turner escaped but was captured two months later (Starobin 1970, 88; Morgan 1986, 44). Many southerners blamed the Prosser, Vessey, and Turner uprisings on industrial slavery. By mid-century, and probably somewhat earlier, many white southerners reconsidered the use of industrial slavery (Foner and Lewis 1989, 98–99; Foner 1995).

Southerners often criticized the northern free labor market, insisting that workers were "wage slaves." Laborers, they claimed, enjoyed the right to starve as they searched for temporary work after they were no longer employed by a particular factory. Wage labor was seen as the "most intolerable slavery that men can suffer" (quoted in Egerton 1996, 219; also see Foner 1995).

Barbara Fields (1985) questions whether industrial slavery could ever work in an industrial society affected by the tides of a fluctuating economy. Various supporting services, such as sailing, carting, oystering, food processing, and construction relied on the rhythm of trade, weather, and economy; Fields argues that the slave system could not profitably meet those irregular demands. Slavery in an industrial context was not the problem, rather it was excessive profit seeking by industrialists that made entrepreneurs uneasy about having enslaved people idle for parts of the day or year. Industrial slavery could not adequately fill the needs of support occupations compared to organized free labor. "Objective structural requirements, not subjective individual preferences, explain the prevalence of free labor in urban employment" (Fields 1985, 55). As market relations replaced the household paternalistic structure of the preindustrial economy, the coherence of enslavement disintegrated.

Fields's interpretation is viable, but other issues related to local social and political structures and shifting racist ideologies complicate this scenario. While industrial slavery seemed to level off or slightly decline by the mid-nineteenth century in the rural South (see Starobin 1970; Dew 1966, 1994a), some industries such as iron and sugar continued to rely heavily on bonded workers. Other issues regarding racism and the continued subordination of African Americans are worth considering in the context of the decreasing use of industrial slavery. For instance, Gov. James Hammond's protest against industrial slavery before the South Carolina Institute in 1850 is not based on the lack of efficiency of industrial slavery in a capitalist society. Rather his letter reveals racist motives for discouraging industrial slavery. He noted: "Whenever a slave is made a mechanic, he is more than half freed, and soon becomes, as we too well know, and all history attests, with rare exception, the most corrupt and turbulent of his class. Whenever slavery has decayed the first step in the progress of emancipation, has been the elevation of the slaves to the rank of artisan and soldiers" (Hammond 1989 [1850], 94). By the 1830s a growing number of whites feared competition and protested against the use of black artisans. Euro-Americans increasingly enacted legislation that relegated African Americans to secondary roles in industrial society, and they were pushed to the periphery of industrial capitalism. They became the carters, draymen, food processors, and laborers. African Americans were excluded from most craft shops, and by the 1840s Irish immigrants replaced blacks as laborers and in various carrying occupations (Boydston 1990, 59–61). Even though the African Americans' economic role changed through the nineteenth century, ideological mechanisms ensured their subordinate status in an industrializing society and disfranchised them from the increasingly dominant industrial culture.

Free African Americans who labored in a growing industrial system faced many legal and societal restrictions. Through the second quarter of the nineteenth century an increasing number of legislative acts in various communities restricted African American rights and further relegated them to the peripheral and supportive roles of the dominant culture. For example, in 1835 St. Louis passed an ordinance that prohibited African Americans from operating ordinaries, which served food and drink (St. Louis City Council 1836, 143–46). Whites feared that free blacks would sell liquor to enslaved people and that the alcohol would embolden them to revolt against their masters. Whites also feared that free blacks would traffic stolen goods from plantations, thus encouraging pilfering. Therefore, in the first half of the nineteenth century, the Maryland legislature passed laws that prohibited African Americans from being involved in the transport of agricultural products (Brackett 1889, 143–46). Whites quickly sought legislative means to restrict black employment and competition. Several times Baltimore residents petitioned the legislature to restrict black employment. In 1827 they asked that African Americans be prevented from driving hacks, carts, or drays. In 1837 they requested the prohibition of African Americans from engaging in artisan trades; in 1844 they asked for African Americans' exclusion from the trade of carpentry and to tax all free blacks employed in any other artisan capacity (Brackett 1889, 15; Curry 1981, 17). Washington, D.C., had some of the most restrictive laws for black employment. In 1836 free African Americans could not be issued a license except for menial jobs such as driving carts, drays, hackney carriages, or wagons, and after November 9, 1836, any newcomer would not be issued a license (Curry 1981, 17).

Societal pressures also proved restrictive. Significant amounts of documentation exist to demonstrate that even free African Americans who did menial jobs, such as carting, were often refused licenses because of their color (Curry 1981, 18; Block 1969). They also encountered strong opposition when trying to enter artisan trades in northern cities. In New York no African Americans were employed in shipbuilding until after the War of 1812, and in 1835 the Boston city directory lists only seven black artisans. "The president of the Mechanical Association of Cincinnati was tried before the society in 1830 for having accepted a black apprentice, an (action) few other master workmen apparently made then or later" (Curry 1981, 19).

In antebellum America, especially in the North, more than half the black men were employed in low-opportunity jobs, such as carters, while only a few could obtain the status of artisan. Contrary to our conventional wisdom, more opportunity for higher-status artisan jobs existed in the Deep South. For instance, more than 65 percent of the free African Americans in urban areas in the lower south, such as New Orleans and Charleston, were artisans, while about 8 percent of free African Americans in New England and the Middle Atlantic

States held these more lucrative jobs. Before the American Revolution, an urban free labor shortage existed in the rural Deep South (Curry 1981, 31). In southern cities African Americans were extensively employed as skilled workers to create a support system for a new growing urban elite, especially in cities like New Orleans. Therefore, whites did not originally perceive black artisans as strange or a threat to the jobs of white artisans. Generally through the 1800s free-black employment patterns in the North did not improve significantly; in fact, by 1850 African Americans were faced with declining access to more promising occupations (Curry 1981, 26–31).

AFRICAN AMERICANS IN THE INDUSTRIAL TOWN OF HARPERS FERRY

The example of Harpers Ferry, one of the earliest industrial towns in America, shows the various roles that African Americans played in government-operated weapons manufacturing. The Harpers Ferry armory was established in 1794, when the U.S. Congress decided to establish armories for the manufacture and storage of arms. Harpers Ferry was chosen along with its counterpart, Springfield, Massachusetts. Construction of the armory began in 1799, and the first guns were produced by 1801 (Smith 1977; Shackel 1996).

Skilled craftsmen carried out production at the armory during the first several decades of the facilities' operations. This task-oriented production entailed a high degree of manual skill and knowledge on the part of the armory worker of many different aspects of gun making. In general, these craftsmen perceived the introduction of labor-saving machinery as a threat to their way of life. "Above all, they considered themselves artisans, not machine tenders, and, as such, believed in the dictum that an armorer's task consisted in making a complete product—lock, stock, and barrel" (Smith 1977, 67–68).

In the 1840s the armory labor system experienced major revisions. A military superintendent replaced the civilian management system and proceeded to enforce a more intricate division of labor. A clock was installed in the armory and all workers labored to standardized time. Rules and regulations reinforced the type of factory discipline found at many Middle Atlantic and New England industrial enterprises. In order to easily accommodate the change in work habits it was necessary to change the work environment. Most of the armory buildings were unsuited for the implementation of a division of labor, as they lacked architectural and functional unity. Surveillance of workers was extremely difficult under this seemingly chaotic factory layout. The Harpers Ferry facilities contrasted sharply with the orderly layout of other factory systems, especially those in the North. In 1844, Supt. Maj. John Symington, an engineer, introduced new labor saving machinery and he created a plan for the armory's renovation. Symington imposed a grid over the existing town plan and he standardized the factory plan for the armory. The gridlike factory design allowed for easier surveillance of workers, and the creation of a wall around the factory grounds with only one gate allowed for the control of people and information in and out of the armory. Armory workers protested the introduction of new factory design and machinery. They feared that they would become mere tenders of machinery, which is how they saw their New England counterparts.

African Americans did not play a purely industrial or agricultural role during the development and redesign of the armory. Enslaved and freed blacks were not allowed to participate in the operation of the U.S. armory directly, nor were many enslaved or freed African Americans required for intense year-round agricultural labor on cash crops like tobacco or cotton. Yet a significant number of African Americans lived and worked in Harpers Ferry and the surrounding area. Three hundred of the town's population of 3,000 were African Americans, half of which were enslaved (Bureau of the Census 1810–60). Not employed by local industry or used in field gangs, most of Harpers Ferry's African Americans provided domestic service and general labor, while a few worked in skilled positions. The presence of the gun factory in Harpers Ferry created a need for support services filled by both enslaved and free African Americans. Various sources reveal these African Americans were involved in many social and economic interactions within the town, were oppressed and resisted oppression, were sometimes successful in bettering their circumstances, and were sometimes defeated.

Mainly, African Americans and whites in Harpers Ferry lived and worked close to each other. Deed records and census figures reveal that most buildings in town, at one time or another, housed both blacks and whites. Enslaved people most often lived with their owners, and there are many examples of free African Americans living with white families. While there were a few small enclaves of free African American households, the town was not segregated into distinct neighborhoods. Some evidence suggests that African Americans were sometimes quartered in outbuildings or in basements. Most houses that contained both whites and blacks were dominated by whites who owned or hired one to three African Americans (Bureau of the Census 1810–60; U.S. Census Slave Schedules 1850–60; Jefferson County Deed Book [JCDB] 20:586; 21:404; 23:120; 24:453; 35:36, 73, 216–17; Snell 1959b; African American

Research Report [AARR] 1992). There are a few instances in which boarding-houses or homes occupied by blacks also had a minority of whites residing there (Bureau of the Census 1830, see for instance Philip Coontz).

Both enslaved and free blacks provided services and labor important to the efficient workings of the local economy. Many members of white society depended on blacks for domestic service, cooking, laundry, nursing, and farm labor. Most of the enslaved people in Harpers Ferry were women and children who performed these tasks. One-third of the enslaved population were men who primarily worked as laborers and farmhands. A few enslaved males acquired skills like carpentry and quarry work (Bureau of the Census 1810–60; U.S. Census Slave Schedules 1850 and 1860; advertisements in *The Virginia Free Press [VFP]*, 1829–61; National Archives RG 217; Snell 1959a).

The U.S. armory hired a few enslaved males from their owners as laborers, cartmen, and carpenters. The gun factory also engaged free blacks as canal lock-keepers, plasterers, quarrymen, and stonemasons (National Archives RG 217; Snell 1959a). Citizens hired contractors that used African American work crews to build their stores and homes. Other plied their trades as blacksmiths and butchers. Although evidence shows that few if any African Americans joined Harpers Ferry's merchant class, the preponderance of black boatmen and draymen indicates many retailers depended on them to deliver their merchandise (Bureau of the Census 1810–60; *VFP* 1829–61). African Americans supplied much of the town's labor foundation.

AFRICAN AMERICANS IN THE U.S. ARMORY

Jobs in the U.S. armory were key to the town's economic, political, and social life. First and foremost, the U.S. government owned and operated the gun factory, and it became a public concern. Those who ran the armory were not preoccupied by gaining a profit from their production. Rather, efficiency was necessary only to the degree that they satisfied superiors and fulfilled their own political agendas (Smith 1977; Barry 1903; Shackel 1996). From its very inception, those who managed the factory were faced with a choice: Was the factory to be primarily operated to benefit the United States as a whole or primarily to benefit the region around Harpers Ferry? Merritt Roe Smith (1977) persuasively argues that through patronage and politics, the latter agenda was adopted for much of the factory's history. There are instances, however, of superintendents who tried to run the factory to the benefit of the country. Even when in power, these men were constantly challenged by the local public, who believed that the factory existed for their own benefit. In simple terms, those who held positions of power in the armory relied on the support and votes of those they employed. For the most part, those who held power could rely on that support by supplying jobs and seeing to the needs of their employees. Such a system reinforced the rural values held by many local workers. The control of jobs in the gun factory translated to social and political power (Smith 1977:151).

For most of Harpers Ferry's antebellum history, there was no shortage of white labor eager to work in the gun factory. Local residents as well as Irish and German immigrants were ever willing to step into any vacancies. As long as workers understood and did not challenge the system of patronage, armory employees were treated well, as they were able to make social demands of their "superiors" in exchange for their political support. Because white workers were readily available and represented votes, the social and political position of African Americans—enslaved or free—for the most part, prevented their direct participation in the workings of the armory.

In the very early days of the gun factory, however, skilled white labor was not always so easy to acquire. Before mechanization, weapons could only be produced by craftsmen who had years of training and experience. Until 1818, the factory experienced difficulty in maintaining a workforce of skilled craftsmen large enough to meet production goals. Though a significant minority of African Americans were skilled blacksmiths, stonemasons, and carpenters, there is no evidence that any were gunsmiths. Antebellum-period southern states passed many laws restricting African Americans from gaining access to firearms (Stampp 1956, 208). As a result, it might be inferred that African Americans were prohibited from gunsmithing. While a detailed study of this massive record group is still required, a brief survey of the 1840s armory records (Snell 1959a) reveals many pay vouchers showing that the U.S. armory hired enslaved males. An 1845 armory slave roll indicates that six local slave owners rented seven slaves to the armory. Six of the seven slaves were male and were rented for twenty-six days. The seventh, also male, was rented for four. Their occupations are listed as one cartman, four laborers, one carpenter, and, finally, one horse and cart driver (Snell 1959a, form 18, March 1846). Except for the carpenter, these enslaved males performed unskilled work. Similarly, the January 26, 1847, armory account of expenditures from July 1845 to June 1846 also indicates that the armory used the enslaved labor for menial tasks. The voucher states that the U.S. government spent $1,160.49 on miscellaneous slave labor and $346.35 on slave construction (Snell 1959a). This last piece of data is currently the only known evidence indicating skilled work performed by enslaved males in the gun factory. There is no evidence to suggest these slaves worked on guns. As there is evidence that the armory employed slaves as carpenters, it is probable that the government confined the "slave workmanship" to areas other than the production of weapons.

Other armory records reveal that free African Americans were also employed by the armory. A voucher from January 1842 listed John Butler, a free African American, as a lock-keeper for the armory canal. The same voucher indicates that another free black man, Thomas Spriggs, was a wagoner. Other pay records show Jeremiah Harris, a plasterer, frequently worked on government projects. A sampling of armory correspondence provides further evidence of the presence of free African Americans in armory operations. On August 11, 1840, the superintendent of the armory wrote the Ordinance Department asking for advice on paying the accounts of deceased workers in cases "where free men of colour have died having small balances due … there being little if anything more than enough to pay funeral expenses" (Snell 1959a). While the specific occupations of these men are not listed, as often happens with enslaved labor, no evidence suggests that free African Americans helped produce weapons.

John Gust, a stonemason, is one of the most striking and successful examples of free African Americans working for the armory. Gust can best be described as a contractor. Armory pay records from 1824 to 1831 provide copious evidence of Gust and his crew quarrying, hauling, paving, building embankments, and laying stone (Snell 1959a). On June 11, 1830, armory superintendent George Rust wrote the Ordinance Department: "For the latter [Gust], a contract had been prepared, but he being a coloured man, and some doubt arising whether he was actually entitled to his freedom or not, the contract was not signed. Upon inquiry I learned that his character was good, and ascertaining that he had faithfully executed the work at which he had been employed, I permitted him to continue at it, observing, however, the caution never to pay him for as much work as had been actually completed." Superintendent Rust went on to report that Gust and a fellow contractor were due $2,000 to $3,000 (National Archives RG1 56, 1830–31 8R:3).

It is very likely that some white contractors used enslaved or free African Americans as labor when working for the armory. When contemplating African American presence in the gun factory, researchers must consider how often blacks were employed by white contractors or individuals not known to be black. Those African Americans' identities would not have been revealed on pay vouchers.

An incident involving a white contractor named Collins suggests that on at least one occasion a white contractor did use free black labor. On July 3, 1849, Collins wrote Gen. George Talcott of the Ordinance Department complaining that workers in Harpers Ferry were interfering with his employees and preventing him from completing his work (Snell 1959a). Maj. John Symington, superintendent of the U.S. armory, responded to Talcott's investigation of the matter on July 6, 1849. Symington stated the town magistrate, Fontaine Beckham, received citizen complaints of the "disorderly and riotous conduct of negroes who were nightly in the habit of assembling at houses in their vicinity, particularly occupied by a family of free negroes" (quoted in Snell 1959a). Beckham authorized a police officer to summon a "patrole" and "proceed against the offenders." Six African Americans were arrested and conducted across the Potomac River to the Maryland side "with a warning not to return again." The report continued, "One of the offending negroes, having twice before been sent across the bridge was insolent to the party and was flogged for it." Beckham claimed the proceedings did not mean to single out Collins's free blacks, "but the fact of two or three of his hands being notoriously bad fellows, gave character to the whole of them" (quoted in Snell 1959a).

Collins existed as a threat because he did not belong to the patronage system. In a second letter written on July 12 to a Captain Magruder, Symington revealed that Collins, an outsider, blamed the incident on people who did not want him in Harpers Ferry. Symington spelled it out, "Our people, you must know, claim exclusive right to employment about these parts" (quoted in Snell 1959a). Symington wrote that one of those people was a brick maker named Larubaugh. Because of Collins, Larubaugh lost work on some government buildings and "hence Larubaugh and his cliques [sic] opposition." Mr. Collins was away at the time, but later blamed "this attack upon his negroes: to this party and others of their way of thinking" (Snell 1959a). Hence, Collins's free black employees were not harassed just because they were black. Indeed, they were harassed because they represented the threat of the outsider Collins *and* because they were black.

The Collins incident illustrates that African Americans were present in and around the U.S. armory. One may only wonder how many worked there in some unofficial or indirect capacity. Though they may have been viewed cautiously by white society, African Americans were not entirely excluded from the factory grounds. While a great deal of specific evidence is lacking, there are some indications that privately owned enslaved males were often sent on errands to the factory. Black cartmen and boatmen probably delivered wood, coal, and machine parts and enslaved women carried lunch to their masters. Certainly, African Americans lived all around the gun factory and with many of the armory's white employees.

CONCLUSION

Historical archaeologists have increasingly shown the importance of using a variety of historical sources to understand the meanings and uses of material culture (for example, see Beaudry 1988; Little 1992; Little and Shackel 1992). The diversity of sources available for archaeologists is outlined in Little's (1992, 2–3) review. Knowing the breadth of historical documentation is an important tool for comprehending the material record. Understanding the context for the growth and development of the town, as well as the social and political relations among the townspeople of Harpers Ferry, aids in deciphering the variability found in the archaeological record.

A history of African American and Euro-American interactions provides a complex picture of group dynamics, social relations, and settlement patterns. While the armory operated by a patronage system and African Americans were excluded from higher paying jobs in the facility, many whites and blacks at one time shared housing, work space, and probably many commodities. An archaeological site identified as being solely inhabited by African Americans does not exist in Harpers Ferry. Historic neighborhood boundaries did not exist and African Americans lived in almost every house in Harpers Ferry, often at the same time as whites. Armory officials often had slaves in their households who were boarded in either their house, basement, or outbuilding.

The dominant culture created mechanisms to maintain African Americans' subordinate status. Close physical proximity to African Americans in the workplace was an important control mechanism. Surveillance techniques were also active when slaves lived in the same house with their masters, or free blacks lived with their employers. Increasing African Americans' accountability to their masters or sponsors curtailed their social life. This integration became essential to the success of Harpers Ferry's economy and was important to the maintenance of the existing social system. The new design of the armory grounds, the grid system, the systematic layout of buildings, and the enclosure of the armory complex also allowed for the subordination of laborers, as well as the increased surveillance of enslaved and free African Americans (see Shackel 1996).

Legislation also became an essential tool used to maintain African Americans' subordinate position. The most striking of these was the 1806 Virginia law that constantly threatened all free blacks with possible reenslavement. The law also curtailed the activities of free African Americans and made their possible contribution to slave insurrection less of a threat (Russell 1969; Berlin 1974).

Another control mechanism was the economic role relegated to blacks. The realm of opportunity and upward mobility was quite limited. African Americans were denied access to the very economic engine of the town, the U.S. armory. Direct influence and participation of African Americans in the armory was minimal, although their presence could not be ignored. Euro-Americans dominated the factory system and denied African Americans access to political power and influence. Although demographic analyses show that African Americans in Harpers Ferry were physically integrated into the community, other evidence indicates that they remained a peripheral group in the armory for its entire existence. African Americans served no direct purpose in the patronage system. The fact that African Americans in Harpers Ferry were unable to vote meant they could not gain access into the manufacturing system and therefore were subjugated to subordinate roles in a factory town. The patronage system allowed whites to obtain comparatively higher status and higher-paying craft positions. Even when the government transformed the armory into a wage-labor system in 1841, African Americans were still excluded from jobs that entailed factory discipline. Considering these cases shows that African Americans' changing role in the factory system in the context of wage labor is a complex issue dictated by many national and local, as well as social and political, ideologies.

A national context of industrial slavery provides some insight into the changing ideologies and perceptions of African Americans in factory and urban labor situations. An examination of urban labor also enlightens us about other disfranchised groups. On the national level, the increasing relegation of a group out of the factory and into support occupations for a white male-centered industrial society from the second quarter of the nineteenth century was not solely an African American phenomenon. In the early nineteenth century women comprised a large workforce in many northeastern industries. Entrepreneurs reassured an agrarian-based society that women and children could easily be employed in mills without disrupting the harmony of the agrarian-based society and economy that dominated American culture (Boydston 1996, 183–206; Cowen 1983; Dublin 1977, 1979, Stansell 1986; Vogel 1977). Many work roles show a predominance of women laboring in factories while males always played a dominant role as supervisors. African Americans and women were relegated to the docile, repetitive, unrewarding factory work that created a new group of free white male individuals. By the middle of the nineteenth century many

Americans lost hope for a sustained agrarian culture as factory labor increased exponentially throughout most urban areas. Women were no longer the dominant labor force in the factories as their role became increasingly relegated to domestic services (see Wall 1994).

Since industrialization removed traditional professions and crafts from the house to the factory women became excluded from traditional fields. Traditional goods could be purchased and middle-class women focused on the care of the children and the home. Boundaries and roles became increasingly codified and the home developed as a separate sphere from the rest of society (Strasser 1982, 5; Mintz and Kellog 1988). Households adapted to the industrial workers' routines and women increasingly participated in the economy by organizing consumption. In an industrialized society the emphasis of public order was replaced by stressing private discipline and self-control. Etiquette and social rules provided restrictive guidelines for behavior. Women's roles also became more narrowly defined as they cared for the children and prepared workers for the workday (Cowen 1983; Boydston 1990, 1996; Strasser 1982).

It is no coincidence that African Americans and women played decreasing roles in factory labor by the mid-nineteenth century. A new ideology dictated that profit-seeking capitalists could not allow men (and women) to be truly free, and therefore laborers needed to be alienated from their labor. The ideological tide turned to convince men that wage labor was the free men's choice instead of the slave's or woman's role (Little, pers. comm.). As factory labor became the dominant mode of production in the United States, industrialists, who were predominantly white males, relegated groups that could have posed a threat to the new dominant culture to a subservient and supportive role in a developing industrial society.

NOTE

We appreciate Jim Delle, Robert Paynter, and Stephen Mrozowski for inviting us to participate in this volume, and we thank them for their comments on earlier versions of this paper. Barbara Little also provided helpful suggestions and comments during the writing of this manuscript. We are also grateful to Randy McGuire for his comments on this chapter.

REFERENCES CITED

African American Research Report [AARR]. 1992. On file, Harpers Ferry National Historical Park, Harpers Ferry, W.Va.

Barry, Joseph. 1903. *The Strange Story of Harpers Ferry*. Shepherdstown, W.Va.: Shepherdstown Register.

Beaudry, Mary, ed. 1988. *Documentary Archaeology in the New World*. Cambridge: Cambridge Univ. Press.

Berlin, Ira. 1974. *Slaves without Masters: The Free Negro in the Antebellum South*. New York: Oxford Univ. Press.

Block, Herman D. 1969. *The Circle of Discrimination: An Economic and Social Study of the Black Man in New York*. New York: New York Univ. Press.

Boydston, Jeanne. 1990. *Home and Work: Housework, Wages, and the Ideology of Labor in the Early Republic*. New York: Oxford Univ. Press.

————. 1996. The Woman Who Wasn't There: Women's Market Labor and the Transition to Capitalism in the United States. *Journal of the Early Republic* 16 (2): 183–206.

Brackett, Jeffrey R. 1889. *The Negro in Maryland*. Baltimore: Johns Hopkins Univ. Press.

Christian, Marcus Bruce. 1972. *Negro Ironworkers in Louisiana, 1718–1900*. Gretna, La.: Pelican.

Cowen, Ruth Schwartz. 1983. *More Work for Mother: The Ironies of Household Technology from the Open Hearth to the Microwave*. New York: Basic Books.

Curry, Leonard. 1981. *The Free Black in Urban America, 1800–1850: The Shadow of the Dream*. Chicago: Univ. of Chicago Press.

Dew, Charles B. 1966. *Ironmaker to the Confederacy: Joseph R. Anderson and the Tredegan Iron Works*. New Haven: Yale Univ. Press.

————. 1994a. *Bonds of Iron: Master and Slave at Buffalo Forge*. New York: Norton.

————. 1994b. David Ross and the Oxford Iron Works: A Study of Industrial Slavery in the Early Nineteenth-Century South. *William and Mary Quarterly* 31 (2): 189–224.

Dublin, Thomas. 1977. Women, Work, and Protest in the Early Lowell Mills: "The Oppressing Hand of Avarice Would Enslave Us." In *Class, Sex, and the Woman Worker*, ed. M. Cantor and B. Ware, 43–63. Westport, Conn.: Greenwood Press.

————. 1979. *Women at Work: The Transformation of Work and Community in Lowell, Massachusetts, 1826–1860*. New York: Columbia Univ. Press.

Eaton, C. 1961. *The Growth of Southern Civilization*. New York: Harper.

Egerton, Douglas R. 1996. Markets without a Market Revolution: Southern Planters and Capitalism. *Journal of the Early Republic* 16 (2): 207–21.

Fields, Barbara J. 1985. *Slavery and Freedom on the Middle Ground: Maryland in the Twentieth Century*. New Haven: Yale Univ. Press.

Fisher, Charles. 1989 [1828]. A Report on the Establishment of Cotton and Woolen Manufacturers, on the Growing of Wool; Made to the House of Commons of North Carolina, by Mr. Fisher, from Rowan, on Tuesday, Jan. 1, 1828. In *Black Workers: A Documentary History from Colonial Times to the Present*, ed. P. S. Foner and R. L. Lewis, 84–85. Philadelphia: Temple Univ. Press.

Foner, Eric. 1995. *Free Soil, Free Labor, Free Men: The Ideology of the Republican Party before the Civil War.* New York: Oxford Univ. Press.

Foner, Philip, and Ronald Lewis, eds. 1989. *Black Workers: A Documentary History from Colonial Times to the Present.* Philadelphia: Temple Univ. Press.

Hammond, James. 1989 [1850]. "Progress of Southern Industry," Gov. Hammond's Address before the South Carolina Institute, 1850. In *Black Workers: A Documentary History from Colonial Times to the Present*, ed. P. Foner and R. Lewis, 90–94. Philadelphia: Temple Univ. Press.

Jefferson County Deed Book [JCDB]. Jefferson County Courthouse, Jefferson County, W.Va.

Jones, Thomas P. 1989 [1827]. The Progress of Manufacturers and Internal Improvements in the United States, and Particularly on the Advantages in the Manufacturing of Cotton and Other Goods. In *Black Workers: A Documentary History from Colonial Times to the Present*, ed. P. Foner and R. Lewis, 77–82. Philadelphia: Temple Univ. Press.

Lewis, Ronald L. 1979. *Coal, Iron, and Slaves: Industrial Slavery in Maryland and Virginia.* Westport, Conn.: Greenwood Press.

Little, Barbara J., ed. 1992. *Text-Aided Archaeology.* Boca Raton, Fla.: CRC Press.

Little, Barbara J., and Paul A. Shackel, eds. 1992. Meanings and Uses of Material Culture. *Historical Archaeology* 26 (3).

Litwack, Leon. 1961. *North of Slavery.* Chicago: Univ. of Chicago Press.

Marx, Leo. 1964. *The Machine in the Garden: Technology and the Pastoral Ideal in America.* New York: Oxford Univ. Press.

Miller, Randall. 1981. The Fabric of Control: Slavery in Antebellum Southern Textile Mills. *Business History Review* 55:487.

Mintz, Steven, and Susan Kellog. 1988. *Domestic Revolutions: A Social History of American Family Life.* New York: The Free Press.

Morgan, Philip, ed. 1986. *"Don't Grieve After Me," The Black Experience in Virginia, 1619–1986.* Hampton: Hampton Univ. Press.

National Archives. RG 156, 1830–31. File 8R:3. Records of the Office of the Chief of Ordnance, National Archives Branch Depository, Suitland, Md.

————. RG 217. Records of the U.S. Treasury Dept. Records of the Second Auditor, 1817 to 1841, Relating to the U.S. Armory, Vol. 1. National Archives Branch Depository, Suitland, Md.

National Bureau of Economic Research. 1966. *Output, Employment, and Production in the United States after 1800.* New York: National Bureau of Economic Research.

Olmstead, Frederick J. 1861. *Journey in the Seaboard Slave States.* New York.

Paynter, Robert. 1989. The Archaeology of Equality and Inequality. *Annual Review of Archaeology* 18:369–99.

Paynter, Robert, and Randall McGuire. 1991. The Archaeology of Inequality: Material Culture, Domination, and Resistance. In *The Archaeology of Inequality*, ed. R. McGuire and R. Paynter, 1–27. Cambridge, Mass.: Basil Blackwell.

Prude, Jonathan. 1996. Capitalism, Industrialization, and the Factory in Post-Revolutionary America. *Journal of the Early Republic* 16 (2): 237–55.

Russell, John H. 1969 [1913]. *The Free Negro in Virginia, 1619–1865.* New York: Dover Publications.

St. Louis City Council. 1836. *The Revised Ordinances of the City of St. Louis.* St. Louis: Missouri Argus Office.

Scott, James C. 1985. *Weapons of the Weak: Everyday Forms of Peasant Resistance.* New Haven: Yale Univ. Press.

Scott, James C. 1990. *Domination and Resistance.* New Haven: Yale Univ. Press.

Shackel, Paul A. 1996. *Culture Change and the New Technology: An Archaeology of the Early American Industrial Era.* New York: Plenum.

Smith, Merritt Roe. 1977. *Harpers Ferry Armory and the New Technology: The Challenge of Change.* Ithaca, N.Y.: Cornell Univ. Press.

Snell, Charles. 1959a. Extracts from National Archives RG 217, Records of the U.S. Treasury Dept. Records of the Second Auditor, 1817 to 1841, Relating to the U.S. Armory. Vol. 1. On file, Harpers Ferry National Historical Park, Harpers Ferry, W.Va.

————. 1959b. The Town of Harpers Ferry in 1859, A Physical History. Manuscript on file at Harpers Ferry National Historical Park, Harpers Ferry, W.Va.

Stampp, Kenneth M. 1956. *The Peculiar Institution: Slavery in the Ante-Bellum South.* New York: Vintage Books.

Stansell, Christine. 1986. *City of Women: Sex and Class in New York, 1789–1860.* New York: Alfred A. Knopf.

Starobin, Robert S. 1970. *Industrial Slavery in the Old South.* New York: Oxford Univ. Press.

Strasser, Susan. 1982. *Never Done: A History of American Housework.* New York: Pantheon Books.

United States Census for Jefferson County Virginia. 1810, 1820, 1830, 1840, 1850, 1860. On file, Harpers Ferry National Historical Park, Harpers Ferry, West Virginia.

United States Slave Schedule. 1850, 1860. On file, Harpers Ferry National Historical Park, Harpers Ferry, West Virginia.

Vogel, Lise. 1977. Hearts to Feel and Tongues to Speak: New England Mill Women in the Early Nineteenth Century. In *Class, Sex, and the Woman Worker,* ed. M. Cantor and B. Ware, 64–82. Westport, Conn.: Greenwood Press.

Wade, R. 1964. *Slavery in the Cities.* New York: Oxford Univ. Press.

Wall, Diana diZerega. 1994. *The Archaeology of Gender: Separating the Spheres in Urban America.* New York: Plenum.

Williamson, J. 1965. *After Slavery.* Chapel Hill: Univ. of North Carolina Press.

CHAPTER THREE

Lemuel's Garden

CONFRONTING ISSUES OF RACE, CLASS, AND POWER THROUGH THE DIFFERENTIAL PRESERVATION OF ARCHAEOLOGICAL SITES IN NORTHERN UTAH

William B. Fawcett
Walter Robert Lewelling

Situated along the Bear River east of Tremonton, Utah, is a river terrace that is classified as "prime agriculture land" (map 3.1). Today there are numerous successful farms in the area. The neat, well-kept fields are mostly planted in alfalfa, barley, and corn. Modern homes show the care and attention of people deeply committed to the land. A close examination of their fields reveals scatters of articles from forgotten settlers' homesteads. This area was the scene of a unique agricultural and social experiment in the late 1800s.

In 1994 several farmers and landowners from the northern Utah community of Tremonton contacted Fawcett (1996, 9). They had discovered that much of their land had been owned by Native Americans during the late nineteenth and early twentieth centuries. It came as a surprise to both the present owners and to us that Native Americans not only obtained title to this land under various Homestead Acts but were also members of the Church

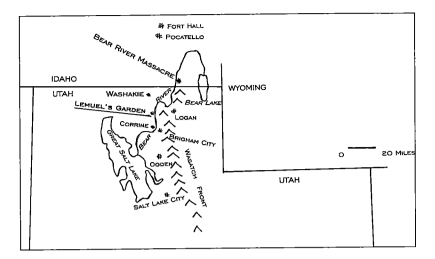

Map 3.1. Places associated with the northwestern Shoshoni
in northern Utah and surrounding states.

of Jesus Christ of Latter-Day Saints (LDS), also known as the Mormon church. Most of the current landowners have lived near Tremonton all of their lives but had not heard about the Native American homesteads that once existed there. While prompted by historical curiosity, they also hoped to forge an alliance among the archaeological community and the Shoshoni descendants of the original homesteaders to protect the land from inundation by the proposed Honeyville Reservoir on the lower Bear River. This led to an ongoing investigation involving Utah State University, volunteers from the Utah Statewide Archaeological Society, members of the Northwestern Band of the Shoshoni Nation, and the current landowners.

The Native American homesteads have been largely ignored and forgotten within the communities of northern Utah. Many of the physical remains of the Native American homesteads have been destroyed, while those associated with Anglo LDS pioneers are celebrated and preserved, often as highly visible monuments located in public parks. We argue that the differential preservation of the archaeological and historical records not only reflects but also fuels race and class struggles over political and economic power, extending beyond the confines of Utah. An integral part of these struggles is, the way in which the past is viewed and constructed.

In recent years, archaeology has contributed important insights about people presumed to lack history because they were illiterate or were prevented from writing histories. The case we examine here is different. The archaeological record of the Native American homesteads has largely been destroyed. Instead, archival data and written accounts by Native American homesteaders exist to supplement oral traditions. Yet, the telling of this history has gone unnoticed by historians and anthropologists who have focused on official records or the reconstruction of a more distant and, falsely presumed, pristine past. Part of our task is to resurrect the Native American accounts, which differ substantially from the prevailing view that the "failure" of the homesteads marked the end of a Native American presence in northern Utah.

HISTORICAL BACKGROUND

Anthropologists generally agree that Numic-speaking ancestors of the Shoshoni were present in northern Utah by at least A.D. 1400, although no consensus exists about how long before that date they may have been present, or about the nature of the migration(s) (Rhode and Madsen 1994). Julian Steward (1938) described the Shoshoni and their fellow Numic speakers (for example, Paiutes, Comanche, and Utes) as mobile bands of egalitarian hunter-gatherers who occupied much of the region in and around the Great Basin. From Europeans the Shoshoni acquired horses, firearms, and other technologies. The Shoshoni adopted many of the trappings of Plains Indians as they used the fur trade to acquire new forms of mass-produced material culture from Euro-Americans. They encountered, supplied, and guided Euro-American explorers, including Lewis and Clark. The Shoshoni suffered like other Native Americans from diseases introduced by Europeans.

From the 1840s on, the Shoshoni were greatly effected by Euro-American travelers on their way to California and Oregon, and even more so by the arrival of Mormon pioneers to Utah. Cattle grazed on the grasses that had provided seeds the Shoshoni gathered and consumed. Euro-American settlers and travelers burned and cleared the piñon pines that provided the nuts so essential to the Shoshoni diet. Irrigation projects diverted water from streams and springs. Euro-American farmers occupied the foothills along the Wasatch Front, driving a wedge of foreign settlers between highland mountains and lowland wetlands. Shoshoni found it increasingly difficult to sustain the wide-ranging mobile lifestyle that they had formerly used. They and other Native Americans turned to raiding and begging to supplement their increasingly meager returns from hunting and gathering, and to demonstrate their defiance toward the newcomers.

On the morning of January 29, 1863, Col. Patrick E. Connor led 220 men from the Third California Volunteers in an attack on Northwestern Shoshoni camped near Franklin, Idaho. This attack was probably opportunistic—an ambitious colonel in charge of a paramilitary force of questionable military proficiency who sought to chastise the most available Indian encampment (Madsen 1985, 199). Although the attack was a retaliation for warlike acts by some Indians, no attempt was made to identify or apprehend the guilty parties (197). After initially being repulsed, the volunteers gained the high ground above the Shoshoni. Their concentrated fire power killed about 250 Shoshoni men, women, and children in what is now known as the Bear River Massacre (200). No warriors were taken prisoner. A few Shoshoni escaped by diving into the icy river. Shoshoni survivors and Mormon observers reported that the soldiers executed some of the wounded, raped women, and bayoneted and smashed infants against rocks. None of these allegations was investigated (Hart 1982, 121–38; Parry 1976, 147). Fourteen soldiers were buried on the field, nine more died of wounds over the next month, and approximately ninety were discharged for disability resulting from wounds or cold injury incurred during the massacre (Madsen 1985, 194–97).

The Bear River Massacre was one of the largest in the western Indian wars (Madsen 1985, 20–24). While it was widely reported in the regional press at the time, it was overshadowed by the Civil War in terms of national attention.

Following the massacre, Shoshoni survivors in northern Utah and southeastern Idaho had little remaining land base. The native plant and animal resources on which they depended for their subsistence were rapidly disappearing as their traditional territories were occupied by Anglo-American farmers, miners, and soldiers who were transforming the landscape into an urban-based agrarian environment. The Shoshoni were increasingly linked to the larger capitalist economic system that would neither sustain nor tolerate "primitive" hunting and gathering involving mobility and relatively egalitarian communal organizations.

Between 1863 and 1873, the Shoshoni negotiated with the United States and Utah governments in the attempt to secure some form of subsistence annuities and a permanent land base or reservation as compensation for land they had lost. The U.S. government was bound by the Treaty of Box Elder, signed July 30, 1863, to pay $5,000 annually to support approximately 1,200 members of the ten recognized Northwestern bands. The sum would have been adequate had the funds been available, but they seldom were (Madsen 1985, 212–13). In ratifying the treaty, Congress added an amendment: "The Northwest Shoshoni could claim no more land than that which they had occupied formerly under Mexican law." Although the northwestern Shoshoni had occupied most of northern Utah during the period of Spanish and Mexican rule, their rights to that area had not been recognized. The treaty amendments effectively dispossessed the Shoshoni of all their traditional lands in Utah (Madsen 1985, 212).

After signing the Treaty of Box Elder, the Northwestern Shoshoni clustered around Anglo settlements in Cache Valley (around Logan) and Box Elder County. They begged for food and clothing, pastured their horses in cultivated fields, and stole watermelons while awaiting their annuities.

The Treaty of Fort Bridger, signed July 3, 1868, led to the establishment of a reservation at Fort Hall, Idaho (Madsen 1980a, app. C; 1986, 69). Although the majority of the Shoshoni in Utah and Idaho eventually settled on or near Fort Hall, several hundred of the surviving members of the Northwestern Band, and possibly also members of several other tribal groups from Idaho, Nevada, Wyoming, and the Dakotas,[1] were baptized into the LDS church (Hill 1873–83). They became the Native American homesteaders on the lower Bear River near present-day Tremonton.

Since the 1840s, the LDS church has been the dominant political and economic force in Utah and southeast Idaho. While the LDS dispossessed the Shoshoni from their lands, the official position of the church was one of relative benevolence. The church perceived itself as having a special relationship with Native Americans, whom they believed to be "Laminites," descendants of an early migration of chosen people from the Mediterranean who had been punished for apostasy by being changed into Native Americans (LDS 1993). The church genuinely wanted to assist the Shoshoni to become Christian agriculturists and to assimilate them into the dominant society to fulfill LDS prophecy.

These Native American converts became the nucleus for an agricultural settlement in northern Utah (map 3.2) known as "Indian Town" to the Anglo residents and often referred to as "Lemuel's Garden" by missionary George Washington Hill in his reports to the president of the LDS Church (Hill 1873–83). In the 1870s they filed on and patented homestead claims along the lower Bear River, incorporated an agrarian capitalist subsistence base, employed mechanized farming techniques, relied upon wheeled vehicles (including wagons and rail transportation), constructed irrigation canals, participated in the construction of the LDS temple in Logan, contributed to church and community activities, suffered economic and social hardship arising from racism and ethnocentrism, and sent their children on LDS missions (Christensen 1995, 154–81; Hill 1873–83; Hunsaker 1983a, 1983b). While the

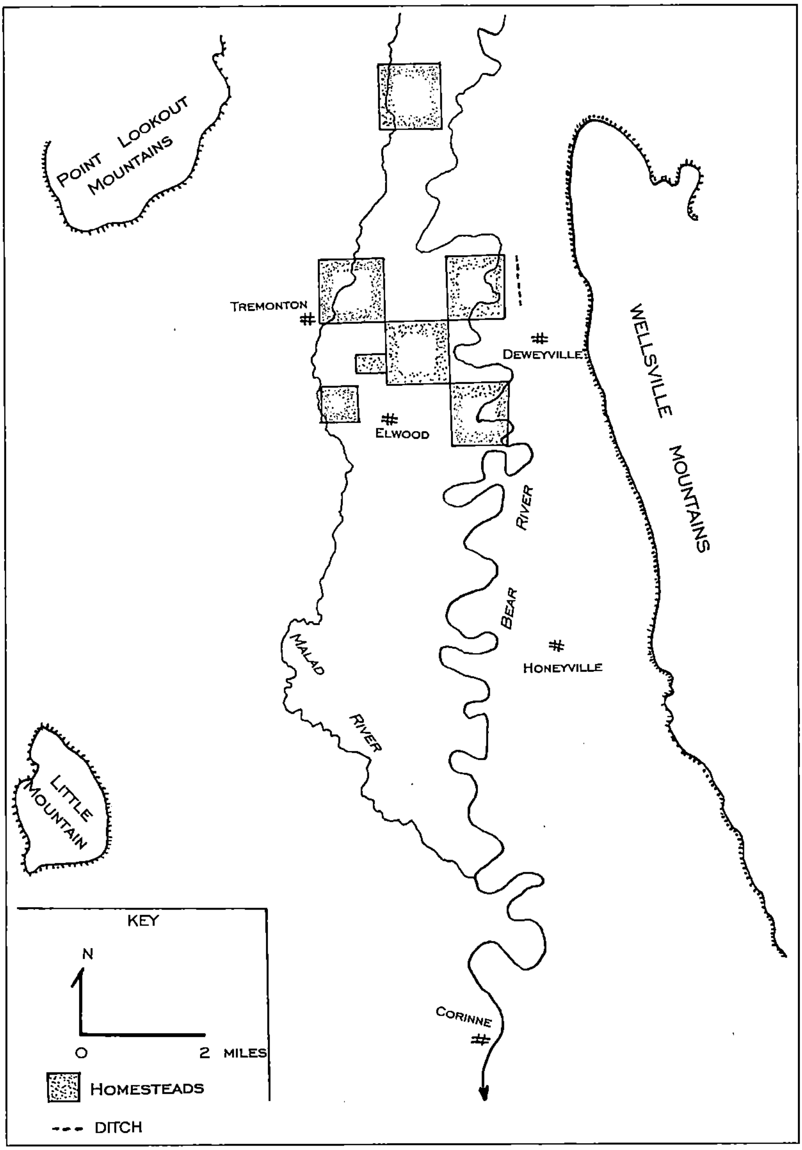
POINT LOOKOUT MOUNTAINS
TREMONTON
DEWEYVILLE
ELWOOD
WELLSVILLE MOUNTAINS
RIVER
BEAR
HONEYVILLE
MALAD
RIVER
LITTLE MOUNTAIN
KEY
N
0
2 MILES
HOMESTEADS
DITCH
CORINNE

Map 3.2. Native American homesteads located at Lemuel's Garden.

residents of Lemuel's Garden were no longer the hunter-gatherers of even a decade before, many traditional practices persisted, including aspects of religion, utilization of wild resources, residential mobility, and a preference for working and sharing communally.

Ownership of the Shoshoni homesteads was frequently contested by both public and private sectors of the Anglo community. Land was lost through bureaucratic process and court action, often resulting from misinterpretation and reinterpretation of federal statutes (Knack 1992). All forms of chicanery, fraud, and deceit were employed to induce the transfer of lands to Anglo ownership. Often, when threatened with loss of their land because of liens or back taxes, the Shoshoni would relinquish part of their claim in an attempt to save the remainder. Frequently, the Indian agent, the Government Land Office agent, and land speculators would visit Shoshoni landowners to encourage land transfers (Bureau of Land Management n.d.; Box Elder County Deed Records; Shoshoni interviews in Fawcett and Lewelling 1996).

Because of their proximity to the non-Mormon Anglo community at Corrine, which was hostile to both the Mormons and the Shoshoni, misunderstandings were frequent, and relations between the homesteaders and the townspeople were contentious.

Fueled by a sensationalist press that warned of thousands of hostile Lakota warriors lurking in the mountains awaiting the signal to join the Shoshoni in driving the Anglos from Corrine, most of the Shoshoni homesteaders were forcibly removed by the U.S. Army in August 1875 (Madsen 1980b, 283–84). Many Shoshoni continued to farm at Lemuel's Garden while residing at the LDS mission at Washakie, established in 1880, further north in Box Elder County (Christensen 1995, 181).

The enforced nonresidency created a problem in meeting the occupancy and structure requirements of the Government Land Office for patenting the homesteads at Lemuel's Garden. Although structures had been constructed on many of the homesteads when first occupied, by the 1880s many of them were torn down to be used by the local Anglo farmers for building pig corrals. Government Land Office inspectors appeared to be particularly vigorous in applying the structure and residence requirements to the Shoshoni homesteads (Hill 1886).

By the 1920–30s, Lemuel's Garden was largely lost to Anglo settlers. Shoshoni elders were very concerned about that loss, as detailed in numerous newspaper accounts written by Willie Ottogary, a resident of Lemuel's Garden and Washakie (fig. 3.1). In February 1920, a commissioner from Washington, D.C., was sent to Utah to address the Shoshoni concerns. (We have placed our edits in brackets to add clarification or contextual information; otherwise, we have let Ottogary speak for himself, quoting entire passages from his newspaper columns.)

> The commission is been here in our town one 17 Feb '20. He come from Washington, D.C. and he want to see the Indians. But he had chance happen to see them and talk with [LDS] Bishop George M. Ward. He want[ed to see] the him pretty bad and he is not [here] long enough to see him. I supposed we need some help from government. We haven't see out agent yet. But we heard a agent been our little town some time ago.
>
> Their is some Indians visiting Brigham City some time ago on the land business. But some of our boys trying to get land here just. The commissioner come here[.] we are going [to] see him and get some land. And their is so many haven't got no land. (Ottogary 1920)

A year later, Ottogary focused another newspaper column on the continuing loss of homesteads through probate and purchase:

> Well, we are been holding a consil last Monday night, the business was to [be] the land [and] also about our treaties here in the years 1863 made in Brigham City, Utah. But was not forfill yet. We want get Government [to] look after that thing. And also our [Willie's] father had some land took up about forty year ago. These was a homestead land. Then the land is bad condition. About three year ago the[re] was probate. But the Indian have not money for probate matter. The court was forced Indian pay up the probating. Some white men are buying land from our people. I see they didn't paying enough money. They was cheating Indian. Some the land for $60.00 to $100 dollars for acres. These only half the land worth. Some land is valuable. I will telling one reason. Our people are uncitizen. They are not paying tax. Because they can sell land we want took up these matter with the New President U.S. We are going send one man to Washington D.C. to settle up this. We are donating some money that count. (Ottogary 1921a)

Willie Ottogary was part of the Shoshoni delegation to Washington, D.C., in March 1921:

I am coming Washington City and was very surprise [to] see so many Indians from different tribes of the nation. But pretty well acquainted with them. And seen a inauguration day on 4th day of the March. Their is a big crowd of the people was here. Well and listen what other Indians say about our Indian right and more other thing. We seen Congress M.H. Welling, Senate Reed Smoot and more other men, I

Fig. 3.1. Willie Ottogary, probably taken during his visit to Washington, D.C. National Anthropological Archives, Smithsonian Institution.

cannot remember it all. We was seen President Harding 8 day of March and shake hand with him. We was in that bunch too. We was very glad that day. This Indians delegated for their people. Some of them went home last week. I surprise some Latter-day Saints here at Washington, D.C. I been Sunday School with them and very glad when found some I know from our own country. (Ottogary 1921b)

In September 1921 the Northwestern Band hired an attorney to represent their interest in the nation's capitol. Although they paid a $1,000 retainer fee and probably sent additional sums of money, no action was ever taken (Ottogary 1921c, 1921d). Within a year, the Shoshoni lost their confidence in the government to deal impartially with their complaints.

In March 1922 Willie Ottogary wrote a vivid account of some irregular land deals involving the Indian agent:

The agent is here at Washakie about two week ago. He was in the sand business or some other matter. Well not understand what he come here for and he took some business with our white man [LDS] Bishop. I like [to] see him when he comes here. Bue [But] he is kind some crook work on our people some away rather. We want know his business. He didn't care for our people. That is all I know about him. I though his business come here and talking with the Indians. And make everybody understand his especial business is. We are under his jurisdiction now or his [he] is our agent. . . . We are very poor this year. And we have no money. (1922)

Today, the Anglo community tends to view the agricultural experiment at Lemuel's Garden as a political and economic failure, if indeed they have even heard of it. The realities of homesteading are often ignored or romanticized. In fact, homesteads often failed, especially where they were located on marginal land, irrespective of their residents' racial or cultural identity (Allen 1987, 79–82; Bowen 1994, 73–85).

Native American accounts stress how they were illegally or unfairly deprived of their homesteads. Little consensus exists between the Anglo accounts and those of Native Americans, although it is also a mistake to believe that discrepancies and disagreements did not exist among Native Americans, as well as Anglos. The archaeological record provides another source of information about the histories of Native American and Anglo farmers along the lower Bear River.

EXAMINING THE ARCHAEOLOGICAL RECORD

While there is an excellent record for contemporary and historic settlement in northern Utah, very few Native American sites dating to the past two centuries have been investigated. Most of the sites that have received attention are monuments to battles in which Native Americans were defeated (for example, Bear River Massacre), or to the locally dominant, non-Native American LDS pioneers.

We thought that the archaeological record could be used in conjunction with the ethnographic histories to evaluate the relative success or failure of the Native American homesteads. Through archaeological survey we documented the material remains currently visible on the ground surface near Tremonton.

Our archaeological survey team received full cooperation from the present landowners. They were not only granted access to the areas but were given additional information and guidance regarding structures and sites associated with the Shoshoni homesteads. The Tribal Council of the Northwestern Band of Shoshoni fully supported and participated in the survey. Approximately 80 percent of the area is now under cultivation. The remainder is covered by residential and commercial developments or road right-of-way.

The survey team examined all of the land parcels involved in Lemuel's Garden (shown as homesteads in map 3.2). Other homesteads scattered north from Lemuel's Garden to Washakie and even further into southeastern Idaho will be examined later as the focus of our investigations shifts to Washakie. None of the original homesteads in Utah are now owned by members of the Northwestern Band.

Today, few late-nineteenth- or early-twentieth-century structures are standing on any of the homestead parcels. During our intensive walkover survey the most intact artifactual and structural evidence was found at the former LDS Mission House (42BO833). While the structure was moved and later demolished, a scatter of ceramics and glass remain within an agricultural field. Many of the fields have been mechanically leveled, eliminating any trace of buildings associated with the original homesteads (for example, the Ottogarys' home [42BO830] and 42BO834). Not only has the surficial archaeological record been obliterated, but foundations, chimneys, wells, and walls have been removed.

A structure, known locally as the "Indian House" (42BO831), may represent the last standing building from the community of Lemuel's Garden. This house was recently covered with siding, and it and the surrounding land has been severely altered by agricultural activities.

Our survey did locate a ditch that follows the contours along the east slope of the valley (map 3.2). While no mention has been found of an irrigation ditch in the records at the county courthouse or local irrigation companies, some local residents maintain that this ditch was constructed by the Shoshoni homesteaders to provide water to their fields along the floodplain (Fawcett and Lewelling 1996). Today, the ditch (42BO832) is overgrown, but archaeological test excavations, in conjunction with an examination of the soils and ditch morphology, might resolve questions about the origins, relative age, and use of this ditch.

We suspect that subsurface features (for example, wickiups, storage pits, hearths, privies, cellar holes, and/or building foundations) may extend below the plow zone at several sites (including the LDS Mission House, Ottogary's home, and the Indian House) where artifact scatters are visible. These features would probably be scattered over too large an area to systematically expose them through excavation without doing considerable damage to agricultural fields. Instead, we plan to use aerial and historic photography, magnetometers, and other remote sensing techniques to pinpoint suspected features that could then be examined with smaller, less intrusive test excavations. At present, no definitive evidence exists that any features have survived the current intensive agricultural use of the land.

Both local farmers and Northwestern Band Shoshoni are intrigued by the possibilities for less intrusive remote sensing, and they share some concerns for the recognition of cultural resources in the vicinity of Lemuel's Garden. They are using the value of cultural resources to challenge the construction of the proposed Honeyville dam, which would inundate farmland in the vicinity of Tremonton. In addition, the Shoshoni want to use the recognition of Lemuel's Garden to support their land claims. Despite these seemingly different agendas, the archaeology is fostering greater communications among these groups. One outcome might be the development of a greater consensus among the rural people of Utah.

DISCUSSION AND IMPLICATIONS

The differential preservation and interpretation of Native American historic sites in northern Utah, as compared to sites associated with Anglos, reflect and contribute to the notion that Native American history is relatively unimportant. Essentially, local Native American history ends when they were evicted from Lemuel's Garden and Washakie. Although ownership of many of the homesteads remained under Shoshoni control into the 1920–30s and most of the descendants still reside in the area, they are largely invisible in contemporary cultural and historical interpretations and writings. Native American historic sites have been vandalized, destroyed, or gone unrecorded while Anglo sites have been protected and preserved.

Anglo sites are more frequently deemed to be significant and worthy of preservation through nomination to the National Register of Historic Places. Of the twenty-nine historic sites listed from Box Elder County on the National Register, only one (Washakie) is associated with historic Native Americans. Four other sites and a district (with many sites) are associated with more ancient, prehistoric times (National Register 1989, 718; Utah State Historical Society files, December 1996). These sites may not be directly ancestral to those of the Shoshoni. Because Native Americans of northern Utah did not build elaborate architecture, like Puebloan peoples of the American Southwest, few of their settlements have been placed on the National Register. Native American sites are not included in plans to develop heritage tourism in northern Utah.

During the 1870s, the major building contractor in northern Utah was Shadrach Jones. He was a stonemason and craftsman who constructed numerous houses that have survived into the twentieth century and have been listed on the National Register of Historic Places (Utah State Historical Society files). Jones (n.d.) constructed chimneys and possibly even structures at Lemuel's Garden. Unlike the sites associated with the Anglo community, none of the Native American homesteads that he helped to build have been recognized or preserved.

Based on various written sources and our survey, the material culture used in the Native American homesteads consisted of essentially the same mass-produced goods prevalent in Euro-American sites from the late nineteenth and early twentieth centuries. We know that Native Americans used the same artifacts as their fellow Anglo settlers, but in distinctively different ways and contexts (for example, recycling and modifying tin cans to make tools for food preparation and consumption). The absence of drastically different objects, such as the elaborate pottery once made and used by Puebloan peoples of the American Southwest—things of great value on the antiquity market and among collectors—probably has also contributed to the lack of interest in the preservation or recognition of the Native American homesteads.

While the archaeological record of Lemuel's Garden has been severely disturbed, other sources are available. Willie Ottogary and several other Shoshoni residents wrote detailed accounts. They describe everyday life in their community and relations with surrounding people. Yet, even historians and anthropologists very knowledgeable about the Great Basin have largely ignored or misunderstood the significance of Lemuel's Garden and the Native American sources relating to it. Willie Ottogary wrote hundreds of columns that were published in several northern Utah newspapers between 1909 and 1923.

Brigham Madsen, the foremost historian of the northern Shoshoni, mentions Willie Ottogary in connection with his arrest for illegal hunting (1980a), but never cited any of Ottogary's columns, even though he cited other newspaper accounts in his histories. It seems unlikely that he was unaware of Ottogary's columns—he taught at Utah State University in Logan for many years, and most of Ottogary's columns were published on page 1 of the Logan newspaper. Julian Steward during the mid-1930s interviewed Shoshoni at Washakie for his classic Great Basin ethnography (1938, 217–20), yet he never mentions the recently deceased Willie Ottogary (1867–1929). Ottogary is still widely remembered and revered by contemporary Shoshoni. Perhaps we have too readily presumed that Native Americans were illiterate. In this instance, some of them were not.

The dominant Mormon (LDS) culture professed a policy of helping the Shoshoni, but when is "help" really help? The class structure in Mormon society tends to reward material acquisition and financial gain (Arrington 1958). The Mormon pioneers were immigrants from the East. Most of them were recent arrivals in the United States, and they perceived themselves as a disadvantaged minority. To many of them, the reality of Shoshoni warriors and their extended families gleaning food from the pioneers' fields was intolerable.

After the Shoshoni converts claimed the prime farmland along the lower Bear River for their homesteads, it was inevitable that Anglo Mormons would covet the same land as their population grew and native populations declined. The soil survey of Box Elder County confirms that Lemuel's Garden was located on the most productive farmland in the county (Chadwick et al. 1975, table 2). As discussed earlier, various means were used to displace the Native American homesteaders from this prime land.

LDS officials tended to adopt a patronizing attitude toward the "Laminites." The Native Americans were explained as a remnant of the lost tribes of Israel, who had been cursed with a dark skin and doomed to run wild in the wilderness (Stegner 1942, 147). They could be saved by conversion to the LDS faith. While this view engendered a degree of sympathy toward the Native Americans (uncommon in nineteenth-century America), it also justified a prejudice based on "God's word" that the Laminites were sinners and lesser people. One outcome of LDS beliefs was the rationalization of the displacement and destruction of the Native American homesteads.

CONCLUSIONS

Understanding the recent archaeological record of northern Utah requires far more than just documenting it with greater empirical detail. Historic sites and settlements associated with Anglos have been recognized and preserved, while those associated with Native Americans have not. The differential preservation of the archaeological record has occurred despite the shared religious faith (LDS) and agrarian economy of both Native American and Euro-American residents. Whether intentional or not, the destruction of the Native American homesteads perpetuates the notion that native peoples no longer live in northern Utah, and it denies us the possibility of examining their more recent past with (archaeological) sources other than written or oral accounts.

Historical archaeology is becoming increasingly important in the examination of recent Native American history. It often provides a source of information with which to challenge dominant or standard histories preserved by more powerful institutions. While we may have conceptualized the beaded and feather-wearing mobile warriors as representing pristine or natural societies in tune with their environment and worthy of study, we have often characterized Native Americans who moved onto reservations or into the dominant society as being uninteresting and having no valid culture. This becomes a self-fulfilling prophecy. If we perceive a people as lacking historical or cultural identity, then the record of that people also becomes unimportant and prone to destruction, fulfilling the prophecy. This presumption is particularly vicious to Native Americans attempting to preserve a distinct cultural identity while surviving within American society. Dominant and powerful individuals often reduce perceptions of the failings of Native Americans to stereotypes, eliminating the possibility of variation within or between culturally defined categories or groups. Thus, success or failure becomes attributable to race or class. By giving greater significance to the more distant or elaborate past of indigenous peoples while denying the existence of contemporary Native Americans in northern Utah, we commit genocide far more effectively than the U.S. military was ever able to do.

NOTES

The work would be impossible without the generous assistance of several groups of individuals: landowners near Tremonton, the Northwestern Band of the Shoshoni Nation, Bill and Sarah

Yates (Utah Statewide Archaeological Society volunteers), Scott Christensen, and our academic colleagues, particularly Steven R. Simms, Richley Crapo, Larry Zimmerman, and Alice Kehoe. They may not agree with all that we have said, but we believe that our discussions are developing a more inclusive recognization of heritage in Utah.

1. Places of birth for residents of Lemuel's Garden and Washakie listed in the U.S. Bureau of the Census, 1880, 1900, 1910, and 1920. Washington, D.C.

REFERENCES CITED

Allen, Barbara. 1987. *Homsteading in the High Desert.* Salt Lake City: Univ. of Utah Press.

Arrington, Leonard J. 1958. *Great Basin Kingdom: Economic History of the Latter-Day Saints, 1830-1900.* Cambridge: Harvard Univ.

Bowen, Marshall E. 1994. *Utah People in the Nevada Desert: Homestead and Community on a Twentieth-Century Farmers' Frontier.* Logan: Utah State Univ. Press.

Box Elder County Clerk. Landownership Records. County Courthouse, Brigham City, Utah.

Bureau of Land Management. N.d. Homestead Records. Government Land Office, Salt Lake City.

Chadwick, R. S., M. L. Barney et al. 1975. *Soil Survey of Box Elder County, Utah, Eastern Part.* USDA Soil Conservation Service, Washington, D.C.

Christensen, Scott R. 1995. *Sagwitch: Shoshoni Chieftain, Mormon Elder, 1822-1884.* Master's thesis, Utah State Univ., Logan.

Dibble, Charles E. 1947. The Mormon Mission to the Shoshoni Indians. *Utah Humanities Review* 1:53–73, 166–77, 279–93.

Fawcett, William B. 1996. Encouraging Research in Cultural Resource Management. *Public Archaeology Review* 4:3–14.

Fawcett, William B., and Walter Robert Lewelling. 1996. Field Notes, Box Elder County Native American Homestead Project. Manuscript on file, Anthropology Program, Utah State Univ., Logan.

Hart, Newell S. 1982. *The Bear River Massacre: Being a Complete Source Book and Story Book of the Genocidal Action against the Shoshones in 1863—And of General P. E. Connor and How He Related to and Dealt with Indians and Mormons on the Western Frontier.* Cache Valley Newsletter, Preston, Idaho.

Hill, George Washington. 1873–83. George Washington Hill Papers, 1873–1883. Microfilm Manuscript, Church of Jesus Christ of Latter-Day Saints Archive, Salt Lake City.

——. 1886. Letter to LDS Church President, John Taylor, Oct. 11. CRI/180 box 21. Church of Jesus Christ of Latter-Day Saints Archive, Salt Lake City.

Hunsaker, Kenneth D. 1983a. Indian Town, Utah: A Pre-Washakie Settlement. Manuscript, Utah State Univ. Merrill Library, Special Collections, Logan.

————. 1983b. Feeding the Indians of Northern Utah. Manuscript, Utah State Univ. Merrill Library, Special Collections, Logan.

Jones, Shadrach. N.d. Journal. Manuscript, Church of Jesus Christ of Latter-Day Saints Archive, Salt Lake City.

Knack, Martha C. 1992. Utah Indians and the Homestead Laws. *State and Reservation: New Perspectives on Federal Indian Policy,* ed. George Pierre Castle and Robert L. Lee, 63–91. Tucson: Univ. of Arizona Press.

LDS. 1993. *The Book of Mormon.* Salt Lake City: Corporation of the President of the Church of Jesus Christ of Latter-Day Saints.

Madsen, Brigham D. 1980a. *The Northern Shoshoni.* Caldwell, Idaho: Caxton Printers.

————. 1980b. *Corinne: The Gentile Capital of Utah.* Salt Lake City: Utah State Historical Society.

————. 1985. *The Shoshone Frontier and the Bear River Massacre.* Salt Lake City: Univ. of Utah Press.

————. 1986. *Chief Pocatello "The White Plume."* Salt Lake City: Univ. of Utah Press.

National Register. 1989. *National Register of Historic Places, 1966-1988.* Washington, D.C.: National Park Service.

Ottogary, Willie. 1920. Willie Ottogary's Washakie Letter. *Logan Journal,* Feb. 26, 1.

————. 1921a. Willie Ottogary's Washakie Letter. *Logan Journal,* Jan. 22, 1.

————. 1921b Willie Ottogary in Washington. *Logan Journal,* Mar. 22, 1.

————. 1921c Willie Ottogary's Washakie Letter. *Logan Journal,* Sept. 5, 1.

————. 1921d Willie Ottogary's Washakie Letter. *Logan Journal,* Oct. 24, 1.

————. 1922 Willie Ottogary's Washakie Letter. *Logan Journal,* Apr. 1, 1.

Ottogary, Willie, and E. Edlefsen. 1967. *Willie Ottogary's Letters to "The Journal."* Davis, Calif.: Danewel.

Parry, Mae T. 1976. Massacre at Bia Ogoi. *The Bear River Massacre,* ed. N. Hart, 143–52. Preston, Idaho: Cache Valley Newsletter.

Rhode, David, and David B. Madsen. 1994. Where Are We? *Across the West: Human Population Movement and the Expansion of the Numa,* ed. D. B. Madsen and D. Rhode, 213–22. Salt Lake City: Univ. of Utah Press.

Shoshone-Bannock Nation. 1968. Public Domain Allotments, Washakie Utah. Manuscript on file, Fort Hall, Idaho.

Stegner, Wallace. 1942. *Mormon Country.* New York: Duell, Sloan and Pearce.

Steward, Julian H. 1938. *Basin-Plateau Sociopolitical Groups.* Bulletin 120. Bureau of American Ethnology, Washington, D.C.

U.S. Bureau of the Census. 1880a. Population Schedules of the 10th (1880) Census of the United States, Box Elder County, Utah. National Archives, Washington, D.C.

—————. 1900. Population Schedules of the 12th (1900) Census, Box Elder County, Utah. National Archives, Washington D.C.

—————. 1910. Population Schedules of the 13th (1910) Census of the United States, Box Elder County, Utah. National Archives, Washington, D.C.

—————. 1920. Population Schedules of the 14th (1920) Census, Box Elder County, Utah. National Archives, Washington, D.C.

Utah State Historical Society, Cultural Resources and National Register Files, Dec. 1996, Salt Lake City.

CHAPTER FOUR

Panoptic Plantations

THE GARDEN SIGHTS OF THOMAS JEFFERSON AND GEORGE MASON

Terrence W. Epperson

At first glance, the phrase "panoptic plantations" appears as a puzzling paradox unrelated to garden or landscape studies. In a realm far removed from the plantation, the concept of the panopticon was initially formulated as a factory design by Sir Samuel Bentham (1757–1831) while employed by Prince Potemkin during a massive effort to transplant English manufacturing methods to White Russia. In 1785 Samuel's older brother Jeremy (1748–1832) visited him in Russia and, in a series of letters back home, extolled the applicability of the design to the various disciplinary institutions of emergent capitalism. These letters formed the basis of Jeremy Bentham's 1791 three-volume work entitled *Panopticon; or, The Inspection House: Containing the idea of a new principal of construction applicable to any sort of establishment, in which persons of any description are to be kept under inspection: and in particular to penitentiary-houses, prisons, houses of industry . . . and schools . . . .* Samuel returned to England soon after *Panopticon* was published, and the brothers collaborated on the construction of a panoptic prison designed to confine one thousand inmates (Bentham 1791; Dictionary of National Biography 1909).

The ideal panopticon consists of an observation tower within a large circular courtyard surrounded by an annular cellblock several stories high but only one room deep. Each cell should be occupied by only one surveillant who is subject to constant observation from the tower; yet the design of the panopticon simultaneously prevents communication between inmates. Ideally, the central tower is screened, so the inmates never know who (if anyone) is in the observatory at any particular time.

According to Michel Foucault's analysis of panopticism in *Discipline and Punish,* this design has a number of effects. Since the observer is screened from the gaze of the inmates, the see/being-seen dyad is dissociated, inducing "in the inmates a state of consciousness and permanent visibility that assures the automatic functioning of power." Furthermore, the exercise of power is dispersed, depersonalized, and internalized by the inmates. It is irrelevant to the functioning of the mechanism who, if anyone, actually occupies the tower so long as the inmates (or patients, students, workers, shoppers) behave *as if* they were under constant surveillance by the director. "[In short], the inmates should be caught up in a power situation of which they are themselves the bearers." Although the panopticon in its pure and literal form was relatively rare, it was—and remains—an extremely pervasive "political technology," deployed in many disparate realms of capitalist society (Foucault 1979; Davis 1992).

By contrast, the plantation—with its spectacular displays of extremely personalized sovereign power and its rule through the constant threat (and occasional application) of physical violence—would seem to belong to an earlier, less "rational" order. Indeed, I have elsewhere suggested that attempts to impose a unified spatial disciplinary grid upon the plantation were in fundamental contradiction with the oppressor's desire to construct "difference" through social and spatial segregation. Because life within the slave quarter was largely "invisible" to the planter, a vibrant culture of resistance survived and flourished, belying the image of the plantation as a "total institution" (Epperson 1990a, 1990b, 1999; Sider 1976).

Yet, notwithstanding these objections, I will argue that the gardens of George Mason's Gunston Hall (begun in 1753) and Thomas Jefferson's Monticello (begun by 1771) represent a significant departure from earlier plantation landscapes, and that the principal of panopticism is absolutely essential for an adequate "reading" of these houses, gardens, and associated landscapes. While earlier plantation mansions embodied and conveyed power and status primarily through ostentatious display within a dynamic landscape, Gunston Hall and Monticello are, in outward appearance, relatively unimposing structures. The one-and-one-half story, five-bay mass, and diminutive porticos of Gunston Hall give it an "almost vernacular" appearance. Similarly, Jefferson rejected the overbearing Georgian architecture of his day and eventually adopted the model of a Greek garden temple for Monticello. Indeed, the design of Monticello incorporates a number of optical illusions that actually diminish the apparent size and importance of the house within the garden (McLaughlin 1988, 248–57; Tafuri 1976, 25–30; Whiffen and Koeper 1981, 88–91; Whitehill 1976, 105–7).

Gunston Hall and Monticello were preeminently designed as observation posts. Power was embodied in, and expressed by, the ability to see rather than to be seen. This study is inspired in part by Dell Upton's analysis of early Virginia landscapes: "While Monticello could not be seen, its builder commanded the prospect of a vast territory around it.... Here was the articulated landscape in its most optimistic and most egocentric form; the natural and human worlds were refashioned to converge on a single individual at its center.... Everything at Monticello was made to be absorbed from a single point of view by the central actor" (1990, 84).

The argument of this paper is bolstered by the knowledge that contemporaneous landscape observation towers in England were among the inspirations for Bentham's panopticon as well as some rather surprising linkages between the architectural practices of Bentham and Jefferson (Foucault 1979, 317). After separate analyses of Mason's Gunston Hall and Jefferson's Monticello, the paper offers speculations on the possible linkages between panopticism in the landscape and the political philosophies of these two founding fathers. I close by examining the ramifications of a panoptic reading for the preservation and presentation of these houses and landscapes.

While previous studies of "power gardens" have focused on the manipulation of landscape and architectural space to assert social or political legitimacy or to impose spatial discipline, in this essay I would like to focus our gaze upon the subjectivity of the eye/I that constructs and controls these landscapes. To do so will require us to invert and subvert the usual emphasis of Foucaultian analysis. Despite Foucault's purported dual focus on both the dominatory and enabling functions of power, consideration of "the subject" (regardless of position) is generally subsumed by discussion of disembodied power relations (Sangren 1995; Smith 1988). An important exception to this tendency is the essay "The Eye of Power," where Foucault is specifically concerned with how "spaces of constructed visibility" serve to "constitute the subject" (Foucault 1980; Rajchman 1988). I would like to propose a reading that retains a primary focus upon relations of domination and resistance between human beings in different class positions (Billinage, 1984; Duncan and Duncan, 1988; Jameson, 1985; Kryder-Reid, 1991, 1994; Leone, 1988, 1995; Leone, et al., 1988). Unlike the case of the ideal panoptic prison, it makes all the difference in the world who occupies the privileged vantage point within the panoptic plantation.

GUNSTON HALL ⌐7

George Mason (1725–1792) of Fairfax County, Virginia, is known today primarily as the author of the 1776 Virginia Declaration of Liberties, an immediate precursor of Jefferson's Declaration of Independence. As a delegate to the constitutional convention in 1787 he delivered some 136 speeches in favor of replacing the Articles of Confederation; yet he ultimately refused to sign the completed document because of the absence of a Bill of Rights and joined other anti-Federalists in an unsuccessful attempt to block Virginia's ratification of the Constitution in 1788 (Bisbee 1994; Miller 1975, 1987; Rutland, 1970).

Construction of Gunston Hall was initiated in 1753, apparently under Mason's direct planning and supervision. Two years later he brought William Buckland (1734–1774), a young London carpenter-joiner, to Virginia under a four-year indenture to finish the interior of the house. Buckland subsequently established an architectural practice in Maryland where the 1774 Hammond-Harwood House in Annapolis was his last commission (Beirne and Scarff 1958).

In stark contrast to Monticello, there is a disappointing scarcity of contemporary documents detailing the day-to-day plantation operations and formal landscapes of Gunston Hall. In addition, archaeological investigations conducted to date have met with limited success. The important exception to this pattern is a remarkably detailed set of recollections written by George and Ann Mason's fourth son, John (1766–1849), during the late 1830s (Fauber Garbee, Inc. 1986; Mason, n.d.; Outlaw, 1973; Rowland, 1964).

The formal garden was located on the south (river) side of the house and contained, according to John Mason, "exactly one acre." (The present garden is considerably larger.) The garden was laid out "on a simple plan in rectangular squares and gravel walks." John recalls that his father "was fondest of his Garden," and during periods of "close occupation" he took most of his exercise here. From his study, in what is now known as the "Little Parlor," George Mason could move directly into the garden. The family knew he was not to be disturbed during his garden walks, and John remembers that his father would often "pass out of his Study and walk for a considerable time wrapped in meditation, and return again to his desk, without seeing or speaking to any of the Family" (Mason n.d., 8).

John Mason provided the following description of the south front of the house, which had a commanding view of the Potomac River:

From an elevated little portico you descended directly into an exten-
sive garden touching the house on one side & reduced from the natural
irregularity of the hill top, to a perfect level platform, the southern
extremity of which was bounded by a spacious walk running eastwardly
& westwardly, from which there was by the natural & sudden declivity
of the hill a rapid descent to the plain considerably below it. On this
plain adjoining the margin of the hill opposite to & in full view from
the garden was a deer park studded with trees kept well fenced and
stocked with native deer domesticated. (40–41)

The longest passage in John Mason's recollections is devoted to the description of the north or landward front of the mansion, where his father
maintained "an extensive lawn kept closely pastured." Within this vista George
Mason commissioned an intriguing exercise in point-perspective landscape
manipulation. The carriageway, described as a "spacious avenue," was flanked
by two footpaths. Beginning at a point about 200 feet from the house and
extending away from the house for about 1,200 feet, the carriageway and foot
paths were lined and shaded by four rows of "black-heart" cherry trees, each
row containing over fifty trees. These trees were sited and trimmed in rows
that diverged from the eye of an observer standing in the middle of the front
doorway of the mansion:

A common center was established, exactly in the middle of the outer
door way of the mansion, on that front—from which were made to
diverge at a certain angle the four lines on which these trees were
planted—the plantation not commencing but at a considerable dis-
tance there from (about 200 feet as before mentioned) and so carefully
and accurately had they been planted, & trained, and dressed in ac-
cordance each with the others, as they progressed in their growth, that
from . . . the common center . . . only the first four trees were visible.
More than once have I known my Father, under whose special care,
this singular and beautiful display of trees had been arranged and pre-
served, and who set great value on them, amuse his friends by inviting
some Gentleman or Lady (who visiting Gunston for the first time, may
have happened to have arrived after night, or may have come by the
way of the river and entered by the other front and so not have seen the
avenue) to the north front to see the grounds, and then by placing
them exactly in the middle of the door way, and asking—"How many

trees do you see before you"—? "four" would necessarily be the answer, because the fact was, that those at the end of the four rows next to the house, completely, and especially when in full leaf, concealed, from that view, body & top all the others—tho' more than fifty in each row— then came the request—"be good enough to place yourself now close to either side of the door way, & then tell us how many you see?" The answer would now be with delight and surprise, but as necessarily, "A great number, and to a vast extent, but how many it is impossible to say" and in truth to the eye placed at only about 2 feet to the right or left of the first position, there were presented, as if by magic, four long and apparently close walls of wood, made up of the bodies of the trees— and above as many, of rich foliage constituted by their boughs stretching, as seemed to an immeasurable distance. (41–43)

In an essay on the origins of linear perspective, Denis Cosgrove traces the history of the landscape idea as an individualist, bourgeois "way of seeing" linked to the emergence of merchant capitalism. Cosgrove notes that linear perspective utilizes the same geometry as accounting, navigation, land survey, mapping, and artillery. Unlike earlier artistic conventions that did not assert a dichotomy between the observer and the depicted scene, representation of three-dimensional space on a two-dimensional surface through linear perspective directs the external world toward the viewer located outside of the space. The depicted space therefore becomes the visual property of detached, individual observer (Cosgrove 1984, 1985; Jackson 1989, 44).

The formal landscape of Gunston Hall is thus a superb example of "aesthetic appropriation," although in this instance the process is reversed. Rather than being used to depict a three-dimensional scene on a flat surface, the principals of point perspective have been deployed to construct a landscape that exists for only one privileged viewer. The massive landscape feature consisting of over 200 large, carefully trained cherry trees could be appreciated from only one point in space (the center of the front doorway) by only one person at a time. It would be difficult to imagine a more extreme exercise in alienated, individualized perception of the landscape.

In much the same way that vanishing-point perspective in painting or the omnipotent third-person narrative voice in fiction places the viewer outside of—yet in full control over—the scene being observed, this landscape manipulation asserts that a single person, specifically the plantation owner or his privileged guest, controls the landscape visible from the front porch. Furthermore, the formal garden appears to have been constructed primarily for George Mason's private enjoyment, and his claim to mastery over nature was bolstered by the native deer kept in captivity in the deer park just beyond the formal gardens.

In his essay "Foucault's Art of Seeing," John Rajchman draws our attention to "spaces of constructed visibility," or "how spaces were designed to make things seeable, and seeable in a specific way" (1988, 103). Yet, we must also consider "spaces of constructed invisibility." While trees were planted and groomed at Gunston Hall to assert symbolic (and literal) control over the formal landscape, they were also used to mask the less idyllic aspects of plantation life from view, severely limiting the power of the panoptic impulse.

> To the west of the main building were first the school house—and then, at a little distance masqued by a row of large English walnut trees were the stables—to the east was a high paled yard, adjoining the house, into which opened an outer door from the private front within or connected with which yard were the kitchen, well, poultry houses and other domestic arrangements;—and beyond it on the same side, were the corn house and granary—Servants houses (in those days called Negroe quarters) hay yard & cattle pens, all of which masqued by rows of large cherry and mulberry trees.... The west side of the lawn or enclosed grounds was skirted by a wood, just far enough within which, to be out of sight, was a little village called Log-Town—so called because most of the houses were built of hewn pine logs—here lived several families of the slaves, serving about the mansion house—among them were, my father's body servant James, a Mulatto Man & his family, and those of several Negroe carpenters. (Mason n.d., 43–44)

According to John Mason, the enslaved laborers at Gunston Hall included "carpenters, coopers, sawyers, blacksmiths, tanners, curriers, shoemakers, spinners, weavers, knitters, and even a distiller" (46).

By the early 1780s George Mason's holdings included thirty major outbuildings and structures at Gunston Hall as well as approximately ninety enslaved laborers (Bisbee 1994). However, his control over the labor force was tenuous at best. On July 15, 1784, Mason placed an advertisement in the *Virginia Journal and Alexandria Advertiser* offering a reward of ten pounds for the return of two slaves who had absented themselves from their plantation duties. Clem was described as a well-set "BLACK NEGRO lad of about 19 years of age." Dick, his companion, was "a stout lusty MULATTO FELLOW, about

22 years of age, has large features and eyes, a very roguish down look, beats a drum pretty well, is artful and plausible, and well acquainted in most parts of Virginia and Maryland, having formerly waited upon me."

Dick was apparently returned to Gunston Hall, but not for long. Just over two years later Mason again advertised a reward for the return of Dick and a companion (*Virginia Journal and Alexandria Advertiser,* September 30, 1786). In this notice Dick was described as "a very lusty and well made mulatto fellow about 25 years of age, has bushy hair or wool, which he generally combs back, large teeth and eyes, a glum down look when spoken to, is a subtle and artful fellow, well acquainted both with Virginia and Maryland, beats a drum pretty well, and formerly a waiting-man. . . . He ran away some time ago, when working on board a bay craft by the name of Thomas Webster."

This time Dick was accompanied by Watt, "a stout Negro fellow, remarkably black, about 35 years of age . . . has had cross paths lately shaved on his head, to conceal which he will probably shave or cut close the rest of his hair." Subscribers are warned, "They will perhaps change their names and pass for freeman: and it is probable they may have a forged pass.—They will probably make for the Eastern-Shore, or for the State of Delaware or Pennsylvania. . . . All Captains or Skippers of vessels are hereby forewarned, at their peril, from taking them on board, or employing them."

These advertisements exemplify the geography of resistance. Dick's service as Mason's waiting man and later as a mariner gave him a wide range of topographic knowledge and mobility, which he apparently used to advantage upon at least two occasions. In both advertisements Mason also mentioned Dick's skill as a drummer; perhaps indicating an awareness of an important cultural tradition that was suppressed by law in colonial Virginia. Watt, Dick's companion on the second excursion, is even more intriguing. Although the "cross paths" shaved on Watt's head may have been an imposed identifying mark, they may instead represent an instance where an enslaved man has inscribed a geographical metaphor of cultural resistance upon himself. Leland Ferguson's essay "The Cross Is a Magic Sign: Marks on Pottery from Colonial South Carolina" suggests a tantalizing hypothesis regarding the possible significance of Watt's "cross paths." In coastal South Carolina Ferguson has found designs on the bottoms of small African American colonoware bowls that are remarkably similar to cosmograms documented in southern Zaire and Angola. These bowls are almost always recovered from underwater contexts, indicating possible use in water-related ceremonies (Ferguson 1992, 1999). Perhaps the "crosspaths" represented a cosmogram related to Watt's employment as a mariner.

Archaeological research conducted northeast of the mansion in 1952–53 resulted in the discovery of three eighteenth-century features: a rectangular refuse pit, a small brick foundation, and small rectangular pit paved with unmortared salvaged brick. The 1953 report noted in passing that these features could be related to the "Negro quarters" indicated by John Mason's description, but no further work was done in this area (Fauber 1953). Subsequent archaeological investigations, particularly at Kingsmill Plantations and Monticello, have found that wood- or brick-lined subfloor "root cellars" are a ubiquitous feature of Chesapeake slave dwellings, and the features at Gunston Hall certainly deserve reexamination in light of these recent discoveries (Kelso 1984a). Although they are not unique to African American contexts, these features probably provided slaves with a relatively secure place to conceal valued items (Kimmel 1993; Sanford 1996). In any event, we suspect that there was a great deal happening behind the English walnut, cherry, and mulberry trees that masked the quarters from the gaze of Gunston Hall.

MONTICELLO

Thomas Jefferson began designing Monticello as early as 1767 and had initiated construction by 1771. The first phase of construction was completed over the next ten years. By 1776, eighty-three enslaved African Americans lived and labored on Jefferson's "Little Mountain" (Upton 1998, 27). In 1789 Jefferson returned from extensive travels abroad, inspired by the neoclassical architecture of Paris and the ruins of classical antiquity he had visited in southern France. By 1796 he had initiated the second phase of building at Monticello, and in 1804 he designed extensive alterations for the grounds of Monticello on the basis of his thorough knowledge of English landscape design. From his retirement from public life in 1809 until his death in 1826 Jefferson was constantly "putting up and pulling down" at his beloved mountaintop estate, described by architectural historian Dell Upton (1998, 20) as a "densely layered, half resolved agglomeration of visual images, social ideas, and spatial relationships." When we speak of the "landscape" of Monticello, we are therefore referring to an extremely dynamic (and astonishingly well-documented), ongoing process. Nevertheless, the principle of panopticism—whether or not it was consciously articulated—provides a unifying theme for understanding Jefferson's manipulations of architectural and landscape space (Beiswanger 1984; Brown 1990; Kelso 1984b, 1986; Martin 1991; Nichols and Griswold 1978).

In formulating the basic plan for Monticello and its dependencies, Jefferson

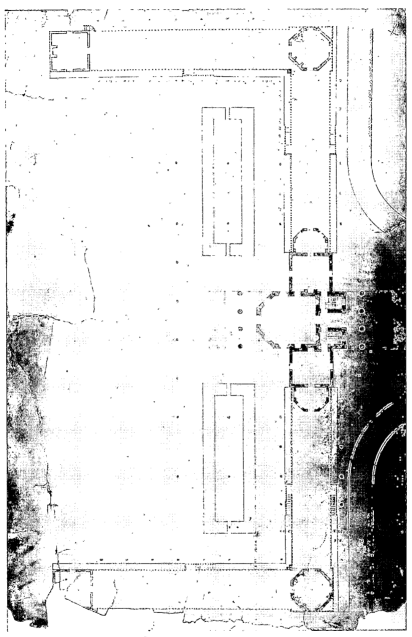

Fig. 4.1. Jefferson's design for the ground floor and dependencies at Monticello.
Courtesy of the Massachusetts Historical Society.

basically turned the classical Palladian villa "inside out." While dependencies typically opened into a central courtyard, Jefferson's design suppressed the dependencies into the hillside to provide an unimpeded view of the surrounding landscape (fig. 4.1). These dependencies also framed and defined the formal gardens of the west front of the house, and the roofs of the wings could be used as promenades from the ground floor of the house. The two L-shaped dependencies themselves could be entered only from the outside edge of the complex (Adams 1976, 275). By leveling and redesigning the top of his mountain, Jefferson accomplished the same visual screening effect that Mason achieved by the judicious planting of English walnut, cherry, and mulberry trees. There was, however, one important difference. While Mason's masking impulse was primarily exclusionary, Jefferson was able simultaneously to preserve his view of the surrounding landscape, mask the dependencies from view, yet still incorporate them into the rigid, symmetrical space of the immediate plantation nucleus.

In the same year he began construction of Monticello, Jefferson took steps to couple literal and aesthetic appropriation of the landscape surrounding Monticello. In exchange for legal services provided to Edward Carter, Jefferson noted in his memorandum book that he was to receive "as much of his [Carter's] nearest mountain as can be seen from mine, and 100 yards beyond the line of sight." Carter's Mountain, renamed Montalto ("high mountain") by Jefferson, was 400 feet higher than Monticello ("little mountain") (Beiswanger 1984, 174–75). This portion of Jefferson's vista was the subject of several landscape design schemes, most of which were never implemented. Jefferson was quite taken by the concept of the *ferme ornée* (ornamental farm), and he had hoped to construct several farms on the flank of Montalto to improve the prospect from Monticello.

During their tour of English gardens in 1786, Jefferson and John Adams visited Stowe, the estate of the Grenville family, which included an octagonal column 115 feet high. This monument was "intended by Lord Cobham as a prospect tower from which to survey the landscape achievements of a lifetime." Jefferson was fascinated by the concept of the observation tower and formulated at least three designs for a tower to be constructed on Montalto, none of which were ever executed (fig. 4.2). Jefferson's first tower design was to have been one hundred feet high and constructed in five stories, each of which was to present a different example of the Roman orders. The columns and entablatures were to be cut out of plank and appear only on the facade facing Monticello, indicating that the tower was primarily intended as a "sham" or eye-catcher to be viewed from Monticello. Jefferson later redesigned the tower to include an

Fig. 4.2. One of Jefferson's never-executed designs for an observation tower
for the summit of Montalto. Courtesy of the Massachusetts Historical Society.

octagonal cupola as illustrated in James Gibbs's 1728 *Book of Architecture* (Beiswanger 1984, 175; Dumbauld 1976, 145–47).

Visitors to Monticello were generally more impressed by the view from the gardens than by the gardens themselves. For example, when the duc de La Rochefoucault-Liancourt visited in 1796, he wrote:

> *in the back [west] part the prospect is soon interrupted by a mountain [Montalto] more elevated than that on which the house is seated. The bounds of the view on this point, at so small a distance, form a pleasant resting-place, as the immensity of prospect it enjoys [to the east] is perhaps already too vast. A considerable number of cultivated fields, houses, and barns enliven and variegate the extensive landscape, still more embellished by the beautiful and diversified forms of mountains. (Rochefoucault-Liancourt 1799, 2:69–72).*

We should remember that everything the Monticello visitor could see on Montalto (plus 100 yards beyond the line of sight) was owned, controlled, and contrived by Jefferson. While the landscape manipulations and the placement of a dome atop the rebuilt plantation house "transformed Jefferson into an all-seeing I," the Master of Monticello also went to extraordinary lengths to render his enslaved workforce invisible (Upton 1998, 37).

During a visit to Monticello, Margaret Bayard Smith noted that the slave dwellings along Mulberry Row created "a most unpleasant contrast with the palace that rises so near them" (quoted in Adams 1983, 164–67). In 1804 Jefferson drafted "General Ideas for the improvement of Monticello," initiating a new phase of rebuilding and landscape modification. In order to improve the view of the surrounding countryside, the landscape alterations included construction of a ha-ha at the base of the gardens and the removal of the wooden buildings (including slave dwellings) along Mulberry Row and the integration of additional plantation functions into the "southeastern offices" beneath the terrace edge. The reconstruction of Mulberry Row coincided with Jefferson's conscious efforts to further "rationalize" the management of his enslaved laborers. Within the house, Jefferson developed devices such as dumbwaiters, lazy Susans, and a *garde-robe* privy that could be emptied from the basement to minimize intimate contact with his slaves (Upton 1998, 30).

In his writings, Jefferson often proclaimed the necessity to maintain separation of the races, stating that "amalgamation produces a degradation to which no one . . . can innocently consent" (quoted in Gordon-Reed 1997,

134). However, Jefferson's well-documented disdain of miscegenation, as well as his manipulation of landscape and architectural space to render African Americans "invisible," must be interpreted in light of recent genetic research. A recent study has proven that Thomas Jefferson was the father of Thomas Easton Hemings (1808–1856), youngest son of Sally Hemings, an enslaved domestic laborer who also happened to be the half-sister of Jefferson's deceased wife, Martha. (Lander and Ellis 1998; Foster et al. 1998). This connection reminds us of the irreconcilable contradiction between incorporation and exclusion that characterizes all modes of oppression.

In addition to his plantation interests, Jefferson had a longstanding interest and involvement in prison design. While he was in Paris during the 1780s, the directors of public buildings for the capital in Richmond requested plans for a state capital building, a governor's house, and a prison. Jefferson's August 13, 1785, reply regarding a prison plan reads in part: "Having heard high commendations of a plan of a prison at Lyons I sent there for it. The architect furnished me with it. It is certainly the best plan I ever saw. It unites in the most perfect manner the objects of security and health, and has moreover the advantage, valuable to us, of being capable of being adjusted to any number of prisoners, small or great and admitting of execution from time to time, as it may be convenient" (quoted in Adams 1976, 230; Rice 1953).

The prison architect Jefferson admired was Pierre-Gabriel Bugniet (?– 1806). In addition to Bugniet's plan, Jefferson submitted his own scaled-down plan for a prison to be constructed in Richmond. Neither plan survives, but a design by Bugniet for an ideal prison is probably quite similar. While not a literal panopticon, this design does incorporate a central observation tower surrounded by a circular courtyard.

In his *Autobiography* Jefferson also indicates his awareness of English prison reform movements: "With respect to the plan of a prison . . . I had heard of a benevolent society, in England, which had been indulged by the government, in an experiment of the effect of labor, in *solitary confinement*, on some of their criminals; which experiment had succeeded beyond expectation" (quoted in Adams 1976, 204).

Among Jefferson's surviving architectural papers is a sketch in his own hand for a prison block that includes a cell for solitary confinement. The annotations for the remaining six cells are: "white female criminals, female blacks, white male criminals, male blacks, white male debtors, and white female debtors."

Jefferson was indisputably knowledgeable about Jeremy Bentham's writings on panoptic institutions and was probably personally acquainted with the prison reformer and pragmatic philosopher. Jefferson's library included the three-volume 1791 London edition of *Panopticon,* and on October 20, 1824, Bentham presented Jefferson with an autographed copy of his 1791 book *Essays on Political Tactics* (Sowerby 1955).

In 1796 the Commonwealth of Virginia sponsored a competition for the design of a new prison consistent with reforms instituted the preceding year. The commission was awarded to Benjamin Henry Latrobe (1764–1820). In his autobiography Jefferson indicates that Latrobe's prison was based on his own design formulated several years earlier. Unlike Jefferson's surviving sketch, Latrobe's plan does not include provisions for racial segregation. For the men's portion of the prison, Latrobe's design employs the panoptic principals of the central observation tower, circular courtyard, and annular cell block three stories high but only one cell deep (see also, Leone and Hurry 1998). The cornerstone for the new prison was laid on August 7, 1797 (Adams 1976, 232).

PANOPTIC POSSESSIVE INDIVIDUALISM

Historian Page Smith has documented the extent to which Jefferson relied upon Mason's Virginia Declaration of Rights when drafting the Declaration of Independence (Smith 1976, cited in Gunston Hall Board of Regents 1991). However, this parallel also reminds us of Mason and Jefferson's thorough mutual grounding in, and reliance upon, the political philosophy of John Locke. Since Mason and Jefferson were the two founding fathers most urgently concerned with the definition and protection of individual liberties, it is particularly significant that political theorist C. B. Macpherson characterizes Locke's work as the epitome of "possessive individualism" (Laslett 1960; Macpherson 1962).

In the *Second Treatise* Locke reminds us, "The great and *chief end* therefore, of Mens uniting into Commonwealths, and putting themselves under Government, *is the Preservation of their Property*" (Laslett 1960, 124). Yet it is "property" (in its broadest connotation) which accounts for inequalities between "men" within civil society, and in Locke's view this "disproportionate and unequal Possession of the Earth" was arrived at through the "tacit and voluntary consent" of all parties (50). For Locke, the capacity to labor is a form of property that can be voluntarily alienated in return for a wage. However, since property was the basis and "chief end" of government, propertyless persons (particularly wage laborers) could legitimately be excluded from governmental participation, even though they were still subject to governmental control (Macpherson 1962, 231).

This political philosophy had tangible manifestations within plantation landscapes and gardens. Since, in Locke's words, God gave the earth "to the use of the Industrious and Rational" (34), one could assert political legitimacy by manipulating the landscape to demonstrate one's command over the natural laws of perspective (Kryder-Reid, 1991, 1994; Leone, 1988; Leone et al. 1988). Yet, within the panoptic plantations we see something even more specific occurring, the constitution of individual political identity through manipulation of landscape space.

Mason and Jefferson were not merely demonstrating their control over property for the rest of the world to see, they were constituting *themselves* as political beings and manifesting a radical new political philosophy through their control over spatial and social relations. Their political vision was, of course, extremely individualized and alienated. At Gunston Hall the land-scape could be appropriately appreciated by only one person at a time, from only one point in space, to the exclusion of all other individuals and points of view. At Mason's discretion, the privileged visitor could briefly occupy the focal point of the landscape and know what it felt like to be in a position of power. At Monticello, Jefferson combined literal and aesthetic appropriation to create a landscape that could be only appreciated from the top of "his" little mountain. The enslaved human beings that actually constructed the gardens and landscapes and made the plantation economy possible were rendered invisible to the observer occupying the position of privilege. This "invisibility" within the constructed landscape was—not surprisingly—reflected by a political invisibility in the founding documents of our nation.

POSTSCRIPT

The two Jeffersonian institutions of Charlottesville, Virginia, were recently embroiled in a fratricidal struggle involving Jefferson's landscape vision. In 1988 the University of Virginia unveiled plans to construct two office buildings on the approach to Monticello, within the "viewshed" of the mansion. The response from the Thomas Jefferson Memorial Foundation was predictable and swift. Executive Director Daniel P. Jordan announced that the proposed development would be a "major intrusion" into Monticello's access corridor, "an area that is pristine and rural—zoned that way by the county—and an intrusion that would adversely affect the larger setting of Monticello." Expressing a sentiment that resonates with the present analysis, he added, "You can't understand Jefferson unless you understand the setting." Although plans for the development were abandoned in January of 1990, "viewshed preservation" has become a "front burner" issue for the foundation, requiring an innovative combination of several preservation approaches, since a large-scale land purchase is not a viable option. Again, quoting Jordan: "We don't have a permanent endowment, much less a fund for acquiring property .... It is absolutely impossible to even think about buying enough land to preserve the view shed. You cannot buy up the view of Monticello" (Larson 1991).

This statement, of course, elides the fact that Jefferson himself went a fair distance toward buying—and reconfiguring—the view from Monticello. Although landscape preservation is indeed an important preservation issue, the trustees of Monticello should not be uncritical in their attempts to reproduce Jefferson's sovereign gaze. Even in Jefferson's day the view was not "pristine," but was carefully contrived and controlled. The half-million citizens who visit Monticello every year might well consider the connections between this landscape and Jefferson's sense of himself as a political individual.

NOTE

A version of this paper was presented at the 1993 American Anthropological Association Annual Meeting in Washington, D.C., in a session entitled "Vision and the Human Landscape: Approaches to Site and Sight." Elizabeth Kryder-Reid, D. Fairchild Ruggles, and Mark P. Leone provided valuable comments. My research at Gunston Hall was facilitated by the generous assistance of Susan Borchadt, archivist, and Ann Baker, librarian.

REFERENCES CITED

Adams, William Howard, ed. 1976. *The Eye of Thomas Jefferson*. National Gallery of Art, Washington, D.C. Reprint, Charlottesville, Va.: Thomas Jefferson Memorial Foundation; Columbia and London: Univ. of Missouri Press.

Adams, William Howard. 1983. *Jefferson's Monticello*. New York: Abbeville Press.

Beirne, Rosamond Randall, and John Henry Scarff. 1958. *William Buckland, 1734–1774: Architect of Virginia and Maryland*. Baltimore: Maryland Historical Society.

Beiswanger, William L. 1984. The Temple in the Garden: Thomas Jefferson's Vision of the Monticello Landscape. In *British and American Gardens in the Eighteenth Century*, ed. Robert P. Maccubbin and Peter Martin, 170–87. Williamsburg, Va.: Colonial Williamsburg Foundation.

Bentham, Jeremy. 1791. *Panopticon; or, The Inspection House* .... London.

Billinage, Mark. 1984. Hegemony, Class, and Power in Late Georgian and Early Victorian England: Towards a Cultural Geography. In *Explorations in Historical Geography: Interpretative Essays*, ed. Alan Baker and Derek Gregory, 28–67. Cambridge: Cambridge Univ. Press.

Bisbee, M. Lauren. 1994. *Of Land and Labor: Gunston Hall Plantation Life in the Eighteenth Century*. Lorton, Va.: Gunston Hall Board of Regents.

Brown, C. Allan. 1990. Thomas Jefferson's Poplar Forest: The Mathematics of an Ideal Villa. *Journal of Garden History* 10:117–39.

Cosgrove, Dennis E. 1984. *Social Formation and Symbolic Landscape.* Totowa, N.J.: Barnes and Noble.

———. 1985. Prospect, Perspective and the Evolution of the Landscape Idea. *Transactions, Institute of British Geographers* New Series, 10:45–62.

Davis, Mike. 1992. *City of Quartz: Excavating the Future in Los Angeles.* New York: Verso.

Dictionary of National Biography. 1909. London: Smith, Elder & Co.

Dumbauld, Edward. 1976. Jefferson and Adams's English Garden Tour. In *Jefferson and the Arts: An Extended View,* ed. William Howard. Adams, 146–47. Washington D.C.: National Gallery of Art.

Duncan, J., and N. Duncan. 1988. (Re)reading the Landscape. *Society and Space* 6:117–26.

Epperson, Terrence W. 1990a. Race and the Disciplines of the Plantation. *Historical Archaeology* 24 (4): 29–36.

———. 1990b. "To Fix a Perpetual Brand": The Social Construction of Race in Virginia, 1675–1750. Ph.D. diss., Dept. of Anthropology, Temple Univ. Ann Arbor, Mich.: University Microfilms.

———. 1999. Constructing Difference: The Social and Spatial Order of the Chesapeake Plantation. In *"I, Too, Am America": Archaeological Studies of African-American Life,* ed. Theresa A. Singleton, pp. 159–72. Charlottesville and London: Univ. Press of Virginia.

Fauber, J. Everette, Jr. 1953. Archaeological Survey—Gunston Hall. Report on file at the Gunston Hall Library, Lorton, Va.

Fauber Garbee, Inc. 1986. Consolidation of All Archaeological Research Concerning the Dependencies around the Mansion "Gunston Hall," Lorton, Virginia. Report on file at the Gunston Hall Library, Lorton, Va.

Ferguson, Leland G. 1992. *Uncommon Ground: Archaeology and Early African America.* Washington, D.C.: Smithsonian Institution Press.

———. 1999. "The Cross Is a Magic Sign": Marks on Eighteenth-Century Bowls from South Carolina. In *"I, Too, Am America":* Archaeological Studies of African-American Life, ed. Theresa A. Singleton, pp. 116–31. Charlottesville and London: Univ. Press of Virginia.

Foster, Eugene A., M. A. Jobling, P. G. Taylor, P. Donnelly, P. Knijff, Rene Mieremet, T. Zerjal, and C. Tyler-Smith. 1998. Jefferson Fathered Slave's Last Child. *Nature,* Nov. 5, 1998, 27–28.

Foucault, Michel. 1979. *Discipline and Punish: The Birth of the Prison.* New York: Vintage.

———. 1980. The Eye of Power. In *Power/Knowledge: Selected Interviews and Other Writings, 1972–1977,* ed. Colin Gordon, 146–65. New York: Pantheon.

Gordon-Reed, Annette. 1997. *Thomas Jefferson and Sally Hemings: An American Controversy.* Charlottesville and London: Univ. Press of Virginia.

Gunston Hall Board of Regents. 1991. *Gunston Hall Return to Splendor: The Colonial Home of George Mason, Father of America's Bill of Rights.* Lorton, Va.: Gunston Hall Board of Regents.

Jackson, Peter. 1989. *Maps of Meaning.* London: Unwin Hyman.

Jameson, Fredric. 1985. Architecture and the Critique of Ideology. In *Architecture, Criticism, Ideology,* ed. Joan Ockman, 51–87. Princeton: Princeton Architectural Press.

Kelso, William M. 1984a. *Kingsmill Plantations, 1619–1800: Archaeology of Country Life in Colonial Virginia.* New York: Academic Press.

———. 1984b. Landscape Archaeology: A Key to Virginia's Cultivated Past. In *British and American Gardens in the Eighteenth Century,* ed. Robert P. Maccubbin and Peter Martin, 159–69. Williamsburg, Va.: Colonial Williamsburg Foundation.

———. 1986. The Archaeology of Slave Life at Thomas Jefferson's Monticello: "A Wolf by the Ears." *Journal of New World Archaeology* 6 (4): 5–20.

Kimmel, Richard H. 1993. Notes on the Cultural Origins and Functions of Sub-Floor Pits. *Historical Archaeology* 27 (3): 102–13.

Kryder-Reid, Elizabeth. 1991. Landscape as Myth: The Contextual Archaeology of an Annapolis Landscape. Ph.D. diss., Dept. of Anthropology, Brown Univ. Ann Arbor, Mich.: University Microfilms.

———. 1994. The Archaeology of Vision in Eighteenth-Century Chesapeake Gardens. *Journal of Garden History* 14 (1): 42–54.

Lander, Eric S., and Joseph J. Ellis. 1998. Founding Father. *Nature,* Nov. 5, 1998, 13–14.

Larson, Chiles T. A. 1991. Alarm on "Little Mountain." *Historic Preservation* 43 (2): 46–49.

Laslett, Peter, ed. 1960. *John Locke: Two Treatises of Government.* Cambridge: Cambridge Univ. Press. (All Second Treatise quotations are by section number.)

Leone, Mark P. 1988. The Georgian Order as the Order of Merchant Capitalism in Annapolis, Maryland. In *Recovering Meaning: Historical Archaeology in the Eastern United States,* ed. Mark P. Leone and Parker Potter, 235–61. Washington, D.C.: Smithsonian Institution Press.

———. 1995. A Historical Archaeology of Capitalism. *American Anthropologist* 97:251–68.

Leone, Mark P., and Silas D. Hurry. 1998. Seeing: The Power of Town Planning in the Chesapeake. *Historical Archaeology* 32 (4): 34–62.

Leone, Mark P., Elizabeth Kryder-Reid, Julie H. Ernstein, and Paul A. Shackel. 1988. Power Gardens of Annapolis. *Archaeology* 42:34–39.

Macpherson, C. B. 1962. *The Political Theory of Possessive Individualism: Hobbes to Locke.* Oxford: Oxford Univ. Press.

Martin, Peter. 1991. *The Pleasure Gardens of Virginia: From Jamestown to Jefferson.* Princeton: Princeton Univ. Press.

Mason, John. n.d. "Recollections" Original manuscript and unabridged transcription on file, Gunston Hall Library, Lorton, Va. (Pagination refers to original manuscript.)

McLaughlin, Jack. 1988. *Jefferson and Monticello: The Biography of a Builder.* New York: Henry Holt and Company.

Miller, Helen Hill. 1975. *George Mason: Gentleman Revolutionary.* Chapel Hill: Univ. of North Carolina Press.

————. 1987. *George Mason: The Man Who Didn't Sign.* Lorton, Va.: Board of Regents of Gunston Hall.

Nichols, Frederick Doveton, and Ralph E. Griswold. 1978. *Thomas Jefferson, Landscape Architect.* Charlottesville: Univ. Press of Virginia.

Outlaw, Alain C. 1973. Archaeological Excavations at Gunston Hall. Report on file at the Gunston Hall Library, Lorton, Va.

Rajchman, John. 1988. Foucault's Art of Seeing. *October* 14:89–119.

Rice, Howard C., Jr. 1953. A French Source of Jefferson's Plan for the Prison at Richmond. *Journal of the Society of Architectural Historians* 12 (4): 28–30.

Rochefoucault-Liancourt, François. 1799. *Travels through the United States of America.* London.

Rowland, Kate Mason. 1964. *The Life of George Mason, 1725–1792.* 2 vols. New York: G. P. Putnam's Sons.

Rutland, Robert, ed. 1970. *The Papers of George Mason, 1725–1792.* Chapel Hill: Univ. of North Carolina Press.

Sanford, Douglas. 1996. Searching and "Researching" for the African Americans of Eighteenth Century Virginia. In *The Archaeology of Eighteenth Century Virginia,* ed. Theodore. R. Reinhart, 131–48. *Archaeological Society of Virginia Special Publication* 35. Richmond: Archaeological Society of Virginia.

Sangren, P. Steven. 1995. "Power" against Ideology: A Critique of Foucaultian Usage. *Cultural Anthropology* 10:3–40.

Sider, Gerald. 1976. When Parrots Learn to Talk, and Why They Can't: Domination, Deception, and Self-Deception in Indian White Relations. *Comparative Studies in Society and History* 29:3–23.

Smith, Page. 1976. *A New Age Now Begun: A People's History of the American Revolution.* New York: McGraw-Hill.

Smith, Paul. 1988. *Discerning the Subject.* Minneapolis: Univ. of Minnesota Press.

Sowerby, E. Millicent, comp. 1955. *Catalogue of the Library of Thomas Jefferson.* Washington D.C.: Library of Congress,

Tafuri, Manfredo. 1976. *Architecture and Utopia: Design and Capitalist Development.* Cambridge, Mass.: MIT Press.

Upton, Dell. 1990. Imagining the Early Virginia Landscape. In *Earth Patterns: Essays in Landscape Archaeology,* ed. William M. Kelso and Rachel Most, 71–86. Charlottesville: Univ. Press of Virginia.

————. 1998. *Architecture in the United States.* Oxford and New York: Oxford Univ. Press.

Whiffen, Marcus, and Frederick Koeper. 1981. *American Architecture.* Vol. 1, *1607–1860.* Cambridge, Mass.: MIT Press.

Whitehill, Walter M. 1976. *Palladio in America.* New York: Rizzoli.

CHAPTER FIVE

The Divide in Post-Fifteenth-Century Southern Africa

ARCHAEOLOGY OF THE COLOR LINE AND WHITE SETTLER HISTORY

Warren R. Perry

In the late eighteenth and early nineteenth centuries the political and cultural form of southeastern Africa changed in an irreversible way. This period, known as the Mfecane or the Difaqane, Zulu and Sotho respectively for "the crushing," is symbolized by the transformations wrought in Zulu society by Shaka. The rise of the Zulu state under Shaka in the context of the Mfecane/Difaqane is one of the great problems in the social sciences and one of the great moments in the history of southern Africa. The existence of the Zulu state has played a central role in defining the black and white color line in southern Africa from the nineteenth century up until today. With a few exceptions most contemporary historians and social scientists continue to reproduce that line in their speculations about the emergence of states in southern Africa.

This chapter considers the political and economic forces underlying state formation in southeastern Africa. Most of the previous work on this topic is based on documentary and oral sources. However, an increasing body of information from archaeological contexts can be brought to bear on examining various hypotheses on the causes of the Mfecane/Difaqane. Key to many of these theories is an underlying model, ironically named "the settler model." In this model the European settlers virtually disappear as players on that southeastern African landscape. As a result, the settler model has excluded European colonial culture as a major cause of the dislocations of the Mfecane/Difaqane. When subjected to archaeological data, this model serves as a poor basis for understanding this crucial period of history.

THE SETTLER MODEL AND THE MFECANE/DIFAQANE

Much of the current research on southern Africa has focused on the pivotal role of the Mfecane/Difaqane and the consequent formation of the Zulu state as the most important events in later south African history (Denoon and Nyeko 1986; Guy 1980, 1982; Hamilton 1995; Omer-Cooper 1966, 1988, 1995; Shillington 1987). Explanations of these events have been posed in terms of African internal economic dynamics. They emphasize catastrophic population pressures, ecological conditions such as soil erosion, and naturally increasing cattle herds resulting in depleted resources and overgrazing as the forces behind the Mfecane/Difaqane. These forces caused culture change and state formation in the late eighteenth and early nineteenth centuries.

According to settler model theorists, during the late eighteenth and early nineteenth centuries, social relations in southern Africa were drastically reorganized from clan-organized ranked social relations to age-grade military institutions with a bureaucracy of military elite of the newly forming state. Productive cycles were disrupted and trade relations realigned. People shifted their allegiances and reformulated group identities many times as warfare and famine swept the region. By all accounts it was a period of great strife, suffering, sorrow, and, for some, triumph.

The settler model of South African history, most clearly espoused by Omer-Cooper, is anchored in three assumptions regarding pre–European-contact southern African people. The first is the idea that southern African society was composed of a number of relatively discrete ethnic groups that had their origin in the past and persisted into relatively recent times. The second is that these ethnic groups were poorly articulated one to the other—that there was little systemic interaction between the groups that can be used to understand cultural transformation. The third is the Zulucentric focus, namely that these social relations were disrupted in the early nineteenth century by the Mfecane/Difaqane when local conditions led the pre-Zulu ethnic group to become a predatory state.

The consensus is that there were three major groups of people in southern Africa during the last five hundred years, two of whom, the Nguni and the Sotho-Tswana (Sotho and Tswana), belong to the southern "Bantu." The third major group, the Ju/'hoansi (Khoi-Khoi and San or Khoisan), are thought to be the original inhabitants of southern Africa. The traditional wisdom holds that Nguni and Sotho-Tswana agropastoralism allowed much more rapid population growth and relatively high population densities and encouraged a more complex sociopolitical organization than the pastroforaging Ju/'hoansi (Khoisan) groups they encountered. Culture change came about in Zululand with the resultant development of an expansionist state which disrupted the social relations among these various ethnic groups.

Settler model theorists argue that late-eighteenth-century political upheavals within local polities in the Mfolozi-Phongola region, the area that was to become the Zulu heartland (see map 5.1), were the result of various internal conditions focusing upon anthropogenic environmental change. The standard versions suggest that conflict between different groups in the Mfolozi-Phongola region over the need for grazing land resulted in livestock raiding by the more powerful polities, and extensive migrations by the less powerful. Refugees on the move were attacking other polities in their path as they fled the Mfolozi-Phongola region. The scale of devastation is said to have been heretofore unknown in southern Africa. The state of contention among the groups in this region culminated in the emergence of a hierarchy of centralized military polities, at the apex of which stood the Zulu state (Omer-Cooper 1966).

The emergence of the Zulu state had continuing impact on the wider region of southern Africa. The effects of the Zulu state were to continually create refugees, demand tribute, create subordinate allegiances of predatory military states, and confiscate territory and resources. These activities created impacts in the outlying peripheries of Zululand. They drastically altered regional power relations, having significant consequences for the political economy of nineteenth-century southern Africa far beyond the margins of the Zulu state. The violent dislocation of, and incursions by, African polities inspired by the Zulu against other agropastoral communities prompted further political and economic transformations in outlying peripheral communities.

Omer-Cooper (1988, 66) argues that these chaotic conditions invited European intervention. European missionaries, traders, and others living beyond the encroaching European frontiers were caught-up in the African

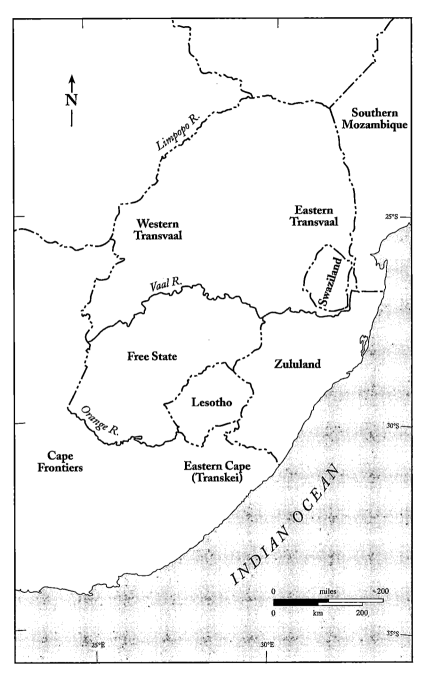

Map 5.1. *Zululand and other areas used in the analyses within the context of southeast Africa.*

inspired turmoil. He explains that: "The previously thriving population of Natal was particularly disrupted. Many fled south. Others hid themselves in extensive areas of dense bush leaving most of the land apparently deserted apart from the vicinity of Port Natal where a community of about five thousand lived under the *protection* of the English traders" (emphasis added).

Various theories have been advanced to explain these changes. For instance, demographic arguments have emphasized varying kinds of population stress (for example, Gluckman 1960; Omer-Cooper 1966, 1988; 1995; Service 1975; Shillington 1987; Stevenson 1968). Gluckman (1960) was the first to suggest that population pressure led to increased competition for land, generating conflict that led to intra-African warfare. Omer-Cooper (1966), in his classic *The Zulu Aftermath,* offered a detailed explanation of Zulu state emergence based on catastrophic population pressure and a lack of grazing land. In this work he popularized the idea that the Mfecane/Difaqane was a unique and violent historical event that brought a sudden and dramatic end to centuries of southern African social stagnation (Hall 1990; Webster 1991). He has since amended his original formulation, adding the factor of the effects of the ivory trade at Delagoa Bay (Omer-Cooper 1988, 53).

Other explanations have also stressed the imbalance between populations and resources, but they have drawn attention to the degradation of the environment as the cause of the crisis. For instance, Guy (1980, 1982) and Marks (1967) suggest that a lack of grazing land due to extensive overgrazing and a decline in land productivity resulting from soil erosion, drought, disease, and increasing human and stock densities were major causes for the rise of the Zulu state.

Several Africanist historians have emphasized the importance of trade as a factor in causing the social disruption of the Mfecane/Difaqane (Carlson 1984; Hedges 1978; Slater 1976; Smith 1969; Wilson and Thompson 1969–1971). Still others linked the contraction of this trade to the rise of later states (Bonner 1977, 1980, 1983; Delius 1983; Legassick 1969). The trade proponents argue that inter-European and intra-African political and economic conflicts over control of trade resulted in indigenous transitions in African sociocultural institutions. Trade intensified class conflict and maneuvering, becoming an exclusive prerogative of the elite for distribution of rare items to other elites, favorite retainers, and others within the prestige systems with regard to generating aristocratic wealth accumulation and power.

Eldredge (1995) has presented an important synthesis of the demographic and trade proponents. She argues that the Mfecane/Difaqane involved factors governed both by the physical environment and by Delagoa Bay trade. An environmental crisis, presumably a drought, initiated a scarcity of food resources which resulted in famine and increased competition over productive resources. Groups with locational advantage had greater access to food resources and were differentially empowered. Furthermore, as the local and regional ivory trade grew, elephant herds declined, reducing ivory exports. This combination of elements, she concludes, may have provoked violent struggles for dominance and survival and promoted the political consolidation of elite power and economic growth at the expense of peripheral communities who were differentially incorporated into the lower hierarchical levels of the dominant polities (Eldredge 1995).

In the United States some early African American scholars challenged the prevailing views of colonialist historiography, explaining the Zulu revolution as a fight to consolidate southern Africans and resist European penetration (Diop 1974, 169; Du Bois 1969, 31; Clarke 1970, 35; Rodney 1981, 128–32). This explanation was generally ignored by South African and other European scholars until recently.

Chanaiwa (1980) presented an African vindicationist argument that Zulu state formation was the result of embryonic, institutionalized class development and wealth concentration exacerbated by aristocratic/commoner antagonisms. He suggested that the Zulu chose military resistance to maintain autonomy over migration or refugeeism. This might have freed them from ethnic and territorial boundaries, despair, and inaction. Finally, he concluded that the Zulu revolution may have offered every able-bodied man an opportunity to acquire cattle, despite earlier disadvantages of birth, rank, class, and political power.

Threads of an alternative analysis that undermines the geographic localization and European passivity of the settler model can be found in the work pioneered by Macmillian and his student de Kiewiet during the late 1920s and early 1930s—work that was dismissed by the academy and political institutions of South Africa (Saunders 1995). This work has most recently been resurrected and elaborated upon by Cobbing (1988), his students (Webster 1991, 1995), and later others (Wright 1990, 1995a, 1995b). Cobbing contends that the Mfecane/Difaqane is linked to disruptive, destabilizing European forces emanating from the Cape, southern Mozambique, and other European colonies in southern Africa, which were in turn inextricably bound to the developing global capitalist social formation (Cobbing 1988; Etherington 1991a, 1991b, 1995). This scope and scale have previously been purposely ignored by a settler version of South African history that considered the simultaneous events of the Great Trek of the Dutch colonists to the interior and the alleged African self-destruction of the Mfecane/Difaqane as fortuitous occurrences.

Cobbing focuses on the role of slave raiding in the precipitation of internal conflicts and asserts that slaving was the most consequential determinant disrupting African societies in the Delagoa Bay and Cape areas. Slaving, he argues, altered demographics and social relations, incited political instability, and converted social reproduction, forcing a restructuring of African polities in the region. Furthermore, he insists that European farmers, traders, and missionaries were in collusion and that their agents, the Griqua and Korana, were the principal sources of violence in the interior (see Eldredge 1995; Hamilton 1995; and Hartly 1995; they challenge Cobbing's views on the role of European collusion).

Cobbing concludes that the Mfecane/Difaqane served as a "multiple alibi," removing any need for an explanation of the African past by ignoring and/or concealing massive external imperial agency and thereby authenticating white occupation of the land through an ideology of separate development. His explanations of the nature of white population movements augmented by the dearth of evidence for Zulu agency make very compelling grounds to repudiate the Mfecane/Difaqane myth as an explanation for the depopulation and destruction of the interior African societies. Cobbing argues that the concept of Mfecane/Difaqane is Zulucentric, ideologically "loaded," and historically erroneous. Its ponderous baggage renders it untenable as a neutral descriptive historical category, and being devoid of any analytical utility it must be abandoned (Cobbing 1988, 487, 519).

In sum, the settler model sees the rise of the Zulu state as being responsible for the Mfecane/Difaqane. Moreover, the Zulu state rises because of local factors involving, variously, the environment, the social structure of agropastoralist communities, and/or long distance trade in European exotics. The result of Zulu state formation appears to be the conquest of and disruption of life for the various independent African cultures of southeastern Africa. Cobbing's alternative vision suggests a much more fluid set of cultural interactions among the various indigenous groups, with Europeans playing an active role in a complex colonial field. The Europeans were interested not only in high-prestige exotics, but most importantly in human beings as enslavable labor. The quest for captives was the central disruptive process that led to the disasters of the Mfecane/Difaqane as well as Zulu state formation.

The scale of the phenomena as well as the timing of disruptions are open to archaeological analysis. The use of material remains can be brought to bear on assessing the relative significance of the settler model and Cobbing's alternative thesis. Material remains are especially important for assessing Cobbing's model since he argues that few, if any, documents of slaving should exist, since this was an outlawed trade. It is to the archaeological assessment of these ideas that I next turn.

ARCHAEOLOGY IN SOUTHERN AFRICA

Archaeology in southern Africa has primarily focused on the "Stone Age" (Hall 1993; Perry 1999). However, in recent years a considerable number of Africanist archaeologists have conducted research on later historical southern African sites (Chatterton et al. 1979; Collett 1982a, 1982b; Daniel 1973; Denbow and Wilmsen 1983; M. Hall 1980, 1981, 1984; Hall and Mack 1983; S. Hall 1995; Maggs 1982, 1984, Maggs and Whitelaw 1991; Marker and Evers 1976; Mason 1968, 1973; Mason et al. 1981). Many have demonstrated the utility of combining archaeological and ethnohistorical approaches by focusing on the connection between archaeological data and oral traditions (Cruz-Uribe and Schrire 1991; Evers 1984; Maggs 1976, 1977; Marker and Evers 1976; Perry 1991; Schrire 1988, 1996; Schrire et al. 1995; Scully 1978; van der Merwe and Scully 1971; Wright and Kus 1979).

In particular, the Historical Archaeology Research Unit of the University of Cape Town has embarked on several Cultural Resource Management projects (Hall and Malan 1988; Hall et al. 1990a, 1990b; Markell et al. 1995). One major focus is designated "the archaeology of impact" by Hall (1993). This theme assumes the concept of the frontier as an intricate, volatile zone of interaction where the economic and political impact of European penetration was felt by Africans long before actual colonial settlement (Hall 1990, 1993). If this were the case, then archaeological evidence of "impact" encounters should be present at a variety of southern African sites. Early European sites, such as mission stations, are locations where "impact" may be seen. European pastoralists' homesteads, forts, and trading posts all aimed at interactions with African communities. Early African sites, such as the various African capitals and some Ju/'hoansi pastroforager sites, contain large numbers of glass trade beads, indicative of the "impact" of trade between Europeans and various African groups. A broad survey of mostly published and some unpublished archaeological materials from the period of the Mfecane/Difaqane was conducted and combined with data from a site survey in Swaziland (Perry 1996, Perry 1999) to establish a data base to evaluate the utility of the settler model in explaining southeast African political economy. Interactions between Europeans and pastroforagers are especially significant because many mixed groups exiled from the Cape later turned to cattle and slave raiding but have received no archaeological attention (Hall 1993).

One example of archaeology on the fluid frontiers of southern Africa is Schrire's archaeological research on Oudepost I, a seventeenth- through eighteenth-century Dutch trading outpost and military garrison at the Western Cape. This was an important excavation of a historical military site whose focus was European and Ju/'hoansi social relations. Schrire's research has contributed significant insights into the devastating impact on both the wild and domestic food resource base of the Ju/'hoansi pastroforaging economy by Europeans that resulted in dispossessing Ju/'hoansi from their lands and forcing them into dependence on Europeans (Cruz-Uribe and Schrire 1991; Schrire 1988, 1996; Schrire and Deacon 1989; Schrire et al. 1995).

Zulu state emergence has been the subject of archaeological study. For example, Hall (1980, 1981) has conducted an ecologically focused settlement pattern study. He concluded that the Zulu state could have arisen from internal ecological stress as grazing availability declined and stock density increased (Hall 1981). The Zulu state could also have resulted from "overall increases in demand following internal reorganization of the Iron Age economy, for instance as a result of a political need to support a non-productive class or to meet the demands for tribute imposed by a more powerful neighbour" (Hall 1981, 166).

More recently, Simon Hall (1995) used archaeological data from seventeenth-through nineteenth-century Sotho-Tswana settlement transformations and locations through time to examine the impact of the Difaqane in the western and southwestern Transvaal. He argues that the post-fifteenth-century western Transvaal shows three types of settlement strategies. The first type includes stone-walled hilltop defensive settlements with abnormally low frequencies of cattle bone and glass beads. Between 1650 and 1750 these type settlements began to aggregate rapidly into larger towns with perimeter stone walling. Simultaneously, another settlement type with different layout and form of dwelling appears on the sides of steep hills. By the nineteenth century Sotho-Tswana were found in underground cavern systems, suggestive of loose, fragmented communities under severe stress (S. Hall 1995, 309). The initial impulse toward settlement aggregation may have had local causes, but the accelerated regional aggregation after 1750 followed by the occupation of large-scale underground refuge villages was possibly due to increasing impact toward the end of the eighteenth century of the northern Cape frontier (S. Hall 1995, 321).

· The small amount of historical archaeology performed on European and

African sites tantalizingly demonstrates the creative and productive integration of historical documents, oral texts, and archaeological data and is indicative of a promising future for such research in southern Africa. This work has reached the point of maturity that it can now be brought to bear on the question of the utility of the settler model.

ASSESSING THE MFECANE/DIFAQANE WITH ARCHAEOLOGICAL DATA

On the basis of my review of the literature and work in Swaziland, there are 159 sites that can be brought to bear on the utility of the settler model (Perry 1996, 348–479). They have been grouped into the major ecological and geopolitical regions of southeastern Africa: Zululand, Swaziland, the eastern and western Transvaal, and the Free State. Since the settler version sees Zululand as the main area where the Zulu state emerged, it is considered a "core" area. All of the other areas are viewed as peripheral to Zululand. I was able to use a number of variables to group the sites into pre– and post–Mfecane/Difaqane sets. Given the way I have organized the data, this means that pre–Mfecane/Difaqane population should be larger in the core area Zululand and smaller in the others.

Another potential source of information on "impact" is rock art scenes (Lewis-Williams 1981, 1982, 1984, 1989; see Campbell 1986 and Dowson 1995 for examples of studies more concerned with the relations of rock art and European penetration).

The settler model has specific temporal and spatial trajectories that can be compared with archaeological results. Key variables include population growth, ecological degradation, social hierarchy formation, state formation, native and external European trade, and the geographic spread out of settlement disruption. Most importantly, the settler model assumes a general change from local scale social interactions to increasingly larger spatial interactions integrating southeastern Africa relative to the Zulu core region.

Table 5.1 summarizes both the expectations for key archaeologically recoverable variables under the assumptions of the settler model and the results of the archaeological analyses. Discussion of the analyses follows; Perry (1996, 1999) gives a much fuller accounting of the analyses.

Demography
Another prediction of the standard model is that population sizes in specific regions will have a certain pre–Mfecane/Difaqane pattern, and that these

TABLE 5.1

Southeast African Changes from Pre– to Post–Mfecane/Difaqane

Site	Population Size		Social Hierarchy		Cattle (no. of encounters)		Rank Size (type of curve)		Trade European Goods	
	Exp	Obs	Exp	Obs	Exp	Obs	Exp	Obs	Exp	Obs
Zululand	↑	↑	↑	↑	↑	↓	LL to C	C to DC	↑	↑
Swaziland	same	↑	↑	same	↑	↓	LL to V	C to DC	same	↑
Eastern Transvaal	↑	↓	same	↓	↓	↑	LL to LL	DC to DC	↓	↓
Western Transvaal	↑	↓	same	same	↑	↓	LL to V	C to C	same	same
Free State	↑	↓	↑	↓	↓	↓	V to V	C to V	same	↓
Southeast Africa	↑	↓	↑	↓	↑	↓	V to V	C to LL	↑	↓

Notes: *Exp = Expected; Obs = Observed;* ↑ *= Increase;* ↓ *= Decrease; LL = Log-linear; C = Concave; DC = Double Convex; V = Convex.*

population sizes will change in specific ways after the Mfecane/Difaqane. Is that what the archaeological record shows?

This population pressure and stress argument is also an internal explanation of the Mfecane/Difaqane. The basic proposition suggests that a population explosion in the Zulu heartland led to increased competition for land, generating overgrazing, environmental degradation, and intra-African warfare. If this argument were correct, then we might expect a dramatic increase in population in the area of Zululand during pre–Mfecane/Difaqane times resulting in the Zulu state. The rest of southeastern Africa should show relatively low population sizes that increase with the arrival of the Zulu state.

There are several references to population size estimates and site sizes in the ethnographic, historic, and archaeological literature on southern Africa for various polities and groups. These estimates range from the general to the specific. Various authors (Bryant 1929; Chanaiwa 1980; Edgerton 1988; Fortes and Evans-Pritchard 1967; Gluckman 1960; Guy 1982; Hoernle 1946; Kinsman 1984; Krige 1965 [1936]; H. Kuper 1947, 1965, 1970, 1986; Lee 1993; Lye and Murray 1980; Morris 1965; Mostert 1992; Omer-Cooper 1966, 1988; Roberts 1974; Schapera 1967, 1970; Service 1975; Shillington 1987; Stevenson 1968) have attempted to estimate population sizes from ethnohistorical data. Problems with this approach are numerous, not the least of which is that information for pre–Mfecane/ Difaqane is much scarcer than from post–Mfecane/Difaqane. Without a baseline to compare against, the high population densities of the ethnohistorical period could be evidence for population pressure causing state formation, or conversely could be evidence of state-induced population growth. Archaeological data, though it too has its problems, provides another source of information on population growth.

I calculated settlement areas from a variety of archaeological reports. These areas are taken to be rough indicators of population size (Derricourt and Evers 1973; Evers 1975; Evers and van der Merwe 1987; Goudie and Price-Williams 1983; Hall 1990; Huffman 1984, 1986; Inskeep 1979; Maggs 1976, 1977, 1982; Marker and Evers 1976; Mason 1973; Parkington and Cronin 1979; Perry 1991; Taylor 1975; van der Merwe and Scully 1971; Watson and Watson 1990). The results are interesting for the role of population growth in southern African state formation.

Although reliable estimates of absolute population sizes in early historical documents are rare, the figures compiled by Stevenson, Huffman, and others for Zululand, along with population estimates for other southern African polities (see Perry 1996, app. 2) were calculated to derive hypothetical population estimates for pre– and post–Mfecane/Difaqane sites and times based upon mean population densities and mean territorial sizes.

Site size data (see Perry 1996, app. 1) were used to produce population estimates for Zululand, Swaziland, the eastern Transvaal, the western Transvaal, and the Free State. Local population in Zululand, as indicated by total site size, increased substantially, going from 1 hectare to 78 hectares, an increase of 77 hectares. Local Swaziland population, as indicated by total site size, increased 18 hectares, going from 21 to 39 hectares in settlement. Eastern Transvaal's local pre–Mfecane/Difaqane population decreased dramatically, going from 214 hectares in settlement to 80 after the Mfecane/ Difaqane, a decrease of 134 hectares. Local population in western Transvaal decreased only slightly. Hectares in settlement went from 17 pre–Mfecane/ Difaqane hectares in settlement to 13 post–Mfecane/Difaqane hectares, a decrease of 4 hectares. Free State population suffered the most precipitous decrease, falling from 204 pre–Mfecane/Difaqane hectares in settlement to only 13 post–Mfecane/Difaqane hectares, a decrease of 191.

Based on the total number of sites per time period, overall population in southeast Africa seems to have increased slightly. At the same time, the total number of hectares in settlement in the southeast African sample dropped 441 hectares, going from 637 hectares during the pre–Mfecane/Difaqane period to 196 for the post–Mfecane/Difaqane period. Thus, although site number appears to have remained somewhat stable despite increases and decreases in certain areas, overall area in settlement was reduced by about 31 percent. These results suggest that populations abandoned certain areas and clustered in others after the Mfecane/Difaqane. Furthermore, the transition from pre–Mfecane/Difaqane to post–Mfecane/Difaqane in southeast Africa was accompanied by a 34 percent decrease in total sites for all areas except for Swaziland and Zululand, which showed a 33 percent increase in total sites.

The demographic situations in the eastern Transvaal and Free State are perhaps the most interesting. In terms of regional demographics, it seems that during the earlier periods the eastern Transvaal and the Free State populations were significantly larger than that of Zululand, but during the later periods, as the Zululand population increased, the eastern Transvaal and Free State populations underwent an overall reduction, suggesting a population shift from these areas into Zululand and Swaziland.

What seems to have been going on are massive shifts in population from one region to another and a shift from more uniform to more clustered distributions of sites across the landscape, such as would be expected if warfare was the stimulus for this population movement. Thus the Mfecane/Difaqane is associated with an unprecedented increase in the amount of movement induced by violence. In other words the general principle that peace has a centrifugal tendency, spreading primary producer sites across the landscape, and war is a centripetal force, pulling primary producer populations into centers, rather than demographic pressure, seems to have been operative in southern Africa.

Social Hierarchy

Anthropological archaeologists have noted a general relationship between settlement hierarchy and social hierarchy. They generally posit that the number of tiers in a settlement hierarchy is related to the number of tiers within a social hierarchy. The more stratified the settlement hierarchy, the more stratified the social hierarchy. Various proposals have been offered linking the number of settlement tiers to specific forms of social hierarchy (Evers and Hammond-Tooke 1986; Huffman 1986; Taylor 1975; Wright 1977; Johnson 1977, 1980a, 1980b; H. Wright and Johnson 1975). One of the most famous propositions is Wright and Johnson's (1975), which suggests that states have a minimum of three settlement tiers. Huffman (1986) has done the most extensive work with this proposition for southern African settlements.

My studies do not rely upon establishing a particular correlation between the number of settlement tiers and the form of social organization. Rather, the propositions from the settler model indicate relative similarities or differences in hierarchy at any particular time and directional change in hierarchy for different regions. In particular, the pre–Mfecane/Difaqane regions should display relatively unstratified social and settlement hierarchies, with the possibility that the Zulu heartland may have been slightly more stratified. After the Mfecane/ Difaqane, social stratification should be quite marked in the heartland and less so in the peripheries.

Settlement hierarchies were developed using information on site size and site function. Site sizes were plotted as frequency distributions and "natural" breaks in the distribution were taken as indicative of the breaks in settlement tiers (Johnson 1973, 1980b). Unimodal distributions have no "natural" breaks and are indicative of relatively nonstratified social relations; bimodal distributions have one break and are indicative of more stratified social relations; trimodal distributions have two breaks and are even more stratified; and so on.

The settler model assumes the existence of egalitarian and rank-ordered agropastoral communities according to age and sex prior to the formation of the Zulu state. Under the settlement model the heartland of Zululand might exhibit slightly greater degrees of social inequality prior to state formation; the independent agropastoralists and pastoralists of the eastern Transvaal, western Transvaal and Free State should exhibit marked social equality.

Social hierarchy can be assessed from the southern African data with such indicators as the presence of exotic materials, the existence of socially central settlements, the size of cattle enclosures, the culling patterns of herds from more and less prestigious settlements, and the overall organization of the settlement hierarchy. My studies drew on all of the these variables, but here I will report on the settlement hierarchy studies.

The general results of the regional site size analysis and artifactual analysis are complex and varied. Only the settlement hierarchies from Zululand show an increase in social hierarchy, with all other regional hierarchies decreasing. This result supports the settler model's assumption that after the Mfecane/ Difaqane, Zululand became more stratified.

Simultaneously, there are other kinds of archaeological evidence in all regions to indicate discrepancies with the settler model. The most intriguing area is the Free State, whose early bimodal distribution contained a very large site four times larger than the largest in Zululand and is the largest site in the entire southeast African sample. This elite site is particularly interesting for other reasons besides its huge size. The faunal assemblage, although dominated by wild game and containing marine resources, is characterized by an elite cattle culling pattern along with the presence of sheep/goat. There is evidence of glass beads and bead production, copper, rock gongs, and miniature pots, suggesting initiation or other rituals. There are also burials with stone-lined tombs and many grave goods. Stone tools, red ochre chunks, bored stones, and undecorated grass-tempered pottery typical of ethnographic pastroforagers is also present. Finally, there is evidence of at least one burnt dwelling and no evidence that the site was occupied during the later periods.

The marked concentrations of sites noted in all regions suggest that earlier periods were perhaps more peaceful than later times since the smaller (primary producer) and large (production) sites, were more evenly distributed spatially across the region. Furthermore, since the largest early site in Zululand was an iron production site, this could suggest less stratified social relations and iron production for local markets. Finally, the larger production sites were all outside of Zululand.

In sum, the structural evidence from settlement hierarchies alone can be very misleading, the evidence for social hierarchy is quite complex and dependent on the number and kinds of evidence selected for analysis. Furthermore, different regions were experiencing social hierarchy differently at different times. Whatever the case, the settler model's prediction of universally increasing social hierarchy after the Mfecane/Difaqane is not supported. The evidence from these limited analyses indicates that the situation was far more complex.

Cattle Enclosures

Differential possession and accumulation of cattle are key indicators of social inequality among southern African polities. Consequently, cattle enclosure size can heuristically be used as a surrogate to inform on status, wealth, and power, and hence class and state formation, in southern African societies. The cattle enclosure sizes were estimated from the archaeologically recovered remains, and from them an estimate of the number of animal units was developed. As prestige items, cattle should become increasingly concentrated in the hands of state elites in the Zululand and Swaziland state formation areas and should generally decline in both number and level of concentration in other areas.

Cattle served several significant roles in the pre- and post-fifteenth-century southeast African political economy. Earlier elders' authority at the homesteads was dependent upon their control over access to cattle for bride-wealth payments for juniors in exchange for labor services. Later, cattle accumulation was necessary for local elites to increase their own herds and to reward local homesteaders for valor in battle to better keep the peace within their domain of control and to have access to rare prestige goods through exchange. Hence, cattle accumulation was a way to balance fissioning and facilitate the political and economic transactions that characterize the emergence of social inequality, class and state formation, and power over people.

The cattle enclosure analysis shows that all areas had unimodal enclosure size distributions during both periods, except for eastern Transvaal, which had a trimodal distribution for both periods. This suggests differential possession of cattle in the eastern Transvaal before and after the Mfecane/Difaqane. In addition, every region, except eastern Transvaal (which gained three enclosures), showed a decrease in the number of cattle enclosures through time. However, if we look at each region in terms of total enclosure areas presumably housing livestock, and mean enclosure size, a different, more complex pattern emerges. Zululand showed an increase in both areas enclosed and mean cattle enclosure size. Swaziland exhibits a decrease in areas enclosed and an increase in mean cattle enclosure size. Eastern Transvaal, like Zululand, increased in both categories while western Transvaal decreased in both categories. The Free State, like Swaziland, increases in areas enclosed and decreases in mean enclosure size. A similar pattern is found if one looks at estimates of animal units, namely increasing numbers of animals in Zululand and the eastern Transvaal and declining numbers of animals in the other three regions.

Only Zululand and the eastern Transvaal show increases in the number of cattle. This suggests the presence of a strong social hierarchy in these two areas. There is also evidence for nonstate societies before the Mfecane/Difaqane in Zululand; state formation appears to have begun after the Mfecane/Difaqane. The existence of evidence for a long and continuous social hierarchy in the eastern Transvaal is at odds with the settler model and suggests that state formation in Zululand was not the first such incident in southeast Africa. Furthermore, the enclosure size evidence from eastern Transvaal indicates interaction with Europeans in the Delagoa Bay area well before the Mfecane/Difaqane.

In Swaziland, western Transvaal, and the Free State there was a decrease in the very categories (enclosures, animals, and the like) that increased in Zululand

and eastern Transvaal. Though consistent with the settler model for the western Transvaal and the Free State, it is a surprising result for Swaziland.

Rank Size

The settler model argues that social interactions went from the scale of regional integration to the scale of multiregional integration with the onset of state formation among the Zulu. The spatial scale of integration has been studied by archaeologists through the analysis of rank-size relations. Rank-size analysis was developed by geographers interested in the mathematical relationship between the size of any given place in a settlement system and its rank order relative to size. To conduct such studies, well-integrated settlement patterns were studied by ordering all the places in the system from largest to smallest and assigning each a rank, with the rank of one being assigned to the largest place. Plots of the size of places against the rank of places disclose a number of interesting patterns (Haggett 1966).

The expected plot for well-integrated settlement systems is a log-linear relation. When rank and size are transformed to their logarithms, a plot of this relation is a straight line. Issues of scale of integration can be seen in deviations from this straight line. So, for instance, geographers (for example, Berry 1961; Haggett 1966) have argued that when a settlement pattern is affected by outside influences, the observed distribution drops below the expected line, a pattern referred to as a concave distribution. Johnson (1977, 1980a, 1980b) has identified a pattern of another kind. When the settlements studied are actually the result of compounding two or more independent settlement systems, the result is a line that rises above the expected straight line. Paynter (1982) argues that such a pattern can also occur when the settlement system is drawn from the marginal settlement of a much larger settlement system. Finally, Falconer and Savage (1995) have discovered a distinctive pattern indicative of the effects of colonialism. They argue that a double-convex deviation, one in which the observed lines falls above the expected, drops to the expected, and then falls above again, results from the operation of a colonial system imposed on part of a formally well-integrated settlement system. This model—the rank-size linear relation—and its deviations can be used to assess whether various settlement systems in the pre– and post–Mfecane/Difaqane were essentially independent, well-integrated settlement systems or systems reflecting the impact of outside influences. The settler model would lead one to expect that pre–Mfecane/Difaqane settlement systems would either disclose independence from significant outside influences or possibly the effects of observer bias in improperly compounding two or more independent settlement systems in the same analysis. In other words, under the settler model, straight line and convex distributions should be most common. After the Mfecane/Difaqane, with the Zulu state making its influence felt throughout southern Africa, the heartland regions of Zululand should show their central role in this larger process through the development of concave deviations, whereas other regions might show their increasing peripheral position through convex or double convex deviations, or their relative independence in straight lines or the error created convex distributions.

As can be seen from table 5.1 the results hardly are consistent with the settler model. With the exception of the eastern Transvaal, the regions display a concave pattern in the early period, indicative of the operation of larger-scale settlement systems. Zululand, the supposed heartland of the process, Swaziland, and the eastern Transvaal display double convex patterns in the post–Mfecane/Difaqane period, indicative of being a colonial region. Western Transvaal and the Free State continue to display participation in larger settlement systems. I also analyzed all sites for which I had site size data in southeast Africa. Johnson (1977, 498) has cautioned that the larger the scale, the greater the probability for various stochastic processes to effect the rank-size curves. The rank-size curve for southeast Africa should be convex in both periods since such an analysis is, according to the settler model, compounding many settlement systems.

Instead, the pre–Mfecane/Difaqane rank-size curve for southeast Africa is concave. The post–Mfecane/Difaqane rank-size distribution for southeast Africa produced a more log-linear distribution with larger settlements lying along the linear rank-size line, while smaller sites show lower limb concavity being smaller than predicted. These results are at odds with the settler model expectations of the operation of numerous independent polities in both periods.

There clearly were very complex settlement processes happening in post-fifteenth-century southeast Africa, and the analysis points to effects beyond the regions and indeed beyond the scale of southeast Africa. Throughout southeast Africa the pre–Mfecane/Difaqane period was marked, to varying degrees, by concave rank-size patterning, patterns of a relatively few large places and many small places. Post–Mfecane/Difaqane patterns show a more complex situation— Zululand, Swaziland, and the eastern Transvaal show double-convex patterning, while the Free State appears convex. Generally, all of southeast Africa moves from a concave pattern to a log-linear pattern for larger sites and an increasingly concave pattern as sites become smaller. All of these patterns indicate the effects of large-scale processes, even in the pre–Mfecane/Difaqane period, processes certainly larger than any of the individual regions and processes beyond the scale of southeast Africa. This is evidence for the involvement of Europeans in state formation in southeastern Africa, yet leaves open the issue of the nature of that involvement.

European Trade Goods

Twenty-one sites from the pre–Mfecane/Difaqane period and twenty from the post–Mfecane/Difaqane period contained European goods. These ranged from items such as trade beads to gunflint. Under the settler models that emphasize trade in exotics disrupting local political processes, there should be a concentration of these items at the elite royal sites in the core areas of Zululand and Swaziland, with barely any evidence at primary production sites and in the other regions.

Many site reports do not provide artifact counts, which can be used to develop a sense of relative quantity. I assumed that authors using the term "abundant" felt that the amounts of glass beads were above those amounts "normally" expected. Therefore, I chose to use this description in quotation marks to generally interpret quantities from the data.

A number of observations can be made about the distribution of these items. First, mineral production sites contain the most glass beads during earlier times. Second, royal residences, although either first or second in numbers of glass beads for both periods, take the lead only after the Mfecane/Difaqane and never contain "abundant" numbers. Furthermore, of the four earlier sites with large numbers of glass beads, only one is a royal residence, two are mineral production sites, and the other is a military site. It is noteworthy that the mineral production sites are in the eastern Transvaal while the royal residence and fort are located in the Free State. On the other hand, there is only one later site with "abundant" amounts of glass beads and this is a fort located in the Free State. Of the six pre–Mfecane/Difaqane and seven post–Mfecane/Difaqane sites with European military items (including horses) all are in the eastern and western Transvaal, the Free State, and the Cape Frontier, while none are located in Zululand.

The Free State had the most pre–Mfecane/Difaqane sites with European goods (nine); the eastern Transvaal was second with seven. The eastern Transvaal had the most post–Mfecane/Difaqane sites with European goods (seven), and the Free State was second with six. These areas also had the most diverse kinds of European trade goods for both time periods (Perry 1996, 469–78). It must be emphasized that the amount and diversity of artifacts is conditioned by, among other things, the differential intensity of the archaeological research. Surprisingly, royal sites, especially in Zululand, have very little evidence of European trade items.

These data present serious problems for the settler model. Evidence for trade with Europeans is more prevalent in the pre-state-formation period than after states formed. This would seem to suggest that something other than access to European trade goods was the goal of the Zulu state, or if it was their goal they were not successful (Carlson 1984; Hedges 1978; Slater 1976; Omer-Cooper 1988; Smith 1969). Moreover, it is interesting that the one place with evidence for trade was a fort, possibly indicative of the frontier nature of forts or of the possibility of trade for arms. The distribution of pre–Mfecane/Difaqane trade goods shows a distinct bias toward mineral production sites, suggesting that the European goods functioned as payment for goods rather than as prestige items in elite competitive duels. The production sites have no evidence of elite residences or other indications of elites.

CONCLUSIONS

The settler model with its local-level integration that gives way to state formation in Zululand, a development that spreads havoc throughout the rest of southeastern Africa, does not provide a good description of the historical geography evident in the archaeological record. Southeastern Africa is better modeled in the pre–Mfecane/Difaqane period as a network of interrelated social groups, some emphasizing agropastoralism, some pastoralism, and some, from Europe, seeking exotic items and human captives. Processes of accumulation involving the use of cattle and prestige ranking systems came into conflict with processes of accumulation based on capturing human labor and engaging in long-distance mercantile trade. Their collision resulted in the population dislocations, famines, state formations, and wars of the Mfecane/Difaqane. Shaka was one of the principal geniuses acting in this complex colonial field, but only one. Until the interpretive net is cast widely enough to incorporate the actions of Europeans at Port Natal and Delagoa Bay, and their agents operating in the hinterlands of the Free State and western Transvaal, as well as Zululand, the history of the period will remain hidden.

My research and analysis suggest that the settler model of the Mfecane/ Difaqane is wrong: it has the wrong people in the wrong places with the wrong political organization, and it incorrectly assumes a lack of political/economic ties between regions. This raises two questions: How did we wind up with this situation, and Where do we go from here?

The reason we wound up in this situation is that everybody believed the settler version because it served European colonial interests and the interests of African elites. The Europeans, for example, had an interest in obscuring the role and magnitude of slaving and the effects that slaving had on African populations. The post-1820 African elites had an interest in legitimizing their own superordinate status and therefore had reason to disguise the nature of pre-1820 polities (Perry 1996, 1999).

How archaeology can be used to investigate the emergence of lines of social inequality in the past, and in its ability to provide an alternative data base to the information encoded in documents and stories, also help disclose the lines that continue to affect our understanding of the world of the present. Where do we go from here? Archaeology has an important role to play in the recovery of the past of southern Africa. We must survey and excavate sites in the eastern Cape, Lesotho, and southern Mozambique. The historical documents and oral texts indicate that these archaeologically under-investigated areas were the key areas impacted by Europeans and Africans involved in African captive and cattle raiding. But collecting more sites is not enough. Archaeologists need to be more attentive to issues of power, issues concerning how it was exercised in African and European communities and how it was resisted, internally and externally. Archaeology can contribute by identifying and explaining the contradictions between the archaeological and documentary records caused by the context of colonialism. Such "ambiguities" in the different lines of evidence are places where power lies—power that has resulted in telling histories that affect social relations today (Leone and Potter 1988). Thus we need renewed investigations of both documentary and material records.

How can historical archaeology use archaeological methods for collecting, analyzing, and interpreting data to understand issues of power and the theoretical and historical discourses regarding colonialism, domination, and resistance in post-fifteenth-century southern Africa? Crucial to understanding these historical global processes are the roles of African captivity in both African and European societies. In colonial situations we need to formulate new research topics with questions that challenge the settler versions of history. We must identify the contrastive case, the "native" version of history, to direct future archaeological research strategies. We must also examine the spatial distribution of European settlement types and structures at colonial entrepôts and elsewhere.

We must look beyond explanations of the Mfecane/Difaqane posed by the settler version. It is possible that the transition to military polities and to exports like cattle and humans was based upon African resistance to European penetration. This resistance can be found in the demand for firepower superimposed onto preexisting structures like the Amabutho during the Mfecane/Difaqane. European weapons facilitated both the ability to exact tribute over wider areas by raw military force and the ability to resist raiders. Unlike earlier wealth forms that maintained and lubricated ruling-class alliances, European weapons could be used by local groups to confront competing Africans and Europeans. European hegemony was facilitated by providing collaborating African polities with the advantage of firearms, along with horses and alliances for augmenting their captive- and cattle-raiding capabilities, further accelerating and entrenching African dependence.

Racial commodity slavery sponsored captive- and cattle-raiding, which transformed African labor without military protection into an available labor pool for external plantations and internal colonies (Wilmsen 1989). From the beginning, however, these local and global transformations engendered forms of African resistance and contestation, which must be reflected in the material world and cultural landscapes of southern Africa. Investigating these processes of domination and resistance, rather than the social isolates of the settler model, is how archaeology can contribute to a history of the impact of colonialism in southern Africa.

REFERENCES CITED

Berry, Brian J. 1961. City Size Distributions and Economic Development. *Economic Development and Cultural Change* 9:573–88.

Bonner, Phillip L. 1977. *Rise, Consolidation, and Disintegration of Dlamnini Power.* London: Univ. of London Press.

———. 1980. Classes, the Mode of Production and the State in Pre-Colonial Swaziland. In *Economy and Society in Preindustrial South Africa,* ed. S. Marks and A. Atmore, 80–101. London: Longman.

———. 1983. *Kings, Commoners, and Concessionaires: The Evolution and Dissolution of the Nineteenth-Century Swazi State.* Johannesburg: Raven Press.

Bryant, A. T. 1929. *Olden Times in Zululand and Natal.* London: Longmans.

Campbell, Colin. 1986. Images of War: A Problem in San Rock Art Research. *World Archaeology* 18 (2): 255–68.

Carlson, Swen H. 1984. *Trade and Dependency: Studies in the Expansion of Europe.* Stockholm: Almqvist and Wiskell International.

Chanaiwa, David. 1980. The Zulu Revolution: State Formation in a Pastoral Society. *African Studies Review* 23 (3): 3–20.

Chatterton, J. F., D. P. Collett, and J. T. Swan. 1979. A Late Iron Age Village Site in the Letaba District, Northeast Transvaal. *South African Archaeological Society* 3:109–19. Goodwin Series.

Clarke, John Henrik. 1970. Introduction. In *Introduction to African Civilizations*, ed. J. G. Jackson, 3–35. New York: University Books.

Cobbing, Julian. 1988. The Mfecane as Alibi: Thoughts on Dithakong and Mbolompo. *Journal of African History* 29:487–519.

Collett, D. P. 1982a. Excavations of Stone-Walled Ruin Types in the Badfontein Valley, Eastern Transvaal, South Africa. *South African Archaeological Bulletin* 37:34–43.

————. 1982b. Ruin Distributions in the Stone-Walled Settlements of the Eastern Transvaal, South Africa. *South African Journal of Science* 78:39–40.

Cruz-Uribe, Kathryn, and Carmel Schrire. 1991. Analysis of Faunal Remains from Oudepost I, an Early Outpost of the Dutch East India Company, Cape Province. *South African Archaeological Bulletin* 46:92–106.

Daniel, J. B. McI. 1973. A Geographical Study of Pre-Shakan Zululand. *South African Geographical Journal* 55 (1): 23–31.

Delius, Peter. 1983. *The Land Belongs to Us*. Johannesburg: Raven Press.

Denbow, James R., and Edwin N. Wilmsen. 1983. Iron Age Pastoralist Settlements in Botswana. *South African Journal of Science* 79:405–8.

Denoon, Donald, and Balam Nyeko. 1986. *Southern Africa since 1800*. London: Longmans.

Derricourt, R. M., and T. M. Evers. 1973. Robertsdrift, an Iron Age Settlement on the Banks of the Vaal and Klip Rivers near Standerton, Southeastern Transvaal. *African Studies* 32:183–96.

Diop, Cheikh Anta. 1974. *The African Origin of Civilization: Myth or Reality*. Westport: Lawrence Hill and Co.

Dowson, Thomas A. 1995. Hunter-Gatherers, Traders, and Slaves: The "Mfecane" Impact on Bushmen, Their Ritual and Their Art. In *The Mfecane/Difaqane Aftermath: Reconstructive Debates in Southern African History*, ed. C. Hamilton, 51–70. Johannesburg: Witwatersrand Univ. Press.

Du Bois, W. E. B. 1969. *The World and Africa*. New York: Monthly Review Press.

Edgerton, Robert. 1988. *Like Lions They Fought*. New York: The Free Press.

Eldredge, Elizabeth. 1995. Sources of Conflict in Southern Africa, c. 1800–1830: the "Mfecane" Reconsidered. In *The Mfecane/Difaqane Aftermath: Reconstructive Debates in Southern African History*, ed. C. Hamilton, 35–50. Johannesburg: Witwatersrand Univ. Press.

Etherington, Norman. 1991a. The Aftermath of the Aftermath. Report on the Colloquium, The "Mfecane" Aftermath: Towards a New Paradigm, at the Univ. of Witwatersrand. *South African Historical Journal* 25:154–62.

————. 1991b. The Great Trek in Relation to the Mfecane: A Reassessment. *South African Historical Journal* 25:3–21.

————. 1995. New Wine in Old Bottles: The Persistence of Narrative Structures in the Historiography of the Mfecane and the Great Trek. In *The Mfecane/Difaqane Aftermath: Reconstructive Debates in Southern African History,* ed. C. Hamilton, 35–50. Johannesburg: Witwatersrand Univ. Press.

Evers, T. M. 1975. Recent Iron Age Research in the Eastern Transvaal, South Africa. *South African Archaeological Bulletin* 30:71–83.

————. 1984. Sotho-Tswana and Moloko Settlement Patterns and the Bantu Cattle Pattern. In *Frontiers: Southern African Archaeology Today,* ed. M. Hall, G. Avery, D. M. Avery, M. L. Wilson, and A. J. B. Humphreys, 236–51. Oxford: British Archaeological Reports.

Evers, T. M., and W. D. Hammond-Tooke. 1986. The Emergence of South African Chiefdoms: An Archaeological Perspective. *Journal of African Studies* 45 (1): 37–41.

Evers, T. M., and Nicholaas van der Merwe. 1987. Iron Age Ceramics from Phalaborwa Southeastern Transvaal Lowveld, South Africa. *South African Archaeological Bulletin* 42:87–106.

Falconer, Steven E., and Stephen H. Savage. 1995. Heartlands and Hinterlands: Alternative Trajectories of Early Urbanization in Mesopotamia and the Southern Levant. *American Antiquity* 60 (1): 37–58.

Fortes, Meyer, and E. E. Evans-Pritchard. 1967. *African Political Systems.* London, New York, Toronto: Oxford Univ. Press.

Gluckman, Max. 1960. The Rise of the Zulu Empire. *Scientific American* 202 (4): 157–68.

Goudie, Andrew S., and David Price-Williams. 1983. *The Atlas of Swaziland.* The Swaziland National Trust Commission, Occasional Paper No. 4, Lobamba, Swaziland.

Guy, Jeff. 1980. Ecological Factors in the Rise of Shaka and the Zulu Kingdom. In *Economy and Society in Preindustrial South Africa,* ed. S. Marks and A. Atmore, 103–19. London: Longmans.

————. 1982. *The Destruction of the Zulu Kingdom.* Johannesburg: Raven Press.

Haggett, P. 1966. *Locational Analysis in Human Geography.* New York: St. Martin's Press.

Hall, Martin. 1980a. *The Ecology of the Iron Age in Zululand.* Cambridge: Univ. of Cambridge.

————. 1980b. *Patterns in the Iron Age in Zululand: An Ecological Interpretation.* Oxford: British Archaeological Reports.

————. 1984. The Myth of the Zulu Homestead: Archaeology and Ethnography. *Africa* 54 (1): 65–79.

————. 1990. *Farmers, Kings, and Traders: The People of Southern Africa,* 200–1860. Chicago: Univ. of Chicago Press.

————. 1993. The Archaeology of Colonial Settlement in Southern Africa. *Annual Review of Anthropology* 22:177–200.

Hall, Martin, David Halkett, P. Huigen van Beek, and J. Klose. 1990a. "A Stone Wall Out of the Earth That Thundering Cannon Cannot Destroy?": Bastian and Moat at the Castle, Cape Town. *Social Dynamics* 16:22–37.

Hall, Martin, David Halkett, Jane Klose, and Gabrielle Richie. 1990b. "The Barrack Street Well:

Images of a Cape Town Household in the Nineteenth Century." *South African Archaeological Bulletin* 47:73–92.

Hall, Martin, and Kathleen Mack. 1983. The Outline of an Eighteenth-Century Economic System in Southeast Africa. *Annals of the South African Museum* 91 (2): 163–94.

Hall, Simon. 1995. Archaeological indicators for stress in the western Transvaal region between the seventeenth and nineteenth centuries. In *The Mfecane/Difaqane Aftermath: Reconstructive Debates in Southern African History*, ed. C. Hamilton, 307–22. Johannesburg: Witwatersrand Univ. Press.

Hamilton, Carolyn A. 1995. The Character and Objects of Shaka: A Reconsideration of the Making of Shaka as "Mfecane" Motor. In *The Mfecane/Difaqane Aftermath: Reconstructive Debates in Southern African History*, ed. C. Hamilton, 183–212. Johannesburg: Witwatersrand Univ. Press.

Hartley, Guy. 1995. The Battle of Dithakong and "Mfecane" Theory. In *The Mfecane/Difaqane Aftermath: Reconstructive Debates in Southern African History*, ed. C. Hamilton, 395–416. Johannesburg: Witwatersrand Univ. Press.

Hedges, David. 1978. *Trade and Politics in Southern Mozambique and Zululand in the Eighteenth and Nineteenth Centuries.* London: London School of Oriental and African Studies.

Hoernle, Winifred. 1946. Social Organization. In *The Bantu Speaking Tribes of Southern Africa*, ed. I. Schapera, 67–93. London: Routledge and Sons.

Huffman, Thomas N. 1984. Archaeological Evidence and Conventional Explanations of Southern Bantu Settlement Patterns. Paper presented at the South African Association of Anthropologists, RAU Island.

———. 1986. Iron Age Settlement Patterns and the Origins of Class Distinction in Southern Africa. *Advances in Archaeology* 5:291–337.

Inskeep, R. R. 1979. *The Peopling of Southern Africa.* New York: Barnes and Noble.

Johnson, Gregory A. 1973. Local Exchange and Early State Development in Southwestern Iran. Anthropological Papers 51. Ann Arbor: Univ. of Michigan Museum of Anthropology.

———. 1977. Aspects of Regional Analysis in Archaeology. *Annual Review of Anthropology* 6:479–508.

———. 1980a. Rank-Size Convexity and System Integration: A View from Archaeology. *Economic Geography* 56 (3): 234–47.

———. 1980b. Spatial Organization of Early Uruk Settlement Systems. In *L'archeologie de L'Iraq due debut de L'epaque Neolithique a 333 avant notre ere—Perspectives et limites de l'interpretation anthropologique des document*, ed. M. T. Barrelet, 580:223–63. CNRS Colloque International. Paris: CNRS.

Kinsman, Margaret. 1984. The Impact of the Difaqane on Southern Tswana Communities, with Special Reference to the Rolong. Paper presented at the University of Witwatersrand history workshop, "Class, Community, and Conflict."

Warren R. Perry

Krige, E. H. 1965 [1936]. The Military Organization of the Zulus. In *Peoples and Cultures of Africa*, ed. E. Skinner, 483–502. New York: National History Press.

Kuper, Hilda. 1947. *An African Aristocracy: Rank among the Swazi*. Oxford: Oxford Univ. Press.

———. 1965. The Swazi of Swaziland. In *Peoples of Africa*, ed. J. L. Gibbs, 479–512. New York: Holt, Rhinehart and Winston.

———. 1970. Kinship among the Swazi. In *African Systems of Kinship and Marriage*, ed. A. R. Radcliffe-Brown and D. Forde, 86–110. London: IAI Oxford.

———. 1986. *The Swazi: A South African Kingdom*. New York: Holt, Rhinehart and Winston.

Lee, Richard. 1993. *The Dobe Ju/'hoansi*. New York: Holt, Rhinehart and Winston.

Legassick, Martin. 1969. The Sotho-Tswana Peoples before 1800. In *African Societies in Southern Africa*, ed. L. Thompson, 86–125. London: Praeger.

Leone, Mark P., and Parker B. Potter, eds. 1988. *The Recovery of Meaning*. Washington: Smithsonian Institution Press.

Lewis-Williams, David. 1981. *Believing and Seeing: Symbolic Meanings in Southern San Rock Paintings*. London: Academic Press.

———. 1982. The Economic and Social Context of Southern San Rock Art. *Current Anthropology* 23 (4): 429–49.

———. 1984. A Dream of Eland: An Unexplored Component of San Shamanism and Rock Art. *World Archaeology* 19 (2): 165–77.

———. 1989. Southern Africa's Place in the Archaeology of Human Understanding. *South African Journal of Science* 85 (1): 47–52.

Lye, William F., and Colin Murray. 1980. *Transformations on the Highveld: The Tswana and Southern Sotho*. Cape Town: David Phillip.

Maggs, Tim O. 1971. Pastoral Settlements on the Riet River. *South African Archaeological Bulletin* 26:37–63.

———. 1974. Early Farming Communities on the Southern Highveld: A Survey of Iron Age Settlements. Ph.D. Diss., Univ. of Cape Town, South Africa.

———. 1976. Iron Age Settlement Patterns and Soho History on the Southern Highveld, South Africa. *World Archaeology* 7:318–32.

———. 1977. The Iron Age: Sequence South of the Vaal and Pongola Rivers: Some Historical Implications. *Journal of African History* 21 (1): 1–15.

———. 1982. Mabhija: A Pre-Colonial Industrial Development in the Tugela Basin. *Annals of the Natal Museum* 25 (1): 123–41.

———. 1984. Iron Age Settlement and Subsistence Patterns in the Tugela River Basin, Natal. In *Frontiers: Southern African Archaeology Today*, ed. M. Hall, G. Avery, D. M. Avery, M. L. Wilson, and A. J. B. Humphreys, 194–206. Oxford: British Archaeological Reports.

Maggs, Tim O., and Galvin Whitelaw. 1991. A Review of Recent Archaeological Research on Food-Producing Communities in Southern Africa. *Journal of African History* 32:3–24.

Markell, Ann, Martin Hall, and Carmel Schrire. 1995. The Historical Archaeology of Vegelegen, an Early Farmstead at the Cape of Good Hope. *Historical Archaeology* 29 (1): 10–34.

Marker, M. E., and T. M. Evers. 1976. Iron Age Settlement and Soil Erosion in the Eastern Transvaal, South Africa. *South African Archaeological Bulletin* 31 (3–4): 153–65.

Marks, Shula. 1967. The Rise of the Zulu Kingdom. In *The Middle Ages of African History*, ed. R. Oliver, 85–91. London: Oxford Univ. Press.

Marshall, Lorna. 1965. The Kung Bushmen of the Kalahari Desert. In *Peoples of Africa*, ed. J. L. Gibbs, 479–512. New York: Holt, Rhinehart and Winston.

Mason, Revil. 1968. Transvaal and Natal Iron Age Settlements Revealed by Aerial Photography and Excavation. *African Studies* 27 (4): 167–80.

————. 1973. First Early Iron Age Settlement in South Africa: Broederstroom 24/73, Brits District, Transvaal. *South African Journal of Science* 69:324–26.

Mason, Revil, M. Houmoller, and R. Steel. 1981. Archaeological Survey of the Magalies Valley. *South African Journal of Science* 77 (7): 310–12.

Monstert, Noel. 1992. *Frontiers: The Epic of South Africa's Creation and the Tragedy of the Xhosa People.* New York: Alfred Knopf.

Morris, Donald. 1965. *The Washing of the Spears.* New York: Simon and Schuster.

Omer-Cooper, J. D. 1966. *The Zulu Aftermath: A Nineteenth-Century Revolution in Bantu Africa.* London: Longmans.

————. 1969. Political Change in the Nineteenth-Century Mfecane. In *African Societies in Southern Africa*, ed. L. Thompson. New York: Praeger.

————. 1988. *History of Southern Africa.* London: Heinemann.

————. 1995. The Mfecane Survives Its Critics. In *The Mfecane/Difaqane Aftermath: Reconstructive Debates in Southern African History*, ed. C. Hamilton, 277–301. Johannesburg: Witwatersrand Univ. Press.

Parkington, John, and Mike Cronin. 1979. The Size and Layout of Mgungundlovu, 1828–1838. In *South African Archaeological Society*, ed. N. V. D. Merwe and T. N. Huffman. 3:133–48. Goodwin Series.

Paynter, Robert. 1982. *Models of Spatial Inequality: Settlement Patterns in Historical Archaeology.* New York: Academic Press.

Perry, Warren. 1991. Problems in the Integration of Oral History and Archaeological Data in Swaziland, Southern Africa. *Anthropology of Work Review* 12 (2): 1–6.

————. 1996. Archaeology of the Mfecane/Difaqane: Landscape Transformation in Post-Fifteenth-Century Southern Africa. Ph.D. diss., Dept. of Anthropology, City Univ. of New York.

————. 1999. *The Archaeology of Colonial Impact in Southern Africa, 1500–1900.* New York: Plenum.

Roberts, Brian. 1974. *The Zulu Kings.* New York: Charles Scribner's Sons.

Warren R. Perry

Rodney, Walter. 1981. *How Europe Underdeveloped Africa.* Washington: Howard Univ. Press.

Saunders, Christopher. 1995. Pre-Cobbing Mfecane Historiography. In *The Mfecane/Difaqane Aftermath: Reconstructive Debates in Southern African History,* ed. C. Hamilton, 21–34. Johannesburg: Witwatersrand Univ. Press.

Schapera, Issac. 1967. *Government and Politics in Tribal Societies.* New York: Schocken.

———. 1970. Kinship and Marriage among the Tswana. In *African Systems of Kinship and Marriage,* ed. A. R. Radcliffe-Brown and D. Forde, 111–39. London: IAI Oxford.

Schrire, Carmel. 1988. The Historical Archaeology of the Impact of Colonialism in Seventeenth-Century South Africa. *Antiquity* 62 (235): 214–25.

———. 1989. The Indigenous Artifacts from Oudepost I, a Colonial Outpost of the VOC at Saldanha Bay, Cape. *South African Archaeological Bulletin* 44:105–13.

———. 1996. *Digging through Darkness: Chronicles of an Archaeologist.* Charlottesville, Va.: Univ. Press of Virginia.

Schrire, Carmel, and Janette Deacon. 1989. "The Indigenous Artifacts from Oudepost I, a Colonial Outpost of the VOC at Saldanha Bay, Cape." *South African Archaeological Bulletin* 44: 105–13.

Schrire, Carmel, K. Cruz-Uribe, and J. Klose. 1995. *The Site History of the Historical Site at Oudepost I, Cape.* Goodwin Series. South African Archaeological Society 7:21–32.

Scully, R. T. K. 1978. Phalaborwa Oral Tradition. Ph.D. diss., State Univ. of New York at Binghamton.

Service, Elman. 1975. *Origins of the State and Civilization.* New York: Norton.

Shillington, Kevin. 1987. *History of Southern Africa.* London: Longmans.

Slater, Henry. 1976. Transitions in the Political Economy of Southeastern Africa before 1840. Ph.D. diss., Univ. of Sussex.

Smith, Alan K. 1969. The Trade of Delagoa Bay as a Factor in Nguni Politics, 1750–1835. In *African Societies in Southern Africa,* ed. L. Thompson, 171–89. New York: Praeger.

Stevenson, Robert F. 1968. *Population and Political Systems in Tropical Africa.* New York: Columbia Univ. Press.

Taylor, Donna. 1975. Some Locational Aspects of Middle-Range Hierarchical Societies. Ph.D. diss., Dept. of Anthropology, City Univ. of New York.

van der Merwe, Nicholas, and R. T. Scully. 1971. The Phalaborwa Story: Archaeological and Ethnographic Investigation of a South African Iron Age Group. *World Archaeology* 3:178–96.

Watson, E. J., and V. Watson. 1990. "Of Commoners and Kings": Faunal Remains from Ondini. *South African Archaeological Bulletin* 45:33–46.

Webster, Alan. 1991. The Mfecane Paradigm Overthrown. Report on the Colloquium, The "Mfecane" Aftermath: Towards a New Paradigm. *South African Historical Journal* 25:170–72.

Webster, Alan. 1995. Unmasking the Fingo: The War of 1835 Revisited. In *The Mfecane/Difaqane Aftermath: Reconstructive Debates in Southern African History,* ed. C. Hamilton, 241–76. Johannesburg: Witwatersrand Univ. Press.

Wilmsen, Edwin N. 1989. *Land Filled with Flies: A Political Economy of the Kalahari*. Chicago: Univ. of Chicago Press.

Wilson, M., and L. Thompson. 1969–71. *The Oxford History of South Africa, South Africa to 1870*. Vols. 1–3. Oxford: Clarendon Press.

Wright, Henry T. 1977. Recent Research on the Origin of the State. *Annual Review of Anthropology* 6:279–89.

Wright, Henry T., and Gregory A. Johnson. 1975. Population, Exchange, and Early State Formation in Southwestern Iran. *American Anthropologist* 77:267–89.

Wright, Henry T., and Susan Kus. 1979. An Archaeological Reconnaissance of Ancient Imerina. In *Madagascar in History*, ed. R. K. Kent, 1–31. Albany, Calif.: Foundation for Malagasy Studies.

Wright, John B. 1990. The Dynamics of Power and Conflict in the Thukela–Mzimkhulu Region in the Late Eighteenth and Early Nineteenth Centuries: A Critical Reconstruction. Ph.D. diss., Univ. of Witwatersrand, Johannesburg.

———. 1995a. Beyond the Concept of the "Zulu Explosion": Comments on the Current Debate. In *The Mfecane/Difaqane Aftermath: Reconstructive Debates in Southern African History*, ed. C. Hamilton, 107–22. Johannesburg: Witwatersrand Univ. Press.

———. 1995b. Political Transformations in the Thukela–Mzimkhulu Region in the Late Eighteenth and Early Nineteenth Centuries. In *The Mfecane/Difaqane Aftermath: Reconstructive Debates in Southern African History*, ed. C. Hamilton, 163–82. Johannesburg: Witwatersrand Univ. Press.

PART TWO

Lines Defining Gender

The Material Worlds of Men and Women

CHAPTER SIX

Family Meals and Evening Parties

CONSTRUCTING DOMESTICITY IN NINETEENTH-CENTURY MIDDLE-CLASS NEW YORK

Diana diZerega Wall

One of the major promises of historical archaeology has been that archaeologists would be able to use material culture as a written text in which to "read" about the lives of people who have been excluded from public arenas of power and consequently from the written record. Women's lives are among those often not recorded in the documents that we traditionally use to write our histories. Jane Austen pointed this out almost two centuries ago in her novel *Persuasion*. In a discussion on the nature of women, her heroine, Anne Elliot, would not allow Captain Harville to cite passages from books to prove his point because "[m]en have had every advantage of us in telling their story. Education has been theirs in so much higher degree; the pen has been in their hands. I will not allow books to prove anything" (1818/1898, 242). As Russell Handsman (1984) and Steve Mrozowski (1984, 43) both noted well over a decade ago, historical archaeology is a particularly appropriate avenue for exploring the experience of women because so much of what we excavate are women's goods—the bits and pieces of crockery and glassware that contribute to the rich fabric of domesticity. More recently, some historical archaeologists have begun to study these goods to understand the lives of women and their experiences in the larger society (see, for example, Burley 1989; DeCunzo 1995; Lucas 1994; Seifert 1991; Scott 1994; Wall 1991, 1994; Yentsch 1991a, 1991b).

In this essay, I use bits and pieces of crockery and glassware to explore the lives of middle-class women in nineteenth-century New York City. In doing this, I draw on some of the work of Pierre Bourdieu. In *Distinction*, Bourdieu (1984) shows how tastes in domestic goods and other phenomena help to create and maintain the power structure among socioeconomic classes in mid-twentieth century France. One of the many examples he provides consists of the symbolic roles of the domestic goods—including crockery and glassware—that are used in French working-class and bourgeois homes. When entertaining, for example, French working-class women tend to set their tables with simple earthenware plates and ordinary glasses, while wives in executive and professional families tend to use more elegant porcelain plates and crystal glasses (198). Bourdieu's rationale for explaining these differences does not rest solely on the cost of these commodities but rather in their meaning to the people who use them. For working-class families, where necessity prevails outside the home, freedom is the watchword for domestic life inside the home. French working-class people restrict invitations to a meal to family members or those who can be treated as family—people they feel "at home with." For Bourdieu's bourgeois families, on the other hand, the home is an extension of the outside world. Since they entertain professional and business acquaintances at home, they incorporate the order, restraint, and propriety of the outside world into domestic life (175–200). These very different meanings of home life both structure and are structured by the material goods that French women use to set their tables.

In this study, I use a perspective similar to Bourdieu's to examine the roles of nineteenth-century middle-class women in New York City. The study builds on earlier work (for example, Wall 1991, 1994, 1999) and is part of a continuing interest in the examination of gender, class, and cultural origin in nineteenth-century American culture. Here, I am interested in seeing whether New York women at different positions along the middle-class spectrum defined their domestic roles in the same way, or whether the rubric of "middle class" veiled a broad array of cultural experience. I use some of the material goods that women appropriated in constructing their domestic roles to explore this issue. These goods consist not only of the crockery on which archaeologists have traditionally focused so much analytical attention, but also glassware—the tumblers and wineglasses that women also used to set their tables—which archaeologists have traditionally ignored. The glassware and crockery were recovered archaeologically from three different middle-class households in New York City's Greenwich Village.[1] First, I briefly describe the cultural context of the urban middle class and the roles of its women during the nineteenth century. Then, I describe the households in which the glassware and crockery from the archaeological assemblages were used and the deposits in which they were found. Next, I examine the context of the meals in which the crockery and glassware appeared in these households. Finally, I look at the vessels themselves and use them and their various styles to discuss the roles of the women who had first purchased and then used them to help construct their visions of domestic life.

CULTURAL CONTEXT

The early nineteenth century was the period that saw the emergence of the urban middle class as we know it today (Blumin 1989). By the 1860s, an article in the *New York Times* defined the middle class as including "professional men, clergymen, artists, college professors, shopkeepers, and upper mechanics" (cited in Blumin 1989, 247). This broad definition suggests that for the men of this class in this period, as today, the rubric of "middle class" veiled a broad spectrum of cultural experience. This was undoubtedly true for their wives as well.

During the nineteenth century, women of the emerging middle class had access to the arenas of politics and the economy only indirectly, through their male relatives: their fathers, brothers, husbands, and sons. But mid-nineteenth-century mistresses of middle-class homes were firmly in charge of domestic life. In this arena, wives were responsible for inculcating in their children those values and behaviors that were appropriate to their class so that their children would succeed in later life. Historians agree that at this time women's roles revolved around two separate, complementary aspects of domesticity and social reproduction (Coontz 1988; Blumin 1989). On the one hand, they were the guardians of society's morals, a role that had become sentimentalized and even sanctified as the homes that they ran came to be perceived as full-fledged sanctuaries in the heartless world of the marketplace. On the other, they were responsible for negotiating the family's social position so that family members (and particularly their children) would continue to have access to the middle class and could even ascend within the perilous class structure. They exercised this role by promoting a refined, genteel, and even fashionable image of their homes and families to their friends, acquaintances, and their husbands' business associates.

Both of these aspects of women's roles were evident in the features of the homes they created—in the architecture of their houses and in the decor of the objects that they used inside them. The uncertainties of the nineteenth century saw the introduction of a profusion of nostalgic styles in architecture and home furnishings. During the 1840s, the neo-Gothic style was introduced into American architecture. In fact, its ecclesiastical associations made it extremely popular for middle-class domestic architecture because it embodied the home's role as a sanctuary. However, although multitudes of churches were built in this style in New York, Gothic never became popular for the facades of domestic buildings in the city (Landau 1982). Instead, the Italianate romantic palazzo style that was introduced into the city for commercial and public buildings and the mansions of the very wealthy at the same time was also popular in its domestic Italianate form for the row houses of the middle class. This style, with its perceived elegance of height and allowance for rich architectural detail, permitted householders to make statements about wealth, fashion, and taste on an unprecedented scale—statements that were much more obvious than those made by the Greek Revival style that it supplanted. Block-long rows of these houses created class-consistent, uniform street fronts on a much broader scale than ever before (Lockwood 1972, 131–32, 143–55). From our perspective, the exteriors of these homes provided the venue for the woman of the house to act as social negotiator in making a visible, public statement of her family's class position and her husband's wherewithal to support it.

Women also used style, though in a somewhat different way, to furnish the interiors of these homes. The different decors they used stressed the different symbolic importance of the various rooms and the activities that took place within them. This is particularly evident in the difference in the ways in which the parlor, which was used for entertaining, and the dining room, which was used for family gatherings, were furnished. The writers of house-plan books, who began their contribution to the prescriptive literature in the 1850s, directed the attention of their readers to the importance of the home as an influence in building character. Although these plans were almost always directed to homes in the newly developing suburbs (because they assumed that it was impossible to create a home encompassing middle-class values in the morally dangerous city), their books were read by city and suburban women alike. These writers, in discussing appropriate styles of room furnishings, argued that the rooms should embody the values that were being emphasized in the activities that took place in them. In 1850, for example, one such writer, Andrew Jackson Downing, wrote that "[t]he prevailing character of the Grecian and Italian styles partakes of the gay spirit of the drawing-room and social life; that of the Gothic, of the quiet, domestic feeling of the library and the family circle" (1850/1969, 23–24). In discussing a slightly later period, Susan Williams, a social historian, points out the parallels between dining rituals and religious rituals. She stresses the stylistic similarities of the Gothic sideboard—the visual focus of the dining room—and the altarpiece—the focus of the church—that became particularly marked in the 1870s and 1880s (1985, 65–67).

Middle-class women in urban areas were active participants in shaping their domestic environments (Blumin 1989, 183–85). In New York, they had begun selecting and shopping for these goods at least as early as the turn of the nineteenth century. For example, at the time of her marriage in 1800 Elizabeth Bleecker recorded in her diary the many shopping expeditions that she made to purchase the household goods that she needed to set up her first home (Bleecker 1799–1806). A half century later, Julia Harkness Lay, a bookkeeper's wife who lived on Allen Street, also recorded making many household purchases in her diary (Lay 1851–78). But though both Bleecker and Lay made entries recording their key role in making household purchases that included crockery and glassware, they specified neither the particular patterns that they selected nor the reasons behind their choices. To understand this aspect of women's roles, we have to turn to the bits of crockery and glassware that turn up in the archaeological record, in this case in the assemblages that originated in the homes of three mid-nineteenth-century middle-class families. These objects too were presumably purchased by the mistresses of the three households where they were used.

THREE FAMILIES

The sites where the archaeological materials were found are located at 25 Barrow Street, 153 West 12th Street, and 50 Washington Square South. All three sites are in New York's Greenwich Village (map 6.1). The houses on these sites were built in the first half of the nineteenth century, during the period when the Village of Greenwich was being developed into one of New York's first residential neighborhoods. For many of its middle-class and wealthy residents, its creation marked the end of the old "walking city," with its pattern of integrated homes and workplaces that had characterized New York throughout the colonial and Federal periods (Wall 1994). Although the suburb was swallowed by the growing city by mid-century, the village area remained a relatively exclusive enclave for the wealthy and the middle class:

153 WEST 12TH STREET

25 BARROW STREET

50 WASHINGTON SQUARE SOUTH

City Hall

Map 6.1. Greenwich Village sites of 25 Barrow Street, 153 West Twelfth Street, and
50 Washington Square South sites. "North" is toward the upper left corner of the map.
Courtesy City of New York, Department of City Planning; photograph by Herbert Seignoret.

in the 1860s, fewer than a quarter of the buildings there were tenements.
Working-class German and Irish immigrants—the most numerous and poor-
est tenement dwellers in the city—were for the most part excluded from the
neighborhood (Ernst 1949, 45, 235).

But although the village as a whole can be characterized as relatively exclusive, the three adjacent areas where the sites were located were in some ways
quite different from each other at mid-century. It is possible to explore some of

TABLE 6.1

1851 Breakdown of Occupations for Greenwich Village Blocks

Occupations	Barrow St. Block		Twelfth St. Block		Washington Square South Block	
	n	%	n	%	n	%
Merchant/ broker	4	11.8	10	27.0	6	46.2
Other commercial	4	11.8	11	29.7	1	7.7
Professional	1	2.9	8	21.6	5	38.5
White collar	2	5.9	4	10.8	1	7.7
Craftsman	12	35.3	4	10.8	0	0.0
Unskilled	3	8.8	0	0.0	0	0.0
Cartman	8	23.5	0	0.0	0	0.0
Total	34	100	37	99.9	13	100.1

SOURCE: See note 2.

TABLE 6.2

Occupancy and Property Values for Greenwich Village Blocks

	Barrow St. Block	Twelfth St. Block	Washington Square South Block
Mean no. of families per house	2.2	1.1	1.0
Mean value of property	$2,291	$4,371	$9,447
% tenant occupied	69.7	86.7	26.7

SOURCE: See note 2.

these differences by examining all the households that occupied the three blocks where the sites were located at this time—by looking at the occupations of the householders who lived there, the values of the homes in which they lived, the number of families that lived in each of the houses, and whether or not these families owned their own homes (see tables 6.1 and 6.2).[2]

The building at 50 Washington Square South was located, as its address implies, on the south side of Washington Square, a park which had been developed as a focus for wealthier homes in the late 1820s. Houses on the southern side of the square were less expensive and therefore less exclusive than those on the square's northern side because of their proximity to a poorer and less desirable neighborhood immediately to the south. Nevertheless, the households on the block were those at the wealthier end of the middle-class spectrum. Almost half the men in these families worked as merchants or brokers—they were actively involved in that sector of the economy that controlled the city's wealth at mid-century (Pessen 1973)—and an additional third were professionals. Most of these household heads owned their own homes; only 27 percent of them were listed as tenants in the tax records. The values of their properties were relatively high; the mean value of their assessments for real estate taxes was $9,447 in 1851. Furthermore, all of the people who lived on the block lived in single-family homes.

The other two homes discussed in this study were located to the west of Sixth Avenue, a shop-lined boundary separating the more exclusive part of the village to the east and the less exclusive part to the west. One-fifty-three West Twelfth Street was located between Sixth and Seventh Avenues, an area that had been developed in the early 1840s with single-family homes for the middle class. Of the men on this block whose occupations were identified, over half worked in the commercial sector of the economy, with over a quarter of them working as merchants or brokers. An additional quarter were professionals. The values of these properties were considerably lower than those on Washington Square South, however; their mean value was $4,371, only half the average value for the properties on the nearby square. For the most part these single-family homes were occupied by tenants and not their owners.

Twenty-five Barrow Street, between Bleecker and West Fourth Streets, was located in a poorer neighborhood that included a mixture of middle-class and working-class residents. Over a third of the people who lived on the block worked as craftsmen or in manufacturing, and almost a quarter of them were cart men who handled the freight of the city. Half of these cart men owned their own homes and had stables on their premises to accommodate their horses. Most of the houses on the block were either occupied by more than one family or lodged families that took in boarders. Six of the properties had been densely developed and were the sites of two houses, with one fronting on Barrow Street and the other located in the rear yard. The mean value of the houses on this block was only $2,291, just slightly over half the value of the Twelfth Street properties. Most of these houses were rented and not owner occupied.

These three houses, then, were located on three blocks that represent three different neighborhoods in Greenwich Village, neighborhoods that typify three different points along the middle-class spectrum, ranging from richer to poorer as we go from the Washington Square to the Twelfth Street to the Barrow Street homes.

The house at 25 Barrow Street was built as a two-and-a-half-story, single-family Federal style house in 1826.[3] During the 1860s (when the archaeological materials were deposited in the ground), the house was home to at least two separate families. In 1858, English-born Emeline Hirst and her husband, Samuel, a baker who was also born in England, and their six American-born children moved into the house as tenants. After Samuel's death a few years later, Emeline and the children continued to live there for almost a decade. The family presumably supported themselves through the earnings of Emeline (who became a nurse and later took in boarders, a common recourse for widows who were financially strapped) and the older children, some of whom were in their twenties when the family moved into the house. Although the Hirst family probably struggled after Samuel's death, they apparently were able to hold on to their position in the middle class. Almost a decade later, their son Edwin, by then in his late twenties but still living at home with his mother, was described in the city directories as a clerk, the quintessential middle-class occupation of the late nineteenth century. Other tenants in the house were there only briefly. Selina Sinclair, who was born in New York, and her Scottish-born husband, David, a locksmith, and their two children lived there for only a few years, from 1858 until 1862. David's locksmith shop was located on nearby Bleecker Street. The Sinclairs were probably succeeded in the house by other families or by boarders taken in by the widowed Emeline Hirst, but their presence has not been documented in the historical records.

The Barrow Street families were close to the poorer end of the middle-class spectrum: they rented rather than owned their home, which they shared with other families for at least part of the time. The value of the house itself was assessed at only $2,600 in 1860. In that same year, the two families that lived in the house (the Hirsts and the Sinclairs) included a total of twelve

Table 6.3

1860 Housing Information for Greenwich Village Sites

	Barrow St.	Twelfth St.	Washington Square South
Home ownership	Rent	Rent	Own
Number of stories	2½	3	3½
Value of home	$2,600	$5,000	$10,200
Number of families	2	1	1
Number of individuals	12	6	4
Number of domestics	0	2	2

SOURCE: 1860 U.S. manuscript census records and City of New York tax assessment records.

individuals. Neither family enjoyed the services of live-in domestic help, an amenity that was fairly common among middle-class New Yorkers at mid-century. (This information is presented as comparative data in table 6.3.)

The three-story Greek Revival house at 153 West Twelfth Street was built circa 1841. The house continued to be a single-family home until the late nineteenth century. In 1855, Henrietta Raymer and her husband, Henry, moved into the house as tenants. They were joined there briefly by Henrietta's sister, Mary Purdy. The Raymers continued to live there for a decade, during the period when it is believed the archaeological materials discussed here were deposited in the ground. In 1860, the household included the Raymers (Henrietta was thirty-four and Henry was forty-two in that year), their two young children, George and Maria (who were then aged two and four and who had both been born while the family was living in the house), and two domestics, Catherine Henn and Anne Hines, who had emigrated from Germany and Ireland, respectively. Henry Raymer was a grocer who commuted downtown to do business on Front Street in the lower city. In 1865 disaster struck the Raymer household when Henry died; shortly thereafter his widow and children moved away from the house.

While they lived on Twelfth Street, the Raymers were solid members of the middle class. They lived in a single-family home and enjoyed the services of live-in domestic servants. In 1860, the house was assessed for $5,000, almost twice as much as the two-family home of their contemporaries on Barrow Street. However, the young family did not own their own home. They were close to the middle of the middle-class spectrum.

The Federal house at 50 Washington Square South was a three-and-a-half-story home that was built in 1826 as part of the development of the elite residential area around Washington Square. In 1841, Eliza Robson (then aged forty-eight) moved into the house with her fifty-five-year-old husband, Benjamin, a physician, and her twenty-six-year-old brother, James Bool. They presumably bought the house because it was close to their twenty-three-year-old daughter, Mary Sage, who lived next door with her husband, a merchant who worked downtown on South Street; the Sages eventually had seven children. The Robsons continued to live on the property until Benjamin's death almost four decades later.

The Robsons were clearly among the wealthier families within the middle class in Greenwich Village. They lived in the relatively exclusive enclave of Washington Square in a three-and-a-half-story single-family home they owned themselves. In 1860, their house was assessed for $10,200, over twice the value of the Raymers' home on Twelfth Street in the same year. They had live-in domestic help (consisting of two Irish-born women) and even kept a carriage driven by an African American coachman for part of the period that they lived there.

These three families, like the respective Greenwich Village neighborhoods in which they lived, represent three different positions along the middle-class spectrum, ranging from lower to upper as we move from Barrow Street to Twelfth Street to Washington Square South.

ARCHAEOLOGICAL CONTEXT

The ceramic and glass assemblages examined for this study came from backyard features behind the homes of the three families described above. One was found in a privy or pit from an outhouse behind the Robsons' home on Washington Square South (Salwen and Yamin 1990). The artifactual data suggest that this material was deposited in the mid-1850s, during the long period when the Robsons lived in the house.[4] The second assemblage was also uncovered in a privy; this one was located in the yard behind the Raymers' home on West Twelfth Street. Here, the artifacts suggest that the material was deposited during the mid-1860s, perhaps at the time when Henrietta Raymer and her children were moving away from the house.[5] The third assemblage came from a cistern in the backyard behind 25 Barrow Street (Bodie 1992). This assemblage was part of the trash used to fill up the cistern after the house got indoor plumbing and the cistern was abandoned, possibly at the time when Emeline Hirst and her children moved away from the house in 1870. In all three cases, the ceramics and glassware as well as the rest of the trash found in the features are assumed to have been used in the households of the people who lived on the lots at the time the features were filled.

Ceramics and Glassware: Context of Use

For this study, the ceramics and glassware from the Barrow Street, Twelfth Street, and Washington Square homes are examined to explore what we can learn about the nature of the quality of the domestic life that Emeline Hirst, Henrietta Raymer, and Eliza Robson constructed in their homes. The goal is to see whether or not these three middle-class women, whose households fall at different points along the middle-class spectrum, shared similar visions of domesticity. Did all three of them conform to the ideology of domesticity of their class and devote themselves to serving as the moral guardians of their families and to presenting the image of their families' gentility in negotiating their positions in the class structure? Or did they construct versions of domestic life that were tempered by their position within the middle class?

Before we address this question directly by looking at the vessels themselves, we need to understand something about their contexts of use: the meals in which the vessels were used in middle-class homes during the mid-nineteenth century and the meanings these meals may have had for the women who presented them. One way to gain an understanding of the arenas where different kinds of plates, cups, and glasses were used is by examining the prescriptive literature that was popular at this time and which instructed middle-class women in how to run their homes. Catherine Beecher (1845, 1846) and Eliza Leslie (1850) authored several works that pay particular attention to the details of setting the table for meals and the accoutrements used to present them during this period. It should be remembered, however, that the extent to which middle-class women of the mid-nineteenth century followed the prescriptive literature is unclear. It is highly likely that their readers were mostly those who were vying for entry into the upper-middle class or even into the upper classes. Nonetheless, the very existence and popularity of this literature are in themselves expressions of a cultural view that was shared at least in part among the middle class.

Both authors agree that breakfast and tea (an evening meal that we might equate with supper today) are to be served in similar ways. In each case, the vessels used include cups and saucers (for tea or coffee) and plates. Furthermore, Beecher specifies that *small-sized* plates should be used for tea (1846, 246).

Since both she and Leslie specify that the table should be set in the same way for breakfast as for tea, we can reasonably infer that small plates were used for the former meal as well. There is no indication that either tumblers or stemware (except for an occasional egg glass) were used at either of these meals (Beecher 1845, 308–9; Leslie 1850, 274–80). Beecher (1846, 244) includes a diagram showing a table properly set for breakfast or tea.

Dinner, the main meal of the day, could be served either in the afternoon or evening. Although the literature describes formal meals consisting of a number of courses, the degree to which this formality might be relaxed at everyday meals is not completely clear. Our informants are fairly explicit however about the vessels the individual diners should use. Each place setting might include a soup plate, a large plate for each of the main courses, and a smaller plate for dessert and fruit courses. In addition, each diner would be supplied with a tumbler and (if wine was to be served) wineglass(es). After dinner, cups and saucers for tea or coffee might be used (Beecher 1845, 309–11; 1846, 236–41; Leslie 1850, 256–68).

Tea or evening parties are also described by both of our informants. These entertainments, which both took place in the evening after family tea had been served, took several forms, depending in part on both the number of guests and the level of elegance to which the hostess aspired. At larger parties, refreshments might be handed around on trays by waiters hired for the occasion, while at smaller parties, tea might be poured by a lady of the house while the guests helped themselves to food. The vessels used at these affairs might include cups and saucers for tea, chocolate, and coffee; glasses with handles for lemonade; and small plates for cake. Supper might or might not be included at these events. If no supper was served, wineglasses for wine and liqueurs and tumblers for water might follow an additional round of desserts. If supper *was* to be served, it would be a "standing supper," or what we would today call a buffet (Leslie 1850, 283–84): an elaborately decorated table would be spread with desserts and other food (Beecher 1846, 241–42; Leslie 1850, 281–87). Although neither Beecher nor Leslie mentions the size of the plates that should be used for these suppers, we may infer that they were relatively small because the guests ate while standing up and large plates would be awkward to hold.[6]

Now, we must address the issue of the meanings that these different meals may have had in terms of the roles of the middle-class women who planned them. Some of these meals provided arenas where we would expect women to exercise their role of moral guardian, while others encouraged the expression of their role of negotiating their families' position in society; the question is which meals belong in each category. The answer to this question for most of these meals is quite straightforward. We would expect women to exercise their role as the arbiters of their families' gentility when entertaining friends and acquaintances of their class. Leslie and Beecher are quite clear that these meals would include the tea or evening parties (which might or might not include standing supper) that took place in the parlor. We would further expect that women would emphasize their role as society's moral guardians at meals that took place in the family dining room and involved family members. We may infer that breakfast and tea were family affairs.

Dinner is more problematic. Both Beecher and Leslie are clearly describing dinners that can vary in their complexity, from small family dinners at one end of the continuum to lavish dinner parties at the other (Beecher 1846, 236–41; Leslie 1850, 267). However, Clifford Clark has argued that house-plan books indicate that among the middle class, dining rooms continued to be used almost exclusively by the family, with only the occasional guest. Dinner parties, a mainstay of upper-class socializing for generations, only became commonplace among the middle class decades after the period discussed here, in the 1880s (Clark 1987, 154–55). This would suggest that the sit-down dinner parties described by Beecher and Leslie that required formal dining rooms were not necessarily adopted by most women of the middle class; in fact, the descriptions of these parties might have been aimed at readers who aspired to ascend into the upper regions of the middle class if not the upper classes.[7] We would therefore expect that dinners in our three middle-class homes were for the most part family

TABLE 6.4

Vessels Used in Mid-Nineteenth-Century Middle-Class Meals

	Glassware			Crockery			Primary
	Tumblers	Stemware		Plates		Cups	Participants
		Wine Glasses	Goblets	Small	Large		
Breakfast	-	-	-	+	-	+	Family
Dinner	+	+	-	+	+	+	Family
Tea	-	-	-	+	-	+	Family
Tea/evening parties	+	+	-	+	-	+	Guests

SOURCE: Beecher 1845, 1846; Leslie 1850.

NOTE: + indicates vessels mentioned as used in that meal; - indicates not mentioned.

Diana diZerega Wall

affairs stressing the respectability and morality of the family. The vessels that we would expect to be used at the various meals in middle-class homes are summarized in table 6.4.

Ceramics and Glassware: Analysis

Four different kinds of vessels from the archaeological assemblages at these three sites are used in this study. They include the ceramic plates and cups and glass tumblers and stemware that people used when partaking of meals. Vessels used for serving food and beverages are not included here because at least some of them were made of silver or silver plate, and therefore their representation in the archaeological record would not be comparable.

Before looking at the vessels from these three homes, let's see how Leslie and Beecher describe the styles of dishes that were appropriate for use in these different arenas. Leslie recommends white crockery consisting of common queensware for plates used in the kitchen (1850, 233). She also advises her readers that "for common, every-day use, china ware of entire white seems now to have superseded all others, and very justly; as when of good quality, it is pure and delicate in its appearance, never looks the worst for wear, (as is the case with much of the gilt china,) and when broken is easily matched" (1850, 290). Beecher informs us that "[f]or table-furniture, French china is deemed the nicest" but is too slippery: "it is liable to the objection of having plates, so made, that salt, butter, and similar articles, will not lodge on the edge, but slip into the centre" (1845, 307). Leslie agrees with Beecher in describing the popularity of French china: "the French is usually preferred to [India china (presumably Chinese export porcelain)], the gilding being more lasting, the colors finer, and the patterns more elegant." She adds, however, that "Worcester china is also very beautiful in quality, gilding, and painting." She rejects "[c]hina of a white ground, sprigged with flowers of different colours" as having "too much the look of calico. The most elegant that we have seen has but one color besides the gilding" (1850, 290). Taken together, although they are not as clear or specific as we would like, our informants can be interpreted as recommending the use of white crockery or common queensware for kitchen use, plain white chinaware for everyday use by the family, and French or English china (presumably porcelain), which may be decorated with gilding and one other color for more "elegant" occasions.

Now let's turn to the archaeological assemblages. Archaeologists regard similarities in the styles of objects that are used in similar contexts (such as evening parties or family meals) within a single cultural system (such as middle-class, nineteenth-century New York City) as implying that both the objects and their arenas of use have similar meanings. They also look on differences in the styles of objects that are used in similar cultural contexts as implying that both the objects and their arenas of use have different meanings.[8] Therefore we might expect that the crockery and glassware used for the family meals of breakfast, dinner, and tea might be similar to each other but would differ in style from those presented to guests at evening parties. Furthermore, based on Downing's statement quoted above, we might expect that the vessels used in entertaining in the drawing room or parlor—evening parties—might tend to be in "Grecian and Italian styles," befitting the "gay spirit" of social life, while those used in family meals—breakfast, dinner, and tea—might tend to be in the Gothic style, befitting the "quiet, domestic feeling of the . . . family circle" (Downing 1850/1969, 23–24).

Ceramic Plates

Let's look first at the plates that were used in the three Greenwich Village homes and explore which styles of vessels might have been used for entertaining and which were probably used for family meals (see table 6.5). The assemblages from all three households include plates in various sizes made out of earthenware, ironstone, and porcelain. We know from the prescriptive literature that the only middle-class meal in which we would expect to find large table plates (plates nine or ten inches in diameter; see table 6.4) is family dinner. In looking over the sizes and kinds of plates from the three assemblages (table 6.5), it is clear that for all of the assemblages, large plates are made only out of ironstone and earthenware; presumably, these women did not use porcelain plates for family dinner or, by extension, for other family meals.

If the porcelain plates are excluded from the sample (see table 6.6), the distributions of the remaining plates from the three households are quite similar to each other. From over a third to slightly over half of the plates from each of the households are white granite ironstone with paneled rims (fig. 6.1), a pattern referred to as "Gothic" in the ceramics literature (Wetherbee 1985). Furthermore, all three of the assemblages include a few transfer-printed plates as well as those in the plain white and blue shell-edged patterns. The last two mentioned were presumably used only for the most informal meals or by the domestics in the kitchen. (The plain white plates are the "common queensware" mentioned by Leslie for kitchen use, referred to above). The popularity of the Gothic ironstone plates and the

TABLE 6.5

Distributions of Plates in Greenwich Village Assemblages by Site and Decorative Type

Ware/ Decoration	25 Barrow St.		153 West Twelfth St.		50 Washington Square South		Relative Value 1846	1850s
	n	%	n	%	n	%		
Earthenware								
CC/plain	5	35.7	4	11.1	4	10.0		
Table plate	(5)		(3)		(4)		11	
Twiffler/muffin			(1)					
Edged	1	7.1	1	2.8	5	12.5		
Table plate	(1)				(4)		1.14	1.12
Twiffler/muffin			(1)		(1)			
Willow	1	7.1						
Table plate	(1)						n/a	1.6
Printed			3	8.3	5	12.5	2.11	1.6
Table plate			(3)		(3)			
Twiffler/muffin					(2)			
Dark-blue printed								
Table plate							2.29	n/a
Flown								
Table plate							2.64	2.4
Ironstone								
Plain			1	2.8			1.93	n/a
Table plate			(1)					
White-granite								
paneled	6	42.9	5	13.9	19	47.5		
Table plate	(4)		(2)		(10)		1.93	n/a
Twiffler/muffin	(2)		(3)		(9)			
Porcelain								
Plain			18	50.0	4	10.0	n/a	n/a
Twiffler/muffin			(18)		(4)			
Molded-paneled			4	11.1			n/a	n/a
Twiffler/muffin			(4)					
Gilt painted	1	7.1			3	7.5	n/a	n/a
Twiffler/muffin	(1)							
Total	14	99.9	36	100	40	100		

SOURCE: Relative values from Miller (1991).
NOTE: Unfortunately, there is no information on the value of porcelain plates during this period.

TABLE 6.6

Distribution of Plates (Excluding Porcelains) by Site and Decorative Type

	25 Barrow St		153 West Twelfth St.		50 Washington Square South	
	n	%	n	%	n	%
Earthenware						
CC/plain	5	38.5	4	28.6	4	12.1
Edged	1	7.7	1	7.1	5	15.2
Willow	1	7.7				
Printed			3	21.4	5	15.2
Ironstone						
Plain			1	7.1		
White-granite						
paneled	6	46.2	5	35.7	19	57.6
Total	13	100	14	99.9	33	100.1

NOTE: A chi-square test of association (Siegel 1956, 175–79) comparing the distribution of the white granite versus all the other wares combined yielded a value of 1.98, a value not significant at the level of p < .05 and 2 degrees of freedom. The data were grouped thus: 25 Barrow St., white-granite paneled: 6; other: 7; 153 West Twelfth St.: white-granite paneled: 5; other: 9; 50 Washington Square South, white-granite paneled: 19; other: 14.

fact that they were bought in both small and large sizes (and thus would have been suitable for serving dessert courses as part of family dinners as well as for breakfast and tea where smaller plates were preferred; see table 6.4) both indicate that all three women saw these vessels as appropriate for their family meals. These plates are also presumably the "china of entire white" that Leslie describes (see above) as the most popular for everyday use at mid-century.

Plates of French or English porcelain were found in all three of the assemblages (table 6.5). In all cases, they were small, in sizes designated as muffins or twifflers in the ceramics literature. As mentioned above, their size precludes their use in family dinner and by extension in other family meals; they were presumably used for entertaining at evening parties. Most of these plates are plain white with flat rims with no painted decoration (fig. 6.2)—a style that might be designated as neoclassical or *Grecian,* to use Downing's term. The

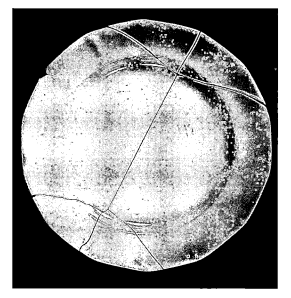

Fig. 6.1. White-paneled ironstone plate in the Gothic pattern, from the Barrow Street site. Department of Anthropology, New York University; photograph by the author.

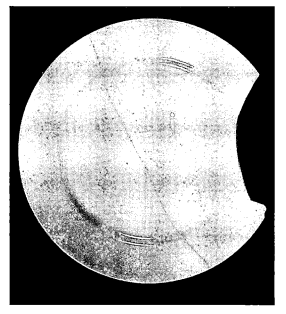

Fig. 6.2. Plain porcelain plate from the Washington Square site. South Street Seaport Museum; photograph by the author.

Twelfth Street assemblage includes an extremely large number of porcelain plates: 60 percent of the plates in the assemblage were made of porcelain. Although most of these plates are plain, a few have rims that are subtly paneled in the Gothic style. In addition, a few of the porcelain plates from Washington Square, as well as the only porcelain plate from Barrow Street, are simply but elegantly decorated with painted gilt circles.

Ceramic Cups and Saucers

Next let's turn to the teacups and saucers (table 6.7)—vessels that according to the prescriptive literature were used in all four of the meals of the middle-class home—breakfast, dinner, tea, and evening parties (table 6.4). In all three households, the most popular style consisted of plain white vessels with molded decoration and most of these vessels—whether made of ironstone or porcelain—were decorated with simple panels in the Gothic style (fig. 6.3). This would suggest that these cups and saucers were used along with the paneled Gothic plates in family meals. The distributions of the other styles of cups and saucers in the three households are strikingly and significantly dissimilar, however (see chi square test in table 6.7). In the poorer Barrow Street household, cups and saucers were present in only one other style: plain vessels with no decoration at all that would match the plates in "common queensware" that Leslie prescribed for kitchen use, mentioned above. The middling Twelfth Street household, however, possessed just as many vessels made of colored European porcelain as of plain queensware. A few of these were hard-paste vessels decorated in an Italianate style with gilt overglaze decoration, while the rest were of white soft-paste porcelain and decorated with blue-figured motifs.[9] Some of the latter were shaped with molded panels, while others showed a white embossed pattern on a white ground (fig. 6.4). Finally, the Washington Square household presented a different pattern still. The Robson assemblage did not include any of the plain queensware vessels—they may have used in their kitchen the sprig-painted whiteware cups that Leslie dismissed as being too similar to calico. Instead, over a third of the assemblage consisted of colored European porcelain vessels. None of these was in the blue-figured patterns found at Twelfth Street; instead, most were in the Italianate style with molded pedestals and gilt overglaze decoration (fig. 6.5). These colored European porcelain vessels were presumably used for entertaining at evening parties in the wealthier Twelfth Street and Washington Square homes.

TABLE 6.7

Distribution of Teacups and Saucers by Decoration and Site

Decoration/ware	25 Barrow St.		153 West Twelfth St.		50 Washington Square South	
	n	%	n	%	n	%
Plain	3	37.5	16	22.5	0	0
CC			(8)			
Ironstone	(3)		(3)			
Porcelain			(5)			
Painted	0		2	2.8	6	13.6
Whiteware "calico"			(1)		(6)	
Chinese export porcelain			(1)			
Printed	0		0		2	4.5
Whiteware					(2)	
Molded only	5	62.5	34	47.9	20	45.4
Panels						
Ironstone	(3)		(14)		(3)	
Porcelain			(16)		(17)	
Other						
Ironstone	(2)					
Porcelain			(4)			
Colored European Porcelain	0	0	19	26.8	16	36.4
Blue-figured						
Paneled			(6)			
Unpaneled			(8)			
Overglaze painted						
Gilt			(4)		(10)	
Gilt and other colors					(3)	
Other colors only			(1)		(3)	
Total	8	100	71	100	44	99.9

NOTE: A chi-square test of association (Siegel 1956, 175–79) comparing the distribution of the decorated European porcelain vessels (that is, those used for entertaining) versus the white plain and molded wares combined (those used in family meals and in the kitchen) yielded a value of 7.02, a value significant with $p < .05$ and 2 degrees of freedom. This indicates that there is in fact a significant difference between the distributions of these three samples. The data were grouped thus: 25 Barrow St., colored European porcelain: 0; plain white and moded wares: 8; 153 West Twelfth St., colored European porcelain: 19; plain white and molded: 50; 50 Washington Square South, colored European porcelain: 16; plain white and molded: 20.

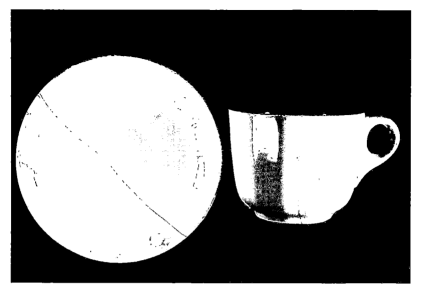

Fig. 6.3. White-paneled cup and saucer in the Gothic pattern from the Barrow Street site. Department of Anthropology, New York University; photograph by the author.

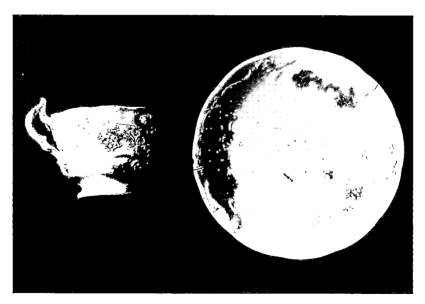

Fig. 6.4. Soft-paste porcelain cup and saucer in the blue-figured pattern from the Twelfth Street site. The Cooper Union for the Advancement of Science and Art; photograph by the author.

Fig. 6.5. Gilded and pedestaled porcelain cup from the Washington Square site.
South Street Seaport Museum; photograph by the author.

Glass Stemware and Tumblers

Now let's turn to the tumblers and stemware that these women used to grace their meals. Unfortunately, although both Leslie and Beecher mention tumblers and wineglasses as playing parts in several meals, they are not as eloquent in describing the preferred styles for these vessels as modern researchers would wish. Leslie makes the only encountered reference to styles of glassware when she recommends "common glass tumblers" as appropriate accouterments for the kitchen (1850, 233). We might expect such "common" or plain tumblers to be confined to kitchen use, while both tumblers and, if wine was served,[10] wineglasses might be used at dinner and at evening parties (table 6.4).

Unfortunately, since the Barrow Street glassware assemblage was extremely small—it includes a single wineglass decorated with panels, a style that would have complimented the paneled ironstone plates and teacups—it will not be considered further here; instead we will have to limit our analysis to the other two households. The styles preferred in both these households include plain tumblers, paneled tumblers and wineglasses, and tumblers and wineglasses

TABLE 6.8

Distribution of Tumblers by Site and Decorative Type

Decoration	25 Barrow St		153 West Twelfth St.		50 Washington Square South	
	n	%	n	%	n	%
Plain	0	0	18	31.0	4	22.2
Paneled	0	0	34	58.6	11	61.1
Other decorated patterns	0	0	6	10.4	3	16.7
Argus	0	0	(3)			
Ashburton	0	0	(3)		(3)	
Total	0	0	58	100	18	100

NOTE: A chi-square test of association corrected for continuity (Siegel 1956, 104–11) comparing the distribution of the paneled versus all the other decoratively patterned tumblers (excluding the plain tumblers) from the Twelfth Street and Washington Square South sites yielded a value of 0.02, a value not significant with $p < .05$ and 1 degree of freedom. The data were grouped thus: 153 West Twelfth St., paneled: 34; other decorated patterns: 6; 50 Washington Square South, paneled: 11; other decorated patterns: 3.

decorated in other pressed patterns. The distributions of the styles of tumblers in the two households are fairly similar to each other (table 6.8). Plain tumblers for kitchen use appeared in both of the assemblages. Paneled tumblers (fig. 6.6) were the most popular style of tumbler in both the households and would have matched the paneled plates, cups, and saucers that appeared at family dinners. Glasses decorated in other, more elaborate patterns made up relatively small percentages of each of the assemblages.

In contrast, the distributions of the styles of stemware in the two households are quite different from each other (see chi square test in table 6.9). By far the large majority of the stemware from the Twelfth Street household is in the paneled style, complimenting the paneled tumblers (fig. 6.6), ironstone plates, and even the paneled blue-figured teacups and porcelain plates in the same assemblage. All of the stemware pieces from the Washington Square assemblage, on the other hand, are in the more elaborate Ashburton pattern (fig. 6.7)— matching all the tumblers in that assemblage that were decorated in a non-paneled pattern. But the meaning of the similarities in the distributions of the tumblers and the dissimilarities in the distributions of the stemware is not completely clear. This issue is discussed more fully below.

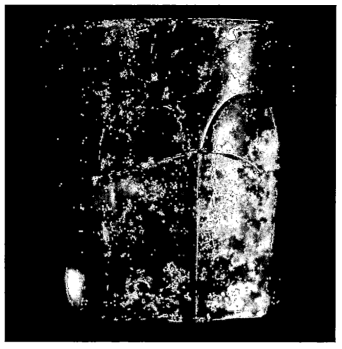

Fig. 6.6. Pressed paneled tumbler from the Washington Square site.

South Street Seaport Museum; photograph by the author.

TABLE 6.9

Distribution of Stemware by Decoration and Site

	25 Barrow St.		153 West Twelfth St.		50 Washington Square South	
Decoration	**n**	**%**	**n**	**%**	**n**	**%**
Paneled	1	100	39	88.6	0	0
Other decorated patterns	0	0	5	11.4	5	100
Ashburton	-		(1)		(5)	
Bigler	-		(3)		-	
Honeycomb	-		(1)		-	
Total	1	100	44	100	5	100

NOTE: A chi-square test of association corrected for continuity (Siegel 1956, 104–11) comparing the distribution of the paneled versus all the other decoratively patterned stemware from the Twelfth Street and Washington Square South sites yielded a value of 16.6, a value significant with $p < .05$ and 1 degree of freedom. The data were grouped thus: 153 West Twelfth St., paneled: 39; other decorated patterns: 5; 50 Washington Square South, paneled: 0; other decorated patterns: 5.

Fig. 6.7. Pressed Ashburton goblet from the Washington Square site.
South Street Seaport Museum; photograph by the author.

DISCUSSION

This comparison of the styles of the plates, cups, and glassware from the three households is quite provocative. It suggests that the women in these middle-class homes were constructing domestic worlds that in some ways were the same as, but in other ways quite different from, each other. Like Bourdieu's working-class French women, middle-class New York women also seem to have used vessels to distinguish domestic life in the home from commercial life in the marketplace. All three women, regardless of their economic position within the middle class, used Gothic paneled plates, cups, and saucers in setting their tables for family meals. Even Eliza Robson, who certainly could have afforded tablewares in the more expensive patterns, consistently chose the Gothic vessels, which were middle range in cost for her family's meals (table 6.5). These Gothic dishes were enhanced by the similarly paneled tumblers and wineglasses that were used with them. Furthermore, these meals that served as the "constant and familiar" reunions of home life (Calvert Vaux, quoted in Clark 1986, 42) may have been held in dining rooms that were also furnished in the Gothic style. This style was not only deemed appropriate for the "quiet, domestic feeling of the ... family circle" (Downing 1850, 23–24) but was the most popular style of architecture for churches in mid-nineteenth-century New York. The New York women apparently equated the rituals of family meals with the sanctity of religious rituals, an equation that could only have enhanced the sacred aspect of woman's role as a moral leader.

The wealthier Eliza Robson and Henrietta Raymer also entertained their friends at evening parties in the parlor, where they negotiated their families' position in the class structure. Many of the vessels that they used for these affairs were neoclassical or Italianate in style, styles befitting "the gay spirit of the drawing-room and social life" (Downing 1850, 24–25). That this was also the style that had become most popular for commercial buildings in the city at mid-century (Lockwood 1976, 89) suggests that, just as for Bourdieu's bourgeois families, "home" for these women and their families was not simply a haven from the competitive world of the capitalist marketplace (after Lasch 1977). In fact, they may have used these dishes in competitive displays designed to impress their friends with the refinement and gentility of their families.

There were some differences, however, in the kinds of fancier tea vessels preferred by these two women. Most of the wealthy Eliza Robson's more elegant cups and saucers were gilt-painted, pedestaled, Italianate vessels and her porcelain plates were plain or neoclassical in style. Although the less wealthy Henrietta Raymer had some of both these kinds of vessels, she also had both blue-figured tea cups and porcelain plates in paneled patterns reminiscent of the Gothic style of the dishes that all the families used for family meals. Perhaps Henrietta Raymer, located close to the middle of the middle class, did not always strive to impress and compete with her friends or did not have the means to do so, but aimed to stress community ties with them at times as well. These ties could have proved important to her when she was left a widow with two small children after her husband's death.

These different social meanings of entertaining might help explain the differences noted above in the glassware in these two households as well. Most of Henrietta Raymer's tumblers and stemware were decorated with panels, a pattern that complimented both her white ironstone Gothic plates and her paneled porcelain party plates. In contrast, all of Eliza Robson's stemware was decorated in the pressed Ashburton pattern, the pattern that matched some of her tumblers as well. Perhaps Eliza Robson only used these vessels for serving wine and water at evening parties, where she felt these patterns were more appropriate than panels for enhancing her neoclassical and Italianate porcelain dishes.

The fact that the Barrow Street family did not have sets of fancy cups and stemware does not necessarily mean that poorer middle-class women simply could not afford them or that they did not have their friends in for tea. It could also mean that when they entertained their friends, the meal had a different meaning. Instead of trying to promote the image of gentility and impressing and competing with their friends for social status, perhaps the Barrow Street tenants (like Bourdieu's working class) only invited those equated with family into their homes for any meal at all. The paneled cups and saucers may have served to elicit the almost sacred values of community—values which could be very useful for those at the lower end of the middle-class spectrum—among the people who were gathering together for tea.

In 1852, Julia Harkness Lay, a bookkeeper's wife who lived in New York City, noted in her diary that she had just "bought some new crockery." However, she described neither the crockery she purchased nor how and why she made her choice. But the analysis of archaeological materials from the homes of contemporary New Yorkers allows us to glimpse parts of the broad spectrum of cultural experience of middle-class women who purchased crockery to construct and maintain domestic life, a spectrum which is otherwise invisible. It lets us hypothesize that, as a bookkeeper's wife keeping house in mid-century New York City, Julia Lay may well have bought most of her tea ware and tableware in the paneled Gothic pattern, and we can begin to understand why she made that choice.

NOTES

Bert Salwen played a leading role in the excavations at the Sullivan Street site (which he co-directed with Arnold Pickman) and the Barrow Street site (which he co-directed with me). I analyzed the ceramics from the upper deposit of Feature 9 at the Sullivan Street site for this study, and Debra Bodie and I together analyzed the materials from the Barrow Street site. Bodie used the Barrow Street materials as the basis of her master's thesis at New York University's Department of Anthropology (1992). I directed the excavations at 153 West Twelfth Street in 1990–91 for the Cooper Union, which owns this property that serves as the home of its president. I am particularly grateful for the kind and generous hospitality of Jay and Leah Iselin, who made the archaeologists so welcome in their backyard. Daphne Joachim, then a student at Cooper Union, was responsible for initiating the Twelfth Street project. She also conducted the original documentary research on the property and worked with us while we were in the field. Nancy Brighton has worked on this project almost from its inception and is now analyzing the results of the excavation as part of her master's thesis in the Department of

Anthropology at New York University. I am particularly grateful to her for sharing her ongoing interpretations for this analysis.

This study has been infinitely improved by the comments of Anne-Marie Cantwell, Randall McGuire, Paul Mullins, Nan A. Rothschild, Donna Seifert, several anonymous reviewers, and the editors of this volume. I am also grateful to Olive Jones for her advice for analyzing the glass. However, all errors of fact or interpretation that appear in the study are, of course, my own.

1. It is obviously "reaching" to attempt to resolve a problem as complex as this one with data from only three households; instead, this study is designed both to explore the question and to show the potential of using data generated by historical archaeology for addressing questions of this nature.

2. The following discussion and tables 6.1 and 6.2 are based on information derived from contemporary city directories and tax records. The names of the heads of the families residing on each of the blocks were looked up first in the reverse or street directory for 1851 (Doggett 1851a). Each name was then looked up, first in the city directory for the same year (Doggett 1851b), in order to uncover information about occupations, and then in the tax records for the same year (City of New York 1851) in order to find out about the value of the property and whether or not the occupant of a house was the one being assessed for its taxes. In cases where the occupant of a house was *not* being assessed for the real estate taxes for the house, it was inferred that the occupant was a tenant and did not own the house.

3. Unless otherwise noted, the data upon which both this discussion of the three households and table 6.3 are based were derived from the tax assessment records (City of New York 1860), the city directories (Trow 1853, 1855–74), and the federal manuscript census records (Bureau of the Census 1860).

4. There were two domestic deposits in this feature (Feature 9) at the Sullivan Street Site. The lowermost one had a *terminus post quem* date of 1840, while the uppermost, more recent one is that analyzed here.

5. Nancy Brighton, personal communication. After the Raymers moved away from the house, the house, which had been owned by the Remsen estate, was sold to a family who lived in it. It is inferred here that the owners probably installed indoor plumbing and thus filled in the privy before it was sold so that the house could fetch a higher price.

6. Supper parties, described by Leslie (1850, 287–88), were also used for entertaining. The accoutrements for this meal are not included in the present analysis because it is unlikely that the middle class participated in these entertainments that took place in formal dining rooms; see the discussion of dinner parties, below.

7. Archaeological data suggest that, contrary to Clark, at least some contemporary middle-class families were having dinner parties at this time. In the nearby suburb of Brooklyn

(which was then not part of New York) archaeologists have found hard-paste porcelain table plates and soup plates and have interpreted their presence as indicating that middle-class Brooklynites were entertaining their friends for dinner (for example, Fitts and Yamin 1996). To my knowledge, these vessel forms have never been found in porcelain in contemporary middle-class assemblages in New York City. Instead, the archaeological evidence for New York (exemplified by the absence of porcelain soup and table plates and the presence of porcelain plates only in smaller sizes) supports Clark's interpretation that the middle class did not entertain at dinner parties. One possible explanation for these differences in entertaining practices in places that are so close to each other could be the distances that guests had to travel to their hosts' homes. Many men of the Brooklyn middle class commuted to work in New York. Therefore, when their wives entertained, some of their guests were probably New Yorkers who had long trips by ferry and omnibus to get from their own homes to their hosts' homes in Brooklyn. It is possible that the length of this trip prevented Brooklynites from entertaining these friends at after-dinner parties (which might or might not include supper); if a New Yorker were to make such a trip, only a longer visit would make the long trip worthwhile.

8. This argument is an extension of Wobst's (1977) and Hodder's (1979) discussions on the importance of style in forming and maintaining boundaries.

9. The designation of "blue-figured" for these cups and saucers was suggested by George Miller (pers. comm. 1998).

10. The extent to which the temperance movement (which included wine as part of its focus by the mid-nineteenth century) was effective in prohibiting the serving of wine and other forms of alcohol in these middle-class homes is unclear. Susan Williams convincingly supports her contention that, although as the arbiters of morality many of these women did not drink wine themselves during the late nineteenth century, they did continue to serve it. She cites the continued appearance of drinking glasses—including those for wine, champagne, ale, and whiskey—in museum collections and trade catalogues whose market included the middle-class housewife (1985, 134–37). W. J. Rorabaugh, on the other hand, avers straightforwardly that "middle-class women did not serve alcohol in the home" (1987, 42). This is a question that could be easily addressed by the analysis of archaeological deposits associated with the homes of late-nineteenth-century middle-class families.

REFERENCES CITED

Austen, Jane. 1818/1898. *Persuasion.* London: J. M. Dent.

Beecher, Catherine. 1845. *A Treatise on Domestic Economy, for the Use of Young Ladies at Home and at School.* New York: Harper and Brothers.

————. 1846. *Miss Beecher's Domestic Receipt-Book, Designed as a Supplement to Her Treatise on Domestic Economy*. New York: Harper and Bothers.

Bleecker, Elizabeth. 1799–1806. Diary kept in New York City. Rare Books and Manuscripts Division, New York Public Library.

Blumin, Stuart. 1989. *The Emergence of the Middle Class: Social Experience in the American City, 1760–1900*. Cambridge: Cambridge Univ. Press.

Bodie, Debra C. 1992. *The Construction of Community in Nineteenth Century New York: A Case Study Based on the Archaeological Investigation of the 25 Barrow Street Site*. Master's thesis, Dept. of Anthropology, New York University.

Bourdieu, Pierre. 1984. *Distinction: A Social Critique of the Judgement of Taste*, trans. Richard Nice. Cambridge, Mass.: Harvard Univ. Press.

Burley, David V. 1989. Function, Meaning, and Context: Ambiguities in Ceramic Use by the Hivernant Metis of the Northwestern Plains. *Historical Archaeology* 23:97–106.

City of New York. 1851, 1860. Tax Assessment Records. Municipal Archives, Dept. of Records and Information Services, New York.

Clark, Clifford E. 1986. *The American Family Home, 1800–1960*. Chapel Hill: Univ. of North Carolina Press.

————. 1987. The Vision of the Dining Room: Plan Book Dreams and Middle-Class Realities. In *Dining in America, 1850–1900*, ed. Kathryn Glover, 142–72. Amherst: Univ. of Massachusetts Press; Rochester, N.Y.: Margaret Woodbury Strong Museum.

Coontz, Stephanie. 1988. *The Social Origins of Private Life: A History of American Families, 1600–1900*. London: Verso.

DeCunzo, LuAnn. 1995. Reform, Respite, Ritual: An Archaeology of Institutions: The Magdalen Society of Philadelphia. *Historical Archaeology* 29 (3).

Doggett, John, Jr. 1851a. *Doggett's New York City Street Directory for 1851*. New York: John Doggett.

————. 1851b. *Doggett's New York City Directory*. New York: John Doggett.

Downing, Andrew Jackson. 1850/1969. *The Architecture of Country Houses*. New York: Dover.

Ernst, Robert. 1949. *Immigrant Life in New York City, 1825–1863*. New York: Kings Crown Press.

Fitts, Robert, and Rebecca Yamin. 1996. *The Archaeology of Domesticity in Victorian Brooklyn: Exploratory Testing and Data Recovery at Block 2006 of the Atlantic Terminal Urban Renewal Area, Brooklyn, New York*. Prepared for Atlantic Housing Corporation and Atlantic Center Housing Associates by John Milner Associates, Inc.

Handsman, Russell G. 1984. Merchant Capital and the Historical Archaeology of Gender, Motherhood, and Child Raising. Paper presented at the annual meeting of the Council for Northeast Historical Archaeology, Binghamton, New York.

Hodder, Ian. 1979. Economic and Social Stress and Material Culture Patterning. *American Antiquity* 44:446–54.

Landau, Sarah Bradford. 1982. Greek and Gothic Side by Side: Architecture around the Square. In *Around the Square, 1830–1890: Essays on Life, Letters, and Architecture*, ed. Mindy Cantor, 12–29. New York: New York Univ. Press.

Lasch, Christopher. 1977. *Haven in a Heartless World: The Family Besieged.* New York: Basic Books.

Lay, Julia Harkness. 1851–78. Diary. Rare Books and Manuscripts Division, New York Public Library, New York.

Leslie, Eliza. 1850. *Miss Leslie's Lady's House-Book; A Manual of Domestic Economy.* Philadelphia: A. Hart.

Lockwood, Charles. 1972. *Bricks and Brownstone: The New York Row House, 1783–1929: An Architectural and Social History.* New York: McGraw-Hill.

————. 1976. *Manhattan Moves Uptown: An Illustrated History.* New York: Barnes and Noble.

Lucas, Michael T. 1994. A la Russe, à la Pell-Mell, or à la Practical: Ideology and Compromise at the Late-Nineteenth-Century Dinner Table. In *An Archaeology of Harpers Ferry's Commercial and Residential District*, ed. Paul A. Shackel and Susan E. Winter. *Historical Archaeology* 28 (4): 80–94.

Miller, George. 1991. A Revised Set of CC Index Values for Classification and Economic Scaling of English Ceramics from 1787 to 1880. *Historical Archaeology* 25 (1): 1–25.

Mrozowski, Stephen. 1984. Prospects and Perspectives on an Archaeology of the Household. *Man in the Northeast* 27:31–49.

Pessen, Edward. 1973. *Riches, Class, and Power Before the Civil War.* Lexington, Mass.: D. C. Heath.

Rorabaugh, W. J. 1987. Beer, Lemonade, and Propriety in the Gilded Age. In *Dining in America, 1850–1900*, ed. Kathryn Grover, 24–46. Amherst: Univ. of Massachusetts Press.

Salwen, Bert, and Rebecca Yamin. 1990. *The Archaeological History of Six Nineteenth Century Lots: Sullivan Street, Greenwich Village, New York City.* Prepared by New York Univ. Law School. Submitted to the New York City Landmarks Preservation Commission.

Scott, Elizabeth M., ed. 1994. *Those of Little Note: Gender, Race, and Class in Historical Archaeology.* Tucson: Univ. of Arizona.

Seifert, Donna, ed. 1991. Gender in Historical Archaeology. *Historical Archaeology* 25:4.

Siegel, Sidney. 1956. *Non-Parametric Statistics for the Behavioral Sciences.* New York: McGraw-Hill.

Trow, John F. 1853. *Trow's New York City Directory.* New York: John F. Trow.

————. 1855–74. *Trow's New York City Directory.* New York: John F. Trow.

U.S. Bureau of the Census. 1860. *Population Schedules, Eighth Census of the United States.* Washington, D.C.: Government Printing Office.

Wall, Diana diZerega. 1991. Sacred Dinners and Secular Teas: Constructing Domesticity in Mid-Nineteenth-Century New York. In *Gender in Historical Archaeology*, ed. Donna Seifert. *Historical Archaeology* 25 (4): 69–81.

————. 1994. *The Archaeology of Gender: Separating the Spheres in Urban America.* New York: Plenum.

———. 1999. Examining Gender, Class, and Ethnicity in Nineteenth-Century New York City. In *Confronting Class,* ed. LouAnn Wurst and Robert K. Fitts. *Historical Archaeology* 33(1): 102–17.

Wetherbee, Jean. 1985. *A Second Look at White Ironstone.* Lombard, Ill.: Wallace-Homestead.

Williams, Susan. 1985. *Savory Suppers and Fashionable Feasts: Dining in Victorian America.* New York: Pantheon Books.

Wobst, H. Martin. 1977. Stylistic Behavior and Information Exchange. In *For the Director: Research Essays in Honor of James B. Griffin,* ed. Charles E. Cleland. Michigan Anthropological Papers 61:317–42.

Yentsch, Anne E. 1991a. The Symbolic Divisions of Pottery: Sex Related Attributes of English and Anglo-American Household Pots. In *The Archaeology of Inequality,* ed. Randall McGuire and Robert Paynter. Oxford: Blackwell.

———. 1991b. Engendering Visible and Invisible Ceramic Artifacts, Especially Dairy Vessels. In *Gender in Historical Archaeology,* ed. Donna J. Seifert. *Historical Archaeology* 25 (4): 132–55.

CHAPTER SEVEN

Doña Luisa and
Her Two Houses

Ross W. Jamieson

Luisa Maldonado de San Juan died in 1664 in the town of Cuenca in the southern highlands of the Spanish colonial Audiencia of Quito (map 7.1). She had been a widow for at least eight years and during this period had maintained control of considerable capital investments in the southern highlands. Luisa's life and the property she owned provide us with a window to the role women played in the seventeenth-century Andean economy.

As a trader and landed property owner, Luisa's role is not the one that has been emphasized for women in mainstream Spanish colonial archaeological research. In her work at St. Augustine in Florida, Kathleen Deagan has dealt largely with the material culture of women of native descent. In her influential model of Spanish colonial domestic material culture, Deagan (1983, 271) proposed that in "socially visible" areas the influence and conservatism of Spanish males predominated. In the socially invisible areas of the house, such as the kitchen, the material culture demonstrates acculturation, based on the incorporation of Indian women into the household. This model of the household has been taken up by a generation of Spanish colonial archaeologists (Ewen 1991; McEwan 1995; South 1988), who have applied it to contexts beyond the garrison town of St. Augustine. Bonnie McEwan, analyzing archaeological evidence of elite women's presence at the Spanish colonial town of Puerto Real, has expanded on this model. For McEwan the work of elite women of Spanish descent in the New World was largely restricted to the home and focused on the domestic responsibilities of maintaining traditional standards (1991, 1995).

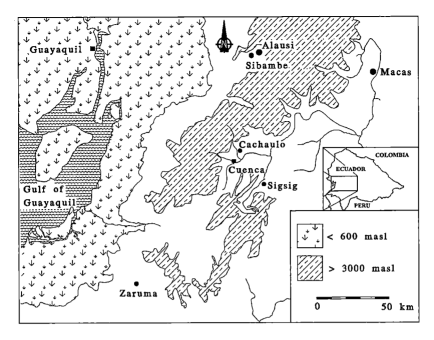

Map 7.1. Southern part of the colonial Audiencia of Quito, now Ecuador.

Examining the life and legacy of Luisa Maldonado de San Juan allows us the opportunity to reexamine women's roles in the Spanish colonies. In this way archaeologists can follow the advice of historians of colonial Latin America, who have warned that "[t]he assumption that colonial women were mostly occupied in familial household activities should be altered" (Lavrin and Couturier 1979, 300). Historical archaeologists have developed an extensive literature on the relationships between power, architecture, and material culture (Beaudry 1988; Paynter and McGuire 1991; Yamin and Metheny 1996). The property that Luisa and her descendants owned, and the material culture they used, provide a useful example of the relationship between the power of a wealthy family in an era of emerging capitalism and their use of material culture as a form of hegemonic discourse (Beaudry et al. 1991). That Luisa was a woman forces us to question the assumption that Spanish families, and particularly women, were peripheral to the emergence of capitalism in the Andes.

DOÑA LUISA AND HER
TWO HUSBANDS

I do not know where or when Luisa Maldonado de San Juan was born, although the names of her parents, Maria Coronado and Pedro Maldonado de

San Juan, are recorded (Borrero Crespo 1962, 37). She was married twice, first to Alonso Fuentes de Navia, with whom she had at least one daughter. Subsequently she married Juan Rodriguez Fernandez, and they had two sons and two daughters. All of her children from both marriages were minors when she died, suggesting that Luisa died well before reaching her fiftieth birthday.[1] Through the institution of marriage Luisa participated twice in a form of church surveillance that was less than a hundred years old at the time. The Tametsi Decree of 1563 had formalized the Roman Catholic ritual of marriage, with requirements for witnesses and the presence of a clergyman. The decree had also given "the church a theoretical tool to curb covert attempts to escape its surveillance," while at the same time civil legislation gave the institution of marriage considerable leverage in inheritance and property rights (Lavrin 1989, 6).

Through marriage Luisa entered into a domestic and private relationship, something which archaeologists of the Spanish colonial period have assumed dominated women's lives. For example, McEwan (1991, 34) asserts, "[i]n most instances, Spanish women in the colonies appear to have worked in the home and maintained traditional standards," and therefore "the archaeological correlates of Spanish women are associated mostly with their domestic responsibilities." The assumption that domestic activities dominated the lives of women both ignores the important role of the family in Andean colonial economic relations and subsumes the huge variation in the lives of women throughout the geographical area of the Spanish empire, and throughout its three-hundred-year history.

WOMEN, FAMILIES, AND THE FORMAL ECONOMY

The political economy of the Spanish colonial Andes was based on a mixture of slave, coerced, and free labor. This system was neither completely feudal nor completely capitalist (Stern 1988). It is important that we do not underestimate the role of women within this formal economy. Archaeologists have portrayed even wealthy women of Spanish descent as "mostly restricted to domestic activities" through which they "lent prestige to their communities, set cultural standards, and, to a lesser degree, exercised financial power" (McEwan 1991, 39). It is vital to understand, however, that in societies that are not fully capitalist the primary association of women with domestic labor and men with monetarily supported labor is not as clear-cut as in capitalist societies. The domestic, private world of the family and the public world of the formal colonial economy were not as clearly separated as is the case in industrial capitalism (Moore 1988; Yentsch 1991, 198). The role of the family, and of women within it, was of essential importance to political and economic power in colonial Latin America. In many regions a small number of families gained great power (Balmori et al. 1984, 8). It has been noted that "[t]hrough marriage and the family, individuals achieved what the formal business organizations and political parties of the time could not: a long-lasting association of power and money" (17).

During the seventeenth century women in the Andes played a very ambivalent role in the economic functioning of elite families. Ethnicity played a key role in this ambivalence. In the early colonial period native Andean women who were either *caciques* themselves,[2] or were related to *caciques*, had considerable access to, and power over, economic resources (Caillavet 1982; Rappaport 1990b; Silverblatt 1987, 115–19; Truhan 1991). For women of largely Spanish descent like Luisa, however, Spanish social norms and legalities placed great restrictions on participation in the money economy (Silverblatt 1987, 119–24; Wilson 1984, 310).

I know nothing of Luisa's first marriage, but by the mid-seventeenth century Luisa and her second husband Juan were *vecinos* (citizens) of the mining town of Zaruma (map 7.1), in the southern highlands of what is now Ecuador, where they were cloth merchants. Zaruma was one of the most important early colonial mines in southern highland Ecuador. The gold and silver deposits there had been discovered in 1560, thirty years after the Spanish conquest of the region, and by 1600 there were thirty mills for processing ore at the site. By 1628, however, mining labor was becoming increasingly problematic in Zaruma, and it became clear that mining was not going to be the mainstay of the southern highland economy (Anda Aguirre 1960, 33; Jácome 1983, 158; Jiménez de la Espada 1965, 3:81–83; Newson 1995, 230; Poloni 1992, 280).

The economic power that Juan and Luisa had access to came from their activities as merchants in Zaruma. There were great social obstacles to women in Spanish colonial society preventing them from participation in long-distance trade on their own. Male traders usually traveled extensively as young men in order to build trade ties and then settled in an area when they were older to reap the benefits of these ties. There was really only one way for women to gain access to this system, and this was via their husbands. The wives of merchants often participated in the administration of the family businesses, particularly when their husbands were away on trading trips (Borchart de Moreno 1992, 364–65, 373). As the wife of a trader, Luisa would have had considerable knowledge of the business before Juan died.

LUISA AS WIDOW

Juan died sometime before 1656, and Luisa was left with considerable investments. Her active participation in maintaining the business after Juan's death indicates that she had been a participant in it during his lifetime. As a widow Luisa sent someone to Panama to buy 8,000 pesos worth of clothing in 1660, and she owned hundreds of yards of cloth in her shop in Zaruma at the time of her death in 1664.[3] Luisa's position as a widow gave her an opportunity for the ownership and management of property, despite the fact that women were considered minors under Spanish colonial law. In most instances, therefore, they required the permission of their father or husband to participate in the formal economy as property owners. The fact that Spanish colonial women often married much older men, however, meant that widowhood such as Luisa's was not a rare occurrence. Widows usually inherited half of their husband's wealth and property and also gained their freedom in terms of undertaking property transactions. Many women, when their husbands had abandoned them or died, used their inheritances to take part quite openly in the management of their own economic resources (Borchart de Moreno 1992, 357–59; Wilson 1984, 316–21).

By 1656 Doña Luisa was a widow twice over. From 1656 to 1659 she purchased more than 7,700 pesos worth of rural and urban properties in the southern highlands of Ecuador.[4] Doña Luisa was a "citizen," a merchant, a property owner, and had considerable wealth in comparison to other seventeenth-century residents of Cuenca. In the Spanish colonial world the role of wealthy women, and particularly widows such as Luisa, with rights to half of the wealth accrued throughout their marriage, gave them significant economic power. Luisa and her descendants negotiated their relationships to others and to the landscape around them through material culture (Beaudry et al. 1991; Gramsci 1971; McGuire 1992, 35–36). We can combine the archaeology, documentary history, and architectural history of Luisa and her family in order to reveal some aspects of how an elite early modern family in the region negotiated these relationships throughout their lives.[5]

CONTROLLING "WILD TERRAIN": DOÑA LUISA'S RURAL ESTANCIA

The native population in the Cuenca region had been decimated in the first sixty years of Spanish rule, with an estimated decline from 58,000 native Cañari people prior to Spanish conquest to a population of perhaps 12,000 in the 1590s (Powers 1995, 17–18, 37–38). Up until the 1560s the majority of native

Andeans in the southern Ecuadorian highlands had lived in dispersed rural communities, with the *cacique's* house as the ceremonial center of their local region and trade systems with lowland groups still intact (Salomon 1983, 114). With the Toledan reforms of the 1570s this changed drastically as dispersed rural inhabitants were congregated in villages founded by the Spanish (Chacón Zhapán 1990, 58).

These reforms made explicit many of the perceptions of the Spanish elite toward Andean peoples. A Jesuit priest writing in 1572 in support of the Toledan reforms said that native Andeans living in scattered hamlets "have not been able to learn the social and political skills that are a prerequisite to becoming capable of the law of God . . . they live in wild terrain like savages" (MacCormack 1991, 276).

Diseases introduced by the Spanish and the mines at Zaruma and Zamora were both major factors in the massive decline in native populations. The mining tribute was frequently equivalent to a death sentence, and many native Andeans fled their home villages to avoid it (Newson 1995, 236). The movement of large numbers of Andeans away from their home villages meant that their control over rural land also dwindled, and as Andean communal lands were taken from them, these lands were sold to private owners, most of them Spanish (Jácome 1983, 137).

Native Andeans who left their home villages settled in the cities or in other Andean villages. By the early seventeenth century the majority of tribute-paying Andeans had abandoned their communities in search of a new life. The *caciques* were still expected to pay the tribute for all of these individuals. In 1651 the situation reached a crisis, and in a form of "punishment as a political tactic" (Foucault 1979, 23), the local *caciques* from the area surrounding Cuenca were imprisoned for failure to pay the tributes of absentee community members. They were only released after a desperate petition stating that there was no way the tribute money could be paid unless the *caciques* were freed to go and find the missing community members (Powers 1995, 149). The tactics used to extract labor from the countryside had changed as *encomienda* tribute from native villages dwindled and citizens like Luisa Maldonado de San Juan bought up land and gained rights to *mitayo* labor.

Grain and livestock dominated the agricultural production of the highland valleys surrounding Cuenca, with livestock traded from Cuenca overland as far as Lima (Aldana Rivera 1989, 113; Espinoza et al. 1982, 39; Newson 1995, 231). After the death of her husband, Luisa began to buy property, purchasing access to this agricultural economy. Families in colonial Latin America aspired to be property owners. It was this access that allowed entrance into the "landed elite," which controlled both church and state (Balmori et al. 1984, 188–90). At the time of her death Luisa had bought four separate rural properties as well as an urban house.[6] The most important rural property was that of an *estancia*, or ranch, called Cachaulo, located northeast of Cuenca on the Machangara River (map 7.1). This name is still given to the hill above the property on modern topographic maps.

Luisa bought the 200-hectare Cachaulo property in 1658 from the estate of another woman, Augustina Ortiz Davila, at a cost of 4,400 pesos. The property was a mixed-grain farm, with 600 sheep and some oxen.[7] Although not a large property by Andean standards, both the size and its cost are quite large for seventeenth-century Cuenca. The architecture on the property at the time of Luisa's death six years later was simple, consisting of an "old house with a thatched roof with wooden doors and windows and a small padlock ... another thatched building for a kitchen ... two small old thatched houses where the Indians live ... and a large building for storing the crops."[8]

The property included the services of four *mitayos*, or tributary native Andeans, who came from the villages of Macas, Sigsig, and Sibambe (map 7.1).[9] The colonial system of *mita* labor had been set up by the Viceroy Toledo in the 1570s and was itself a colonial reworking of the rotating *"mit'a"* labor system of the Inca empire. The *mitayos* were used as a form of state patrimony, assigning a village to supply a certain number of workers on a rotating basis to a mine, city, or Spanish citizen such as Luisa (Stern 1982, 82). The *mitayos* who worked the land and herded the animals at Cachaulo were from villages up to 100 kilometers from Cachaulo, emphasizing the labor shortages caused by the sixteenth- and seventeenth-century decimation of southern highland villages. Each of the four was an adult male and would have brought a family to live at Cachaulo for their limited labor turn.

Upon Luisa's death the Cachaulo property was divided among her heirs, following Spanish laws of partible inheritance, which guaranteed each legitimate child, male or female, an equal share in the property of their mother or father (Lavrin and Couturier 1979, 286). It was essential to the family, however, that such a property be maintained intact as a functioning enterprise. In theory, daughters had inheritance rights equal to sons, but in practice rural properties were negotiated into the hands of a male "heir apparent" (Wilson 1984, 308). In the case of Cachaulo, Luisa's nephew, Alexandro Maldonado de San Juan, slowly bought out or inherited the bulk of the property from the 1660s to 1701.[10]

In 1740 Alexandro Senior was dead, and his widow sold the property to their son, Alexandro Junior. Sometime in the early eighteenth century substantial architectural changes had occurred on the site. The property was reduced to 130 hectares, and the seventeenth-century wattle-and-daub house with tile roof was in ruins. A large new tile-roofed house with "double walls" of adobe brick and a chapel had been built. There were also two other buildings with thatched roofs and a bread oven.[11] This adobe house and chapel (fig. 7.1, buildings B2 and C2) form the core of the buildings still standing on the site today.

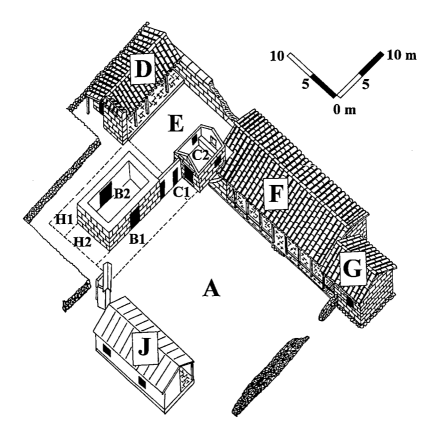

Fig. 7.1. The estancia (ranch) of Cachaulo as it appears today. (A) central courtyard; (B) eighteenth-century house; (C) eighteenth-century chapel; (D) nineteenth-century workrooms; (E) inner courtyard; (F) nineteenth-century house; (G) nineteenth-century chapel; (J) modern workrooms. The roofs of the eighteenth-century buildings (B2 and C2) have been "removed" in this isometric drawing to better represent their orientation within the later architectural additions. The colonial house (B2) is completely embedded within a later (H) building.

The outbuildings and perimeter walls that surround the colonial house and chapel are Republican in date. In eighteenth-century artistic representations (Martínez Borrero 1983) and in other eighteenth-century examples on the landscape (Jamieson 1996) high walls, narrow entranceways, and interior patios typify the colonial architecture of rural highland *estancias*. I would thus propose that the present configuration of Cachaulo's buildings (fig. 7.1) preserves their colonial arrangement. These buildings represent a reification of the Maldonado family's relationship to what they perceived as a rural hinterland. The walls and fences of the valley bottom *estancia* redeployed power over the land, severing the fields owned by the family from the traditional associations with which local Native Andeans had infused the landscape. This had the effect of decorporealizing the experience of the landscape for its inhabitants, setting their gaze toward the rural boundaries of private property (Johnson 1996, 73–74; Lefebvre 1991). The *estancia* complex itself is a physical manifestation of an inward gaze, separating the central patios from the surrounding countryside, as can be seen in the isometric drawing (fig. 7.1). The justified permeability diagram of the current room arrangement (fig. 7.2, compare with Hillier and Hanson 1984, 104) demonstrates how the inner patios (A and E) dominate the flow of traffic and activity within the complex. The colonial chapel (C2) is much less permeable to outside intrusions than the other rooms of the complex. To the Spanish mind there was not only economic wealth in the rural Andes; the devil was waiting in the "remote solitudes" of the rural highlands to lead people away from civilized areas to deceive them more easily (MacCormack 1991, 147). The blank exterior walls of Cachaulo were a barrier separating the Spanish household from the uncontrollable rural territory around it.

A different way of seeing Cachaulo is to look at the inventories. The act of writing inventories was itself an early modern act toward a new will to discipline at the household level, emphasizing the commodification of portable possessions (Johnson 1996, 112). In 1740, when Alexandro Maldonado de San Juan (Jr.) purchased Cachaulo from the estate of his deceased mother, the property was inventoried. Many of the goods listed were agricultural equipment, and it is clear that domestic items were of minimal importance. The main house contained two tables; an *estrado*, or large wooden dais for lounging; a rough bed; two benches; four chairs; and four stools. In the kitchen building there were two tables; a bench; a bronze cooking brazier; two metal buckets; an *ollita*, or small locally made ceramic pot; a small silver saltcellar; and five *botijas*, or large ceramic jars. It is probable that the Maldonado de San Juan family only used these

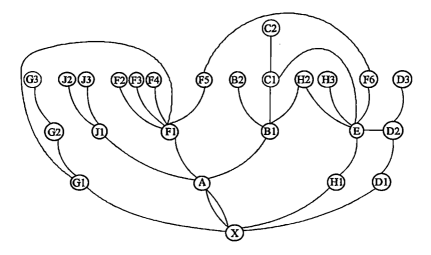

Fig. 7.2. Justified permeability diagram (compare with Hillier and Hanson 1984) of the
estancia of Cachaulo. Each node represents a patio, porch, or room. Each line
represents a connection between nodes through a door, or movement through
space. "X" is the "carrier space," or building complex exterior. Note that C2,
the colonial chapel, is the deepest room in the permeability diagram.

goods on their occasional visits to the Cachaulo property. The goods belonging
to the *mitayos*, who were the full-time residents on this land, would not have
been inventoried as part of the family property and would have been kept in
their own homes.

Of all the inventoried rooms, it is the wealth of material in the chapel that
stands out. The chapel contained a large table with woven cotton tablecloth, a
wooden dais, an altar, and a bench. The art in the chapel consisted of a painting
of a saint; two *bultos*, or religious statues; and a crucifix with silver rays coming
out of it. One of the statues was a virgin with "decent" clothing and flowers in
her hand, and the other was a St. Joseph dressed in silk with silver woven into
it.[12] These are rather expensive investments for what is otherwise a very rustic-
sounding farmstead.

The inventory of 1740 is very detailed, but only in terms of portable goods.
The inherent nature of inventories means architectural features are often not
described and key pieces of evidence can be missed. One impressive architectural feature that is not mentioned in the 1740 Cachaulo inventory is a
series of mural paintings on the chapel walls. These paintings are still present
and are eighteenth century in date (Martínez Borrero pers. comm. 1994).

Consisting of *tromp l'oeil* curtains around the tops of the interior walls, *tromp l'oeil* wainscoting around the lower portions of the walls, and several vases of flowers painted on the sidewalls, these are clearly an attempt to create an atmosphere of opulence using minimal resources. Mural painting on the walls of houses and chapels was common in colonial Ecuador (Martínez Borrero 1983, 80), but preserved examples are now quite rare. The only other private chapel in the region with preserved mural paintings is a chapel completed in 1752 at the Susudel *hacienda* (Martínez Borrero 1983, 100).

From archaeological excavations we can gain a different idea of the material culture of the house, and particularly of the tablewares. Fifteen test pits were excavated around the property (Jamieson 1999). These uncovered very little stratigraphy, suggesting sheet deposits of discarded material and little intensity of occupation in any period. Coarse earthenwares, either plain or slip decorated, made up half of the assemblage, giving testimony to the presence of the *mitayos* and to their ties to the local village economies where the coarse earthenwares were made. The finer red earthenwares were lead-glazed or majolica glazed and were made in the specialist neighborhood of ceramists in Cuenca (Holm 1970, 272; Villavicencio 1858, 429, 433).

Cachaulo was not just a place where agricultural products were produced for urban consumption. It was also a place where the hegemony of an urban Spanish family came into contact with rural native Andean people. Just as anyone else who had tribute laborers working for them, the Maldonado de San Juan family were responsible for the maintenance of "proper" religious practices by the *mitayos* who worked the land and herded the animals of Cachaulo. The ceremonies that took place in the Cachaulo chapel were a microcosm of the native Andean relationship to the Spanish empire and the Catholic Church. The investment in silks, silver, and painted decorations that were all placed in the chapel tells us that this room above all others at Cachaulo was an important expression of this relationship.

The *mitayos* who worked the land at Cachaulo had a worldview very different from the perceptions of the Maldonado de San Juan family. We can best see the perceptions of the world held by native Andean peoples from modern ethnographic research. These are part of the *habitus* of these individuals, as they move through the landscape, learn the traditional stories about it, and learn to associate particular places with particular events in their lived experience (Bourdieu 1977). In the Peruvian southern highlands, rural Quechua people see the landscape divided into three parts, valley bottoms, midslopes, and high mountain areas. For these people the valley bottoms are associated with the Spanish landed estates and with the wage labor of the rural men who walk down to the valleys to work on these estates. There is also an association of these estates with a violent and exploitative "national culture." It is the midslopes that are the benevolent heart of the world, where the dispersed rural villages are positioned to maximize access to agricultural resources. Finally, the high mountain areas are associated with the upland herding done by women, with the wilderness and the uncontrollable, and with the mountain gods, who look down on all of us (Isbell 1978, 57–66; Skar 1981, 37–40). Cachaulo in the seventeenth century can be characterized as an architectural manifestation of the social boundary between forced tribute laborers and a landed upper class (Stern 1982) whose worldviews clashed at a profound level.

Cachaulo is similar to the haciendas of eighteenth-century Cali, Colombia, described as "productive haciendas which existed around an owner's residence constructed in a rustic and cheap manner, although always with a chapel" (Aprile-Gniset 1991, 419, my translation). These rural Cali households led Jacques Aprile-Gniset (1991, 419) to conclude that elite landowners poured their economic resources into their urban houses. To him these symbols of power were of great importance, and the rural houses, far from any major roadway, had no money spent on them because no one "important" was there to see them. And yet there were people of utmost importance who were around to see these buildings—the *mitayos* who worked the land. Luisa and her family understood this. Their Cachaulo house was indeed "rustic," but it was also an enclosed space that created an inward-looking gaze, separating Spanish control from the rural wilds. Most importantly the complex contained the chapel, where significant resources were expended on religious art. Such art was an essential material part of the discourse between Luisa's family and the *mitayos* and their families who worked the land.

"ACQUIRING MORE AUTHORITY": LUISA'S URBAN HOME IN CUENCA

In 1656, two years prior to purchasing Cachaulo, Doña Luisa bought a large (approximately 1,800 square meters) urban property one block from the main plaza of Cuenca (fig. 7.3). At the time of her purchase the property had "some houses with tile roofs, and some constructions of adobe for houses,"[13] suggesting the buildings were actively being expanded. This was one of the more expensive pieces of domestic property in Cuenca, due mostly to its

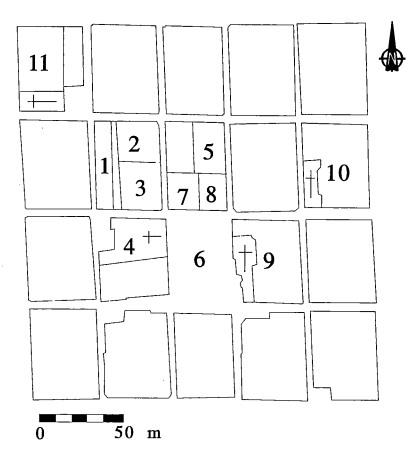

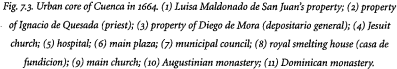

0   50 m

Fig. 7.3. Urban core of Cuenca in 1664. (1) Luisa Maldonado de San Juan's property; (2) property of Ignacio de Quesada (priest); (3) property of Diego de Mora (depositario general); (4) Jesuit church; (5) hospital; (6) main plaza; (7) municipal council; (8) royal smelting house (casa de fundicion); (9) main church; (10) Augustinian monastery; (11) Dominican monastery.

proximity to the *plaza mayor*, directly across from the Jesuit College. Luisa shared the block with Juan Agudo del Alamo and Ignacio de Quesada, a priest. Her other neighbor was Diego de Mora, the *depositario general*, a position on the city council that included the administration of funds and rents for native Andean communities and the custodianship of the goods of people who had died. Luisa's father, Pedro Maldonado de San Juan, had been *depositario general* when he was alive (Chacón Zhapán 1990, 372–73).

This was not an overly "urban" city block in 1652, when the Jesuits sold a portion of it to Juan Agudo del Alamo. The buildings were thatched rather than tiled, and fences rather than walls divided the properties from one another. Juan Agudo's working gardens and livestock are a stark contrast to later ideas of the formal urban garden (Johnson 1996, 148–50).[14] The most important aspect of the property in terms of its elite status was its location as part of the "gridiron" system laid out in Cuenca's act of foundation and its proximity to the central plaza of the town (González Aguirre 1991, 15).

THE SPANISH GRIDIRON TOWN PLAN

Where did the ideas that are manifest in the urban core of Cuenca come from? The gridiron urban plan was instituted in the New World from the earliest Spanish settlements (Deagan 1995; Gutiérrez et al. 1986, 59), and has been characterized as one of the clearest representations of colonial control and oppression (Crouch et al. 1982, xx; Foster 1960). Andean gridiron towns like Cuenca have been seen as descendants of Roman imperial designs, the ideas of Vitruvius, the bastides of France, the garrison towns of the Spanish *reconquista*, and European Renaissance rationality (Crouch et al. 1982; Gutiérrez et al. 1986; Low 1993, 80–83; Stanislawski 1947). The influences of Native American urban planning on Spanish colonial cities have also begun to be emphasized by architectural historians (Crouch et al. 1982, 58, 91–92; Low 1993, 1995). From Taino villages in the Caribbean to Cortes's first views of Tenochtitlán in 1519 (a city which was probably the largest in the world at that time), the Spanish were profoundly impressed with the planned nature of the Native American urban areas they conquered in the sixteenth century. These influences were integral to the development of sixteenth century Spanish colonial urban planning (Low 1995, 754–56). The discourse between European and native Andean versions of urbanism is clear in the Spanish "founding" of Cuzco in 1534, as Pizarro had the all-important gibbet, symbol of Spanish judicial authority, built on top of what was probably the Incaic *ushnu* in the middle of an Inca plaza.[15]

As with Cuzco, Cuenca was founded on the ruins of an Incaic center. The Inca center of Tumipampa had been destroyed in the war of succession just before the arrival of the Spanish (Cieza de León 1962 [1553], 73). It is not really clear how large Tumipampa was, or what parts of Cuenca are pre-Hispanic in layout, but the main plaza and grid plan of Cuenca was laid out in 1557 around 1,200 meters from the central plaza of Incaic Tumipampa (Uhle 1983 [1923]). The spirit of the later 1573 royal ordinances was followed, and Cuenca was founded "where it would be possible to demolish neighboring towns and properties in order to take advantage of the materials that are essential for building" (Crouch et al. 1982, 9). The houses built around the main plaza, where Luisa's house was located, still contain Inca-dressed stone blocks, often in the almost metaphoric function of providing strong pre-Columbian cornerstones for post-Columbian adobe houses. It was clearly not just the building materials that the Spanish were interested in when they laid out Cuenca's urban grid, but also the inherent authority already vested in this pre-Hispanic center of Inca and Cañari power. Rather than a simple "instrument of colonial domination and control," the urban grid of Cuenca "evolved from both indigenous and Spanish influences and models that created a new urban design form." It is a good example of "the cultural tensions of conquest and resistance . . . symbolically encoded in its architecture" (Low 1995, 759).

This is not to deny that the urban grid was built not simply ". . . to be seen . . . or to observe the external space . . . but to permit an internal, articulated, and detailed control" (Foucault 1979, 172). The plaza was the urban center for public displays, an area of "theater," both literally and in terms of the gaze of the public, which always monitored the actions of the individual (Richardson 1980). The church was the focus of this authority, and the 1573 royal ordinances specified that the principal church "ought to be seen from all sides so that it can be decorated better, thus acquiring more authority; efforts should be made that it be somewhat raised from ground level in order that it be approached by steps, and near it, next to the main plaza, the royal council and municipal council and customs houses shall be built . . . in a manner that would not embarrass the temple but add to its prestige" (Crouch et al. 1982, 15). The spirit of this later edict is clear in the 1557 layout of buildings around Cuenca's main plaza (fig. 7.3).

Luisa's purchase of a house one block from Cuenca's main plaza thus placed her at one of the town's more prestigious locations. The tension between private property and the overall goals of state and church are reified in the gridiron plan. Private homes were banned from the main plaza in the 1573 ordinances (Crouch et al. 1982, 15), and encouraged to be "all of one type for the sake of the beauty of the town" (Crouch et al. 1982, 17). There was clearly more than beauty at stake. The tensions between the authority of church and state and the desires of colonial *vecinos* for more local power are manifest in the subordination of the architecture of urban private homes. Houses built on streets without plazas could not be viewed from any great distance and thus could never acquire the visual "authority" of buildings located on plazas. The position of Luisa's property defied these limits, in co-opting not just one facade on the Jesuit plaza south of her property, but also a corner of the Dominican church plaza to the northwest of her property.

There was also an increasing element of ethnic segregation in the spatial ordering of Cuenca when Luisa purchased her house. Cuenca was never a racially segregated town in the seventeenth century, and even in the urban core there were frequent instances of native Andean landowners interspersed with those of Spanish descent (Poloni 1992, 304). Prior to 1620 a significant proportion of native Andean urban land purchases were within the urban core of Cuenca (Poloni 1992, 296–97). The seventeenth century crisis in the rural Andean villages that led to greatly increasing numbers of native Andeans moving into Cuenca (Poloni 1992; Powers 1995, 76), however, increased segregation of native Andeans after 1620 into properties in the two "Indian" parishes rather than in the urban core (Poloni 1992, 296–97). The city block that Luisa's house was on showed no recorded instances of native Andean property owners from 1652 to 1783.[16]

At the time of Doña Luisa's death in 1664 the house was described as having two rooms with a tile roof, and no doubt would have appeared very modest in size to our eyes, especially on such a large urban property. It is not clear whether other family members were living with Luisa in the house. She had four household slaves living with her; Domingo and Ursula (both adults born in Africa); Antonia, who was around fifteen and also born in Africa; and Ursula's four-year-old daughter, Maria, born in the New World.[17]

The contents of the house give us a picture of mid-seventeenth-century elite material culture in Cuenca. Furnishings that the individual conducting the inventory considered worth mentioning included eleven chairs, a buffet, several large wooden chests, nine religious paintings, two carpets, and a stand for a ceramic water bottle. The inventory of Luisa's possessions emphasized her large collection of clothing and jewelry.[18] The chairs, listed first in this and many other elite urban inventories, resonate with the growth of individualism in the early modern world, as benches were replaced by chairs in everyday use (Johnson 1996, 171–72).

The clothing and jewels were both very important to elite Spanish colonial women, in that they were portable forms of wealth and were highly visible (McEwan 1991, 35). The money invested in women's jewelry by the elite was often considerable in the Andes in both the colonial and Republican eras, and jewelry is known to have been used for economic transactions without the consent of a woman's husband (Borchart de Moreno 1992, 358–59). It could also be used to purchase property for a husband who had been "cheated" of his own property inheritance (Wilson 1984, 308).

Included in Luisa's jewelry collection were three gold *topos* with emeralds and pearls and four silver *topos* with small chains.[19] A *topo* is an Incaic pin used to fasten a shawl at the front, and it is clear that the *topo* was an important symbol of female gender. Almost all Inca women and none of the men illustrated in the early seventeenth century by Felipe de Guaman Poma were wearing *topos* (Zuidema 1991, 157–62). *Topos* have been reported previously from early-seventeenth-century wills of several native Andean women in the Audiencia of Quito (Caillavet 1982, 51–52; Rappaport 1990b, 13; Truhan 1991, 139, 145, 149), and they are generally thought to be exclusively associated with women of native ancestry (Truhan, pers. comm. 1996). Luisa's use of such a symbol of Incaic status runs directly counter to the assumption that Spanish women were always associated with conservative European elements of Spanish material culture (McEwan 1991, 34–35). In colonial portraiture, elite women, presumably of native descent, were at times portrayed in Inca dress, including the *topo*. The role of such clothing in the mediation of gender, status, and ethnicity in the colonial Andes is a complex topic that has not been extensively studied (Cummins 1991). Luisa's ethnicity is not stated anywhere, although the fact that she was a *vecina* (citizen) and both of her parents had Spanish names provides some evidence that she considered herself more European than Andean.

Tablewares had a prominent place in the inventory of Luisa's urban possessions. The household tableware included nineteen silver vessels and three gold-plated silver vessels.[20] Although expensive, access to such tablewares was not difficult in Cuenca, as the city was a center for the processing of precious metals and the creation of silver tableware. The main area for such production in the colonial period was the street one block north of the main plaza, a very short distance from Luisa's house (Paniagua Pérez 1989, 127). The prominence of silver tablewares in colonial inventories of elite houses is due to their great economic value, and the fact that they were portable and could be priced accurately based on weight. Their value was not only economic; it was also tied to the ability to display them during meals, an important part of social relations. We should not assume, however, that the social visibility of such tablewares was necessarily tied to males (Deagan 1983, 271), as Carole Shammas has recently proposed that a proliferation of expensive tablewares can be more readily tied to the increasing segregation of women in the home. Women were probably a major force in promoting such enhancements to the domestic environment (Shammas 1990, 186–88).

Four "coconuts for drinking chocolate from the coast" and nine mills or grinders to make chocolate were also inventoried in Luisa's house.[21] Chocolate introduced from Mesoamerica was being cultivated on the Ecuadorian coast by the 1570s (Jiménez de la Espada 1965, 2, 338). By 1617 it was being grown on a large scale and exported from Guayaquil to Peru and New Spain, even though export to New Spain was technically illegal after 1634 (Estrella 1988, 263; Leôn Borja and Nagy 1964, 4–8). Bernabe Cobo described the great popularity of chocolate as a social drink in the seventeenth-century Andes (Cobo 1964 [1653], 258). In the Maldonado de San Juan house the chocolate was served out of coconuts. Coconuts in medieval Europe had been extremely rare and were mounted in precious metals to use as goblets, reliquaries, and other types of containers. By the 1520s, however, the coconut could be bought cheaply in Europe and the New World (Levenson 1991, 128–29). Far from social conservatism in tablewares, Luisa's "coconuts for drinking chocolate from the coast" are an entirely New World social custom, combining two tropical domesticates into a social drink to serve to guests.

It is interesting that there is no listing of any ceramics in the Maldonado de San Juan household. The inventory is very thorough in terms of the more expensive items, so it is clear that no imported porcelains or expensive glassware were present, two assumed essentials of the Spanish colonial elite house. The presence of such a large quantity of silver tableware, and the long treacherous path from the coast through the mountains to highland Cuenca, may go far in explaining why silver was more plausible as an elite tableware than porcelain or glass.

Archaeological test pitting unfortunately could not be undertaken on the property that had been Luisa's, but it was possible to test gardens in the southeastern part of the same city block, on the property that belonged to the *depositario general* in the 1650s (fig. 7.3). In a single one-by-one-meter test pit on this property a midden was encountered with intact stratigraphy dating to before 1671 (Jamieson 1999). The vast majority of ceramics in the midden were locally produced coarse earthenwares, either plain or red slipped, and technologically very similar to prehistoric ceramics in the region. These are reminders that in the houses on this city block native Andean servants and (in the case of Doña Luisa's household) African slaves would have been the workforce in the household kitchen; they also would have controlled the Andean colonoware produced or purchased for that area of the household.

The total lack of locally produced majolicas suggests that the technology for majolica manufacture had not been introduced in Cuenca before the 1670s.

Imported ceramics included fragments of olive jars from Spain and several sherds of Panamanian majolicas with cream to greenish-cream glazes. Panamanian majolicas were only produced from the 1570s until 1671 (Deagan 1987, 24, 29; Long 1964, 104) and are important chronological indicators of early colonial archaeological contexts in the Andes.

The inventory of Luisa's house and the excavations in her neighbor's yard revealed entirely different pictures of material culture. The inventory neglected to mention ceramics, probably because neither the locally produced earthenwares nor the imported majolicas were of any great economic value. Luisa's cloth came from Spain by way of Panama, and the ceramics came from Panama as well, both situating Panama as the conduit for the supply of elite material culture to seventeenth-century Andeans (Borah 1954). It is Luisa's silver tableware and jewelry that were important to those who inventoried her house, but the Panamanian ceramics found archaeologically are just as eloquent reminders of the elite status of the seventeenth-century residents of this block.

After Luisa's death in 1664 her brother, Manuel Maldonado de San Juan, purchased part of the urban property from her estate, and in 1704, as urban pressures increased on the core of Cuenca, he sold the northern half for 500 pesos.[22] The southern half remained in the hands of Luisa's two daughters, Ynes Fuentes de Navia and Magdalena Rodriguez de San Juan. This inheritance of the urban house by female descendants is in contrast to the male inheritance at Cachaulo, demonstrating that urban properties were viewed as valid types of property for females to own and were often built, financed, and inherited entirely by females (Wilson 1984, 310). The house remained in the hands of female descendants of Luisa until 1710, when it was sold outside the family.[23] Neglected for almost fifty years after Luisa's death, the house in 1715 was described as "a one room house with tile roof, with another room with double walls up to the height of installing rafters . . . the said double walls are mostly cracked and the wood of the said house and the room with tile roof is cracked and insect-ridden to the point that two of the rafters have fallen."[24] The 1710 sale did not end the Maldonado de San Juan women's property ownership on this street. Luisa's grand-niece Michaela Maldonado de San Juan, a *vecina* of Cuenca, bought property jointly with her husband on the Jesuit street in the 1770s and "built one building with a double sloping roof, and one room with a single sloping roof," which were "roofed with tile, with one double room with a shop on the street." Michaela's personal belongings were listed as four tables, three benches, four chairs, a wooden bed with mattress, and some religious paintings. There is no listing of any jewelry or silver tableware.[25] It would seem that Michaela, a widow like Luisa at the end of her life, was not nearly as wealthy as her great-aunt had been.

CONCLUSIONS

Kathleen Deagan (1973, 1983) looked at the role of women in colonial St. Augustine and came to the conclusion that the material culture of the houses was related to a relationship between Native American women and "low visibility" activities such as food acquisition and preparation. High visibility objects such as tablewares and the architecture of the houses themselves were associated with males and with Spanish cultural influences. To Deagan "[c]onservatism in certain areas—most notably, those that were socially visible and associated with male activities—was coupled with Spanish-Indian acculturation and syncretism in other areas, especially those that were less socially visible and female dominated" (Deagan 1983, 271). Deagan sees St. Augustine as a particular case, namely a garrison town surrounded by a significant Native American population in the eighteenth century (Deagan 1973, 57). It is important that historical archaeologists do not extend Deagan's model to all other Spanish colonial sites in the mistaken belief that it is "a general Spanish pattern of adaptation to the New World" (Ewen 1991, 102).

Spanish colonialism in the New World cannot be subsumed under any single "pattern." This is evident when we look at the life of Doña Luisa Maldonado de San Juan, who lived at an important intersection between class and gender in the seventeenth-century Audiencia of Quito. Women with access to wealth had advantages that could be argued to show greater equality between the sexes than was otherwise evident. Through participation in her husband's merchant activities, and in taking over the business as a widow, Luisa proved herself a competent actor in an early modern capitalist enterprise. The construction and perpetuation of colonial gender categories come into question when the contradiction of the elite and independent status of wealthy widows like Luisa is emphasized. In this way we can see that "women" did not represent a single undifferentiated category (Wilson 1984, 305).

Even within the life of one woman the relationship of material culture to ideology is quite complex. Doña Luisa's rural property at Cachaulo was a material manifestation of a relationship to the rural tribute laborers she had been assigned, and to the rural lands which provided her with income. Her house in Cuenca was a manifestation of early modern consumption and the display of wealth, tying Luisa into the urban world of the local Spanish elite. In the last ten years of her life Doña Luisa had buying agents in Panama and a shop in Zaruma, a house in Cuenca, and several rural properties. She had built an enduring economic and material legacy for her descendants that transcended and yet did not completely escape the increasingly strict line between public and private in the lives of early modern Andean women.

NOTES

Financial support for the research presented in this paper was provided by a dissertation grant from the Social Sciences and Humanities Research Council of Canada and by the Univ. of Calgary. I would like to thank Jenny Deleski, Kurtis Lesick, and Nancy Saxberg for commenting on earlier versions of the paper. In Cuenca I would thank José-Luis Espinosa, Luz-Maria Guapisaca, Deborah Truhan, and Alexandra Kennedy-Troya. Finally, to Laurie Beckwith, my thanks both for her help in the documentary research on Luisa and for her many useful suggestions.

1. Archivo Nacional de Historia/Cuenca, Ecuador (hereafter cited as ANH/C) C116404a, ff. 6v, 13r, 59r (1664).

2. Andean ethnic leaders.

3. ANH/C C116404a, ff. 26v–29v, 50r, and 59r (1664).

4. ANH/C L514, ff. 362r–362v (1656); L514 ff. 593r–594r (1658); L515, ff. 699v–700v (1659).

5. This study of a single elite family is not intended to deny the existence of other realities in the region at the same time (Beaudry et al 1991, 157). In the colonial Andes groups such as rural villagers of largely native descent, household and plantation slaves of African descent, *mestizo* merchants, and many other groups all existed in relation to each other, and many variations on cultural reality existed. For a few examples (chosen from a massive literature), see Adorno (1986), Rappaport (1990a), Silverblatt (1987), Stern (1987), and Whitten (1974).

6. ANH/C C116404a f. 18v–20v (1664).

7. ANH/C L515 ff. 209r–211v; L514 f. 593r (1658).

8. ANH/C 116404a f. 19r (1664) (my translation).

9. ANH/C L514 f. 593v (1658).

10. ANH/C L528 f. 90r–92v (1693), ANH/C L608 f. 461r (1701).

11. ANH/C L617 f. 49v (1740).

12. ANH/C L617 ff. 49v–50r (1740).

13. ANH/C L514, ff. 362r–362v (1656).

14. ANH/C L514 ff. 55r–56r (1653); L513, f. 547r (1652); C116.404a f. 60r (1664).

15. An *ushnu* is an Inca stone platform symbolizing the *axis mundi* of communication between the above-ground world and the worlds of water and earth below (MacCormack 1991, 72)

16. ANH/C L513, f. 547r (1652); L514, f. 55r–56r (1653); L514, f. 362r (1656); C116404a (1664);

C79.671, f. 6r–84 (1685); L528, f. 556r–561r (1697); L608, f. 462v–466r (1701); L532, f. 530r–531r (1704); L532, f. 525r–526r (1704); L532, f. 904v–905r (1705); L533, f. 637r (1709); L534, f. 967v–970r (1710); L535, f. 644r (1715); L618, f. 204r (1746); L618, f. 278v–279v (1747); L619, f. 568v–569r (1749); L549, f. 223r–226r (1783).

17. ANH/C C116404a, f. 3r (1664).
18. ANH/C C116404a, f. 1v, 4r–5v (1664).
19. ANH/C C116404a f. 5r (1664).
20. ANH/C C116404a, ff. 2r (1664).
21. ANH/C C116404a, ff. 5v, 10r (1664).
22. ANH/C C79671 f. 7v (1685); L608 f. 466r (1701); L532 f. 525r–526r (1704).
23. ANH/C L534, ff. 968r, 970r (1710); L608 f. 462v (1701).
24. ANH/C L535, f. 645r (1715).
25. ANH/C L549 ff. 223r–226r (1783).

REFERENCES CITED

Adorno, Rolena. 1986. *Guaman Poma: Writing and Resistance in Colonial Peru*. Austin: Univ. of Texas Press.

Aldana Rivera, Susana. 1989. Esbozo de un eje de integración: El comercio Piura-Loja-Cuenca, siglo XVIII tardio. *Revista del Archivo Nacional de Historia, Sección del Azuay (Cuenca)* 8:108–32.

Anda Aguirre, Alfonso. 1960. *Zaruma en la colonia*. Quito, Ecuador: Casa de la Cultura Ecuatoriana.

Aprile-Gniset, Jacques. 1991. *La ciudad colombiana*. Bogota, Colombia: Banco Popular.

Balmori, Diana, Stuart F. Voss, and Miles Wortman. 1984. *Notable Family Networks in Latin America*. Chicago: Univ. of Chicago Press.

Beaudry, Mary C., ed. 1988. *Documentary Archaeology in the New World*. Cambridge: Cambridge Univ. Press.

Beaudry, Mary, Lauren J. Cook, and Stephen A. Mrozowski. 1991. Artifacts and Active Voices: Material Culture as Social Discourse. In *The Archaeology of Inequality*, ed. Randall H. McGuire and Robert Paynter, 192–230. Oxford: Basil Blackwell.

Borah, Woodrow. 1954. Early Colonial Trade and Navigation between Mexico and Peru. *Ibero-Americana* 38:1–170.

Borchart de Moreno, Christiana. 1992. La imbecilidad y el coraje: La participacion femenina en la economia colonial (Quito, 1780–1830). In *Mujeres de los Andes: Condiciones de vida y salud*, ed. A. C. Defossez, D. Fassin, and M. Viveros, 357–76. Instituto Frances de Estudios Andinos and Universidad Externado de Colombia.

Borrero Crespo, Maximiliano. 1962. *Orìgenes Cuencanos*. Vol. 1. Cuenca, Ecuador: Universidad de Cuenca.

Bourdieu, Pierre. 1977. *Outline of a Theory of Practice*. Trans. R. Nice. Cambridge: Cambridge Univ. Press.

Caillavet, Chantal. 1982. Caciques de Otavalo en el siglo XVI: Don Alonso Maldonado y su esposa. *Miscelanea Antropologica Ecuatoriana* 2:38–55.

Chacón Zhapán, Juan. 1990. *Historia del corregimiento de cuenca (1557–1777)*. Quito, Ecuador: Banco Central del Ecuador.

Cieza de León, Pedro. 1883 [before 1554] *The Second Part of the Chronicle of Peru*. Trans. and ed. Clements R. Markham. New York: Hakluyt Society.

———. 1962 [1553]. *La crûnica del Peru*. 3d ed. Madrid: Espasa-Calpe.

Cobo, Bernabe. 1964 [1653]. *Historia del nuevo mundo*. Vol. 1. Ed. Marcos Jiménez del la Espada. Madrid: Biblioteca de Autores Españoles.

Crouch, Dora P., Daniel J. Garr, and Axel I. Mundigo. 1982. *Spanish City Planning in North America*. Cambridge, Mass.: MIT Press.

Cummins, Thomas B. F. 1991. We Are the Other: Peruvian Portraits of Colonial Kurakakuna. In *Transatlantic Encounters: Europeans and Andeans in the Sixteenth Century*, ed. Kenneth J. Andrien and Rolena Adorno, 203–31. Berkeley: Univ. of California Press.

Deagan, Kathleen A. 1973. Mestizaje in Colonial St. Augustine. *Ethnohistory* 20 (1): 55–65.

———. 1983. *Spanish St. Augustine: The Archaeology of a Colonial Creole Community*. New York: Academic Press.

———. 1987. *Artifacts of the Spanish Colonies of Florida and the Caribbean, 1500–1800*. Vol. 1, *Ceramics, Glassware, and Beads*. Washington, D.C.: Smithsonian Institution Press.

Deagan, Kathleen A., ed. 1995. *Puerto Real: The Archaeology of a Sixteenth-Century Spanish Town in Hispaniola*. Gainesville: Univ. Press of Florida.

Espinoza, Leonardo, Lucas Achig, and Rubén Martínez. 1982. La gobernación colonial de Cuenca: Formación social y producción mercantil simple. In *Ensayos sobre historia regional: La región centro sur*, ed. Claudio Cordero E., 31–116. Cuenca, Ecuador: Instituto de Investigaciones Sociales de la Universidad de Cuenca.

Estrella, Eduardo. 1988. *El pan de América: Etnohistoria de los alimentos aborígenes en el Ecuador*. 2d ed. Quito, Ecuador: Ediciones Abya-Yala.

Ewen, Charles R. 1991. *From Spaniard to Creole: The Archaeology of Cultural Formation at Puerto Real, Haiti*. Tuscaloosa: Univ. of Alabama Press.

Foster, George M. 1960. *Culture and Conquest: The American Spanish Heritage*. New York: Viking Fund Publications in Anthropology.

Foucault, Michel. 1979. *Discipline and Punish: The Birth of the Prison*. Trans. Alan Sheridan. New York: Vintage Books.

Fraser, Valerie. 1990. *The Architecture of Conquest: Building in the Viceroyalty of Peru, 1535–1635*. Cambridge: Cambridge Univ. Press.

González Aguirre, Iván. 1991. *Cuenca: Barrios de tierra y fuego.* Cuenca, Ecuador: Fundación Paul Rivet.

Gramsci, Antonio. 1971. *Selections from the Prison Notebooks.* New York: International Publishers.

Gutiérrez, Ramón, Cristina Esteras, and Alejandro Málaga. 1986. *El Valle del Colca (Arequipa): Cinco siglos de arquitectura y urbanismo.* Buenos Aires: Libros de Hispanoamerica.

Hillier, Bill, and Julienne Hanson. 1984. *The Social Logic of Space.* New York: Cambridge Univ. Press.

Holm, Olaf. 1970. La cerámica colonial del Ecuador. *Boletín de la academia nacional de historia (Quito)* 116:265–83.

Isbell, Billie Jean. 1978. *To Defend Ourselves: Ecology and Ritual in an Andean Village.* Prospect Heights, Ill.: Waveland Press.

Jácome, Nicanor. 1983. Economía y sociedad en el siglo XVI. In *Nueva historia del Ecuador.* Vol. 3, ed. Enrique Ayala Mora, 123–60. Quito, Ecuador: Corporación Editora Nacional.

Jamieson, Ross W. 1996. Domestic Architecture and Material Culture of Colonial Cuenca, Ecuador, 1600–1800. Ph.D. diss., Dept. of Archaeology, Univ. of Calgary, Calgary, Alberta.

———. 1999. *Domestic Architecture and Power: The Historical Archaeology of Colonial Ecuador.* New York: Plenum.

Jiménez de la Espada, Marcos. 1965. *Relaciones geográficas de Indias: Perù.* 3 vols. Madrid: Biblioteca de Autores Españoles.

Johnson, Matthew. 1996. *An Archaeology of Capitalism.* Oxford: Blackwell.

Lavrin, Asunción. 1989. Introduction: The Scenario, the Actors, and the Issues. In *Sexuality and Marriage in Colonial Latin America,* ed. Asunción Lavrin, 1–43. Lincoln: Univ. of Nebraska Press.

Lavrin, Asunción, and Edith Couturier. 1979. Dowries and Wills: A View of Women's Socioeconomic Role in Colonial Guadalajara and Puebla, 1640–1790. *Hispanic American Historical Review* 59 (2): 280–304.

Lefebvre, H. 1991. *The Production of Space.* Oxford: Blackwell.

León Borja, Dora, and Adám Szászdi Nagy. 1964. El comercio del cacao de Guayaquil. *Revista de historia de Amèrica* 57/58:1–50.

Levenson, Jay A., ed. 1991. *Circa 1492: Art in the Age of Exploration.* Washington, D.C.: National Gallery of Art.

Long, George A. 1964. Excavations at Panama Vieja. *Florida Anthropologist* 17 (2): 104–9.

Low, Setha M. 1993. Cultural Meaning of the Plaza: The History of the Spanish-American Gridplan-Plaza Urban Design. In *The Cultural Meaning of Urban Space,* ed. Robert Rotenberg and Gary McDonogh, 75–93. Westport, Conn.: Bergin and Garvey.

———. 1995. Indigenous Architecture and the Spanish American Plaza in Mesoamerica and the Caribbean. *American Anthropologist* 97 (4): 748–62.

MacCormack, Sabine. 1991 *Religion in the Andes: Vision and Imagination in Early Colonial Peru.* Princeton, N.J.: Princeton Univ. Press.

Martínez Borrero, Juan. 1983. *La pintura popular del Carmen: Identidad y cultura en el siglo XVIII.* Cuenca, Ecuador: Centro Interamericano de Artesanìas y Artes Populares.

McEwan, Bonnie. 1991. The Archaeology of Women in the Spanish New World. *Historical Archaeology* 25 (4): 33–41.

————. 1995. Spanish Precedents and Domestic Life at Puerto Real: The Archaeology of Two Spanish Homesites. In *Puerto Real: The Archaeology of a Sixteenth-Century Spanish Town in Hispaniola,* ed. Kathleen Deagan, 197–229. Gainesville: Univ. Press of Florida·

McGuire, Randall H. 1992. *A Marxist Archaeology.* San Diego, Calif.: Academic Press.

Moore, Henrietta. 1988. *Feminism and Anthropology.* Cambridge: Cambridge Univ. Press.

Newson, Linda. 1995. *Life and Death in Early Colonial Ecuador.* Norman: Univ. of Oklahoma Press.

Paniagua Pérez, Jesús. 1989. *La plata labrada en la Audiencia de Quito (la provincia del Azuay), siglos XVI–XIX.* León, Spain: Universidad de León.

Paynter, Robert, and Randall H. McGuire. 1991. The Archaeology of Inequality: Material Culture, Domination, and Resistance. In *The Archaeology of Inequality,* ed. Randall H. McGuire and Robert Paynter, 1–27. Oxford: Basil Blackwell.

Poloni, Jacques. 1992. Achats et ventes de terres par les Indiens de Cuenca au XVIIE siécle: Éléments de conjoncture Économique et de stratification sociale. *Bull. Inst. fr. études andines* 21 (1): 279–310.

Powers, Karen Vieira. 1995. *Andean Journeys: Migration, Ethnogenesis, and the State in Colonial Quito.* Albuquerque: Univ. of New Mexico Press.

Rappaport, Joanne. 1990a. *The Politics of Memory: Native Historical Interpretation in the Colombian Andes.* Cambridge: Cambridge Univ. Press.

————. 1990b. Cultura material a lo largo de la frontera septentrional Inca: Los Pastos y sus testamentos. *Revista de antropología y arqueología* (Universidad de los Andes, Bogota) 6 (2): 11–25.

Richardson, Miles. 1980. Culture and the Urban Stage: The Nexus of Setting, Behavior, and Image in Urban Places. In *Environment and Culture,* ed. Irwin Altman, Amos Rappaport, and Joachim F. Wohlwill, 209–41. New York: Plenum Press.

Salomon, Frank. 1983. Crisis y transformación de la sociedad aborigen invadida (1528–1573). In *Nueva historia del Ecuador.* Vol. 3. Ed. Enrique Ayala Mora, 91–122. Quito: Corporación Editora Nacional.

Shammas, Carole. 1990. *The Pre-Industrial Consumer in England and America.* Oxford: Clarendon Press.

Silverblatt, Irene. 1987. *Moon, Sun, and Witches: Gender Ideologies and Class in Inca and Colonial Peru.* Princeton, N.J.: Princeton Univ. Press.

Skar, Sarah. 1981. Andean Women and the Concept of Space/Time. In *Women and Space: Ground Rules and Social Maps,* ed. Shirley Ardener, 35–49. London: Croom Helm.

South, Stanley. 1988. Santa Elena: Threshold of Conquest. In *The Recovery of Meaning: Historical Archaeology in the Eastern United States,* ed. Mark P. Leone and Parker B. Potter Jr., 27–71. Washington, D.C.: Smithsonian Institution Press.

Stanislawski, Dan. 1947. Early Spanish Town Planning in the New World. *Geographical Review* 37:94–105.

Stern, Steve J. 1982. *Peru's Indian Peoples and the Challenge of Spanish Conquest, Huamanga to 1640.* Madison: Univ. of Wisconsin Press.

———. 1988. Feudalism, Capitalism, and the World-System in the Perspective of Latin America and the Caribbean. *American Historical Review* 93 (4): 829–72.

Stern, Steve J., ed. 1987. *Resistance, Rebellion, and Consciousness in the Andean Peasant World, Eighteenth to Twentieth Centuries.* Madison: Univ. of Wisconsin Press.

Truhan, Deborah L. 1991. "Mi ultimada y postrimera boluntad," Trayectorias de tres mujeres Andinas: Cuenca, 1599–1610. *Historica* 15 (1): 121–55.

Uhle, Max. 1983 [1923]. Las ruinas de tomebamba. In *Compilacion de cronicas, relatos y descripciones de cuenca y su provincia.* Vol. 1. Ed. Luis A. León, 157–97. Cuenca, Ecuador: Banco Central del Ecuador.

Villavicencio, Manuel. 1858. *Geografía de la república del Ecuador.* New York: R. Craighead.

Wachtel, Nathan. 1977. *The Vision of the Vanquished: The Spanish Conquest of Peru through Indian Eyes, 1530–1570.* Trans. Ben and Sian Reynolds. New York: Barnes and Noble.

Whitten, Norman E. 1974. *Black Frontiersmen: A South American Case.* Cambridge, Mass.: Schenkman Publishing.

Wilson, Fiona. 1984. Marriage, Property, and the Position of Women in the Peruvian Central Andes. In *Kinship Ideology and Practice in Latin America,* ed. Raymond T. Smith, 297–325. Chapel Hill: Univ. of North Carolina Press.

Yamin, Rebecca, and Karen Bescherer Metheny, eds. 1996. *Landscape Archaeology: Reading and Interpreting the American Historical Landscape.* Knoxville: Univ. of Tennessee Press.

Yentsch, Anne. 1991. The Symbolic Divisions of Pottery: Sex-Related Attributes of English and Anglo-American Household Pots. In *The Archaeology of Inequality,* ed. Randall H. McGuire and Robert Paynter, 192–230. Oxford: Basil Blackwell

Zuidema, R. Tom. 1991. Guaman Poma and the Art of Empire: Toward an Iconography of Inca Royal Dress. In *Transatlantic Encounters: Europeans and Andeans in the Sixteenth Century,* ed. Kenneth J. Andrien and Rolena Adorno, 151–202. Berkeley: Univ. of California Press.

CHAPTER EIGHT

Gender, Power, and Space

NEGOTIATING SOCIAL RELATIONS UNDER SLAVERY ON COFFEE PLANTATIONS IN JAMAICA, 1790–1834

James A. Delle

When Donna Seifert (1991a) assembled a thematic volume on the analysis of gender for the journal *Historical Archaeology*, the topic was novel to that field. As has been well stated elsewhere (for example, Conkey and Gero 1991; Scott 1994; Seifert 1991b), archaeology has been slow to fully embrace gender as a primary analytical concept. The contributors to Seifert's volume did well to expose the dearth of interest in historical archaeologies of gender. Their path-breaking work has exerted a positive influence on the field, and, in fact, over the past half decade an increasing number of historical archaeologists have begun to tackle the difficult topic of gender (for example, Bassett 1994; Costello 1998; Hardesty 1994; Kryder-Reid 1994; Little 1994, 1997; Rotman and Nassaney 1997; Seifert 1991a, 1994; Spencer-Wood 1996; Wall 1994; Wehner 1997).

As Seifert herself acknowledged, gender remains a difficult concept for archaeologists to consider, primarily because it is a difficult concept to define. It is well understood by most that the ascription of gender has something to do with defining behavior based on physiological sexual characteristics, and most anthropologically trained archaeologists are aware that some non-Western societies recognize more than two gender categories. Most archaeologists interested in the study of gender agree that observable biological sex traits will influence the ascription of an individual's gender identity; however, most (with the possible exception of the most dogmatic behavioral ecologists) would agree that it is the cultural definition of appropriate behavior, not the genetic makeup of the individual, that determines how members of a given gender group will behave. Most would also agree that gender is one of the primary (if not *the* primary) structuring principles of society; that is, gender will define the role an individual plays in a given social structure, the specific behaviors they will perform over the course of their life, and the nature of the relationships they have with other members of society. For archaeologists, interest lies in analyzing how this structuring principle of gender influences, and is influenced by, material culture (Bassett 1994; Conkey and Gero 1991, 1997; Jackson 1994; Scott 1994; Spencer-Wood 1991; Wylie 1991).

The object of this chapter is to suggest how the construction and negotiation of gender identities impacted the lives of women enslaved on Jamaican coffee plantations in the early nineteenth century. This discussion will be illustrated through the analysis of the documentary and material records of nineteenth-century Jamaican coffee plantations generally, with a particular emphasis placed on case studies drawn from Radnor, Balcarres, and Martins Hill plantations, located in the historical parishes of St. David, St. George, and Manchester, respectively (see map 8.1a and 8.1b).

This essay is part of a larger ongoing archaeological project, the focus of which is the analysis of the material construction of social relations on coffee plantations in early-nineteenth-century Jamaica. Historically, coffee has been most intensively grown in two areas: the Blue Mountains of the east, particularly the uplands contained in the historic parishes of St. Andrew, Port Royal, St. David, St. George, and St. Mary, and the island's central highlands located in the parishes of Manchester, Clarendon, and St. Elizabeth. The specific goal of this project is to analyze how spatial constructions have influenced the negotiation of social relations in these coffee-producing regions. Archaeological work was conducted in the Blue Mountains region between 1991 and 1994 and has been reported on elsewhere (Delle 1998, 1999a); the excavations in the central parishes are scheduled to be conducted over the course of at least three field seasons beginning in the summer of 1999 (Delle 1999b).

As a work of historical archaeology, this project relies on the analysis of

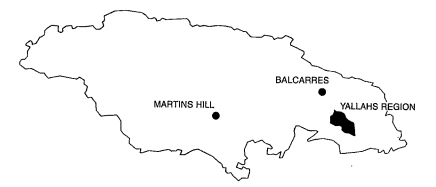

Map 8.1a. Relative location of Balcarres, Martins Hill, and the Yallahs Region.

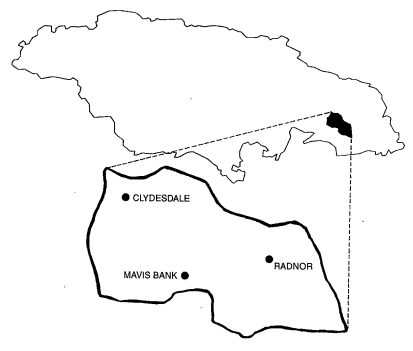

Map 8.1b. Close-up of the Yallahs Region.

James A. Delle

both the material record (articulated in architectural and archaeological evidence) and the documentary record (articulated in public and private archives); most historical archaeologists recognize the need to critically analyze material drawn from both records (for example, Beaudry 1988; Little 1992; Leone and Potter 1988; Shackel 1992). The documentary evidence from slave-based plantations, particularly those located in Jamaica, is exceptionally rich (Armstrong 1990, 17–56; Delle 1996; Hamilton 1992; Singleton 1992), as is the architectural and archaeological evidence for nineteenth-century plantations (Armstrong 1985; Reeves 1997; Singleton 1990). The type of analysis possible in historical archaeology—that is, analysis incorporating both of these data sets—allows a better interpretation of how social relations were negotiated on historic plantations than what could be interpreted from the examination of either set alone (Howson 1990).

As the documentary records of historic coffee plantations located in the Blue Mountains and the central highlands are exceptionally rich, I have been able to incorporate several types of documentary evidence into this study. One type of document that is commonly used by both historians and historical archaeologists is the plantation treatise, a type of book written from the slave master's perspective on how best to structure and organize a plantation. While the information contained within these documents must be analyzed with the greatest care (as, after all, they were written from a racialist frame of reference), the attitudes toward enslaved women that some members of the planter class held are revealed in such tracts. A second important source of documentary material includes plantation accounts kept by estate managers; such accounts exist for each of the plantations discussed in this chapter. While historians of slavery recognize that such documents may not be completely accurate, as oversights (intentional and otherwise) may have been made by the respective estate managers, they have been used by analysts of both North America and the Caribbean to reconstruct the demographic history of enslaved populations (for example, Cody 1996; Craton 1978; Fogel and Engerman 1974, 1979; Higman 1995a, 1995b). Finally, gender is a category of social relation that, like other types of social relations, is negotiated in space (Wehner 1997; Yentsch 1991). The arenas of this negotiation can be revealed and analyzed through the recovery and interpretation of the architectural and landscape records of plantations. To best understand how gender was negotiated under slavery on early nineteenth-century Jamaican coffee plantations, this chapter will analyze data concerning the definition and negotiation of gender from each of these sources.

GENDER, SEXUALITY, AND SOCIAL CONTROL ON JAMAICAN COFFEE PLANTATIONS: EVIDENCE FROM THE PLANTATION TREATISES

The plantation treatise, a book written as an instructive manual on how best to run an estate, was a common literary form of the late eighteenth and early nineteenth centuries. Generally written by men who owned or managed estates, many of these tracts characterized enslaved women as necessary to the plantation economy both as laborers and as "breeders," whose sexual lives required regulation in order to ensure both labor discipline and the reproduction of the enslaved population (Bush 1990, 1996; Dunn 1993; Moitt 1995; Sheridan 1985, 239–41). Of particular note for the analysis of nineteenth-century Jamaican coffee plantations are treatises written by P. J. Laborie in 1798, Dr. David Collins in 1803 (and reprinted in 1811), and Thomas Roughley in 1823. An analysis of these documents reveals how members of the white ruling class imagined gender relations should be constructed.

Controlling Sexuality

Each of the three plantation propagandists commented on the role women played as mothers—or at least as producers of children—simultaneously recognizing that women were crucial members of the workforce. In their discourse concerning these social phenomena, each author underscored the perceived necessity of controlling female sexuality, not only to establish discipline on the plantations, but to ensure that the population would naturally increase.

Laborie, a French émigré planter seeking refuge in Jamaica from the Haitian revolution, was perhaps the least subtle of the three plantations theorists. He recognized that the control of women's sexuality was crucial to the planter's ability to control his workforce. He outlined his opinions on this in an important treatise on the proper management of Jamaican coffee plantations (Laborie 1798). In this volume he recognized that while enslaved women were capable of avoiding pregnancy, those who did become pregnant were liable to induce abortions; he attributed both of these phenomena to women having "an aversion to a situation which checks their amours" (169). He suggested that planters should both encourage pregnancy and punish "voluntary and early miscarriages." Laborie admonished planters to be aware that women could use the bark of certain trees to induce abortion. In order to regulate pregnancy and to prevent abortions, Laborie suggested that the planters require women to declare their menstrual periods. The planter should then verify and register the periods; any woman who had a miscarriage that could not be explained by "evident causes" should be forced to wear an iron collar until her "ensuing pregnancy was well ascertained" (170).

Laborie further suggested that women's sexual partners be limited to men from the same estate, and that they should be rewarded while "in their pregnant state, or while rearing, especially if the fathers are among themselves" (170). However, he suggested that marriages be recognized inasmuch as married women should not be made sexually available to the younger white estate staff (180). Laborie argued that the planter himself should be the father, either metaphorically or biologically, of the children on the plantation. In his opinion this had both an economic and social advantage: "it must be considered that these children are bonds of love, which bind the negroes to the soil and to the master . . . and it affords, in reality, a pleasing sensation, to be surrounded with a black brood of these infants lisping out the word papa" (169).

In his discussion of the prevalence of lockjaw, or tetanus, as a cause of infant mortality, Laborie suggested that the slaves may have been practicing infanticide (173). To counter this strategy of resistance, Laborie suggested that planters reward mothers by granting them one day of liberty per week for each of their living children. After giving birth to six living children, the mother would be granted "household freedom." While no longer required to toil for the estate, the mother would not be allowed legal freedom but would be required to remain on the plantation, tending to her own domestic work. He also suggested that during latter stages of pregnancy women be transferred to light duty like sewing or turning coffee (170–71).

Laborie also recommended that new mothers be given three to four weeks reprieve from work following the birth of a child. After this period, they should be allowed to report to the field an hour after the rest of the gang, presumably to give them time to feed and clothe their child. Prior to weaning, the children were to be brought to the field with their mothers; while the women worked, the children would be attended by one or two girls. However, because the women would be spending time nursing the children, Laborie suggested that prior to weaning, women be employed about the house or in the garden (174). Weaning, suggested Laborie, should occur at the age of sixteen or eighteen months. At this time, the children were to be put into the care of "the keeper" of children, who would be responsible for bathing and feeding the child while the mother was working; the parents could collect their child after the end of the workday. Children would be in the care of the keeper until the age of five or six, when they would be turned back into the custody of their parents (175).

Like Laborie, Dr. David Collins (Collins 1971 [1811]) published a treatise on plantation management prior to emancipation. Originally published in 1803, four years before the abolition of the British slave trade, Collins argued that despite the commonly held convictions of the planters to the contrary, it was less expensive to "breed" slaves than to continually purchase them. In vulgar economic terms, women could be considered "breeding stock." Collins offered advice to the planters on the best way to ensure that women would produce children. Noting that many planters preferred a population that was primarily male, he extorted planters to create an equal gender distribution on their estates. This, he argued, would not only provide the planter with more laborers but would help create sexual discipline: "where a Planter has not his due proportion of women, he should procure them, that each [man] may be accommodated according to the ordinance of nature, and not be under the necessity of trespassing on his neighbor; though it will be difficult to fix their desires to their respective plantations, and prevent them from wandering after novelties abroad" (133).

Although evasively written, Collins suggested that an equal proportion of men to women on each plantation would prevent sexual jealousies from erupting between men over sexual partners. In order to accommodate "the ordinance of nature," the planter should encourage stable monogamous relationships by providing each male laborer with a wife. It is unclear in this passage whether Collins was concerned with the morality of existing relations; he did, however, believe that relationships such as he described would inevitably lead to better labor discipline as well as a larger working population.

Collins seems to have been somewhat obsessed with the necessity of regulating the sexuality of the enslaved population. For example, although he admonished the planters to do what they could to prevent sterility in women, he resigned himself to the peculiarly sexist and racist assumption that enslaved women would be oversexed and as a result less fertile: "negro women have ardent constitutions, which dispose them to be liberal of their favours; and it has been found by experience, that they who resign themselves to the indiscriminate caresses of men, are seldom very prolific; therefore, you must expect that there will be many of your female slaves, who will contribute but little to the population of your estate" (Collins 1971 [1811], 133).

As had Laborie, Collins warned planters against the possibility of pregnant women inducing abortions. However, he suggested a less intrusive method of ensuring that pregnancies were brought to term. Collins recommended that a woman's work load be lightened during pregnancy, and that she be indulged with days off in the hospital; these measures, Collins suggested, would lessen the burdens of pregnancy. By thus rewarding pregnancy, women would be more likely to bring their pregnancies to term.

Unlike Laborie or Collins, Thomas Roughley (1823) published his ideas on plantation management after the British legally abolished the African slave trade in 1807. He therefore explicitly expressed the need to regulate procreation as necessary to the social reproduction of labor within the slave system. According to Roughley: "We have not for some years imported, neither is it ever likely to take place, that we should have a fresh supply of slaves thus brought into the British colonies. The old Africans are daily wearing out and dropping into the grave; our care is to support the present stock, encourage healthy propagation, lessen their propensity for vice ... not to excite their hatred or jealousy by lewdness or wicked practices with their wives—a baneful custom" (76–77).

In this passage, Roughley stated his opinion of the role women needed to play in the "propagation" of the slave labor force while revealing the nature of sexual tension on the plantations. He suggested that the white estate staffs—and perhaps the planters themselves—were involved in "lewd practices" with enslaved women who were recognized as being married. Unfortunately, he did not explicitly state whether these lewd practices included rape per se; however, if these sexual liaisons were inciting jealousy and hatred, it seems likely that the women involved were coerced into sexual relations, either directly through the use or threat of force, or else through the misuse of social power within the plantation social hierarchy. In a remark appearing earlier in the monograph in which he discussed the qualities of a good overseer, Roughley suggested the importance of maintaining sexual discipline: "Above all things, [an overseer] must not encourage the spirit of Obea in [the slaves] ... or dishearten them by cohabiting with their wives, annulling thereby their domestic felicities ... for it very often happens, that well disposed slaves by such freedoms taken with their wives ... become runaways" (41–42).

Clearly, Roughley was concerned that sexual trespass on the part of the overseer could lead to the disruption of labor on the estate. Interestingly, although he suggested how *men* might react to overseer/slave liaisons, he never suggested how *women* would react. Implicitly, he argued that the sexual violation of slave women was an affront to their husbands' rights to women's sexuality; he does not directly address the rights women had to accept or reject the sexual advances or impositions made by the white estate staff. He does, however, reveal a rather patronizing attitude by implying that enslaved women might not only welcome the advances of the overseer, but actually fight amongst themselves for his attention. To prevent this, Roughley admonished the overseer to do nothing to excite jealousy among the women. In discussing the discipline of house servants (or domestics), Roughley states: "When an orderly set [of domestics] is once in a house, they are with little trouble kept to their duty. As jealousy is apt to creep in among the females, the overseer should give them little or no cause for it; it is a raging, unforgiving, relentless pestilence" (98).

As he, too, was concerned with the social reproduction of labor, Roughley discussed how enslaved children were, and should be, brought into the world. In doing so, he described the role midwives played on Jamaican estates. He described midwives as being elderly women who "attend the breeding-women, in time of childbirth" (95). According to his account, midwives were responsible for the delivery of children, unless there were some complications beyond their control, at which time they would ask the overseer to send for a doctor. Roughley recognized that midwives played a crucial role in social reproduction; thus he suggested that should a woman give birth to a viable infant, both she and the midwife should be rewarded.

Evidence for Sexual Behavior

In social contexts where there is marked inequality between genders, sexuality can be used as an expression of power. This was most certainly the case under plantation slavery, where enslaved women would have little if any recourse against forced or coerced sexual relations with white male planters and their employees. Beyond accounts and descriptions recorded by European males, however, relatively little is known about the sexual lives of enslaved women. Much of what we do know is clouded by the exaggerating myths about African sexuality promulgated by European men in the eighteenth and nineteenth centuries, exemplified by Collins's description of female African sexuality discussed above (Collins 1971 [1811], 133). All the documentary evidence and historical interpretations of female sexuality under the slave regimes with which I am familiar exclusively discuss heterosexuality. Clearly our knowledge of this intimate topic remains limited.

The information on sexual behavior at the coffee plantations under consideration here is typically limited. At Radnor, for example, the plantation account book suggests that two individuals may have contracted a venereal disease. A more extensive source of information concerning sexual behavior exists in the records of births on the plantation. Using this information, one can identify those young women whose sexual activity resulted in the birth of children. At Radnor another clue is provided in the data concerning the deaths of children; in sixteen cases the fathers of the deceased children were listed; some sexual liaisons may thus be revealed, though this line of evidence may only reveal who was socially recognized as a father; each individual so recognized was also enslaved on the plantation. Elfrida is the only woman that can be tentatively identified as having children with more than one man. Where a man identified as Mulatto Bob was listed as the father of her daughter Grace, Murray was identified as the father of her son George. This same source of evidence reveals that Murray fathered at least one other child; he was listed as the father of Myrtilla's son Richard.

There is evidence to suggest that at least one woman on the plantation was engaged in a sexual relationship with a member of the white estate staff, probably the overseer. In 1823 Penney gave birth to Sylvia, who was identified as a mulatto female child; two years later, she gave birth to Maggy, who was classified as a sambo child. Although the precise meanings of these attributions were flexible, in his history of Jamaica, Edward Long (1774, 260–62) suggested that the term *mulatto* was used to describe a child whose father was a "White Man" and whose mother was a "Negroe Woman," while the term *sambo* was applied when the child was parented by a "Negroe" man and a "mulatta" woman. It is difficult if not impossible to determine who fathered Penney's children; at most times there were three whites employed at the plantation, an overseer, a bookkeeper, and a head bookkeeper; it is likely that the father was one of these men. If the plantation recorders followed the conventional racial attributions discussed by Long, it is possible that two different men, one white, one African, may have each fathered one of the children; it is also possible that the racial attribution *sambo* was used to conceal the fact that one of the white estate staff fathered not one, but two children by Penney. The plantation account ledger indicates that at one point the plantation purchased a pessary, an intrauterine contraceptive device used in the nineteenth century, listing it under purchases. It would appear that at least one of the white males on the estate was engaged in a sexual relationship with an enslaved woman.

Similar conclusions can be drawn from the plantation record of Martins Hill, which noted the racial attribution for each of the enslaved workers. In the case of Martins Hill, the plantation ledger defines each member of the enslaved population by gender, occupation, age, race, and whether they were African-born or Creole. The racial categories in use at Martins Hill included black, sambo, mulatto, and quadroon; the latter, again according to Long (1774, 260), was applied to a child whose mother, grandmother, and great-grandmother were of African descent, but whose father, grandfather, and great-grandfather were white. In practice, it may be the case that this term was used to describe children whose mothers were mulatto and whose fathers were white, while the term sambo was applied to those whose mothers were mulatto and whose fathers were black. At Martins Hill, of the fifty-five children listed in the ledgers, forty-eight were defined as black, five as sambo, two as quadroon, and ten as mulatto; thus it is possible that as many as seventeen of these children were fathered by white men. This distinction seems to have been important to the planters; not only did they define race by these categories, but mulatto children seem to have been tracked away from the most onerous field occupations. Both adult mulatto women listed in the 1825 population ledger were domestics; the occupation filled by adult mulatto males included carpenter, mason, domestic, and stockman; all four sambo women were fieldworkers, while only one of the five sambo men worked in the field. Of the other four, one each was assigned to poultry keeping, stock minding, and domestic service; the fourth was a driver. Racial assignation as well as gender identification seem to have played a definitive role in the organization of the division of labor on coffee plantations.

GENDER AND THE DIVISION OF LABOR ON JAMAICAN COFFEE PLANTATIONS, 1790–1834

By its very definition plantation slavery limited the range of occupations a woman could pursue in her life. As was the case on most New World plantations, the workforce on early-nineteenth-century coffee plantations was divided into a series of task-based occupations, which incorporated not only agricultural fieldwork but also domestic service in the planters' houses, health care, food preparation both for the planters and the workers, livestock supervision, and a number of skilled artisanal employments, including carpentry, coopering, masonry, and sawyering. While Beckles (1989), among others, has argued that women who worked as domestic servants may have been socially or materially privileged by their occupation, the number of women so employed was relatively limited; the vast majority of women toiled in the fields.

Coffee plantations operated under a gender-based division of labor; a wider range of positions was available to men, including most of the skilled positions, while women were relegated to what were destined after emancipation to become lower-paying and lower-status jobs as domestic servants and unskilled field laborers.

Agricultural field labor was organized on many Jamaican coffee plantations using what was known as the "gang" system, by which the fieldworkers would be divided into three or more gangs, based on age, strength, and ability. Children began to work in the third gang as early as age five or six, the common age for children to join the productive workforce in early-nineteenth-century Jamaica (Higman 1995a, 189; Roughly 1823, 108). Each of the coffee plantation accounts record that when children reached the age when they could contribute to the economy of the plantation (age five or six), their employment status was upgraded from the category of "unserviceable children" into the working population; most if not all were moved into the third gang. When they were young adolescents, children would be elevated to the second gang; when they reached adulthood, they would join the first gang. Higman has suggested that throughout the West Indies, children aged five to twelve would work in the third gang; adolescents aged twelve to eighteen would work in the second gang alongside weaker adults; healthy adults aged between eighteen and forty-five would be members of the first gang (Higman 1995a).

An examination of the plantation records for the three plantations indicates that by the mid-1820s, the bulk of the agricultural fieldwork was being done by women (table 8.1). In each case, a larger proportion of the adult women, at least as defined by the plantation records, were occupied with fieldwork as compared to adult men. At Radnor, 86 percent of adult women were identified as fieldworkers, while 85 percent and 79 percent of adult women at Martins Hill and Balcarres, respectively, were field laborers. In comparison, 65 percent of adult men at Radnor were identified by the plantation account book as field laborers, while only 59 percent were so identified at Martins Hill, and 55 percent at Balcarres. The field labor gangs comprised a female majority; while 56 percent of all fieldworkers at Radnor were women, 62 percent of fieldworkers were women at Martins Hill. The proportions were even higher at Balcarres, where 66 percent of the field population was female.

The gender division of labor was such that a wider range of occupations, particularly skilled occupations, were open to men than were open to women. At Radnor, for example, men were trained as carpenters, doctors, boatswains, masons, saddlers, and sawyers (Delle 1999a). In comparison, there were few

TABLE 8.1

Field Labor by Gender at Radnor, Balcarres, and Martins Hill

	No. of Female Field Workers	% Total Adult Females	No. of Male Field Workers	% Total Adult Males	% Total Labor Force Comprised of Women
Radnor, 1825	70	86	55	65	56
Martins Hill, 1825	167	85	104	59	62
Balcarres, 1825	62	79	32	55	66

skilled occupations open to women on any of the three plantations in the 1820s; besides cooking for the field gangs, such occupations were limited to health-caregiving; for example, a few women served as midwives, nurses, and doctors. No women occupied supervisory positions at Radnor, while on Balcarres and Martins Hill, the only supervisory positions open to women were as the drivers of the smaller labor gangs, which usually were composed of children and the elderly. Unskilled occupations filled by women on the plantations included domestic servant and washer woman.

On Radnor, most of the women who can be identified as being of child-bearing age worked in the first gang. Within the plantation's population of about 220, 28 of 81 adult women can be identified as either having or bearing children between 1822 and 1826, the duration of the record appearing in the plantation account book. Given the short duration of the record, and the nature of the evidence (that is, births reported by the white estate staff), it is possible, if not likely, that there were more mothers on the estate who cannot at this time be identified. Nevertheless, of the 28 identifiable mothers, all but 1 woman, identified as a nurse, worked in the first gang. The only other occupational category that might include women of childbearing age is domestic worker. Although it is possible that some of the 5 domestics on Radnor were in this demographic group, it is also possible that the domestics were either mature women who were no longer useful to the planter as field laborers or young women who were not yet old enough to be useful as field laborers. While it is as yet impossible to prove the age structure of the domestic workers at Radnor, as the plantation book did not list the ages of the enslaved people, Barry Higman (1995a, 197) has demonstrated that in 1822 at Maryland Plantation, a coffee property located in nearby St. Andrew, domestic work was dominated by girls and older women. Five of the 11 female domestics at Maryland were below the age of twenty, 3 being younger than ten. There were only 4 male domestics at Maryland, 3 in their teens or younger, and 1 in his forties. No women in their twenties and only two in their thirties worked as domestic servants; the remaining 4 were forty or older. If the same pattern held at Radnor, it would seem that few women in their strongest and most fertile years worked as domestics, though this is speculative at best.

Unlike the Radnor Plantation Book, the plantation records for Martins Hill and Balcarres noted the ages of the enslaved workers attached to the estates; more can thus be said about the age composition of the various occupations filled on the estates. In 1825, the average age of a worker on Martins Hill was 25.8; although calculated separately, the overall average age for working women and working men (that is, discounting children) turned out to be statistically identical. On average, women fieldworkers and domestic servants were the same age; the mean age of the 167 female fieldworkers (who ranged in age from 6 to 57) and the 5 house workers (who ranged in age from 14 to 42) was 26.7. Male field and house workers were statistically slightly younger; the average age of the 104 male fieldworkers was 26.0, while the average age of the 3 male house workers was 15.4. The only other occupations open to women at Martins Hill were filled by older women: the average age of a washer woman was 49, and a driver 46; the sole midwife and cook were 34 and 31, respectively (see tables 8.2 and 8.3).

The working population on Balcarres was slightly older than that at Martins Hill; overall, the average age of the workforce (discounting children under age 7) was 27.1; the average age of males was slightly older than that for females, 38.7, as opposed to 33.4. Despite the older male population, the average age of women fieldworkers (31.4) was considerably higher than the average age of men fieldworkers (24.6). As was the case on the other plantations, there were more occupations filled by men than women (tables 8.2 and 8.3).

Each of the plantations depended on women to perform the bulk of the agricultural work. On Radnor, for example, women made up the majority of full-time field laborers, 70 as compared to 55 men; on Balcarres, the field gangs comprised 66 women and 38 men, while on Martins Hill, the gangs consisted of 167 women and 104 men. These figures corroborate an overall trend toward the feminization of agricultural work on Jamaican plantations noted by the historians Barry Higman (1995b) and Marietta Morrissey (1989, 77) (see fig. 8.1).

TABLE 8.2

Occupational Data for Balcarres

	Number	Avg. Age	Age Range
Women			
Field	66	31.4	7–51
House	1	11	n/a
Midwife	2	59	57–61
Nurse	3	52.3	41–61
Washerwoman	2	45.5	41–50
Driver	1	37	n/a
Cook	1	41	n/a
Invalid	4	40.1	20–51
Child	17	3.8	0–7
Unknown	1	7	n/a
Total	98	28.3	0–61
Discounting children	81	33.4	7–61
Men			
Field	38	24.6	7–56
Carpenter	6	39.2	16–56
Cooper	1	43	n/a
Mason	3	29.7	21–46
Watchman	5	56.8	51–66
Sawyer	1	45	n/a
Driver	2	34.5	33–36
House	0	n/a	n/a
Mule man	1	43	n/a
Stock keeper	1	27	n/a
Invalid	0	n/a	n/a
Gardener	1	66	n/a
Children	15	3.7	0–7
Total	74	32.3	0–66
Discounting children	59	38.7	7–66

James A. Delle

TABLE 8.3

Occupational Data for Martins Hill, 1825

	Number	Avg. Age	Age Range
Women			
Field	167	26.7	6–57
House	5	26.7	14–42
Midwife	1	34	n/a
Nurse	n/a	n/a	n/a
Washerwoman	3	49	35–62
Driver	2	46	37–55
Cook	1	31	31
Invalid	15	55.8	36–71
Child	29	3	0–7
Unknown	3	14.7	12–18
Total	226	25.8	0–71
Discounting children	197	29.2	6–71
Men			
Field	104	26	6–50
Carpenter	11	33.5	19–61
Cooper	9	31.7	16–51
Mason	7	34.7	15–41
Watchman	15	41.3	31–46
Sawyer	4	42	36–50
Driver	5	41	34–60
House	5	15.4	11–19
Cowboy/cowman	4	33	19–55
Stockman	2	30	18–42
Invalid	4	61.5	50–70
Poultry keeper	5	22	10–41
Children	36	2.8	0–5
Unknown	1	27	n/a
Disabled by yaws	1	19	n/a
Total	213	25.8	0–70
Discounting children	177	30.1	6–77

Gender, Power, and Space

Fig. 8.1. As can be seen in this nineteenth-century depiction of a sugar plantation, women worked alongside men, doing some of the heaviest field labor on both sugar and coffee plantations. Courtesy of the National Library of Jamaica.

WOMEN AND THE REPRODUCTION OF LABOR

Following the legal abolition of the African slave trade in 1807, Jamaican planters felt the need to pay closer attention to the natural increase of the enslaved population attached to their various estates. It is generally recognized that plantation recorders underreported births as a means to mask the high rates of infant mortality, and perhaps to disguise the rates at which infanticide was practiced among the enslaved population as a form of resistance to the slave regime (Bush 1996; Higman 1995a; Trouillot 1995). Nevertheless, a consideration of demographic trends based on these records does provide some sense of how the rhythms of pregnancy, childbirth, and child rearing affected gendered life on the coffee plantations.

Between January of 1822 and the end of 1825, 25 women gave birth to 32 children on Radnor plantation. As reported in the plantation book, the sex parity ratio was remarkable—21 girls and 11 boys were born, for a parity ratio of 52 boys for every 100 girls born; in comparison, Higman's figures for recorded births for Jamaica as a whole in the decade of the 1820s indicates that the islandwide parity ratio was 101 boys for every 100 girls born (Higman 1995a, table S8.1). This recorded disparity cannot yet be fully explained; it may, in fact, simply be a statistical anomaly resulting from the small sample size and the short span of the plantation record (forty-eight months); it may have resulted from some other more nefarious phenomenon. Although no evidence as yet exists to directly support the idea, it may be that the plantation managers underrecorded male births to mask the fact that something was happening to the male babies. In a remote location like Radnor during a time when chattel slavery was the predominate labor system, it does not seem too far-fetched to speculate that the plantation managers were engaged in a black market for male children, underreporting the number of children to hide the fact that they were selling them for their own profit (Medford 1999, pers. comm.). Although no evidence for this has yet been uncovered, it is an intriguing idea. Nevertheless, some more definite statements can be made about infants at Radnor. The plantation records indicate that six women gave birth to more than one child. The other nineteen identifiable mothers bore one child each over these years. This represents a crude birthrate of 145 per 1,000. This figure is high for Jamaican plantations; Barry Higman has calculated crude birthrates of 23 births per 1,000 for Jamaica as a whole, and 23.8 for St. David, the parish in which Radnor is located, for the period 1823–26, roughly the same period recorded in the Radnor Plantation Journal (Higman 1995a, table 21).

Information on birth spacing on Radnor is limited to just three instances. Of the six women who gave birth more than once during the four years recorded in the plantation journal, only three had children who were viable after the first year of life. Each of these women gave birth to a second child approximately three years after the birth of a previous child. The mean interval between births for this sample is 36.3 months, just over three years. These results suggest that women were breast-feeding infants for approximately two years after birth and were soon after both sexually active and fertile.

Primarily because the records cover a longer period of time, the information available to determine birth spacing on Balcarres is more extensive than is the case for Radnor. The Balcarres plantation accounts indicate that between 1818 and 1831, twenty-two women gave birth more than once. Within this sample, the shortest interval was 10 months, while the longest was 82 months. Statistically, the mean interval between births at Balcarres plantation was 34.6 months, with a standard deviation of 15 months. This statistic can be somewhat refined to be more comparable to the Radnor data. In twenty of the thirty-six births, involving eleven women, all of the children involved were viable after one year. In this sample, the mean birth spacing was 33.2 months, with a standard deviation of 12 months. In the remaining sixteen cases, involving twelve women, the mean birth spacing was 36.4 months, with a standard deviation of 18.3 months. These statistics indicate that, as was the case on Radnor, women on Balcarres were nursing viable children for about two years after birth. Statistically, women whose children died in infancy seem to have spaced their births at a slightly longer interval.

The demographic data for Martins Hill is somewhat more problematic. Although the population records are extensive for this plantation, there is a gap between June 1824 and July 1825; during this year the owner of the plantation died; the documents imply that the plantation was in some state of disarray. To further complicate matters, in 1827 the entire plantation population either were assigned or chose new names, making the ascription of maternity difficult in some cases. To account for these mitigating factors, I have bracketed the data into two subsets. The first subset includes the data from the beginning of the plantation records in July 1818 to the break in the record in 1824. The second subset includes the data from the resumption of the plantation accounts in July of 1825 through June of 1831.

In the first bracket ten women can be identified as haven given birth to a total of twenty-three children. The resulting sample size used to calculate birth spacing is thirteen instances. However, of these thirteen, one can be considered an outlier. In one case, there was a space of 60 months between births, a full 19 months longer than the next largest interval. Discounting this outlier, the mean interval between births was 30.3 months, with a standard deviation of 7.5 months, n = 12. With the outlier calculated in, the mean interval was 32.6 months with a standard deviation of 10.75 months, n = 13. In the second bracket, fourteen women gave birth to a total of twenty-nine children; the sample size used for calculating birth interval was sixteen instances. The mean birth interval in this sample was 31.7 months, with a standard deviation of 5.0 months. If both samples are calculated together, again excluding the 60-month outlier, a combined mean of 31.1 months results, with a standard deviation of 6.3 months. If the outlier is included, the mean interval rises to 32.1 months, with a standard deviation of 8.1 months.

The Balcarres plantation data indicates the ages of many of the enslaved. Using this information, it is possible to draw some conclusions about the ages at which women gave birth on the plantation. Of the thirty-seven women known to have given birth, we know the ages of twenty-nine (at least according to the plantation managers). The age at first recorded birth during their enslavement at Balcarres for eight of these twenty-nine women can be confidently identified; the remainder apparently had children prior to the beginning of the plantation record. Of the eight women, the youngest recorded age at first birth is 16, while the oldest is 23. The mean age at first birth is 19.4 years, with a standard deviation of 2.3 years; thus most of the young women on Balcarres who are known to have had children began their childbearing between the ages of 17 and 21. Using this same source of information, the age at which women bore their last child during their captivity can also be calculated. There are twelve women whose final birth can be confidently identified. The age range at final birth of these twelve women was 33 to 42 years. The mean age at final birth was 36.8 years, with a standard deviation of 2.2 years. Statistically, therefore, the mean fertility range of childbearing women on Balcarres plantation was 19.4 through 36.8 years of age, a range of 17.4 years. Taking these two calculations together, if one divides mean birth spacing into mean fertility range, the evidence suggests that the average childbearing woman bore six live children during her fertile years.

As is the case with Balcarres plantation, the Martins Hill accounts include information on the ages of enslaved people. Because of the 1824–25 gap, however, it is difficult to confidently identify either the first or last child delivered by any given woman, as in many cases it is possible that a woman could have given birth to a child either during the gap in the records, before 1818, when the record begins, or else after 1831, when it effectively ends. Be this as it may, it is possible to tentatively suggest some demographic trends concerning fertility. For example, it is possible to suggest a reasonable range of ages at birth at Martins Hill; no woman is identified as having given birth younger than age 16 or older than 44. It is also possible to identify the ages at first birth for nine woman. Within this subset, the range at first birth was between 16 and 21. The mean age at first birth for this group was 17.45, with a standard deviation of 1.43 years. It is much more difficult to confidently suggest the mean age of final birth, as the age at final birth for only three women can be confidently identified. The mean age at last birth for this small sample was 40.67, with a standard deviation of 2.87 years. This figure may not be a very reliable indicator, however, given the small number of instances. It may be more fruitful to offer an impressionistic interpretation of the upper range of childbearing years. It seems that it was fairly common for women on Martins Hill to have children into their late thirties and even into their forties. At least ten women had children after age 37; five of these women had children while in their forties.

GENDER, SPACE, AND POWER

Gender, like all social categories, is negotiated in spatial as well as social contexts; as such, historical archaeological interpretation should take into account that landscapes and buildings, both past and present, help to shape and reinforce the social construction of gender relations (Hood 1996; Kryder-Reid 1996; Yentsch 1991). If we accept the proposition that such spatial artifacts do indeed shape social hierarchies, the analysis of the built environment should include the consideration of how spaces were engendered.

Although the design and production of space on Jamaican coffee plantations differed from sugar plantations in the type and number of buildings required, the planters adapted some of the preexisting spatial logic of sugar plantations—an industry that pre-dated large-scale coffee production by a century and a half—to the demands of coffee agriculture. Thus, in the early nineteenth century, when the estates under discussion here were new, they would have easily been identifiable as plantations by a visitor unfamiliar with the specific spatial layout of a coffee estate. While it is relatively easy to reconstruct the class-based segregation of domestic space incorporating the living areas of the planters, the white estate staff, and the enslaved African laborers (Delle 1999a), it is much more difficult, archaeologically, to reconstruct how gender was negotiated in these particular spaces. As no maps or plans of the specific plantations discussed in this chapter have yet been uncovered, the following analysis is based on a series of estate plans from one coffee-producing region, the Yallahs River drainage, which is located in the Blue Mountains of eastern Jamaica (maps 8.2 and 8.3), and which was the focus of a more detailed consideration of social space on Jamaican coffee plantations (Delle 1998).

Defining Plantation Space

African workers enslaved on Jamaican plantations tended to live in nucleated villages clustered in areas on the plantation defined by the planters as marginal to commodity production. Unlike the industrial works and elite housing on the estates, which were often made of stone and were monumental in scale, houses built by and inhabited by enslaved workers in Jamaica were impermanent structures. During the 1994 field season, I conducted a surface reconnaissance of five historic plantations in the Yallahs region; historic maps were used as a source to locate the position of village sites. In each case the areas identified cartographically as village sites were

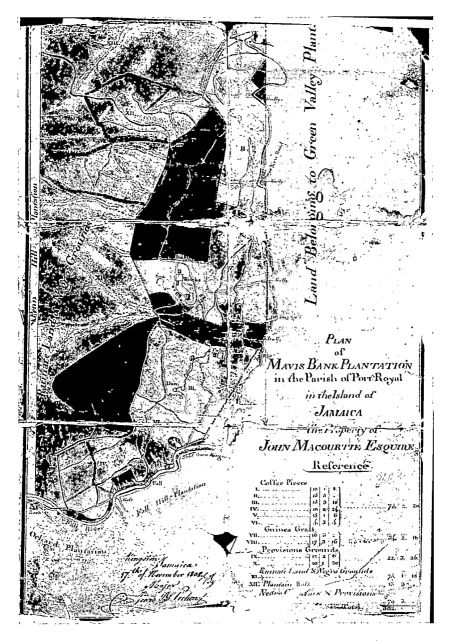

Map. 8.2. A pre-emancipation plan of Mavis Bank, drawn circa 1810. For these plans, boundaries of entire estates were emphasized, most of which were owned by men of European descent. Courtesy National Library of Jamaica.

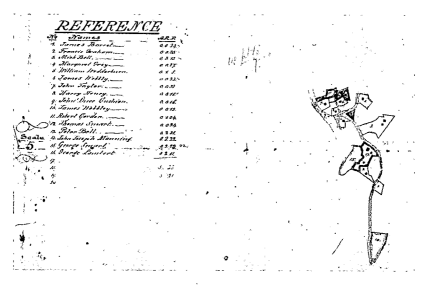

Map 8.3. A post-emancipation map of homesteads owned by emancipated workers of Arcadia Plantation in 1842. At least one of these eleven plots was owned by a woman, Margaret Grey. Courtesy of the National Library of Jamaica.

heavily disturbed; no surface evidence of a village was discovered. At Radnor, for example, the village locations identified by the historic maps had recently been planted in coffee; subsurface testing could not be conducted without disturbing the valuable coffee trees. On each of the other plantations, modern disturbances and erosion caused by a horrific flood that plagued the region in the early twentieth century had either destroyed or obfuscated the archaeological record of the villages.

The analysis of cartographic evidence for villages is subject to another set of methodological limitations. Few of the preemancipation coffee plantation plans depict villages. More commonly, a parcel of land within the plantation is referred to as "Negro grounds," suggesting that the surveyors and their patrons, the planters, took less interest in the spatial organization of the villages than, for example, the coffee fields. Despite these limitations, there are some conclusions that can be drawn about the organization of villages on coffee plantations in the Blue Mountains. In an analysis of the cartographic record of Jamaican coffee plantations, Barry Higman offers a few conclusions relevant to this study. It should be noted that his study included maps from the entire island, spanning the dates 1780–1860. Higman's study was primarily a statistical analysis designed to produce generalizations about the internal structure of Jamaican coffee plantations. In analyzing his sample,

Higman calculated that the mean size of a slave village on a Jamaican coffee plantation during this eighty-year period was 2.7 acres (Higman 1986, 81). It seems reasonable to suggest that villages on Blue Mountain coffee plantations were of a similar size.

Some tentative conclusions can be made by drawing analogies with other villages on the island; unfortunately, few archaeological studies have specifically looked at the internal arrangement of villages attached to Jamaican plantations. The most significant study that has looked at the arrangement of houses was that conducted by Douglas Armstrong on Seville Estate, a sugar plantation located on Jamaica's north coast. Armstrong was able to locate two distinct slave villages, one dating to the early eighteenth century, the other to the late eighteenth century. Using cartographic information supplemented by excavation of numerous houses, Armstrong has been able to discuss how the spatial arrangement of the villages differed. The earlier of the two villages was organized linearly. It was composed of four symmetrically organized rows of houses, two located on either side of a road. The later village consisted of a number of houses organized around a common, reflecting a more dispersed circular village. Armstrong concludes that the settlement pattern of the later village reflects a situation of decreased surveillance of the slaves. Noting that the great house experienced a phase of reconstruction at approximately the same time as the later village was constructed, Armstrong concludes that the planter elites may have been too preoccupied with the reconstruction of the house to dictate the construction of a symmetrically organized village (Armstrong 1996, pers. comm.; Armstrong and Kelly 1990).

Using Armstrong's conclusion as a basis for deduction, it can be hypothesized that the settlement pattern of villages on coffee plantations should more resemble the later slave village at Seville than the earlier. Contemporary observers noted that the daily labor regime, and thus perhaps the intensity of surveillance, on working coffee plantations was less severe than on sugar plantations (for example, Thome and Kimball 1838, 406–7). Yallahs coffee plantations were constructed over a relatively brief period, during which time significant forest clearing, terracing, planting, and construction of industrial works and elite housing would have been simultaneously accomplished. Furthermore, many of the coffee plantations in eastern Jamaica were carved on steeply sloped hillsides; some 50 percent of coffee plantations were located in areas with mean slopes exceeding 20 percent (Higman 1986, 77). Thus, one can hypothesize that due to the investment of capital and attention to the construction of productive space, the coffee planters would have left the construction of villages to the enslaved. Furthermore, the rugged terrain undoubtedly inhibited the construction of symmetrically ordered villages.

Although both the archaeological and cartographic evidence for villages in the Yallahs region are poor, some preliminary observations can be made about the spatial organization of villages based on the cartographic record of two plantations. The first is for Radnor, which is based on a redrawn plan of the estate published by Higman (1986, 1988). In his cartographic analysis of Radnor, Higman represented the village as a cluster of thirty buildings located in a small meadow, approximately 3 acres in size (Higman 1986). According to the parish vestry accounts, in 1806 the enslaved population at Radnor numbered some 252 people. If the estate plan accurately depicted the number of houses, if not their specific location, this would suggest that, on average, 8 people were living in each house. Regardless of the accuracy of the number of houses, if all 252 people were indeed living in the 2.7-acre meadow, the slave village would have been a very densely populated place indeed, with a population density of approximately 93.33 people per acre. A similar analysis of the only other known preemancipation depiction of a Yallahs region village, a plan of Clydesdale Plantation drawn in 1810, suggests that 109 people were living in eleven houses in a 10-acre village (Delle 1998, 147).

It is most likely that the houses of enslaved workers in the Blue Mountains were constructed of wattle and daub with thatched roofs. Entries for the first few weeks of the Radnor plantation book indicate that while three or four people were "making huts," one person was cutting thatch, suggesting that the thatch was used during house construction. Contemporary drawings of African Jamaican houses usually depict houses with thatched roofs; a nineteenth-century sugar planter, Matthew Lewis, described workers housing on his estate as being constructed of wattle and daub (Lewis 1929 [1834], 197). It seems likely that houses in the Yallahs region were similarly constructed.

In Jamaica it was customary for the owners and managers of both sugar and coffee plantations to require the enslaved population to feed itself. As a result, portions of the plantation lands were dedicated to what were known as "provision grounds," areas in which the enslaved population would build and tend gardens. Provision grounds were arguably the most important space to the enslaved populations. The plots that were gardened provided not only food for the sustenance of the workers and their families, but were spaces in which the enslaved were free to produce surplus for sale. Mintz and Hall

(1960) have argued that the individual people were allotted a small plot in the provision grounds, which were sometimes located miles from the villages. In 1790 William Beckford observed that a "quarter acre ... will be fully sufficient for the supply of a moderate family, and may enable the [slave] to carry some to market besides" (Beckford 1790, 257). Another contemporary observer elaborated on this: "Each slave has ... a piece of ground (about half an acre) allotted to him as a provision ground. This is the principal means of his support ... this spot will not only furnish him with sufficient food for his own consumption, but an oversurplus to carry to market" (Stewart 1969 [1823], 267).

Although an extremely important space to the laborers, provision grounds are perhaps the most difficult material space to identify and analyze archaeologically. As they tended to be located away from the centers of the plantations, and may not have had any permanent built landscape features associated with them, it is all but impossible to find these spaces today.

As the provision grounds were a space occupied and utilized by the slaves for their own use, little information on preemancipation provision grounds appears in the cartographic record of the Yallahs region, although a few things can be gleaned from this scanty evidence. For example, an 1808 rendition of Mavis Bank plantation identifies 79¾ acres, approximately 26 percent of the plantation's 302 acres, as "Negro Grounds and Provisions." A similar plan of Radnor indicates that of the estate's 689 acres, 133 acres were in "Negro grounds and provisions," and an additional 222 acres were in "woodland and Negro grounds" (Higman 1986). In both cases although most of this land was located on what could be considered as the material periphery of the estate, it seems clear that the provision grounds were central to the African Jamaican definition of social space.

Engendering Plantation Spaces

On a basic level, the material space of a coffee plantation can be conceptualized as having been divided into several spheres: the domestic space of the elite comprised the great house, overseer's house, and their dependencies; the domestic space of the enslaved comprised the slave villages. The agricultural space of elite commodity production comprised coffee fields and pastures for draft animals; the agricultural space of food and commodity production of the enslaved comprised provision grounds; the industrial space of production comprised the mill complex and what we might define as intermediate space—that is, the areas of the plantations that were neither under production of coffee nor provisions and which were sometimes defined as "ruinate" or forest. These various spaces were the arenas for gender negotiation between enslaved and free, man and woman. As spaces controlled by male planters but cleaned and serviced by female domestics, great houses and overseers' houses would have been contested locations where the negotiation of power would have been contested between the white male planters and the enslaved women forced to work there. As spaces lived in by Africans, the villages would have been areas in which African Jamaican definitions of gender relations would have been expressed. Finally, the pro-

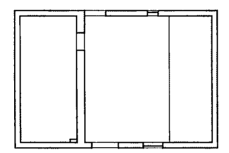

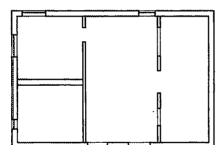

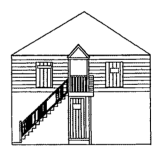

0'   5'   10'

Fig. 8.2. Clydesdale overseers' house–drawing.

Fig. 8.3 Clydesdale overseers' house–photo. Photo by James Delle.

vision grounds were spaces in which both men and women worked to feed themselves and their children and express some measure of economic autonomy.

Take for example the overseers' house at Clydesdale (see figs. 8.2 and 8.3). This building was constructed to mediate the relationship between the overseers and the enslaved, as it was located between the African village and the mill works on the estate in such a way that the workers would have to pass by it on their way from their houses to either the coffee fields or the mill, allowing the overseer the power of surveillance over the workers. Similarly, the interior of the building is divided so as to provide the overseer with power over any workers who may have been inside. The interior, divided into three rooms, was insulated from the external world of the enslaved by stone walls more than twenty inches thick. Once in this space, the overseer could exert an extreme level of authority over the domestic servants; this was more than likely the space within which sexual coercion would have occurred. In this space, women would be physically separated from the external world, and in a real sense would have been trapped; with shutters closed, this space would have been visibly and aurally isolated and under the control of the overseer.

In contrast, the provision grounds in which enslaved women grew food for themselves and their families, and in which they produced surplus to sell at market, would have been spaces controlled by enslaved women. The records seem to indicate that the planters rarely if ever ventured into the provision grounds on the coffee plantations. In these spaces, women would have had more control over their own action, the products of which were theirs to use and sell, in contrast to the degree of alienation they would have experienced both in the planters' houses and the mill works. A similar degree of autonomy may have existed around the house yards in the village, as there is some indication that commodities grown or produced there were also sold by enslaved men and women for cash (PP1842/13/469, 741).

It is well known that slave women throughout the Caribbean participated in a cash economy by producing their own agricultural commodities and selling them in nearby market towns (Beckford 1790, 257; Mintz and Hall 1960; Stewart 1969 [1823], 267). However, as documents like the Radnor plantation book were created to monitor and record the production of the coffee plantation, they are relatively silent about how the enslaved African population experienced the spaces of the provision grounds. Nevertheless, the Radnor account indicates not only that on every Sunday and alternate Saturdays the enslaved were either "cultivating their provision grounds" or else were "employed in their provision grounds," but that the estate managers actually bought provisions from the very people they enslaved. The account also suggests that cultivating certain plants and raising certain animals may have been an important part of the material negotiation of gender. For example, in the plantation accounts, there are numerous entries concerning the purchase of provisions for the estate staff from the enslaved workers, the most common being fresh pork, castor oil, and cocoas—a squashlike vegetable. Pork was sold to the estate almost exclusively by men; of the 584.25 pounds of pork purchased by the estate from known individuals, all but 19 pounds were bought from men. It thus seems likely that hog raising was primarily, although not exclusively, the domain of men. Of the women on the estate, only Rebecca sold pork, and that was on only one recorded occasion. In contrast, castor oil—a product made of an Old World herb—was a commodity that was far more frequently purchased from women; in all, nine separate women made and sold castor oil to the estate during the years covered by the plantation book. A gendered division of productive space—the pigpen versus the herb garden—may well have existed.

CONCLUSION

In capitalist society, generally, there has existed an unequal relationship between those members of the two recognized gender categories. The negotiation of this inequality is nowhere better exemplified than under the conditions of plantation slavery. Women under slavery were subject to extreme forms of sexual violence, ranging from rapes to the indignity of having white planters force them to reveal their menstrual cycles. Sexual exploitation and sexual control were a part of everyday reality for many enslaved women, to the point where the planters kept tight records on where and when children were born and how they died. Under slavery, women were relegated to thankless tasks on the plantation, what one plantation theorist would call "the works of drudgery" (Laborie 1798). Whereas some men were allowed to develop into skilled artisans, few women developed what would become marketable skills in the days following the end of slavery. However, despite the institutional nature of gender inequality, women did express autonomy in a number of ways: midwives helped women through pregnancy and childbirth and no doubt assisted with abortions and infanticides; women grew provisions and sold them for profit, creating an economy independent of the patriarchal plantation system. These elements of gender relations were negotiated spatially. It would serve archaeologists well to recognize that all activity areas on plantations—from the great house to the house garden—were contested arenas for the negotiation of gender.

NOTE

I would like to thank the Earl of Crawford for allowing access to the papers of his ancestors, the former owners of Martins Hill and Balcarres estates, and to thank all those who commented on earlier versions of this paper, including Susan Malin-Boyce, Bob Paynter, Randy McGuire, Steve Mrozowski, Paul Mullins, and Mary Ann Levine. This research was funded, in part, by the Wenner-Gren Foundation for Anthropological Research.

REFERENCES CITED

Armstrong, Douglas V. 1985. An Afro-Jamaican Slave Settlement: Archaeological Investigations at Drax Hall. In *The Archaeology of Slavery and Plantation Life*, ed. Theresa Singleton, 261–87. San Diego: Academic Press.

——. 1990. *The Old Village and the Great House: An Archaeological and Historical Examination of Drax Hall Plantation, St. Ann's Bay, Jamaica.* Urbana: Univ. of Illinois Press.

Armstrong, Douglas V., and Kenneth G. Kelly. 1990. Settlement Pattern Shifts in a Jamaican Slave Village, Seville Estate, St. Ann's Bay, Jamaica. Paper presented at the 23d Annual Conference on Historical and Underwater Archaeology, Tucson, Ariz.

Bassett, Everett. 1994. "We Took Care of Each Other Like Families Were Meant To": Gender, Social Organization, and Wage Labor among the Apache at Roosevelt. In *Those of Little Note: Gender, Race, and Class in Historical Archaeology*, ed. Elizabeth Scott, 55–79. Tucson: Univ. of Arizona Press.

Beaudry, Mary C. 1988. Words for Things: Linguistic Analysis of Probate Inventories. In *Documentary Archaeology in the New World*, ed. Mary C. Beaudry, 43–50. Cambridge: Cambridge Univ. Press.

Beckford, William. 1790. *A Descriptive Account of the Island of Jamaica.* London: T. and J. Egerton.

Beckles, Hilary McD. 1989. *Natural Rebels: A Social History of Enslaved Black Women in Barbados.* New Brunswick, N.J.: Rutgers Univ. Press.

Bush, Barbara. 1990. *Slave Women in Caribbean Society, 1650–1838.* Bloomington: Indiana Univ. Press.

———. 1996. Hard Labor: Women, Childbirth, and Resistance in British Caribbean Slave Societies. In *More Than Chattel: Black Women and Slavery in the Americas,* ed. David Barry Gaspar and Darlene Clark Hine, 193–217. Bloomington: Indiana Univ. Press.

Cody, C. A. 1996. Cycles of Work and of Childbearing: Seasonality in Women's Lives on Low Country Plantations. *More Than Chattel: Black Women and Slavery in the Americas,* ed. David Barry Gaspar and Darlene Clark Hine, 61–78. Bloomington: Indiana Univ. Press.

Collins, David. 1971 [1811]. *Practical Rules for the Management and Medical Treatment of Negro Slaves, in the Sugar Colonies, by a Professional Planter.* Freeport, N.Y.: Books for Libraries Press.

Conkey, Margaret W., and Joan M. Gero. 1991. Tensions, Pluralities, and Engendering Archaeology: An Introduction to Women and Prehistory. In *Engendering Archaeology: Women and Prehistory,* ed. Joan M. Gero and Margaret W. Conkey, 3–30. Oxford: Basil Blackwell.

———. 1997. Programme to Practice: Gender and Feminism in Archaeology. *Annual Review of Anthropology* 26:411–37.

Costello, Julia. 1998. The Sporting Life of 1890's Los Angeles Parlor Houses. Paper presented at the annual meeting of Society for Historical Archaeology, Atlanta.

Craton, Michael. 1978. *Searching for the Invisible Man: Slaves and Plantation Life in Jamaica.* Cambridge: Harvard Univ. Press.

Delle, James A. 1996. An Archaeology of Crisis: The Manipulation of Social Spaces in the Blue Mountains of Jamaica, 1790–1865. Ph.D. diss., Dept. of Anthropology, Univ. of Massachusetts, Amherst.

———. 1998. *An Archaeology of Social Space: Analyzing Coffee Plantations in Jamaica's Blue Mountains.* New York: Plenum.

———. 1999a. The Landscapes of Class Negotiation on Coffee Plantations in the Blue Mountains of Jamaica, 1790–1850. *Historical Archaeology* 33 (1): 136–58.

———. 1999b. The Baptist Church and the Making of Free Jamaica. Paper presented at the World Archaeology Congress 4, Cape Town, South Africa.

Dunn, Richard. 1993. Sugar Production and Slave Women in Jamaica. In *Cultivation and Culture: Labor and the Shaping of Slave Life in the Americas,* ed. Ira Berlin and Philip D. Morgan, 49–72. Charlottesville: Univ. Press of Virginia.

Engels, Fredrick. 1972. *The Origins of the Family, Private Property, and the State.* New York: International Publishers.

Fogel, R. W., and Stanley L. Engerman. 1974. *Time on the Cross: The Economics of American Negro Slavery.* Boston: Little, Brown.

————. 1979. Recent Findings in the Study of Slave Demography and Family Structure. *Sociology and Social Research* 63 (3): 566–89.

Hamilton, Donny. 1992. Simon Benning, Pewterer of Port Royal. In *Text-Aided Archaeology,* ed. Barbara J. Little, 39–53. Boca Raton: CRC Press.

Hardesty, Donald L. 1994. Class, Gender Strategies, and Material Culture in the Mining West. In *Those of Little Note: Gender, Race, and Class in Historical Archaeology,* ed. Elizabeth Scott, 129–45. Tucson: Univ. of Arizona Press.

Higman, Barry. 1986. Jamaican Coffee Plantations, 1780–1860: A Cartographic Analyses. *Caribbean Geography* 2: 73–91.

————. 1988. *Jamaica Surveyed: Plantation Maps and Plans of the Eighteenth and Nineteenth Centuries.* Kingston, Jamaica: Institute of Jamaica.

————. 1995a. *Slave Populations of the British Caribbean, 1807–1834.* 2d ed. Mona, Jamaica: Univ. of the West Indies Press.

————. 1995b. *Slave Population and Economy in Jamaica, 1807–1834.* 2d ed. Mona, Jamaica: Univ. of the West Indies Press.

Hood, J. Edward. 1996. Social Relations and the Cultural Landscape. In *Landscape Archaeology: Reading and Interpreting the American Historical Landscape,* ed. Rebecca Yamin and Karen Bescherer Metheny, 121–46. Knoxville: Univ. of Tennessee Press.

Howson, Jean E. 1990. Social Relations and Material Culture: A Critique of the Archaeology of Plantation Slavery. *Historical Archaeology* 24 (4): 78–91.

Jackson, Louise M. 1994. Cloth, Clothing, and Related Paraphernalia: A Key to Gender Visibility in the Archaeological Record of Russian America. In *Those of Little Note: Gender, Race, and Class in Historical Archaeology,* ed. Elizabeth Scott, 27–53. Tucson: Univ. of Arizona Press.

Kryder-Reid, Elizabeth. 1994. "With Manly Courage": Reading the Construction of Gender in a Nineteenth-Century Religious Community. In *Those of Little Note: Gender, Race, and Class in Historical Archaeology,* ed. Elizabeth Scott, 97–114. Tucson: Univ. of Arizona Press.

————. 1996. The Construction of Sanctity: Landscape and Ritual in a Religious Community. In *Landscape Archaeology: Reading and Interpreting the American Historical Landscape,* ed. Rebecca Yamin and Karen Bescherer Metheny, 228–48. Knoxville: Univ. of Tennessee Press.

Laborie, P. J. 1798. *The Coffee Planter of Saint Domingo.* London: T. Caddell and W. Davies.

Leone, Mark, and Parker B. Potter Jr. 1988. Introduction: Issues in Historical Archaeology. In *The Recovery of Meaning: Historical Archaeology in the Eastern United States,* ed. Mark Leone and Parker B. Potter Jr., 1–20. Washington, D.C.: Smithsonian Institution Press.

Lewis, Matthew. 1929 [1834]. *Journal of a West Indian Proprietor, 1815–17.* Edited with an introduction by Mona Wilson. Boston: Houghton Mifflin.

Little, Barbara J. 1992. Text-Aided Archaeology. In *Text-Aided Archaeology,* ed. Barbara J. Little, 1–6. Boca Raton: CRC Press.

———. 1994. "She Was . . . an Example to Her Sex": Possibilities for a Feminist Historical Archaeology. In *Historical Archaeology of the Chesapeake,* ed. Paul A. Shackel and Barbara J. Little, 189–204. Washington, D.C.: Smithsonian Institution Press.

———. 1997. Expressing Ideology without a Voice, or Obfuscation and the Enlightenment. *International Journal of Historical Archaeology* 1 (3): 225–41.

Long, Edward. 1774. *The History of Jamaica.* London.

Mintz, Sidney, and Douglas Hall. 1960. *The Origins of the Jamaican Internal Marketing System.* New Haven: Yale Univ. Publications in Anthropology.

Moitt, Bernard. 1995. Women, Work, and Resistance in the French Caribbean during Slavery, 1700–1848. In *Engendering History: Caribbean Women in Historical Perspective,* ed. Verene Shepherd, Bridget Bereton, and Barbara Baily, 155–75. New York: St. Martins Press.

Morrissey, Marietta. 1989. *Slave Women in the New World: Gender Stratification in the Caribbean.* Lawrence: Univ. of Kansas Press.

Reeves, Matthew. 1997. "By Their Own Labor": Enslaved Africans' Survival Strategies on Two Jamaican Plantations. Ph.D. diss., Syracuse Univ.

Rotman, Deborah L., and Michael S. Nassaney. 1997. Class, Gender, and the Built Environment: Deriving Social Relations from Cultural Landscapes in Southwest Michigan. *Historical Archaeology* 32 (2): 42–62.

Roughley, Thomas. 1823. *The Jamaican Planter's Guide.* London: Longman, Hurst, Rees, Orme and Brown.

Scott, Elizabeth. 1994. Through the Lens of Gender: Archaeology, Inequality, and Those "of Little Note." In *Those of Little Note: Gender, Race, and Class in Historical Archaeology,* ed. Elizabeth Scott, 3–24. Tucson: Univ. of Arizona Press.

Seifert, Donna J. 1991a. Gender in Historical Archaeology. *Historical Archaeology* 25 (4).

———. 1991b. Within Sight of the White House: The Archaeology of Working Women. *Historical Archaeology* 25 (4): 82–108.

———. 1994. Mrs. Starr's Profession. In *Those of Little Note: Gender, Race, and Class in Historical Archaeology,* ed. Elizabeth Scott, 149–73. Tucson: Univ. of Arizona Press.

Shackel, Paul A. 1992. Probate Inventories in Historical Archaeology: A Review and Alternatives. In *Text-Aided Archaeology,* ed. Barbara J. Little, 195–203. Boca Raton: CRC Press.

Sheridan, Richard B. 1985. *Doctors and Slaves: A Medical and Demographic History of Slavery in the British West Indies, 1680–1834.* Cambridge: Cambridge Univ. Press.

Singleton, Theresa. 1990. The Archaeology of the Plantation South: A Review of Approaches and Goals. *Historical Archaeology* 24 (4): 70–77.

———. 1992. Using Written Records in the Archaeological Study of Slavery, an Example from the Butler Island Plantation. In *Text-Aided Archaeology*, ed. Barbara J. Little, 55–66. Boca Raton: CRC Press.

Spencer-Wood, Suzanne M. 1991. Toward an Historical Archaeology on Materialistic Social Reform. In *The Archaeology of Inequality*, ed. Randall H. McGuire and Robert Paynter, 231–86. Oxford: Basil Blackwell.

———. 1996. Feminist Historical Archaeology and the Transformation of American Culture by Domestic Reform Movements, 1840–1925. In *Historical Archaeology and the Study of American Culture*, ed. Lu Ann De Cunzo and Bernard L. Herman, 397–445. Winterthur, Del.: Henry Francis DuPont Winterthur Museum.

Stewart, John. 1969 [1823]. *A View of the Past and Present State of the Island of Jamaica*. New York: Negro Univ. Press.

Thome, James A., and J. Horace Kimball. 1838. *Emancipation in the West Indies. A Six Months' Tour in Antigua, Barbados, and Jamaica in the Year 1837*. New York: American Anti-Slavery Society.

Trouillot, Michel-Rolf. 1995. *Silencing the Past: Power and the Production of History*. Boston: Beacon Press.

Wall, Diana diZerega. 1994. *The Archaeology of Gender: Separating the Spheres in Urban America*. New York: Plenum.

Wehner, Karen Bellinger. 1997. Through the Lens of the Built Environment: Material Life and Social Organization in a Nineteenth-Century Chesapeake Plantation Household. Master's thesis, New York Univ.

Wylie, Alison. 1991. Gender Theory and the Archaeological Record: Why Is There No Archaeology of Gender? In *Engendering Archaeology: Women and Prehistory*, ed. Joan M. Gero and Margaret W. Conkey, 31–54. Oxford: Basil Blackwell.

Yentsch, Anne. 1991. The Symbolic Divisions of Pottery: Sex-Related Attributes of English and Anglo-American Household Pots. In *The Archaeology of Inequality*, ed. Randall H. McGuire and Robert Paynter, 192–230. Oxford: Basil Blackwell.

PART THREE

Lines Defining Class

Archaeologies of Ownership and Production

CHAPTER NINE

Building Biographies

SPATIAL CHANGES IN DOMESTIC STRUCTURES DURING THE TRANSITION FROM FEUDALISM TO CAPITALISM

Patricia Hart Mangan

If space can be understood as the context in which human behavior takes place and therefore helps to shape its form, then its study can illuminate changing economic, political, and ideological relationships. Demonstrating this relevance is the goal of this chapter. In particular, I focus on the role of space in the built environment as it can help us understand the historical transition from feudalism to capitalism that took place early on in Montblanc, a town in Catalonia, Spain. By explaining the manner in which the socially constructed landscapes of Montblanc served to represent and reproduce the historically changing economic, political, and ideological relations that influenced the community's development, I show how changing spatial relations in the eighteenth century expressed social distinctions based both on class and gender, and reinforced people's understanding of where they belonged in the social and physical world.

As I shall show in providing several case studies of changes in Montblanc's built environment, societal and individual conceptions of space were altered in accordance with socioeconomic variables and local traditions. In effect, space was transformed and transformative in the eighteenth-century urban landscape of Montblanc as capitalist relations of inequality and class differentiation became increasingly defining variables in people's lives. As these variables took material form, public space became private space, work space became domestic space and gendered space became redefined—and all in manners that reflected the development of capitalism (for similar studies in other contexts, see Delle 1998, Johnson 1996, McGuire 1988, 1991, Orser 1988, Paynter 1982, Yentsch 1991).

In exploring changes in the built environment I focus on the townscape and domiciles of Montblanc, where much of the medieval past is still visible. While many buildings have been renovated, most of their original structures remain and the phases of their alteration can be discerned. What we shall see, thus, in examining the changing morphological structure of various domiciles in Montblanc are important manifestations of change in the built environment that served to transform the feudal mode of production by creating new spatial forms associated with capitalist patterns of accumulation.

The conceptual framework employed in this study of Montblanc's built environment during the transition to capitalism stresses the discursive relationship between social action and social structure (Bachelard 1964; Bourdieu 1977; Lefebvre 1991; Rappaport 1982). Social structure is understood as being produced and reproduced through social action by individuals and groups, and in this study I focus specifically on how a given people reproduce their society in space (Hirsch and O'Hanlon 1995; Spain 1992).[1] How do they live? Where do they live, and with whom? How do they meet their subsistence needs? In other words, who does what where? In addressing these questions, I analyze the materiality of social life, a materiality which pivots on the productive forces and social relations that enable a society to reproduce itself (Marx 1970; Wolf 1982). It is to a sketch of these relations under feudalism and capitalism that I now turn.

THE SPATIAL CORRELATES OF FEUDALISM AND CAPITALISM IN MONTBLANC

Before turning to the data, let me briefly lay out some of the historical, economic, and spatial correlates of both feudalism and capitalism.

Feudalism

Under feudalism the peasantry had direct access to the means of production (land), while the ruling class extracted surplus in the form of rent through a variety of extra-economic means (Duby 1974). Feudal relationships encompassed a bundle of political-legal ties, customary obligations, and more blatantly coercive means by which lords appropriated surplus from the peasantry (Bloch 1962, 1967).

In economic terms, the feudal system of production was primarily concerned with meeting subsistence rather than market needs; use value predominated over exchange value. Land was most often transmitted by inheritance and rarely sold. Labor power was individually owned and, for most people, was accompanied by local legal restrictions. Ultimately, by the twelfth century, labor services were replaced by taxation as the primary form of feudal rent (Hilton 1984). Peasants increasingly were taxed for the use of various monopolies that the lord owned. Monopolies, both domestic and legal in nature, included the right to access oil and grape presses, cereal mills, and ovens, as well as judicial services granting the right to marry or bury one's dead. Steadily, feudal exploitation was transformed from one of obligation regarding vassalage, military, and labor services, to one of payment of labor rent and dues as calculated by the amount of land held by the peasantry (Anderson 1974).

By the close of the High Middle Ages (1000–1300), significant changes had occurred in feudal society. Most importantly there was a change in the appropriation of surplus labor, in which money rents replaced labor services as the primary form of rent. In effect, changes in labor extraction from the peasant by the lord had altered the social relations that had constituted serfdom. Despite these changes, by the late Middle Ages (1300–1500), the basic tenets of feudal society still remained—that is, the domination of a small, landowning class over the peasantry in which the former continued to extract surplus value via jurisdictional means (Bloch 1967).

While these changes in feudal relations between lord and peasant have been understood by some as a form of peasant enfranchisement (Hilton 1976a), this conclusion is hard to reach if one looks at the built environment. An analysis of space shows that it was increasingly manipulated to perpetuate and enhance the exploitative relationship between the peasantry and the landowning class during the feudal period in Western Europe. Significantly, the enduring webs of asymmetrical relationships that characterized the social structure of feudalism developed within, and were reinforced by, the use of the landscape (Dodgshon 1987). The economic, political, and social hierarchy of feudalism also depended on a hierarchy of space and land use rights in which the smallholder both extracted surplus from his subordinates and paid out part of this surplus to his superiors. Political and economic integration, along with the stability and growth of the feudal mode of production, were directly tied to spatial hierarchies: individuals were granted access to and surplus from distinct spatial areas. The boundedness of feudal space, coupled with packed settlements and a relatively stable political environment, contributed to a particular form of exploitation of the peasants by the lords. And so while variation existed across time and space, feudalism can be generally understood as a vertically integrated economic and political system that was spatially characterized by a modular, relatively homogeneous, and regulated built environment.

Capitalism

The development of capitalism entailed the replacement of feudal relations of landed property with those that were based on the accumulation of capital. As mentioned previously, under feudalism the use of land was granted to the peasants in exchange for payment in rent, labor services, or in kind. The commutation of labor services to money rents forced an increase in the sale of peasant surplus production on the market, which encouraged further increase in commodity consumption by both landlords and peasants alike (Hobsbawm 1976). Landlords, in turn, encouraged rents to be paid in money (Duby 1974, 221; Hilton 1975). During this process a critical change occurred as land came to be viewed increasingly as a financial asset and as a commodity. Landlords soon began to lease, and then to buy and sell land.

One of the central changes occurring during the demise of feudal socio-economic relations and the subsequent rise of capitalist relations was the relaxing of regulated markets and the emergence of competitive price fixing. This trend is best understood as the incorporation of large-scale exchange relations, which entailed a broader integration of industries operating at the regional or continental scale (Braudel 1960, 1982; Thompson 1964, 1983; Wallerstein 1974, 1979). Local processes, including, for example, which crops to grow and sell, also encouraged involvement in new competitive markets, which contributed to the eventual shift in the production of commodities for exchange rather than use (Kriedte et al. 1981)

Capitalism as an economic system involves a process whereby laborers sell their labor power as a commodity, and in which profit is achieved through the exchange of commodities produced by laborers. However, surplus value is not realized solely by the exploitation of labor within the production process; the spatial integration of distribution is also very important in assuring the realization of a profit. The costs of production are compounded by costs of distribution, and the greater distance that needs to be overcome generally correlates with higher prices (Harvey 1982, 1985). Flexibility in the settlement patterns of the laborers becomes necessary as they are expected to go where there is work, following the trail of capital on its path toward accumulation. Thus, the inception and maintenance of the capitalist system generally results in considerably more geographical mobility in the population.

Much has been written about the transition from feudalism to capitalism (Aston and Philpin 1985; Brenner 1978; Dobb 1963; Hilton 1976b; Sweezy 1976). Space does not allow for a lengthy discussion of the complexities of this transition, but certain points bear examination with respect to the present research. Many scholars argue that feudal and capitalist economic and social organizations are mutually exclusive and often explain the transition from one to the other as the result of external forces (Pirenne 1952; Sweezy 1976). In sharp contrast, others understand the aforementioned transition in processual terms and posit that social systems can be and often are transformed by their own internal contradictions (Giddens 1979; Godelier 1977; Hilton 1975; Hobsbawm 1976). The built environment, however, gives evidence to support the position that the transition from feudalism to capitalism was not the replacement of one separate and competing mode of production by another. Spatial analysis of Montblanc clearly shows that feudalism and incipient capitalism coexisted locally and regionally while competing for the relations and forces of production, and for access to and the definition of space.

Along these same lines, when discussing the development of capitalist forces and relations of production, the "urban" centers are given precedence as the crucibles of action. The idea that urbanization takes place with little or no input from the rural countryside is problematic in its assumption of the autonomy of the urban center. In fact, the dichotomy between urban versus rural spheres of activity is historically inaccurate (Chalklin and Havinden 1974; Merrington 1976). Furthermore, this city versus country opposition is also anachronistic with respect to feudal society since the primary geosocial relationship was between town (with the city being the direct outcome of capitalism [Weber 1958]) and country and because the relationship itself was significantly more symbiotic than it was hierarchical. This distinction is important because towns were not always havens of privilege and freedom, nor was the countryside always the bastion of feudal exploitation (Brenner 1985a, 1985b; Holton 1986).

The emphasis, rather, should be placed on the similarities of social life as experienced in the town and country. While towns were perhaps the loci of exchange relations, to posit them as the center of production as well would deny the very significant amount of production that occurred in the countryside (Saunders 1981).

A study of spatial relations in Montblanc, a rural Catalonian town, clearly indicates that capitalism and its related forces and relations of production are not to be found exclusively in the large towns of medieval Europe. It is to this study that I now turn.

MONTBLANC: ITS HISTORY

Montblanc is a walled town located in rural southern Catalonia in the province of Tarragona; it is approximately 100 kilometers southwest of Barcelona and 35 kilometers west of Tarragona, both of which are port cities on the Mediterranean (map 9.1). During the late Middle Ages Montblanc enjoyed an extremely powerful role as an entrepôt, as it was midway along the main route between Tarragona and Lleida, a prominent city along the Catalonia-Aragon border. Furthermore, Montblanc was a ducal city where the king and queen of the Crown of Aragon would hold the *Corts*, or judicial courts; its location ten kilometers to the east of Poblet, one of the most powerful Cistercian monasteries in all of Catalonia, provided it with even more historical and geographical importance.

Southern Catalonia, conquered by the Moslems in the eighth century, was gradually reconquered and recolonized by the Christians of the Carolingian dynasty in the eleventh century (Lewis 1965). By the beginning of the twelfth century, the area around Montblanc was pockmarked with small settlements, castles, and defensive outposts (Miró i Esplugas 1983). Montblanc was founded in 1162 by a royal decree as one of many fortified settlements on the Christian frontier. The development of Montblanc proceeded apace, spurred on by royal concessions that were granted by the monarchy. The earliest construction, which dates to the late twelfth and thirteenth century, include a church, three convents, a hospital, a notary's office, a marketplace, a cemetery, and various neighborhoods, including a Jewish quarter (Bofarull i Sans 1898; Palau i Dulcet 1931; Poblet i Civit 1922–31).

Growth continued throughout the following centuries, with the fourteenth and early fifteenth being periods of cultural, economic, and architectural florescence for Catalonia as it accumulated wealth from extensive maritime activities throughout the Mediterranean (Vicens Vives 1969). During

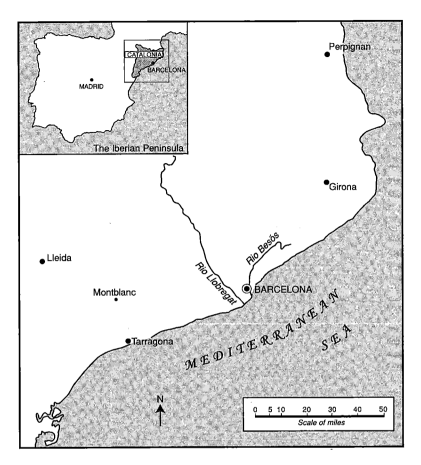

Map 9.1. Montblanc, Catalonia, Spain.

this time, the royalty and their entourages visited Montblanc frequently, holding the celebrated *Corts* and generally showering the inhabitants with favors
and privileges (Canto i Espinach 1894). Public buildings constructed in
Montblanc during the fourteenth and fifteenth centuries included baths,
additional churches, numerous plazas, and a prison. In order for the town to
better defend itself against military attack, the renovation and expansion of
the ramparts that encircled the town were commissioned in the late fourteenth century (Pallàs i Arisa 1967).

  Much of the urban nucleus of present-day Montblanc was constructed
by the end of the fourteenth century. By this time, the Carrer Major, or Main
Street, traversed the town on an east-west axis, and the Plaça Major, or Main

Plaza, served as the other main nuclei of communication and exchange. The plaza was flanked on all sides by municipal offices and impressive stone structures and was also where the weekly market took place. Narrow, winding, cobblestone streets radiated off the central plaza and the upper stories of the structures shielded the sun and light. Even today, upon moving out into the town, one is met by a very compact, mazelike network of streets lined with densely packed houses.

Many of the formal buildings, including palaces, built during Montblanc's heyday in the thirteenth and fourteenth centuries, and which still stand, speak to the wealth of its medieval history. Stylistically, Gothic architecture predominates in the most impressive, well-built structures, both secular and sacred. These architectural gemstones, complete with grounded columns and arches, as well as soaring towers and spires, were the symbolic and material manifestations of petrified wealth that the Catalan aristocracy and merchant class enjoyed during this period of medieval grandeur and prosperity (Villar 1977a; Vicens Vives 1967, 1969).

By the middle of the fifteenth century, however, Montblanc's fortunes were declining, as was much of Catalonia. The combined effects of two civil wars, ravages of the plague, and economic crises left Montblanc's population and infrastructure devastated. Documentary evidence (Albin Sola 1980; Bofarull i Sans 1898; Palau i Dulcet 1931) reveals that many of the houses, churches, and public structures, as well as the ramparts, were badly damaged and in desperate need of repair at this time. During the "long sixteenth century" things went from bad to worse in Montblanc, as well as in the rest of Catalonia and Spain. Spain continued to lose ground internationally and economically as its colonial empire began to fragment and the royal treasury, acquired from the traffic of gold and silver from its colonies, was squandered (Vilar 1967).

The remaining years of the seventeenth century continued much as they had begun with Montblanc and Catalonia mired in an economic and social quagmire. This was the period of Cervantes's Don Quixote, in which Spain's inhabitants dreamed of times of former glory. The final blow was dealt by the last Hapsburg ruler of Spain, Charles II, who ruled from 1665 to 1700 and who was incompetent and unable to exercise control or authority over the various domains within his kingdom (Kamen 1980). Catalonia and Spain suffered under the weight of his decadence during the closing decades of the seventeenth century, a decadence which manifested itself in increased prices and taxes imposed by a bureaucracy encumbered by the demands of a powerful aristocracy. Many emigrated at this time in search of a better life (Harrison 1978).

In 1700, when the aging Charles II lay dying, all of Europe waited nervously to see who he would choose as his successor to the Spanish throne. His choice cannot be underestimated in understanding the demise of feudal society and the development of incipient capitalism, and so I tell the story in some detail here.

As the House of Austria, or the Spanish Hapsburgs, as they were known, had ruled Spain from 1516, they fully expected one of their own to be chosen. But in the final hours of his life Charles II willed Spain and all of its possessions to a young Bourbon prince, Philip II, the grandson of King Louis XIV of France. What looked like a flattening of the Pyrenees and a strengthened union between France and Spain was simultaneously perceived as a call to arms by the rest of Europe. Within a year of Philip's ascension to the throne, war broke out on the continent (Lynch 1989).

Most of all, the Spanish populace feared the centralizing tendencies of the Bourbons and the effect they would have on the privileges enjoyed by many of the country's autonomous regions. Catalonia, along with its neighboring provinces of Valencia and Aragon, were determined to preserve Spain's historic traditions and judicial policies that guaranteed them numerous political and economic privileges, and they swiftly aligned themselves with the Hapsburg heir. By the war's end in 1714, Catalonia found itself on the losing side and under the thumb of a resentful and ever more powerful Philip II. As feared, one of Philip II's first actions was to jettison the regional charters that had for so long embodied the autonomy enjoyed by many of the regional provinces, especially those on the Spanish periphery. In their place a system of reforms known as the Nueva Planta (New Ground Plan) was instituted (Mercader i Riba 1951). Included was the reconfiguration of local government and territories and the replacement of middle-class guilds as representatives of municipal government by members of the elite class (Camps i Arboix 1963). In addition, a new tax known as the *cadastro* (*cadastre* in Catalan) was implemented that appropriated funds from each region in Spain relative to its wealth. Since Catalonia had long enjoyed greater relative prosperity than that of the interior provinces, its tax was substantial and, not surprisingly, met with great resentment.

Within the first decades of the eighteenth century, Bourbon royal authority increased and the absolutist state effectively exercised hegemonic control over all of the provinces of Spain (Lynch 1989). The central government and the bureaucratic elite had successfully wrestled power from the aristocracy, a feat the Hapsburgs had attempted previously without success (Kamen 1980). For the first time in history Catalonia was treated much the same as other regions in Spain, but it set itself apart by engaging in a demographic and economic revival. While the population of Spain nearly doubled over the course of the eighteenth century, rising from 6 to 11 million, nearly a 100 percent growth rate (Vilar 1967), Catalonia's population rose even more strikingly, from approximately 400,000 in 1718, to 900,000 by 1787, a 120 percent growth rate (Iglésies 1967, 1974; Harrison 1978).[2] In addition to an increase in the labor force and, subsequently, in pro- duction, which this demographic boom represented, technological advances also proceeded apace. People were reclaiming new lands and exploiting them more efficiently, and processes of production, distribution, and consumption changed as commercial activities became oriented toward national and inter- national markets.

Significantly, the economic recovery experienced during the early mod- ern period in Catalonia did not develop homogeneously throughout Spain. The transformation of the feudal subsistence-based economy to one in which commercial agriculture boomed, and subsequently underwrote industrial capitalism, occurred most actively along the eastern periphery of Spain, prin- cipally in Valencia and Catalonia (Harrison 1978; Vicens Vives 1967). Not only did these areas produce large quantities of value-added exports, specifically wine and brandy, but they were also able to avail themselves of the maritime industry located in the port cities along the Mediterranean coast.

In an ironic twist of fate, Catalonia's economic renaissance during the eighteenth century was the result of its ability to take advantage of many of the reform policies instituted in the New Ground Plan, policies which were originally intended to repress regional wealth and autonomy by taxation and the denial of age-old rights and privileges. The agrarian recovery began in the countryside and depended on the cultivation of wheat and vineyards (Altisent 1968; Villar 1977b). However, during the course of the century, the production of foodstuffs, in particular cereals, eventually gave way almost exclusively to the increased cultivation of vines (Ardit et al. 1980).

Surprisingly, it was the lower-class peasant households which, despite having the fewest resources with which to engage in economic speculation, took the risk of investing their time, labor, and no doubt limited assets in the cultivation of grapes and, thereby, took a tremendous economic risk; they gambled their "daily bread," so to speak, on the possibility of making money. As a consequence of moving away from polycrop toward monocrop cultivation, Catalonia relied more and more on the import of cereals, both from Spain's interior as well as from foreign markets, while it increased the production, export, distribution, and, ultimately, profit of grapes and their by-products, wine and brandy (Lynch 1989; Vilar 1967).

The economic boom that Catalonia experienced throughout the eighteenth century, which in effect was the early phases of nascent capitalism, served as a model for much of the rest of Spain and Europe (Villar 1962; Tortella Casares 1975). While specific social classes benefited from profits made in agriculture, specifically the sale of grapes, wine, and brandies, it appears that an increase in the standard of living and even in capital gain was experienced by a large percentage of the Catalan population in both urban and rural areas (Harrison 1978). Much of the capital that was realized was the result of extensive international trade, especially with the American colonies, but that is another story.

THE BUILT ENVIRONMENT OF MONTBLANC

The socioeconomic and demographic boom that characterized much of the eighteenth century effected major transformations in the social structure of Montblanc (Grau i Pujol 1988; Solé i Maseres 1982). These social changes and their spatial correlates can be studied via an analysis of building biographies and tax and census records—the cadastros—which the Bourbons recorded from 1731 to 1844. Building biographies document the arrangement and use of space in a given structure over time, as well as when, where, and by whom a building was constructed. The cadastros provide a wealth of economic and demographic data. The cadastros that I analyzed—1731, 1778, and 1825—classify three distinct kinds of houses, first (upper), second (middle), and third (lower) class houses. These designations were assigned according to a house's condition, building materials, and size and location (Porta i Balanyà 1986, 78).[3] After a structure was substantially renovated it was often reclassified as belonging to a higher class in a subsequent cadastro. The population of Montblanc, as estimated from the cadastros, nearly tripled over the course of the eighteenth century; in 1717 it was approximately 896, the lowest it had been since the late fourteenth century, and climbed to just over 3,100 in 1787 (Iglésies 1967, 1974).

Although certain neighborhoods in Montblanc were dominated by the presence of first-, second-, or third-class structures, they also included houses of the other classes. The one exception was the oldest neighborhood in town, the area surrounding the Plaça Major, which was built in the late twelfth and thirteenth centuries. The majority of these structures were assigned first-class status and were differentiated by their expensive building materials, namely stone, and the amount of space they occupied.[4] Many of these structures were constructed with arcades and porticos supported by stone columns that created roofed, open spaces on the ground floor of the buildings. These open, well-lit areas no doubt represented and constituted a spatial extension of the plaza and the markets and allowed for sheltered social and economic exchanges. None of the structures on the plaza are entirely freestanding, but a high number are located on corners. Corner houses were prized because they shared only one or two walls with another structure and because their openness and greater number of windows and doors allowed for increased ventilation and natural light. Other first-class houses, which were built in the fourteenth and fifteenth centuries and located elsewhere, particularly along Carrer Major, extended laterally from one street through to the next. Generally, both sidewalls were shared with other houses, but windows and doors were usually located on both the front and back facades. All first-class houses contained three floors.

Second- and third-class houses shared many common characteristics, and one observes far less structural differentiation between them than between first- and second-class houses. Second- and third-class houses were found scattered throughout the town, but they dominated the peripheral areas closest to the ramparts. The floor plan common to most second- and third-class structures was long and narrow. The facade facing the street had a narrow frontage. These houses were usually flanked on both sides by similar, sometimes identical, structures and shared their posterior wall with another house that was entered from a parallel street, such that the two houses were back to back. This house design, which dates to the High Middle Ages, limited both ventilation and light. The large majority of second- and third-class houses contained three floors, although some houses in each of these classes contained only two floors.

Most first-class houses were constructed entirely from cut stone. Some first-class houses used stone for the first floor and used a mixture of dirt, gravel, and small stones known as *tàpia* for the other floors. *Tàpia* walls were formed when the large slabs of the earthen mixture had dried; the exterior walls were then covered with plaster. Third-class houses were made almost exclusively of *tàpia* and some of wood. The facade of first-class houses often exhibited a family shield carved into the stone lintel. Windows in first-class houses were located on all floors and on all sides of the structure, thereby admitting a considerable amount of light. Windows in second- and third-class houses were also located on all floors; the windows on the ground floor and on the top floor were small, whereas the windows on the second floor tended to be large. The doorways in the facade of first-class houses were large and wide and consisted of two adjoining doors. This style was used to accommodate the width of a carriage, which most first-class households owned. For pedestrian use, a smaller door was built within the panel of one of the larger doors. Second- and third-class houses almost exclusively contained one door, which was small and narrow. Balconies, most of which were small and rarely, if ever, used, were located exclusively in first-class houses.

With respect to the interior of houses, first-class houses exhibited a lot of variation while second- and third-class houses conformed to a given plan. First-class houses, which were generally at least twice the size of their lower-class counterparts, were practically always constructed with a central stairwell. The stairwell was open and ascended from the ground floor to the top floor. First-class houses were also frequently constructed with a walled-in courtyard, a feature that was absent in all second- and third-class structures. Structurally, second-class houses more closely resembled third-class houses than first-class houses. Due to the construction of the buildings, the interior spatial arrangement of second- and third-class houses was long and narrow.

One of the commonalties exhibited by all the classes, although in varying degree, was the presence of a *botiga* on the ground floor. A *botiga* is a small store containing a variety of food items, including olives, oil, nuts, and wine. Analysis of the thirty-two households listed in the 1731 *cadastre* that housed *botigas* shows the following breakdown according to class: sixteen *botigas* in first-class structures (n = 33); four *botigas* in second-class structures (n = 91); and two *botigas* in third-class structures (n = 160) (Porta i Balanyà 1986, 171–72). The spatial use and function of the upper floors in first-class houses revealed no consistent pattern.

The second floor most often contained some or all of the following rooms: a kitchen, the equivalent to a parlor, a study or library, a workshop, and perhaps bedrooms; the third floor usually contained all bedrooms, although studies and workshops were also commonly located on this floor. In terms of room location and function, the use of space in second- and third-class structures resembled one another greatly. The second floor almost always contained a common room in the front of the structure, distinguishing this room as being the only one on that floor to have windows. Behind this room was the kitchen, and farther back small bedrooms separated from the former and from one another by a wall and a doorway. This design of the floor plan, commonly known nowadays as a "shot gun" entailed the movement through one room in order to access the one behind it. The top floor of almost all second- and third-class houses also conformed to the same blueprint. This floor, referred to as the attic, was usually unfinished—that is, with exposed beams and rafters and an absence of plaster. This top floor was used for storage of agricultural surplus and tools, as a place to keep poultry, and as an area to collect water.

Given this understanding of the kinds of houses existing in Montblanc, how, then, did the built environment change over time? In the three case studies that follow, what emerges is the construction of new kinds of spaces demarcating the public and private domains, the work and domestic contexts, and the gendered and neutral dimensions of life.

The Towers

One of the major changes occurring in the built environment of Montblanc during the eighteenth century was the redefinition of public domains into private domains, as evidenced by the reorganization of space in the towers of the wall that encircled Montblanc. The wall is approximately 16 meters high, measures approximately 1,500 meters in length, and has thirty-four towers located at irregular intervals (Guarro 1908). By the eighteenth century, the ramparts that circumscribed Montblanc no longer served a military function. In an effort to increase revenue, the municipality decided to lease the towers on the basis of an *emfiteusi* contract, or hereditary lease. Approximately twenty of the thirty-four towers were leased, renovated, and occupied by about thirty families from 1744 until 1814, a period of seventy years. A deposit was paid by the tenants to the municipality, but the property itself remained in the hands of the local government, which mandated what structural changes could and could not take place.

The municipality reserved the right to collect annual taxes and 10 percent of all payments on any future property transactions. The members of the municipality were elite individuals in Montblanc, generally professional men who had been appointed to office by the dictates of the Bourbon's New Ground Plan. These were men who had different interests at stake than members of the middle-class guilds who were those who had previously presided over municipal affairs.

The towers were not individually listed in any of Montblanc's *cadastros*—

presumably because they were not privately owned, but rather owned by the municipality. Perhaps by virtue of their not being listed, no tax on them was recorded as paid to the state coffers. Thus, I must assign them a "class" by myself and have decided on a fourth-class status by virtue of their extremely small size.

The lease histories of some of the towers provide examples of how space that had once been conceptualized as public was transformed by the local municipality into private domestic space that could be commodified and leased. In order to make the towers inhabitable, floors, stairs, a roof, and one wall were constructed. As the primary structures already existed, relatively little time, labor, and capital needed to be invested in order for this space to be inhabitable. The municipality stipulated that the original structure—that is, the three walls that formed part of the ramparts, was not to be altered in any way. These ordinances were obviously ignored at times since notarial records document that fines were charged and paid by townsfolk who violated the building code by constructing windows or doors in the back wall of the tower (AHT PNM 3649, 111v–113).

In profile the towers are tall and very narrow. Most measure approximately 16 meters high by 5 meters wide and 4.40 meters deep. The stone walls of the towers are thick, averaging approximately 40 centimeters, thereby reducing the interior dimensions of the rooms considerably. From my measurements of the interiors of ten towers that were inhabited during the eighteenth century, the average floor space per floor measured approximately 4.2 by 3.6 meters. The interior surface area was even further reduced as space was used for stairways leading from one story to another.

Each tower contained four floors and each floor contained one room. The ground floor was known as the *entrada,* or entrance, and housed animals and tools. The first floor housed the *cuina,* or kitchen, and doubled as a bedroom during the night. The second floor was referred to as the *sala,* or the sleeping quarters. The top floor, as in other residences, was known as the *golfes,* or attic, which, in the case of the towers, was more like a garret. This floor, the largest of all, since only half as much floor space was taken up by the stairwell, was where crops and secondary products such as wine and olive oil were stored, along with straw for the animals and perhaps live poultry. Each floor contained a window that was built into the front facade. Most towers, although not all, also contained a small narrow window in the rear wall at the top of the tower that had originally served as a sentinel's post from which the goings-on outside the town were observed.

In 1744, the first tower was leased to Francesc Sabater under the condition that he renovate the basic structure while building the front wall in order to make it an enclosed and habitable structure (Guarro 1904, 1908). Sabater paid twelve lliures for the lease of the tower; his occupation was not listed. In the next recorded lease, a decade later, in 1754, the mayor and town councilors are said to have leased a "piece of land and a tower" to the Confraria de la Sang, the Confraternity of the Blood (Guarro 1904). Then, in 1760, there was a boom in the desirability of the towers as the town council leased an additional ten towers to various individuals in the months of October and November. Among those leasing the towers at this time were Andreau and Teresa Albareda, *pagès i muller* (peasant farmer and wife), listed as inhabitants of Montblanc who were ceded the tower next to the Portal del Carlà. Francesc Bordell, the next individual listed in the documents, was also recorded as an inhabitant of Montblanc and a peasant farmer. The subsequent entries are very similar: Pere Joan Forcades, Carlos Foguet, Joseph Muró, Joseph Jordan, and Tomàs Sabate all leased towers, and all were peasant farmers of Montblanc. Anton Escoter, although born in Rojals, a small mountain community to the south of Montblanc, was listed as an inhabitant of Montblanc; he was a woodcutter. Pau Boquer, another resident of Montblanc, is, as we shall see, an important exception, for his occupation is listed as doctor. One wonders why he was leasing a tower or if he ever planned to live in it himself.

In 1772 the municipality leased Joan Llobet the tower next to the gate of San Antoni, which bordered the small industrial neighborhood that was growing outside the northern boundary of the wall known as the Raval, for the price of 250 lliures (AHT PNM 3671, 186–87). The municipality stipulated that Llobet had to "improve the condition of the tower that was almost entirely in ruins" and pay tax to the Ajuntament, or town government, every year on the Day of All Saints, November 1 (AHT PNM 3671, 186). The following year, in 1773, the first tower to be leased, in 1744 for a mere 12 lliures, was released, this time for 165 lliures, a considerably lower price than what Llobet paid, but a lot more than what it went for twenty-nine years earlier (AHT PHM 3735, 42–43).

These sample entries convey the social position of individuals who leased the towers. The majority were peasant farmers. The records do not, however, specify why these farmers were renting the towers. Were they landless laborers who had come to Montblanc in search of work and, without homes of their own, renting the towers? Were they individuals able to accrue an economic surplus which may have enabled them, in time, to purchase property of their own?

In fact, the number of inhabitants living in Montblanc who did not own houses increased throughout the eighteenth century (Mangan 1994). It appears that demographic growth in Montblanc during the eighteenth century in tandem with increased economic opportunities led to a housing shortage in the latter half of the eighteenth century. More importantly, the changes in the conception and use of the space of the towers seems directly related to changing socioeconomic relations characteristic of capitalism. The towers became a site of the reproduction of the labor force, a labor force that was increasingly selling its labor power as a commodity for a wage. But the redefinition and use of the towers was more than this; it was also a means by which capital could be accumulated via rent by a new class of landlords. How else can one explain the leasing of a tower in 1760 by Dr. Pau Boquer? Surely Boquer was not renting this space for himself.

The spatial relationship of rooms in the tower is represented using access graphs (fig. 9.1) (Brown 1986; Hillier and Hanson 1984). The depth of a room is the number of rooms one must pass through from the entrance to the room in question. A room with shallow depth is a room that is close to the main entrance. Permeability is the number of access points into or out of

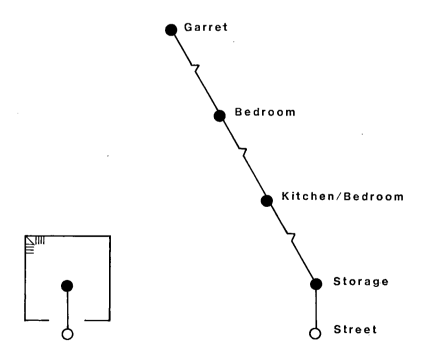

Fig. 9.1. Access graph of tower house.

a given room. A room with one entrance is *unipermeable*, a room with two or more entrances is *bipermeable*.

Old Houses Made New: Renovation of Townhouses

During the eighteenth century, the predominant morphological changes that occurred in most preexisting Montblanc houses, regardless of class designation, were renovations. Instead of tearing down houses, even those in bad need of repair, or moving from one house to another, it appears that Montblanc's inhabitants preferred to renovate their houses by (1) subdividing the interior of the structures, and (2) adding an additional floor to the structure. My analysis showed that most first-class houses did not undergo extensive renovations during this period. This can probably best be explained by the size and comfort these structures already afforded and by the fact that the owners of these homes were wealthy enough to afford the ongoing upkeep. Second-class structures, however, experienced considerable renovation across the board, as did third-class structures, albeit to a lesser extent. Following is a discussion of second-class structures as they were most systematically renovated.

Prior to the mid-eighteenth century, most second-class structures were long and narrow, internally accessed via a side stairway, and bordered on both lateral sides and in the back by similar structures. With these buildings, inhabitants were limited in their options to renovate the external structure of the building. Thus, the most common architectural change that occurred during the eighteenth century involved internal changes, specifically the removal and subsequent reconstruction of the walls that separated rooms on the second floor. The reconstruction of the walls entailed the construction of a hallway that ran the length of the structure and partitioned the kitchen and bedrooms into smaller rooms. This new division of rooms, and the access via the hallway, created a very different traffic pattern than did the previous spatial arrangement. Prior to renovation, all of the rooms on the second floor, except the bedroom at the rear of the structure, had a doorway leading into and out of them. With the construction of the hallway, rooms could no longer be entered directly one from the other. Hallways served not only as passages routing movement from one space to another but also created spatial boundaries; this new spatial division of rooms reflected and promulgated a much greater need for privacy.

The major change that took place on the third floor of many second-class structures often entailed the lowering of the ceiling and the subsequent

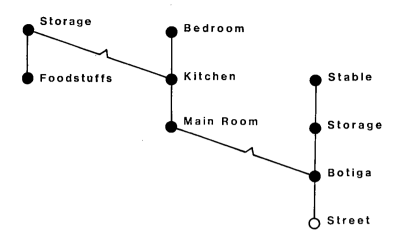

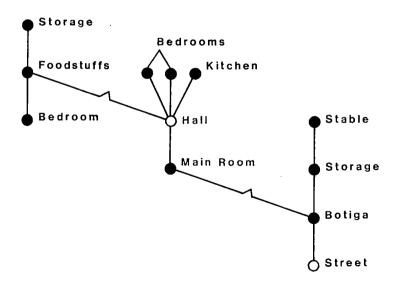

Fig. 9.2. Access graph of second-class house, before (above)
and after (below) architectural changes.

construction of an additional top floor. The third floor was finished structurally and made habitable, while the fourth floor housed the objects and activities that had previously been relegated to the third floor. Since many houses were replastered at this time, this structural change is not always apparent by examining the exterior facades of the structures. Evidence of this change is apparent, however, in the interior of many second-class houses when one examines the walls, rafters, ceiling, and roof of the third and fourth floors. Overall, the internal subdivision of structures resulted in an increase in the number of rooms and floors, in exchange for a reduction of space, light, and air within each room. These changes are represented in figure 9.2. But what else can this change in architectural form tell us?

We must understand that the spatial changes in the residential built space discussed above not only reflect socioeconomic changes operating in Montblanc society, but also the creation and facilitation of them. These structural changes were steps toward the redefinition of public and private arenas of activity. As individuals, families, and communities became involved with social reproduction in a changing economy, private space became more delineated within the domestic realm. Furthermore, the occupants of typical second-class households responded to the socioeconomic changes occurring during the eighteenth century, I would venture, by subdividing their homes in order to rent out part of them, thereby increasing their incomes. In sum, as Montblanc's urban center adapted spatially to new economic changes in society, these changes in the built environment facilitated and furthered said economic changes.

CONSTRUCTION OF NEW DOMESTIC SPACE: THE VILELLA HOUSE

Thus far I have examined how the public space of the towers was redefined and transformed into private space for habitation at a relatively low cost and high return by members of the local town government. In addition, I have presented a detailed analysis of second-class houses renovated in patterned ways. My third and last case study of the changing use of space focuses on a specific building, the Vilella residence, which I have named after the house's builder and first owner. At the time this structure was built, 1793, few other structures existed in this extramural area. More importantly, however, than its relative isolation, this structure was distinct in regard to its functional utilization of space. Looking at the access graph for the Vilella structure (fig. 9.3), one can see the pronounced difference in the location and use of rooms in this structure compared to other second-class structures.

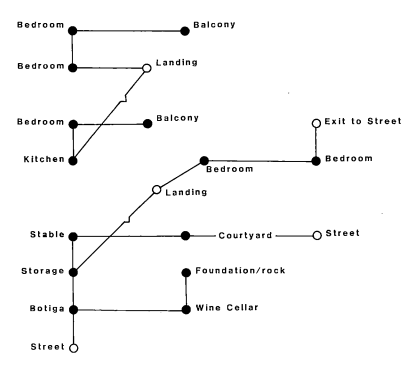

Fig. 9.3. Access graph of Vilella house.

Before elaborating on this unusual utilization of space, it should be noted that relatively little *new* construction was undertaken during the latter half of the eighteenth century, even though Montblanc was experiencing a building boom. Most construction was renovative, and the limited amount of new construction was delineated to the western rampart. Two new neighborhoods came into being in this area, the Raval to the northwest and the Serra to the southwest. The Raval, located next to a small stream, was an industrial neighborhood and included tanning operations, blacksmiths, and distilleries. Although the Raval is located only about 100 meters directly north of the Serra, it lies at considerably lower elevation since the topography climbs rather abruptly to the south along the western border of town. The neighborhood of the Serra was named in honor of the nearby *Convent de la Serra,* or Convent on the Mountain. At the close of the eighteenth century, fewer than ten structures—all domestic, private residences—existed in this neighborhood, compared to the dozens and dozens of houses built in the Raval.

Andreau Vilella initiated plans in the spring of 1793 to construct a house that would border to its west the street that led to the Convent de la Serra. The reason that the construction of Vilella's house is documented at all is due to a dispute between Vilella and his neighbor regarding exactly where he intended to build his house and exactly how high it should be (AHT PNM 3711, 116–17). Josep Anton Foguet, the neighbor, complained that the construction of Vilella's house would interfere with land he owned and cultivated and would also potentially tower above his own house. This dispute was settled when Vilella agreed to do one of two things: he would either build his house no higher than that of his neighbor's, or he would build his house farther from his neighbor's than originally intended. If Vilella agreed to build the house at a distance greater than 46 palmos, approximately 11.5 meters from Foguet's, then he "could raise the walls as high as he liked" (AHT PNM 3711, 116v). Vilella obviously agreed to Foguet's stipulations, as his house was built. Additional documents exist recording Vilella selling land in the vicinity of his home (AHT PNM 3711, 198v–199v) as well as his leasing a grain mill from the municipality (AHT PNM 3714, 210–211v).

The Vilella House in Plan

The Vilella house is located a mere 15 meters west of the ramparts, approximately 30 meters east of the Convent de la Serra, and approximately 100 meters south of the Raval. The house is located at the intersection of two streets. Its main entrance faces south and opens to the *Cami al Convent de la Serra*. Bordering the *Cami Cap al Baluard*, two side entrances face east, one of which is part of the wall of the house and ascends directly to the two adjacent rooms on the second floor, and the other is located in the wall of the courtyard, providing access into the back of the ground floor of the structure. The house itself is perhaps best classified as a three-story with a two-story wing. It is constructed of a stone foundation with *tàpia* and plaster walls supported by beams and has a flat, clay tile roof. The floor plan of the main part of the house is approximately 4 meters wide and 8 meters long; the two-story wing measures 4.5 meters wide and 3.5 meters long.

Upon entering the front door, above which is located a small cement plaque inscribed with the year 1793, one arrives at the first of three rooms located on the ground floor. The first room is documented as having housed a *botiga* from the late 1790s well into the nineteenth century.[5] Wine and brandy were stored and sold there, although it is uncertain if either was produced on the property. The production of wine demands a lot of room, and it is uncommon for individuals to produce it in their own homes (Giralt i Raventós

1952, 1980). The production of brandy, however, can be much more concentrated spatially, and it is entirely possible that individual entrepreneurs both produced and sold brandy in the domicile. Wine and brandy casks still remain on the ground floor of the Vilella residence.

The middle room was where fruits of the harvest were stored and where farm tools were kept; a hayloft was also located there. Along the far end of the eastern wall of this middle room is a stairwell that ascends to the second floor. In the rear room of the ground floor was the stable for farm animals. The eastern wall of this room contains a large door exiting into a courtyard. The courtyard composes one-quarter of the floor plan, the northeast corner, and is bordered by a wall measuring approximately two meters high that has a gate leading out to the *Cami Cap al Baluard*.

As one ascends the stairway, which is located in the middle room of the ground floor, one reaches a landing. To the left or east, through a closed doorway, two adjacent rooms are encountered. The rooms are parallel to one another on a north/south axis. The first room from the landing measures 2 meters wide by 3.5 meters long and contains a window on the south wall. Along the eastern wall of this room a door opens into a second room that borders the street; this room measures 1.5 meters wide by 3.5 meters long. On the northern wall of this room is a doorway which opens into a stairwell that descends directly to another doorway and the street.

Returning to the landing atop the stairs and to the west, one climbs two more stairs, passes through a closed doorway, and enters the kitchen. The kitchen measures 4 by 4 meters. Built into the southern wall of this room is a large window that overlooks the street; no other windows exist in this room. Adjacent to the kitchen to the north is a large bedroom that measures approximately 4 by 4.3 meters. Despite the fact that both the western and northern walls are not built against another structure, there are no windows in either wall. Off the eastern wall of the bedroom is a balcony that measures approximately 1 meter wide and 2 meters long and overlooks the courtyard. At the far end of the eastern wall of the kitchen is a flight of stairs that ascends to the third floor.

This stairwell is identical in dimensions to the stairwell located directly below it. The eastern section of the house, where the two rooms with access to the street are located on the second floor, does not have a third floor. The upper stairwell landing opens, via a closed doorway, into a bedroom with a very small window on the southern wall. This room is almost square, measuring 4 by 3.5 meters. Located to the north of this room is another bedroom, again measuring 4 by 3.5 meters. A balcony extends off the eastern wall of this room, which is located directly above the second-floor balcony.

Having described the internal layout of each floor in the Vilella house, patterns of difference regarding the use of domestic space can be discerned. The Vilella house has three entranceways, two of which lead into the ground floor, and the other, to the second floor. Although it was not uncommon for first-class houses to have a front and rear entranceway, most structures in town comparable (generally) to the second-class Vilella house had only one entrance. The location of the *botiga* directly adjacent to the street in the front section of the ground floor allowed for business transactions to be spatially circumscribed from the domestic functioning of the household. The inhabitants of the Vilella house could enter the property from the side courtyard, pass into the back room, proceed into the middle room, and ascend the stairs located therein, all without passing through the front room. In effect, the shallow depth of the front room and the bipermeability of the ground floor served to spatially separate commercial relations with customers from social relations with the family.

The courtyard is a very important space for several reasons. Aside from allowing additional access to the interior of the house via the ground floor, and thereby channeling traffic in different ways, the courtyard is an area that is laden with symbolic meaning. The fact that the courtyard exists at all in a structure that would otherwise be classified as second class makes it enigmatic as courtyards in structures within the urban nuclei were located exclusively in first-class households. Interestingly, courtyards in traditional first-class structures were very deep and private, usually located at the rear of the house and with no exit leading to the street, unlike the courtyard in the Vilella house. It appears that Vilella was consciously adapting an architectural form from elite houses to different uses. The existence of a courtyard in the Vilella house assumed new meaning within the broader context of capitalist socio-economic changes.

This new meaning is also revealed on the second floor of the Vilella house, which exhibits a very interesting arrangement of rooms. The stairwell leading up to the second floor is located in the middle of the floor plan, as was common in first-class houses. However, unlike the wide open stairwells in first-class houses, the central stairwell in the Vilella house is narrow and enclosed, resembling stairwells common to second- and third-class houses. The placement of the stairwell leading from the ground floor to the second floor also served to horizontally separate the kitchen area and the main bedroom to the north from the two adjacent rooms located in the eastern part of the structure.

The possibility exists that these two rooms were occupied by an extended household member, an offspring, a sister or brother, cousin, widowed aunt, or grandparent, for such family arrangements were typical at the time. However, the fact that the house was constructed with a separate entrance that led from these two rooms to the street was atypical and indicates forethought concerning who might access this space. If in fact these rooms were designed and constructed to house an extended family member, the social relationship of kin would not necessitate spatial segregation and a "private" entrance, features that are present in this structure.

It seems that these two rooms might have been designed as rental property. To support this contention, I would argue that the shallow depth and bipermeability of these two adjacent rooms, which provide easy access to the exterior, were designed as such for a nonfamily member. In view of the fact that Andreau Vilella engaged in numerous economic activities, collecting revenue from a grain mill and selling parcels of land, it is entirely plausible that he could afford to hire paid labor. In so doing, he could accommodate their housing needs by renting them living quarters. Conceivably, he would also be able to easily observe, if not control, the comings and goings of his ward.

There is more to be said about the way space has been changed in relation to incipient capitalism from the Vilella house. Consider, thus, the kitchen, separated from the rooms discussed above by a landing and two stairs. Comparative analysis has shown that kitchens in other structures, regardless of class, were usually located in a deeper space, behind the main sitting room. In this structure, however, the kitchen's location is shallow, though equally as permeable since it is connected via a doorway to another room and to the top floor by a stairwell. In effect, the location of the kitchen above the *botiga*, overlooking the street, places it in a more public space.

I contend that the move of the kitchen into a shallower, more public space is related to an increase in the specialization of gendered activities, particularly domestic reproduction, engaged in by women. Also, the shallow depth of the kitchen would serve to minimize the distance between the private, household space to which the tenants were given access, and the tenants' quarters. If the tenants shared meals with the family or were provided meals by the family, to be consumed in their own quarters, the location of the kitchen would spatially separate the area to which the tenants had access from the rest of the house. These activities might include food preparation and processing, but as likely they may have involved the female head of household's responsibility to serve customers purchasing from the *botiga*. From the kitchen window one could look down into the street to see if someone was there. This possibility is even more likely if women were increasingly staying home rather than going out into the fields to work.

The room behind the kitchen is the main bedroom and its location is in many ways similar to its location in other structures. The difference, however, is its position and permeability in relation to other bedrooms and the balcony that extends off the eastern side of the house. The bedroom, aside from the balcony, which must be considered apart in view of its exteriority, is the room on the second floor, which has the greatest depth. This bedroom is not transversed to access other bedrooms, but rather is segregated from these others. This spatial change can be understood as reflecting and affecting behavioral processes increasingly incorporating privacy into patterns of daily life within the family. In effect, the parents are spatially segregated from their children, who occupy sleeping quarters on the third floor.

Other architectural features that differentiate this structure include the two balconies, located one above the other on the second and third floors, which were built out over the courtyard facing east in the direction of the ramparts and the town beyond. The existence of two balconies in a structure like the Vilella house is unprecedented. Balconies, traditionally the venue of first-class structures, are understood as serving both a practical and symbolic function (Amelang 1986a, 1986b). While they let light and air into a building, thereby contributing to healthier living conditions, they are also highly decorative and connote both leisure time and high status.

A balcony can be seen as a transitional space that both creates and eliminates spatial boundaries; a balcony serves as a spatial interface. Because of its depth, the space of the balcony is difficult to access and is isolated. The spatial relationship that the balcony affords with respect to those who are on it and those in the street below, high versus low, informs, I suggest, a social hierarchy based on privilege. The social interaction that occurs on a balcony is such that both the occupants and the casual passerby can concomitantly see as well as be seen. While the space of the balcony is set apart spatially and is private, both in terms of its location in the air and within the confines of the courtyard below, it is an arena in which behavior is public.

The spatial analysis of this structure is completed with an examination of the third floor. The third floor is more or less a blueprint of the northern section of the second floor, with two square rooms adjacent to one another, but instead of a kitchen and a bedroom, two bedrooms. This floor is "finished" in the sense that it appears to have been both designed and constructed as living quarters. While the beams are still visible, the walls and ceiling were covered with plaster. Traditionally, the space of the top floor in second-class houses was reserved primarily for storage of dried goods and water. The arena for these activities has been moved downstairs in the Vilella house, to the large, bipermeable ground floor. In other words, work, along with the products and tools of labor, have become concentrated in one spatial arena, separate from the living areas.

The third floor, then, has become the domain of bedrooms. The stairwell serves as a boundary, increasing the depth of these two rooms. This pattern may be understood as part of a broader trend toward specialization and privatization of space within the household. The construction of a second balcony, located directly above the one on the second floor, serves various practical and symbolic functions. By its mere existence it reinforces the economic and symbolic message imbued in the lower, slightly larger, balcony beneath it. Each balcony allows members of age classes—parents and children—to display the same privileged social status. Young and old both have access to similar spatial arenas in which behavior can be observed and expressed.

Despite Vilella being classified as a *pagès*, or peasant farmer, in the town records dating to 1793 (AHT PNM 3778, 869v), examination of his house suggests a different story about his economic and social position. Andreau Vilella was, I propose, a member of a new class of entrepreneurs or bourgeoisie. Although not ostentatious in his display of wealth, Vilella utilized spatial forms in the construction of his home that had previously been reserved for first-class houses. He did so as to better carry out the productive and consumptive activities of the new group to which he belonged.

CONCLUDING COMMENTS

In this chapter spatial changes in the built environment have been examined in relation to social and economic processes. In effect, as capitalist relations and forces of production became more embedded in socioeconomic processes, social agents sought to redefine notions of what was public space and what was private space; what was work space and what was domestic space; and in what ways all of these spaces were gendered.

Those who redefined and commodified the urban space of the towers were the people in power, those of the municipal town government, those representing the legal system, and those representing a new type of landlord. Historical evidence from Montblanc suggests that members of this burgeoning social group began to define themselves as members of a new class, a class that saw itself differently from feudal class relations. Actions of members of this new and powerful class may best be understood in relation to the influence they exercised over the populace at large. In essence, these individuals were validated and rewarded for conceiving of space as a commodity to be rented, bought, and sold, and for having the legal right to collect payment in the form of taxes on this newly produced space.

Comparably, those who leased the towers as their private domiciles can also be seen as having actively advanced a reconceptualization of the meaning of space. In fact they did so in a most literal way by transforming the public space of the wall, a space that had for so long circumscribed and defined them as a community, into the private space of the domicile. Realms of both private and public space that had for so long defined Montblanc's medieval past were becoming commodified.

Commodification is also revealed in the renovations made to second-class structures, as formerly private space could be bought and sold by those increasingly inhabiting a world where labor was also a commodity. The compartimentalization of rooms within these structures not only allowed for increased revenue but also for increased privacy among the inhabitants.

Moreover, changes in the location of the Vilella house and the function of space within it are directly related to changing socioeconomic processes that were occurring in Montblanc at the time. This house speaks of an increasing emphasis on social solidarity within the family, of a changing gendered division of labor predicated on a new domesticity for women and of a developing petty bourgeoisie capable of claiming certain first-class privileges and distinctions. The very existence of people such as Andreau Vilella is a solid indication of a more fluid mobility typical of capitalist society; although he is classified as a peasant by ascribed status, documentary evidence clearly indicates that he was a busy entrepreneur.

What we see in all of these cases, then, is that space has provided an arena in which the means of production, distribution, circulation, and consumption could be realized and reinforced as Montblanc moved from feudalism to capitalism. It is, in this sense, an invaluable and long-overlooked focus for historical analysis.

NOTES

This article draws from my dissertation, cited in the bibliography. I would like to thank Robert Paynter, Oriol Pi-Sunyer, and Martin Wobst for comments and suggestions on previous drafts. I would also like to thank Deborah Gewertz for her careful reading on a more recent version and Amherst College for its support.

1. The study of space in strict archaeological or geographical terms involves determining the exact location of a given artifact on a Cartesian plane; the mapping of an object in space is done using Euclidean geometry. The methodological procedure involved in locating an artifact spatially entails collecting empirical measurements of a given object's horizontal and vertical coordinates, which are subsequently plotted in relation to a fixed datum; all other objects in space are located in precisely this same way. The locating of objects of material culture in space, either above or below the ground, allows the investigator to observe said objects in a three-dimensional relationship to other objects.

2. Josep Iglésies (1967) was one of the first historians to work with raw data in estimating population in Catalonia from 1365, when the first known census was taken, up through the nineteenth century. Population estimates were based on the number of *focs*, or heads of households, that existed, a method that is not without its problems. The number of individuals in a household varies across time and space and is influenced by numerous variables including famine, plague, war, poor harvests, available housing, economics, etc. Iglésies estimates that for the second half of the fourteenth century, a period of vitality and prosperity for Catalonia, the number of individuals per household was between four and five. In 1716, a period of decline, the coefficient was estimated to be 3.5, but by the late eighteenth century, a period of economic and demographic recuperation, the estimated number of individuals per household had risen to five.

3. Most of the buildings built in Montblanc prior to the eighteenth century were approximately ten meters high and contained three floors. Occasionally, houses had only two floors and, infrequently, as few as one or as many as four. In 1731, out of the 284 houses recorded in the *cadastro*, 239 had three floors, 38 had two floors, 5 had one floor, and 2 had four floors. All 33 first-class houses had three floors. The 91 second-class houses included the 2 houses with four floors, 88 houses with three floors, and only 1 house that contained two floors. A total of 160 third-class houses made up the majority; most of them contained three floors, although there were a few with only one or two floors. In Catalan vernacular, the floors of a house are known as the *baixo* or *primer pis* (bottom or first floor), the *pis principal* or *segon pis*, (main or second floor), and the *ultim pis* or *golfa* (last or attic floor). The number of floors a given structure has is not in and of itself a good indicator of class, but, rather, it is the ways in which

space was constructed and used within each structure which provide greater insight into class relations.

4. Not all first-class houses were made entirely of stone, but were rather a combination of stone, timber, and plaster. Houses built with a combination of materials used stone, usually local granite, for the foundation and first floor (Solé i Maseras pers. comm.). The upper floors were most often constructed of timber and *tàpia*. *Tàpia* is a combination of soil, gravel and small stones mixed together when wet, pressed into large molds, and dried. *Tàpia* walls are formed out of large slabs of this mixture. The exterior of the walls were then "painted" with *argamassa*, a plaster mixture, to provide a protective coat. Inside the structure, wood beams, mostly of oak, were erected to support the walls and ceilings. Second- and third-class houses were primarily constructed on stone foundations with *tàpia* and plaster walls. The roofs of these houses were supported by large wooden beams on top of which were either clay tiles or *tàpia*.

5. A *botiga* is a small store containing a variety of food, oils, and wine. *Botigas* were most frequently located in first-class houses throughout the eighteenth century. Analysis of the 1731 *cadastro* lists twenty-two houses with *botigas*. The following is a breakdown in relation to class: sixteen first-class houses (n = 33), four second-class houses (n = 91), and two third-class houses (n = 160). The 1778 and 1825 *cadastros* show that the majority of *botigas* are still located in first-class houses, but there is a steady increase in their numbers in second-class houses.

REFERENCES CITED

Arxiu Històric de Tarragona Protocol Notarial de Montblanc.

AHT PNM 3649:111v–113.

AHT PNM 3659 ff. 248v–250v.

AHT PNM 3671 ff. 186–87; 320v–321v.

AHT PNM 3711 ff. 116–17; 198v–199v.

AHT PNM 3714 ff. 210–211v.

AHT PNM 3735 ff. 42–43.

AHT PNM 3778 ff. 869–72.

Albin Sola, Luis. 1980. *Ciudad sin historia.* Manuscript on file, Ajuntament de Montblanc, Montblanc.

Altisent, A. 1968. *Aspectes de la vida agrària de Montblanc al segle XIII.* Circular del Museu-Arxiu de Montlbanc i Comarca 8:1–7.

Amelang, James. 1986a. Public Ceremonies and Private Fetes: Social Segregation and Aristocratic Culture in Barcelona, ca. 1500–1800. In *Conflict in Catalonia,* ed. G. McDonough, 17–32. Gainesville: Univ. of Florida Press.

————. 1986b. *Honored Citizens of Barcelona: Patrician Culture and Class Relations, 1490–1714.* Princeton: Princeton Univ. Press.

Anderson, P. 1974. *Passages from Antiquity to Feudalism.* London: NLB.

Ardit M., A. Balcells, and N. Sales. 1980. *Història dels paisos catalans de 1714 à 1975.* Barcelona: Dalmau.

Aston, T. H., and C. H. E. Philpin, ed. 1985. *The Brenner Debate.* Cambridge: Cambridge Univ. Press.

Bachelard, Gaston. 1964. *The Poetics of Space.* New York: Orion Press.

Bloch, Marc. 1962. *Feudal Society.* London: Routledge & Kegan Paul.

————. 1967. *Land and Work in Medieval Europe.* London: Routledge & Kegan Paul.

Bofarull i Sans, D. Francisco. 1898. Documentos para escribir una monographía de la villa de Montblanc. Memorias de la real academia de buenas letras de Barcelona, 6:423–579.

Bourdieu, Pierre. 1977. *Outline of a Theory of Practice.* Cambridge: Cambridge Univ. Press.

Braudel, Fernand. 1960. *Capitalism and Material Life.* London: Harper & Row.

————. 1982. *The Wheels of Commerce.* Vol. 2, *Civilization and Capitalism: 15th–18th Century.* New York: Harper and Row.

Brenner, Robert. 1978. Dobb on the Transition from Feudalism to Capitalism. *Cambridge Journal of Economics* 2(2): 121–40. Cambridge: Academic Press.

————. 1985a. Agrarian Class Structure and Economic Development in Pre-Industrial Europe. In *The Brenner Debate,* ed. T. H. Aston and C. H. E. Philpin, 10–63. Cambridge: Cambridge Univ. Press.

————1985b. The Agrarian Roots of European Capitalism. In *The Brenner Debate,* ed. T. H. Aston and C. H. E. Philpin, 213–327. Cambridge: Cambridge Univ. Press.

Brown, Frank. 1986. Continuity and Change in the Urban House: Developments in Domestic Space Organization in Seventeenth-Century London. *Comparative Studies in Society and History* 28 (3): 558–90.

Camps i Arboix, Joaquim de. 1963. *El decret de nova planta.* Barcelona: Dalmau.

Canto i Espinach, Ramon. 1894. Historia de la ilustre y real vila ducal de Montblanch, manuscrit inedit. 5 vols. Montblanc, Catalonia.

Chalklin, C. W., and M. A. Havinden, ed. 1974. *Rural Change and Urban Growth, 1500–1800.* London: Longman.

Delle, James A. 1998. *An Archaeology of Social Space: Analyzing Coffee Plantations in Jamaica's Blue Mountains.* New York: Plenum.

Dobb, Maurice. 1963. *Studies in the Development of Capitalism.* London: Routledge & Kegan Paul.

Dodgshon, Robert A. 1987. *The European Past: Social Evolution and Spatial Order.* London: MacMillan Education.

Duby, Georges. 1974. *The Early Growth of the European Economy: Warriors and Peasants from the Seventh to the Twelfth Century.* Ithaca: Cornell Univ. Press.

Giddens, Anthony. 1979. *Central Problems in Social Theory: Action, Structure, and Contradiction in Social Analysis.* Berkeley: Univ. of California Press.

Giralt i Raventós, E. 1952. La vitacultura anterior a la filloxera. *L'avenç* 31:50–57.

———. 1980. Les tècniques de la vitacultura anterior a la filloxera. *L'avenç* 30:64–71.

Godelier, Maurice. 1977. *Perspectives in Marxist Anthropology.* Cambridge: Cambridge Univ. Press.

Grau i Pujol, Josep M. T. 1988 L'exspansio urbanistica de Montblanc a finals del segle XVIII: L'ocupacio dels espais no edificats. *Propiedad i urbanismo.* Montblanc: Imprenta Requesens.

Guarro, Joseph. 1904. Les torres de Montblanch. *La conca de barberà* 56/57.

———. 1908. Noticies històriques des clos amurallat de Montblanch. *La conca de barberà* 252:3.

Harrison, Joseph. 1978. *An Economic History of Spain.* Manchester: Manchester Univ. Press.

Harvey, David. 1982. *The Limits to Capital.* Chicago: Univ. of Chicago.

———. 1985. The Geopolitics of Capitalism. In *Social Relations and Spatial Structures,* ed. D. Gregory and J. Urry, 128–63. New York: St. Martins Press.

Hillier, Bill, and Julienne Hanson. 1984. *The Social Logic of Space.* Cambridge: Cambridge Univ. Press.

Hilton, Rodney. 1975. *English Peasantry in the Later Middle Ages.* Oxford: Oxford Univ. Press.

———. 1976a. *The Transition from Feudalism to Capitalism,* ed. R. Hilton. London: Verso.

———. 1976b. Feudalism and the Origins of Capitalism. *History Workshop Journal* 1 (spring). Oxford: Oxford Univ. Press.

———. 1984. Feudalism in Europe: Problems for Historical Materialists. *New Left Review* 147: 84–93.

Hirsch, Eric, and Michael O'Hanlon, eds. 1995 *The Anthropology of Landscape: Perspectives on Place and Space.* Oxford: Clarendon Press.

Hobsbawm, Eric. 1976. Feudalism, Capitalism, and the Absolutist State: Review of Perry Anderson. *Our History* 68 (summer).

Holton, R. J. 1986. *Cities, Capitalism, and Civilization.* Cambridge: Allen & Unwin.

Iglésies, Josep. 1967. *La població de la conca de barberà a través de la història.* Vol. 8, *Assemblea intercomarcal d'estudiosos a Monblanc,* 75–94. Montblanc, Granollers.

———. 1974. Estadístiques de població de catalunya del primer vicenni del segle XVIII. 3 vols. Barcelona: Vives i Casajuana.

Johnson, Matthew. 1996. *An Archaeology of Capitalism.* Oxford: Basil Blackwell.

Kamen, H. 1980. *Spain in the Later Seventeenth Century.* London: Longman.

Kriedte, P., H. Medick, and J. Schlumbohm. 1981. *Industrialization before Industrialization.* Cambridge: Cambridge Univ. Press.

Lefebvre, Henri. 1991. *The Production of Space.* Oxford: Blackwell.

Lewis, Archibald R. 1965. *The Development of Southern French and Catalan Society, 718–1050.* Austin: Univ. of Texas Press.

Lynch, John. 1989. *Bourbon Spain, 1700–1808.* Cambridge: Basil Blackwell.

Mangan, Patricia Hart. 1994. *Spatial Changes in the Landscape: A Case Study of the Transition from Feudalism to Capitalism in Montblanc, Catalonia, Spain.* Ph.D. diss., Dept. of Anthropology, Univ. of Massachusetts, Amherst.

Marx, Karl. 1970 [1859]. *A Contribution to the Critique of Political Economy.* New York: International Publishers.

McGuire, Randall. 1988. Dialogues with the Dead: Ideology and the Cemetery. In *The Recovery of Meaning: Historical Archaeology in the Eastern United States,* ed. M. P. Leone and P. B. Parker Jr., 435–80. Washington, D.C.: Smithsonian Institution Press.

———. 1991. Building Power in the Cultural Landscape of Broome County, New York, 1880 to 1940. In *The Archaeology of Inequality,* ed. Randall H. McGuire and Robert Paynter, 102–24. Oxford: Basil Blackwell.

Mercader i Riba, J. 1951. La ordenación de cataluña por Felipe: La nueva planta. *Hispania* 43:257–366.

Merrington, John. 1976. Town and Country in the Transition to Capitalism. In *The Transition from Feudalism to Capitalism,* ed. R. Hilton, 170–95. London: Verso.

Miró i Esplugas, Manuel. 1983. L'agricultura medieval a la conca de barberà. *Arrels* 2:221–31.

Orser, Charles E., Jr. 1988. *The Material Basis of the Postbellum Tenant Plantation: Historical Archaeology in the South Carolina Piedmont.* Athens: Univ. of Georgia Press.

Pallàs i Arisa, Camil. 1967. *Recinte emmurallat de Montblanc.* Vol. 8, *Assemblea intercomarcal di estudiosos a Montblanc,* 111–12. Montblanc: Grannolers.

Palau i Dulcet, Antoni. 1931. *Guia de Montblanch.* Barcelona: Imprenta Romana.

Paynter, Robert. 1982. *Models of Spatial Inequality.* New York: Academic Press.

Pirenne, Henri. 1952. *Medieval Cities: Their Origins and the Revival of Trade.* Princeton: Princeton Univ. Press.

Poblet i Civit, J. 1922–31. *Notes Històriques de la Vila de Montblanch.* 3 vols. Montblanc: Indèt.

Porta i Balanyà, Josep Maria. 1986. La vila de Montblanc en el segon quart del segle XVIII. Economia, urbanisme i societat segons la documentació cadastral. Barcelona: Generalitat de Catalunya.

Rappaport, Amos. 1982. *The Meaning of the Built Environment.* Beverly Hills: Sage Publications.

Saunders, P. 1981. *Social Theory and the Urban Question.* London: Holmes Meier.

Solé i Maseres, Mateis. 1982. Síntesí històrico-urbanística. *Espitllera* 5:47–52.

Spain, Daphne. 1992. *Gendered Spaces.* Chapel Hill: Univ. of North Carolina Press.

Sweezy, Paul. 1976. A Critique. In *The Transition from Feudalism to Capitalism.* Introduction by R. Hilton, 33–56. London: Verso.

Thompson, E. P. 1964. *The Making of the English Working Class.* New York: Vintage.

———. 1978. Eighteenth Century English Society: Class Struggle without Class? *Social History* 3 (25). London: Metheun.

————. 1983. *Class Consciousness: History and Class.* Oxford: B. Blackwell.

Tortella Casares, Gabriel. 1975. *Los orígenes del capitalismo en España.* Madrid: Tecnos.

Vicens Vives, Jaime. 1967. *Approaches to the History of Spain.* Berkeley: Univ. of California.

————. 1969. *An Economic History of Spain.* Princeton: Princeton Univ. Press.

Vilar, Sergio. 1967. *Catalunya en España.* Barcelona: S. A. Ayma.

Villar, Pierre. 1962. *Catalogne dans l'Espagne moderne.* 3 vols. Paris: S.E.V.P.E.N.

————. 1977a. *Spain: A Brief History.* New York: Pergamon Press.

————. 1977b. La fi dels elements feudals i senyorials a catalunya al segle XVIII i XIX. Amb alguns punts de vista comparatius per a la resta d'Espanya i per al Roselló. *L'avenç* 1:74–80.

Wallerstein, Immanuel. 1974. *The Modern World System: Capitalist Agriculture and the Origins of the European World Economy in the Sixteenth Century.* New York: Academic Press.

————. 1979. *The Capitalist World Economy.* Cambridge: Cambridge Univ. Press.

Weber, Max. 1958. *The City.* New York: Free Press.

Wolf, Eric. 1982. *Europe and the People without History.* Berkeley: Univ. of California Press.

Yentsch, Anne. 1991. The Symbolic Divisions of Pottery: Sex-Related Attributes of English and Anglo-American Household Pots. In *The Archaeology of Inequality,* ed. Randall H. McGuire and Robert Paynter, 192–230. Oxford: Basil Blackwell.

Archives Consulted

Archivo de la Corona de Aragón, Barcelona.

Arxiu Històric Comarcal de Montblanc.

Arxiu Històric Municipal de Barcelona.

Arxiu Històric de Tarragona: Protocol Notarial de Montblanc.

Biblioteca de Catalunya, Barcelona.

Biblioteca de la Universidad de Barcelona.

CHAPTER TEN

Urban Spaces, Labor Organization, and Social Control

LESSONS FROM NEW ENGLAND'S NINETEENTH-CENTURY CUTLERY INDUSTRY

Michael S. Nassaney
Marjorie R. Abel

On a surprising number of occasions we have been asked why we wish to preserve and admire buildings where severe oppression and exploitation of working people took place
    —*Martha Zimiles and Murray Zimiles,* Early American Mills

The processes of transnationalism and globalization that began in the age of exploration accelerated considerably in the nineteenth century (Orser 1996). Waves of European immigrants were attracted to the opportunities created by American industrial development in the 1830s and 1840s, initially in the mass production of textiles (Mrozowski et al. 1996). The industrial age ushered in numerous types of new machinery, many of which could be operated by unskilled and semiskilled labor. This labor force became the foundation for demographic expansion and population nucleation leading to planned industrial villages and the growth of small and large urban centers through-out the northeastern United States. We are visibly reminded of these early developments through the extant built environment that accompanied in-dustrial culture everywhere (see Gordon and Malone 1994; McGuire 1991; Sande 1978; Shackel 1996).

While the historical preservation movement has succeeded in saving many of these monuments to capitalism, labor historians have been engaged in the study of the relationship between technological change associated with industrialization and the labor process. One of the central debates in the literature on labor organization concerns the linkage between technological innovation, deskilling, and the control of workers (for example, Braverman 1974; Clawson 1980; Marglin 1974; Nassaney and Abel 1993; Noble 1986; Paynter 1988; Shackel 1996; Shaiken 1985). Contrary to neoclassical economic prin-ciples, the centralized organization that characterizes the factory system and the technical deskilling brought about by mechanization did not occur "pri-marily for reasons of technical superiority." The origin and success of the factory can be attributed to new levels of supervision and discipline imposed on workers to promote greater capital accumulation, which led to increasing material disparities between social classes (Marglin 1974, 34). While this is not an entirely new observation, it is important to recognize that the locus of control was not limited to production in the workplace. Rather, industrial-ization and the spatial changes that accompanied it served to create and rein-force relations of economic and social subordination *both in the factory and at home.* Using supervisory and disciplinary tactics, capitalists attempted to control workers in order to increase the likelihood of assuring high rates of productivity and, ultimately, of profit. These lessons emerged from our ex-amination of the archaeological and historical records of Russell Cutlery in Turners Falls, Massachusetts. We use a political-economic theoretical frame-work regarding social control in early American factories to inform our un-derstanding of the conditions that contributed to spatial reorganization in the nineteenth-century cutlery industry. Russell Cutlery provides an ideal case study since, as one author has suggested, the history of the Russell firm is *the* history of the cutlery industry in the United States (Stone 1930, 457).

Cutlery was seldom made in America prior to the nineteenth century. Pro-duced by hand using time-honored techniques virtually unchanged since the Middle Ages, kitchen knives and other edged tools were produced and imported from England, France, and Germany. In the 1830s, American entrepreneurs be-gan to compete in the cutlery industry by introducing two innovations—

mechanization and interchangeability—that revolutionized the trade. These technological changes were important aspects of the so-called American system of manufacture, which developed in the arms-making industry and rapidly diffused to other metal-working trades in the Connecticut River Valley of western Massachusetts (map 10.1). Their implementation led to major changes in labor recruitment, labor organization, and the design of living and working spaces associated with the factory system. In this chapter we explore how spatial reorganizations in the home and in the workplace constitute material expressions of an ideology of order, discipline, and social control that served to create and reproduce class divisions in American society.

The cutlery industry of the Connecticut Valley provides the context for

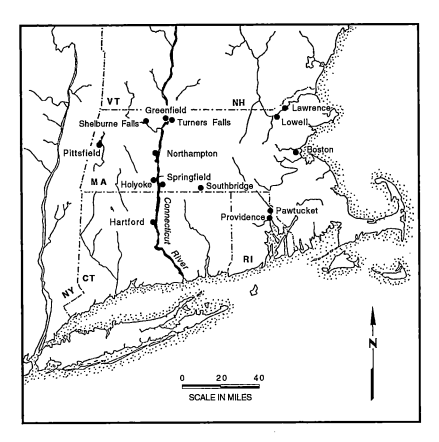

Map 10.1. Southern New England and Connecticut River Valley locations where cutlery production and other metalworking industries flourished in the nineteenth and early twentieth centuries. Also shown are other important industrial and urban centers in the region.

our study. In the late 1980s we had the opportunity to conduct background research and archaeological field investigations of the John Russell Cutlery Company (1833–1933) in Franklin County, Massachusetts. The original cutlery was established in 1833 along the banks of the Green River in present-day Greenfield, Massachusetts. Its founder, John Russell, introduced water- and steam-powered machinery from the cutlery's inception. When the firm relocated to Turners Falls in 1870, it allegedly occupied the largest cutlery factory in the world. One focus of our analysis has been to explore how American cutlers were able to compete successfully with their Old World counterparts.

A unifying characteristic of nineteenth-century American factories was the pervasiveness of technologically defined social relations (Nelson 1981, 173) that were created and reinforced through spatial organization—a critical dimension of the material world. Factory owners and managers used the built environment (that is, factories, housing, landscapes) to discipline agrarian habits to an industrial regime. In doing so, emerging capitalists in the Connecticut Valley and elsewhere attempted to assert control over their workers. Indeed, "the essence of the factory [system] is discipline—the opportunity it affords for the direction and coordination of labor" (Landes 1966, 14; cited in Marglin 1974, 45).

Building design, room location, and the placement of machinery and equipment act to partition space and serve to facilitate some activities while discouraging others. Factory owners used the spatiality of new working and living arenas of cutlers, laborers, supervisors, and managers to create and reproduce the transformation to an industrial order. We recognize that the spatial structures experienced by workers differ from idealized spaces designed by elites. The former emerge out of a struggle between the wishes of capitalists and their employees. While we acknowledge that there is always resistance to power (Foucault 1984, 95), the purpose of this paper is to explore the spatial expressions of some technical and conceptual changes in labor organization and home life. Thus, we emphasize the designs that capitalists implemented to foster economic success. We use material evidence for machinery and the factories of production to illuminate the mechanization process and changes in the technical division of labor. Finally, we argue that spatial tactics of control developed in work-related contexts in industrial New England were often extended beyond the factory and into the home. Employers influenced behavior in domestic settings by designing and owning boardinghouses, tenements, and other essential aspects of infrastructure that workers relied upon daily.

THE HISTORICAL DEVELOPMENT OF
THE AMERICAN CUTLERY INDUSTRY

When large-scale American cutlery production began in the Connecticut Valley in the 1830s, the production methods were already partially mechanized since other metal trades had solved the problem of cutting out irregular shapes in metal (Bishop 1868; Stone 1930; Taber 1955). Cutlery making involves several basic processes: forging, hardening, tempering, grinding, polishing, and hafting. Traditionally, these processes were based on intensive manual labor and were associated with time-honored knowledge and skill.

In knife production, steel is heated to a high temperature prior to pounding with a heavy mass or forging, which hammers the molecules together into a compact mass. The knife is then heated again in a hardening furnace and cooled rapidly in water or oil. Reheating and slowly cooling gives the hardened knife flexibility and resilience in the tempering stage of production. The final shape is achieved by grinding the blade against revolving, abrasive stones of successively finer grain. This also produces the knife's sharp cutting edge. The later stages of grinding actually polish the blade by eliminating grinding marks. In the final stage of production the handle is hafted or attached to the blade by means of a metal extension called a tang. The tang and the blade are usually separated by a bolster which prevents the user's hand from slipping toward the blade (Taber 1955, 32–35).

Until the early nineteenth century, production centers in France, Germany, and especially Sheffield, England, controlled the cutlery trade in the Western world (Lloyd 1913; Smithurst 1987). In Britain, for example, entrance into a specific craft was strictly controlled by apprenticeships and trade unions, resulting in a level of craftsmanship that earned English cutlery worldwide renown well into the nineteenth century. Colonial expansion had assured English producers adequate markets to dispose of their products; however, their prosperity in the trade depended largely upon American consumers.

Prior to the establishment of the American cutlery industry, some knives were made sporadically using traditional techniques (Taber 1955, 1–2). Blacksmiths and a limited number of so-called cutlers made swords, knives, and other tools, but they seldom confined their work to a single product. Blacksmiths passed knowledge to other trades, particularly those that produced items too bulky for transoceanic transport, such as axes, agricultural implements, and occasionally guns.

The establishment of the United States armory (1794) in Springfield, Massachusetts, encouraged the development of the metal trades. Many significant manufacturing innovations in the small-arms industry became potentially transferable to other metalworking industries. The technology for the mechanization of arms making is one of the earliest and most important developments of the American system of manufacture (Smith 1985). A defining characteristic of this manufacturing method is the means by which objects can be assembled using standardized and, hence, interchangeable parts (Hounshell 1984). The system was first used in the late eighteenth century for the production of rifles at the national armories (Oliver 1956; Shackel 1996). By the 1830s, the American system had begun to diffuse beyond firearm factories to various machine shops producing products including cutlery, hoes, scythes, and rakes (Smith 1985, 7).

Grinding was one of the first stages in cutlery production to make use of mechanization. By 1844 forging also became mechanized as leading Connecticut Valley cutleries adopted the use of the tilt, or trip hammer, an innovation that had been introduced earlier at the Springfield armory (Gordon and Malone 1994, 355; Taber 1955, 36). The use of the trip hammer for forging blades increased output dramatically and changed the process of forging from two cooperating workers (a smith and a striker) to a single individual holding the hot metal beneath the hammer that pounded it into the desired shape (Lloyd 1913). By the 1850s, the J. Russell & Company Green River Works and local competitors such as the Lamson & Goodnow Manufacturing Company were using a mechanized process that employed heavy presses and dies to shape blades that had traditionally been hand forged (Taber 1955, 37). In the manual process a smith and striker could forge approximately 150 blades a day, whereas mechanized hammering and die cutting increased daily output twentyfold, to 3000 (Taber 1955, 37).

Besides the obvious increases in production brought about by mechanization, industrialization had a profound effect on workers' lives and helped create a new working class (Thompson 1967). Social and labor historians have noted how industrial work differs qualitatively from agricultural work (Kulik et al. 1982). The demands of the machines fundamentally altered the labor process, and workers of all ages had to adjust to new forms of authority (Kulik et al. 1982, xxx). New relationships of dependency linked workers to wages that were often dictated by fluctuations in market conditions. The shift from an economy based upon independent ownership of land to one increasingly organized on wage labor was one of the most significant historical changes in the experience of the American working class. This structural change precipitated discontent and social tensions with which John Russell, his successors, and other capitalists were inevitably forced to contend.

Though an unlikely innovator in some respects, John Russell established a manufacturing company in 1833 on the Green River in what is now Greenfield, Massachusetts, in direct competition with the guilds of Sheffield, England, and their established reputation for outstanding, high-quality prod-· ucts. This was a completely new enterprise for Russell, and exactly why he decided to pursue the cutlery trade remains unknown. The son of a Greenfield jeweler and silversmith, Russell (1797–1874) spent his early years (ca. 1819–32) in the American South speculating in the cotton market (Jenkins 1982, 76). Within a year of his return to the Connecticut Valley, he advertised his intent to produce cast steel-socket chisels. A Greenfield historian noted that Sheffield was unsuccessful in developing machinery to replace hand processes (Jenkins 1982, 79). He further speculated that Russell may have been "inclined to compete with England in some totally new undertaking," having spent twelve years "in Georgia vying with British agents for the purchase of raw cotton" (Jenkins 1982, 80).

Whatever attracted him to this new endeavor, Russell used the capital gained from his cotton investments, formed a partnership with his brother, Francis, and began to manufacture chisels. In 1834 some of his chisels won a prize for excellence at a fair held by the American Institute (Reader 1973, 80). Soon after Russell diversified production by manufacturing knives and other types of cutlery. In 1844 Russell introduced the use of a water-driven trip hammer into the forging process, a major technological innovation for increasing production output (Taber 1955, 36). He also began to employ heavy dies in power presses to cut out blades. "By 1844 the Russell Company was making a knife in which the blade, tang, and bolster were all forged from one piece of steel," and these knives were advertised as superior in strength and beauty to English ones (Taber 1955, 36).

By the 1840s, Russell's products had achieved widespread recognition and the names "Russell" and "Green River" (stamped, and later etched, on every blade) had earned a prominent standing among cutlers throughout Europe and the Americas. Certain types of Russell knives were extremely popular, especially on the American frontier, and by the 1850s, the name Green River had a special connotation among trappers and mountain men. In *Life in the Far West*, the mid-nineteenth-century serial writer George Frederick Ruxton underscored the effectiveness of a Green River knife when he described how "a thrust from the keen scalp-knife by the nervous arm of a mountaineer was no baby blow, and seldom failed to strike home—up to the 'Green River' on the blade" (Ruxton 1951, 189). From then on, any knife thrust in "up to Green River" indicated a thorough job done, and the expression itself became a part of the American vernacular synonymous with anything well done or well made (Taber 1955, 21).

Russell's business grew steadily and by 1860 it was one of three Franklin County firms to account for almost half (49.4 percent) of the cutlery produced in the United States (Taber 1955, 122). However, the Green River Works were rapidly becoming obsolete. By the end of the decade the management of the Russell Cutlery decided to relocate and modernize their operation, so they began to design a new factory. In 1868 construction of the new plant began nearby in the planned industrial village of Turners Falls across the Connecticut River in the town of Montague (fig. 10.1). When the plant was completed in 1870, it defined the prototype of a modern cutlery factory.

The post–Civil War period witnessed an American economy marked by increased competitiveness and economic instability (Gordon et al. 1982, 95). Economic depressions in 1877 and again between 1893 and 1897, together with unemployment and tensions between labor and industrialists, represented the growing problems in industrial expansion and social unrest (Brecher 1972). Production fell and Russell's firm was in financial crisis. In 1873, the company was financially reorganized and renamed the John Russell Cutlery Company, although John Russell had little to do with the daily operations of the

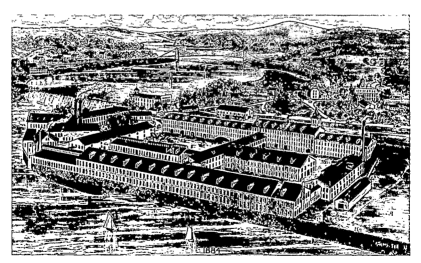

Fig. 10.1. A bird's-eye view of Russell Cutlery in the late nineteenth century. Note the bucolic and idyllic depiction of the landscape. Reproduced from the Centennial Edition of the Greenfield Gazette, 1892, courtesy of The Recorder, Greenfield, Massachusetts.

plant by then. In the 1880s the company initiated a major modernization and rebuilding program that included the construction of new buildings, replacement and rearrangement of machinery, and expansion of certain departments (for example, silver plating, tempering) to meet increased demands. During this period a new inspection room was instituted in the factory to reduce the number of defective knives that left the plant (Merriam et al. 1976, 40). While a certain volume of waste was acceptable (perhaps inevitable) in the production process (see Hounshell 1984, 72, 86 on the early problems with interchangeability), the company sought to ensure that these inferior products were not sold to the public.

By 1900 only 11 percent of the knives produced in the United States were made in Massachusetts. Even though most of the cutlery was still produced by Connecticut Valley firms, this decrease signaled an end to the dominance that the Russell company had once enjoyed in the industry. The Harrington Cutlery of Southbridge, Massachusetts, purchased the John Russell Cutlery Company in 1933, and the two companies merged to form Russell-Harrington Cutlery. By then, the number of employees in Turners Falls had declined to only 150. A major flood in 1936 heavily damaged the factory, and in 1938 the entire operation was moved to Southbridge, where it operates to this day. The once impressive factory complex was abandoned, and only portions of the shop buildings survived until 1958, when they were demolished. In 1976 some of the foundations were visible, as were the remains of a partially collapsed raceway. When archaeological investigations began in 1986, some of the concrete flooring was still exposed, a steel penstock that directed water to one of the turbines protruded from the canal wall, and architectural debris (for example, bricks, wooden beams) was littered about the surface of the site.

THE ARCHAEOLOGY OF
INDUSTRIAL WASTE

In the mid-1980s, the site of the Russell Cutlery in Turners Falls was selected for the construction of a coal-fired electric cogeneration facility (Nassaney et al. 1989). Because of the potential archaeological sensitivity of this location, the site was subjected to an archaeological survey following intensive documentary review. Among the more valuable documents available for this study are a series of detailed Sanborn Fire Insurance Company maps, 1884–1940 (for example, fig. 10.2), which we consulted prior to fieldwork. Subsurface testing led to the identification of relatively intact architectural and artifactual remains associated with the factory. Since these remains had the potential to contribute to questions regarding early industrialization in the region, we developed a data recovery strategy that involved archaeological investigations to explore the development of the American system of cutlery manufacture and how workers reacted to it (Nassaney et al. 1989). Field investigations led to the examination and recovery of portions of the water power system including a water storage tank and a late-nineteenth/early-twentieth century water turbine. We also collected an assemblage of artifacts pertinent to the study of interchangeable parts from along the riverbank adjacent to the former cutting room and trip hammer shop (fig. 10.2). A sample of more than two hundred objects included raw material scraps, cut-out metal, and cutlery wasters (inferior or imperfect manufactured objects) discarded from various stages in the production process (see figs. 10.3–10.5).

Industrialization gave rise to two different production methods that are represented in our artifact assemblage. Mechanized forging, a process repeatedly described in the literature, was used to manufacture dessert knives, among other products, at the plant (for example, Bishop 1868; Taber 1955, 32–35). Early production stages are clearly documented archaeologically (fig. 10.3).

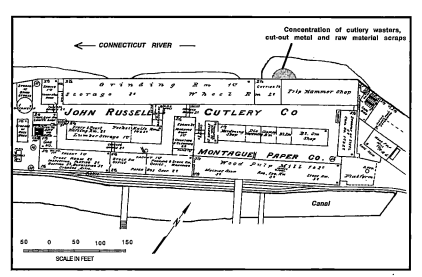

Fig. 10.2. Adaptation of a Sanborn Fire Insurance map (1884) showing the sequential flow of cutlery production and the location where cutlery wasters, cut-out metal, and raw material scraps were recovered during archaeological investigations. Reproduced with modifications from Nassaney and Abel 1993, figure 4, by permission from Kluwer Academic Publishers.

First, the amount of steel required for the blade is measured and cut off with a drop hammer. Next, the metal object is hammered roughly into shape, allowing enough metal for the blade, bolster, and tang to be formed. The bolster and tang are then formed by hammering between dies constructed to give the intended form and size. The blade is completely hammered in the next stage, giving it the appropriate thickness and taper while condensing the steel so as to impart to it a good cutting quality. Finally, dies set into power presses shear off superfluous metal.

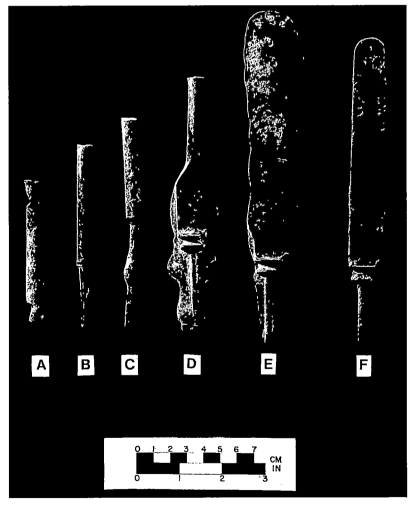

Fig. 10.3. Stages in the production sequence of a dessert knife. From Nassaney and Abel 1993, figure 6, by permission from Kluwer Academic Publishers.

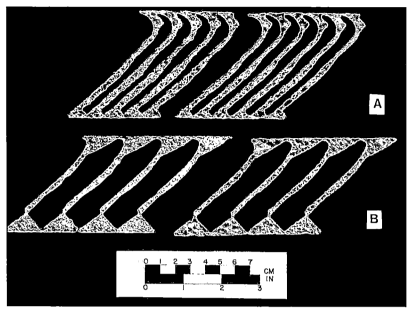

Fig. 10.4. Superfluous metal derived from the stamping or blanking of Barlow knives.
(A) Barlow spring cut-outs; (B) Barlow blade cut-outs. Reproduced from
Nassaney and Abel 1993, figure 5, by permission from Kluwer Academic Publishers.

The second production method was capable of even greater output. It involved the stamping or blanking of sheet metal using dies of appropriate form and size to produce blades and springs for the famous Barlow pocket knives, as well as a variety of other products (fig. 10.4). This method of manufacture has fewer archaeologically recognizable production stages and may have required less skill to perform than forging. Stamping is a much more rapid production technique than forging, more closely resembling what is often thought of as mass production. It was adopted sometime after forging in cutlery manufacture, though these production methods have some temporal overlap.

In addition to identifying stages in the production process, we also inspected a sample of objects to determine why they had been rejected and discarded (fig. 10.5). Most of the objects in our collection represent either scrap metal or wasters. Furthermore, most of the wasters were discarded in the early stages of production (that is, during the forging or stamping stages) before significant amounts of labor and energy were expended on them. Larger samples from controlled contexts are needed to quantify and evaluate this pattern. At least one knife fragment, however, was rejected later in the manufacturing sequence, as indicated by the clearly visible parallel striations on its blade (see fig. 10.5c).

Elsewhere we have argued that production mistakes in our sample may represent fossilized evidence of what Scott (1990) has called a "hidden transcript of resistance" (Nassaney and Abel 1993, 251). Acceptance or consent of the conditions created by management constitutes a "public transcript" in which workers enact expected roles "out of prudent awareness of power"

Fig. 10.5. Additional cutlery wasters recovered from archaeological context. Reproduced from Nassaney and Abel 1993, figure 7, by permission from Kluwer Academic Publishers.

(Kelley 1992, 293). An alternate, yet parallel, "hidden transcript" coexists to challenge ideological hegemony. This dissident political culture often took the form of daily conversations, jokes, songs, foot dragging, stealing, sabotage, and, in the case of cutlery, ruined knives. These forms of resistance arose partly in response to mechanization and may represent efforts to regain some degree of autonomy in the context of exploitative relations of wage labor. Several former employees were asked about the treatment of spoiled production items at the plant. One proud retiree of the Russell firm recalled few production failures, explaining that he and his coworkers were skilled craftsmen. Others noted that in order to avoid having to correct manufacturing mistakes, objects were frequently "thrown out the window, into the river."

Were the Russell cutlery workers able to throw wasters out the window without retribution? Do the cutlery wasters represent acts of defiance committed against the will of management? We reexamined the documentary evidence to improve our understanding of relations between workers and managers. In the late nineteenth century, disputes were frequent between managers and laborers over layoffs, wages, deskilling of jobs, and general work conditions, hinting that these points of contention may have precipitated our sample (Nassaney and Abel 1993, 267–70). The identification of spoiled knives in the archaeological record alerted us to the tensions created by technological innovations and the restructuring of the labor process much as Kulick and his coworkers had predicted (1982, xxx). Our analysis indicates that technological efficiency was not the principal cause for innovation; mechanization and interchangeability served to reorder the organization of production technically and spatially to deskill and control workers as a means of creating conditions of political subordination and relations of social inequality.

SPATIALITY AND SOCIAL RELATIONS

The ability to partition the everyday spaces in workers' lives is a powerful and pervasive means of creating and reproducing social inequality. Researchers have identified numerous contexts in which nineteenth-century America witnessed the planned construction of the built environment to achieve social and economic ends. These include the rural landscape (McMurry 1997; Nassaney et al. 1998) as well as various institutions such as military installations, prisons, schools, and, of course, factories (see contributors to Demers and Voss [1995]; Foucault 1979; Shackel 1993, 14–16). In industrial capitalism, the built environment is a material expression of order and control that is designed to maximize profit through spatial hegemony. What emerged in industrial life was "a new system of domination expressed in new surveillance technology. Discipline and social control of people became a major concern" (Shackel 1993, 15). Spatial hegemony allowed for enforcement of discipline in the factory as the labor process made "bodily behavior routine, repetitive, subject to codifiable rules and accessible to surveillance and calculation" (Tilley 1990, 317). Discipline is the means by which elites exercise control; it allows them to produce "willful subjects who willingly work within the capitalist system" (Shackel 1993, 16). In short, spatiality— the active creation of spatial organization through the built environment— is a means to create, reproduce, and transform social relations. Analysis of the spatial organization of the material world can be used to identify how social spaces serve to reproduce forms of dominant and subordinate ideology and practice.

The notion that spatial organization can inform other aspects of society is not new in the social sciences; but because it has been underemphasized, it is worth reviewing the theoretical foundations that bridge human action with spatial outcome (see Nassaney and Paynter 1995; Rotman and Nassaney 1997; Soja 1989). Three general points should be made. First, people manipulate spatial organization explicitly and implicitly in social interactions (Harvey 1973; Paynter 1982; Soja 1971). Moreover, because human agents actively constitute spatial order as a means to codify social order, space can be construed as a dynamic social outcome rather than a static or passive entity (Lefebvre 1976, 32). From this perspective, spatiality is both a product of, and precedent for, human action.

Second, individuals and social groups actively organize space and constantly strive to restructure it through a dialectical process to produce a pattern that better serves the changing goals and motivations of human action (Gottman 1980, 217). Thus, the landscape serves as a means of social reproduction; it is a text of social action that can be decoded to infer changing relationships of domination, accommodation, and resistance (Lewis 1979, 13; Nassaney 1992; Nassaney et al. 1998). What constitutes an effective spatial order is a product of changing historical conditions.

Third, the built environment has a political-economic dimension; it contributes to the production and accumulation of social surplus (Harvey 1973; Paynter 1982, 32–33). For example, the built environment constitutes the fixed forces of production. It also acts to circulate surplus through transportation networks from its extraction to its consumption. Due to the friction of distance and infrastructural design, the costs associated with the movement of goods are born disproportionately among members of stratified societies. The built environment also codifies relations of inequality through the lavish use of building materials associated with elites (Paynter 1982, 33) or the symbolic metaphors that certain building styles may conjure up to the observer.

Spatiality is an effective medium for transmitting dominant social messages because spatial organization is relatively permanent, pervasive, and capable of fostering redundant messages. Spatial ordering, we should add, occurs at many different scales within the material world of social life, from artifact design (for example, Hegmon 1989; Wobst 1977) to the home lot (for example, Leone 1984; Rotman and Nassaney 1997; Yamin and Metheny 1996), to macro-regional settlement patterns (for example, Linebaugh and Robinson 1994; Paynter 1982; Nassaney and Sassaman 1995). Theoretically, the content of each of these scales underwrites different social behaviors with regard to resource accumulation and labor mobilization. David Harvey (1989, 239) has put it most succinctly:

> *spatial and temporal practices are never neutral in social affairs. They always express some kind of class or other social content, and are more often than not the focus of intense social struggle. That this is so becomes doubly obvious when we consider the ways in which space and time connect with money, and the way that connection becomes even more tightly organized with the development of capitalism. Time and space both get defined through the organization of social practices fundamental to commodity production. But the dynamic force of capital accumulation (and overaccumulation), together with conditions of social struggle, renders the relations unstable.*

In the remainder of this chapter we focus on the ways in which the cutlery factory and associated domestic architecture were designed by industrial capitalists to encourage productive behaviors and discourage unproductive ones. The particular goal of this analysis is to examine how the development of industrial capitalism affected the organization of living and working places. Evidence is drawn from archaeological and historical investigations specific to the Russell Cutlery, as well as material observations on other similarly organized industries in nineteenth-century New England.

LABOR ORGANIZATION IN THE WORK-PLACE AND THE DOMESTIC SPHERE

There is limited documentary evidence regarding Russell's first cutlery factory along the Green River, and no archaeological investigations have yet been conducted to identify and evaluate the significance of potential remains at this site. According to local sources, Russell designed his shop with practical considerations from the start of his business in 1833 (Merriam et al. 1976, 4). Grinding occurred along one side of his small wooden building, whereas trip hammers and tempering and hardening vats were arranged along the other walls (4). Most of the machinery was driven by a sixteen-horsepower steam engine, supposedly the first to be used in Greenfield. Even in these early years, Russell used a spatial division of labor to organize production.

By 1836 Russell moved his operation nearer to a dam on the site of a natural falls along the Green River to obtain access to less expensive water power. Only weeks later a fire and then a flood temporarily suspended cutlery production. Russell gained the support of a local financial backer, and the construction of a new factory soon began. The factory eventually contained several buildings, although strictly speaking not all of the shop processes had been brought under one roof. One building housed a dozen new trip hammers, a second accommodated seventy grindstones and one hundred emery wheels, while a third contained the hardening and tempering apparatus, with the hafting department in the upper story (Merriam et al. 1976, 10). Small sheds on the property held various raw materials. With the new capacity for production, the factory was christened the "Green River Works," and the products were stamped: "J. Russell & Co. Green River Works." The firm achieved considerable success throughout the 1840s and 1850s, particularly as the American market began to take notice of Russell's high-quality products. New buildings were added as the need arose in the 1850s. The factory shops were apparently built of brick, although their interiors were completely constructed of wood. The result was a problem with fires that plagued the cutlery until 1870, when the firm moved to a new brick building in Turners Falls.

Labor Recruitment

The labor force required to operate the cutlery was recruited from home and abroad and was segmented along ethnic and gender lines. Initially, Russell was forced to rely upon native-born labor because skilled German and English cutlers were difficult to attract to Greenfield (Taber 1955, 94–95). As E. P.

Thompson (1967) noted in his discussion of time and work, a major struggle in the establishment of regularity in work habits suitable for capitalist production was the disciplining of workers accustomed to the task-oriented pace of farm production. As Kulik et al. note: "[t]his shift from an economy based upon independent proprietorship of land to an economy increasingly organized around wage labor was one of the most important and deeply felt historical changes in the structure of American social experience, and sharp social conflicts arose from this change in structure" (1982, xxx). In the early years, Russell was forced to hire from an unreliable labor pool. He expressed dissatisfaction with local workers in remarks made in 1850: "Employees were nearly all Americans, and a fine, intelligent lot of men they were, but only so unstable; here today, gone tomorrow; working with desperate energy for a year or so and then away; to the West, to business, to farms, to professions, to scatter the length and breadth of the land" (cited in Taber 1955, 95).

In 1872 Russell observed that American men were "too free and independent" to work long in any factory and this was bad for business: "[n]o business could bear such incessant change of help, such spoiling of work by green hands, so a different system was devised. America retired in favor of Ireland and Germany" (cited in Taber 1955, 95).

Factory work was to become primarily an immigrant experience. Immigration increased the population in the town of Montague significantly, especially in the industrial village of Turners Falls, where three major industries (cutlery, paper, and cotton) were located. Between 1870 and 1880, the foreign-born population in Montague increased from 438 to 1,558 individuals. Whereas immigrants constituted 19.7 percent of the total population in 1870, by 1880 their proportion of the population had risen to 32.0 percent (Abel 1987).

The manufacturing structure, through its demand for specific types of labor, influenced the shape and ethnic composition of the industrial landscape. For example, by the late nineteenth century, Germans were the largest immigrant group in the Massachusetts cutlery industry (Taber 1955, 98). In addition to German workers, Irish, English, and French-Canadian immigrants increased rapidly in the various industries of Turners Falls. In many cases, labor was secured directly from abroad. The Lamson & Goodnow Cutlery in Shelburne Falls was able to obtain English cutlers directly from Sheffield through workers who recruited relatives from abroad. As one former employee put it, "working there was a family affair with certain family names showing on the payroll generation after generation" (interview with a former employee of Lamson & Goodnow Cutlery, 1996). Historically, this was particularly the case for women.

Female immigrants were slightly outnumbered by males in Turners Falls; however, following the over-all demographic pattern, the female population doubled between 1870 and 1880. The female labor force was divided by age and ethnicity according to industry. The cutlery industry employed few women, most of whom were young, single, and related to male employees. Of the thirty-seven females employed at the Russell Cutlery in 1880, the majority (87 percent) were under twenty years of age. The paper industry employed nearly an equal number of single and married women. The married women tended to be older and foreign born, and over half of the foreign born were Irish. French-Canadian men and women tended to be employed in the cotton industry.

The sexual division of labor can reinforce spatial barriers in the factory. For example, men dominated nearly all high-paying jobs in the industry, particularly those that required some degree of "skill," such as grinding (see Abel [1987] and Cockburn [1983] on the social construction of skill). Women were employed in some departments, but men and women rarely shared the same work space (see Spain 1992). Women's work in the cutlery industry was confined to the packaging department, where the tasks of sorting and packaging cutlery for shipment were seen as appropriate for women (Taber 1955).

The Labor Process
In the American system, increases in production and worker productivity, and a decrease in the unit cost of production, resulted from three factors: improved machinery, better design of factory works, and more intensive use of energy. In the metalworking industries such as cutlery, in which mass production was achieved by fabricating and assembling standardized parts, a fourth factor also came into play: designing and managing worker movements (Chandler 1981, 154). This was necessary to coordinate a large workforce that used "a wide variety of skills [and] carried out many different tasks" (Chandler 1981, 155). The spatial organization of Russell's plant resulted from three significant changes in the cutlery industry that distinguished American products from their English counterparts. First, Russell mechanized the production process, which increased the daily output of forged knives tremendously. Second, he subdivided cutlery making into a series of standardized and routinized tasks (see Braverman 1974). Finally, he began to apply principles of scientific management to production, well in

advance of their codification by Frederick Taylor in the twentieth century (see also Bucki 1987, 137).

The driving force in capitalist production is the realization of profit, but both workers and competitors stand between capitalists and this end (Paynter 1988). Capitalists can compete more effectively by producing cheaper commodities, for example by making the workers produce more for less. One tactic to increase worker productivity is to mechanize production, and this is where John Russell excelled. By the 1840s he had fully harnessed water power in all the major production processes.

Russell organized the shop floor to transform the labor process by further subdividing cutlery making into a series of standardized, repetitive tasks. Work was divided so that each worker carried out a single task (Abel 1987, 172). The result was a near complete separation of the conception of production by managers from the execution of labor (Braverman 1974). By segmenting the labor process and separating conception from execution, Russell attempted to deskill the labor force. Grinders and polishers, for example, were engaged in monotonous tasks. Their orderly seating arrangement also homogenized their roles and created interchangeable subjects (fig. 10.6). Young boys brought dull knives to the grinders and moved sharpened products to the next production stage; thus, grinders had few interruptions and were kept working continuously. The tactic of dividing labor to minimize the level of skill needed by a laborer was a means of shifting skill from men to machinery, thereby placing increasing control into the hands of management and reducing the amount of skill and training needed to manufacture a knife (Siskind 1991, 37).

Mechanizing production and segmenting labor serve to increase productivity by (1) making it possible to produce more objects per worker per day and (2) standardizing the labor process so that virtually anyone can do the job. These changes were solutions to the shortage of skilled laborers that initially plagued the industry. As Marx so eloquently noted, the history of technological reorganization and inventions made since the early nineteenth century is simultaneously the history of the ways in which capital supplied itself with weapons against the revolts of the working class (cited in Paynter 1988, 418–19). These design changes and concordant technological innovations reinforced a "theory of dependence" upon which industrial capitalism was based. The premise was that workers "should not be required or encouraged to think for themselves, or give to their own reflection or forecast an influential voice in the determination of their destiny" (Mill 1848, 319; cited

*Fig. 10.6. The Russell Cutlery grinding room (circa 1890), showing the orderly
arrangement of workers and the belts and pulleys that powered the
grinding wheels. Courtesy of the Channing Bete Press.*

in Bendix 1956, 47). In the Collins Axe Company of Connecticut, a class discourse emerged that metaphorically compared a worker and manager to a
horse and its rider (Siskind 1991, 39). Axe makers were seen as "docile and
manageable," or "spirited," in which case they may need to be "bridled and
spurred *every* day" (Siskind 1991, 39). Russell reportedly treated his workers
in such a way as to defuse antagonism, although he also remained "aloof,
exhibiting a sympathetic but distant paternalism that was characteristic of
successful mill owners throughout the 19th century" (Jenkins 1982, 83).

The introduction of new employees to industry posed a continuous problem throughout the nineteenth century as workers struggled with managers
over control of the workplace and "sought to evade the new discipline and
continue more traditional modes of work" (Siskind 1991, 38). At the Collins
Company, employers looked for ways "to mold workers to long hours" and
prevent them from leaving (Siskind 1991, 38). Through planning and design,
Russell was able to rationalize and standardize the production process to coordinate and facilitate the movement and flow of goods. While Russell established a relationship between factory design and efficiency, how much
influence did the process have on disciplining workers? And how did workers find avenues for resistance? The material world of the Russell Cutlery

provides insights into these questions, not only in Turners Falls but in other settings where the so-called labor problem occurred.

The Built Environment of the Workplace

As vehicles for reproducing social relations, space and time can serve to define the technical and human aspects of the production process. The design changes previously discussed were fully put into effect at Russell's new plant in Turners Falls (see figs. 10.1 and 10.2). The cutlery buildings, designed and built by a Philadelphia native, Bernard Farren, comprised a total of 160,000 square feet of work space. Upon completion in 1870, the factory was capable of employing 1,200 workers. Oddly enough, the size of the plant was not its most significant characteristic. What distinguished the cutlery was the spatial organization of production such that goods moved the shortest distance possible from one operation to the next—a veritable blueprint for scientific management in the workplace.

What were the spatial manifestations of these technical and conceptual changes? Material evidence for mechanization and the technical division of labor are reflected in the machinery and factories of production (Paynter 1988, 414). The cutlery buildings were arranged in the form of a large parallelogram with a central courtyard (fig. 10.1). All manufacturing activities took place on the first two floors, whereas managerial offices occupied sections of the upper two stories (Merriam et al. 1976, 24). Similarities to Jeremy Bentham's panopticon were surely intentional; New England factory architecture complies with this principle as a means by which the owners could control their workers through surveillance (Handsman 1987).

Managers long recognized that the layout of a building could play an important role in the success of an industrial enterprise, and Russell was no exception. Nineteenth- and twentieth-century factory designers were attempting to create a rational factory, one that could run automatically as one grand machine (Biggs 1996, 2). They sought organizational plans that provided machinelike predictability as a way of solving various problems associated with production (53). Professionals in the new field of industrial engineering employed an old metaphor in the early years of the twentieth century—the factory as machine. In a study of British industrial architecture, Jones (1985, 11) noted that "an effective design was an integral part of a plant's manufacturing efficiency."

Russell anticipated by decades the field of industrial engineering in his notions of the "factory as machine." He adopted a roughly circular flow for the cutlery production process, although certain technical requirements constrained the ideal movement of goods (Nassaney et al. 1989, 16, 34). Raw materials were brought in by rail, rough-blanked in the drop forge room, shaped with the use of a trip hammer, and then cut using dies to remove excess steel (fig. 10.2). Next, the blanks were hardened and tempered in the eastern courtyard building, ground in the riverside building, and stamped with the company trademark. Polishing and hafting were followed by wrapping and packaging at the end of the circuit near the rail line, where they were shipped to New York for distribution throughout the world.

The ideal interior design and use of space in New England factories were accommodated to specific technical requirements (Zonderman 1992, 64). For example, the distance over which power could be transmitted using belts and pulleys limited the width of the complex (fig. 10.6). Individual buildings were narrow with tall ceilings (fourteen feet) to maximize sunlight. The overall function of the design was to bring people and machines together in one location where they could be effectively supervised (65).

Purposeful design continued to the exterior walls. The physical shapes of factory buildings were often constructed to mediate the tensions between industry and agriculture. In early- and mid-nineteenth-century America, there existed an uncertain relationship between industry and an agrarian way of life (Kulik et al. 1982, xxxi). Most Americans feared the English model of cramped spaces and the social problems that they engendered. Part of the answer was the creation of the factory village. The spatial juxtaposition of the factory in the midst of an agrarian community symbolically reinforced a more rationally ordered industrial operation that blended with the rural structure of the community (Zonderman 1992, 86). The village of Turners Falls was often promoted this way during the 1870s and 1880s in images that depict a bucolic and idyllic landscape marked by numerous shade trees and sailboats along the river (fig. 10.1), even though the landscape likely exhibited a much more urban appearance in reality.

Another way of softening the industrial landscape, particularly in the textile trades, was to build factories that resembled churches or schools (Zonderman 1992, 84–85). These designs were used by owners to mask their participation in "industrial capitalism with the physical and symbolic veneer of a religious presence and purpose" (85). Others have argued that the economy and efficiency embodied in the factory provided the model for campus planning at the Massachusetts Institute of Technology, "in which departments would be located in connected buildings" (Biggs 1996, 53–54). This ideology of order and control also extended to the layout of the community in Turners Falls, which still exhibits a clear rectilinear pattern. The use of space and design both within and without the factory served to create a habitus of hierarchy, even though it could not completely disguise or naturalize an ideology of domination. In Lowell, for example, some saw the orderly city streets and planned factory courtyards as a mere facade aimed at concealing the exploitative conditions of wage labor (Zonderman 1992, 90).

The Built Environment of the Domestic Sphere

The factory was only one of many new institutions (for example, the asylum, prison, school) associated with the disciplinary tactics of capitalism (Foucault 1979, 1980; Paynter and McGuire 1991, 8). While spatial tactics of control were well developed in work-related contexts, they were by no means confined to the shop floor. Factory owners extended the domain of "work" beyond the factory in nineteenth-century New England in general, and Turners Falls in particular, by designing and owning boardinghouses, tenements, and other essential aspects of the infrastructure that workers relied upon daily. Owners also tried to control social excesses among the workers (for example, alcohol consumption) as a way to promote industrial work habits (Zonderman 1992, 144; see also Bond 1989; Levin 1985). The process of control "begins with an elite notion of correct social behavior [and] proceeds to bring about this behavior in others" by grounding the original ideal in action (McGuire and Paynter 1991, 8). By encoding domination and subordination into everyday life—through architecture, town planning, work rules, and etiquette—relationships of power were mystified and naturalized (McGuire and Paynter 1991, 9; Shackel 1993).

In his discussion of working-class struggle over space in Worcester, Massachusetts, Rosenzweig (1979, 32) suggests that while recreational space was a contested terrain of class struggle, "the city's Yankee upper class officially controlled Worcester's parks, as they did the factories and most political offices." Likewise, Langdon Winner (1986, 23), in describing the urban planning and road building of Robert Moses, points out how roads, bridges, and public works can embody systematic social inequality.

Class differences would have also been expressed through the built environment in the different forms of housing for cutlery managers and others who could afford an alternative to tenement life. Not only would managers' housing reflect their relative affluence, but different land-use practices associated with yards and back lots would also exhibit important material means of reinforcing class distinctions. Mrozowski (1991, 91) notes that the yard space around a Lowell mill agents' dwelling was marked by a well-maintained lawn, in contrast to the boardinghouses, where weedy and uncontrolled vegetation thrived. Living conditions for mill workers and their families were allowed to deteriorate in Lowell as owners eventually began replacing native-born employees with immigrant laborers (Mrozowski et al. 1996). Changes in the boardinghouses also indicate increasing neglect as changes in the workforce alleviated labor recruitment problems.

We expect that similar practices occurred in the cutlery industry. By owning the tenements rented to workers, the Russell Company extended their control over workers' lives to their households. The company rented

Fig. 10.7. A contemporary view of the Russell Cutlery tenements on Third Street.
Photo by Thaddeus Kubis.

tenements to workers and, in some cases, paid a worker's board at a boarding-house, deducting the cost from their pay (Taber 1955). Our preliminary analysis of tenements in Turners Falls suggests that workers' housing was another arena used to enforce relations of subordination within the broader context of the built environment. In a parallel case from Lowell, Massachusetts, Mrozowski (1991, 90) has argued that the spatial arrangement of the mill, workers' housing, and overseer's house, all of which were within walking distance, reflects a landscape that was designed to function as a "strict system of moral police" (Miles 1972, 128). The Russell Company did not provide housing for its workers initially because so many of them commuted daily from Greenfield. When changes in transportation scheduling made commuting inconvenient, workers who chose to live in Turners Falls created a housing shortage. The company responded by building a Mansard roof tenement building within walking distance of the factory on Third Street (fig. 10.7) (Merriam et al. 1976, 25). Apparently, the management reluctantly came to realize (as did begrudging employers elsewhere) that better living quarters for workers contributed to greater satisfaction and increased worker efficiency (Comstock 1919, 12). The Russell Cutlery block, as it came to be known, bears a strong resemblance to the Lowell boardinghouses of the 1830s, which mimicked a typical college dormitory of the time, providing a model of "cloistered, academic lifestyles" (Clancey 1989, 7). This architectural style was chosen because it was cheaper to construct than individual buildings. The design would have also served to homogenize the workforce and create standardized subjects (Shackel 1993, 16).

Reuniting Work and Home

How could new norms for industrial behavior be imprinted on workers of the future? The growth of progressive thought in America, with its focus on efficiency and order, provided the cultural and social processes by which the management of production and factory work were connected to the home. During the Progressive Era (1890–1920), a search for order based on rationality, efficiency, and control permeated the economic and social texture of American life (Frederick 1913; Hofstadter 1955; Pattison 1915; Wiebe 1967). A disciplined environment served to Americanize time and space according to the demands of capitalism and the standards of newly emerging middle-class values (Banta 1993; Wiebe 1967). By standardizing work and space in the home, the conditions to reproduce the capitalist class process were established. Most researchers see the movement for efficiency in the home as an outgrowth of the industrial-efficiency movement of the early twentieth century. During this period the standardization of workers' lives in the home and the factory was guided by the growth of a new class of professionals ready to apply scientific knowledge to all of society's problems (see Nassaney et al. 1996).

While the growth of professionalism in the new fields of economics, social work, industrial engineering, and scientific management did not become established in American society until after the turn of the century, there were nineteenth-century forerunners of these disciplines. For example, Ferguson (1981, 8) noted that "an inspection of American homemaker's manuals, published since the 1830s, suggests that an efficiency-ridden populace was waiting to march onto the twentieth-century assembly lines." In her 1841 *Treatise on Domestic Economy*, Catherine Beecher illustrates how a woman, as a professional housekeeper, should organize her domestic duties in a rational way (Hayden 1981). McMurry (1997) also argued convincingly that farmhouse planners of the 1820s and 1830s were designing efficient kitchens that entailed the careful placement of auxiliary rooms and analysis of movement within the kitchen itself, even in advance of Beecher's prescriptions. Likewise, Banta (1993, 280–83) elaborates on how the application of measurement and precision in the arms industry, as well as interchangeable parts for weapons, provided the basis for measurement, standardization, and pattern development for women's clothing, along with other aspects of American lives.

While there was an alternative feminist movement that attempted to socialize housework in the latter half of the nineteenth century, leading advocates of home economics, such as Christine Frederick and Catherine Beecher, provided specific instructions for women on how to standardize household tasks and space (Frederick 1913; Hayden 1981). Domestic chores were to be completed in a rational, time-conscience manner in an ordered, efficient, and functional space. During this period, a woman's proper role was prescribed by the domestic ideal that visualized a woman's life as centered around the social category of "home."

The construction of two distinct spatial domains—one for production (male/public) and the other for reproduction (female/private)—has been accepted as an analytical framework in both Marxist and non-Marxist discourse centered on the household. Yet to a large extent, both spheres inculcated similar behaviors. In order to better document and understand working-class lives, it is necessary to deconstruct the notion of distinct spaces for public and private activities and reassert the importance of female agency (Gardiner 1975; Milroy and Wisner 1994, 84). In traditional Marxist analysis the connection between the household and capitalism has been viewed as one in which the household served capital in its reproduction of labor power. Humphries (1977) provided an early challenge to this functional Marxist perspective when she pointed out the importance of women and the family in the development of class consciousness.

Several recent authors have examined the ways in which women used their agency to the benefit of the working-class family. For example, Cameron (1993, 113) illuminates the role of married women in creating what she refers to as "female consciousness" in her study of Lawrence, Massachusetts. Many women used their associations in the mills and social contacts facilitated through close proximity of housing to engage in various collaborative activities that crosscut ethnic lines (Cameron 1993, 111). Likewise, the living conditions in the tenements and boardinghouses of Turners Falls encouraged women to create social and economic ties among families. The working families who occupied the tenements often kept boarders or had working relatives living with them. Women were usually responsible for the boarders, which indicates that women used domestic spaces to earn an income. There was a broad range of boarding situations, from single boarders to large boardinghouses. Analysis of the 1880 U.S. manuscript census data reveals that of the 902 married women in Montague (which includes the village of Turners Falls), 197, or 21.8 percent, kept boarders (Abel 1990). This was an important source of income for women during the nineteenth and early twentieth centuries as a 1901 survey of 2,577 Massachusetts working-class families shows, which found that 31.4 percent kept boarders, generating an average annual income of $339.68 (U.S. Commissioner of Labor 1904, 362, 366).

Women also made use of back lot space for laundering, gardening, and raising animals. In Lowell, the archaeological record reveals the cultivation of potted plants, grapes, and elderberries for cider (Mrozowski et al. 1996, 47, 58). Historical accounts from Turners Falls document complaints directed at the company about pig raising at the tenements (Merriam et al. 1976, 26). This suggests that self-surveillance served as a form of social control to eliminate unwanted behaviors. Through ownership of living *and* working spaces, the Russell Company was able to exert control and inscribe relations of dominance both inside and outside of the factory. While rental arrangements represented a form of economic control, workers were also able to retaliate by using company space to supplement their income and circumvent this control. For example, one employee used a rental property to keep boarders and pastured a cow on the lot for a fee (Taber 1955, 106).

Women also found employment opportunities in various Turners Falls industries; many women were thus employed both in and out of the home. Their "double duty" reinforces the hegemonic notion that women could be paid lower wages than men because they supposedly provided only supplementary income to male wage earners. Women often entered the cutlery industry through family connections, though they were only allowed to perform tasks deemed appropriate to their gender (Abel 1987). This suggests an overlapping of industrial and private arenas of space. For example, kin relations were used to obtain a position in the workplace, and women did work that reflected their domestic role at home. Thus, the cult of domesticity became a means by which to rationalize and discipline space and time (Ehrenreich and English 1979; Lewis 1980; Welter 1966). Like the workplace, domestic space was increasingly disciplined. The training women received in the efficient, ordered use of domestic space by home economists therefore could be transferred directly to the shop floor. Women's positions in the labor force can best be explained by the complexity of the relationship between the structure of jobs, the household, ideological conceptions of gender roles, technology, employers, and the state (Davin 1978).

It should be clear from the preceding discussion that the physical landscape and social conditions were being reordered in the nineteenth century as cities grew at a rapid pace through immigration and rural to urban migration. The state became particularly alarmed with the growing numbers of immigrants in this country by the end of the nineteenth century, and an anti-immigration sentiment emerged as concerns over the "swarms" of immigrants "invading" America became a social issue (Hunter 1904; Ross 1914). The creation of gendered spaces and the construction of a new image of motherhood were responses aimed at ensuring the reproduction of middle-class values in the face of a burgeoning immigrant population (Davin 1978; Spain 1992).

CONCLUDING COMMENTS

The application of the principles of scientific management in the workplace had its roots in the American system of manufacture. The American system is a means of manufacturing that involves a "sequential series of operations carried out on successive special-purpose machines that produce interchangeable parts" (Ferguson 1968, 298; cited in Hounshell 1984, 15). One reason that the system was so successful in the production of cutlery was that, unlike the annual design changes in some products (for example, reapers) which imposed severe production limitations on the factory, cutlery design changed relatively little in the nineteenth and early twentieth centuries (see Kightlinger 1985). At the core of these new production practices was the substitution of traditional craft production with a hierarchical order, whose latent function was to achieve efficiency in production. The practices associated with an expanded, ordered output became an important factor in the capitalist transformation of the workplace. While the spatial arrangements of the factory may have been adapted to notions of efficiency and order without substantive resistance, how does one change a worker's conception of the execution of the work process? How did capitalists encourage workers to give up their knowledge of the work process and transfer the direction and control of production to management? How can coercive or ideological forms of dominance be legitimized? Much of this was facilitated through a spatial hegemony that permeated the home and the factory and served to naturalize what were in reality arbitrary, rational decisions.

Our emphasis in this chapter has been on the ways in which nineteenth-century elites used spatial organization to reinforce their positions of power and authority in the emergence of industrial capitalism. We underscored the technological innovations and the reorganization of the workplace to argue that technological change is about control and is by no means politically neutral. From our discussion one might get the impression that by the mid- or late nineteenth century, capital had created a well-disciplined workforce that accepted the material conditions of subordination and the logic of the spatial. Nothing could be farther from the truth.

While it is beyond the scope of this chapter to go into detail, let us at least suggest a few of the many ways that workers responded to the coming of the industrial order. First of all, we know that not all Americans flocked to urban centers to embrace industrial culture. Countless alternative, communal societies and religious movements are testimony to an outright rejection of capitalist principles (McBride 1995). There was still a strong agrarian, anti-industrial sentiment in nineteenth-century New England. Furthermore, those who joined the proletariat workforce varied greatly in their degree of consent. As we have suggested above, workers may have spoiled knives intentionally—a form of industrial sabotage—as a way to regain some degree of autonomy on the shop floor, where hierarchy must have seemed immutable for many (see also Nassaney and Abel 1993). Retired cutlers tell us how they made customized hunting knives for their own use in their "spare time" at work (pers. comm. to Abel, 1996). Finally, worker unrest throughout the region took the form of a series of strikes in the 1880s (Taber 1955, 109). In 1884 and 1885 strikes were instigated by grinders over wage cuts at the Lamson & Goodnow and Russell cutleries (Taber 1955, 110). Among the cutlery workers, the grinders were thought to be especially "proud" and "arrogant" in their attitude toward management (Taber 1955, 111). Through these acts, workers attempted to resist social control and reshape the work process to their own ends. In their efforts to accumulate capital, most industrialists were unwilling to tolerate workers who "wanted to reorganize the productive process and the managerial system so that they would get the just value of their labor and some control over their livelihood" (Zonderman 1992, 294). Owners and managers constituted a powerful minority who sought to create and reproduce the conditions of increasing domination in direct opposition to laborers. An efficacious way to do so was through distinctive patterns of speech, gesture, appearance, and material reality, and the "claim that these cultural differences justify their right to rule" (Shackel 1993, 16).

From this discussion we hope to have shown that the contours of the contemporary world are the outcomes of trends that are deeply rooted in the past. Our understanding of late industrial capitalism will be well served by examining the nineteenth-century origins of industry and industrial relations, since some of our twenty-first-century problems have arisen from the contradictions in social life set in motion long ago. Spatial organization—as embodied in the assembly lines, corporate board rooms, back alleys, and cul-de-sacs of contemporary America—constantly serves to reinforce and legitimize social divisions in society, both in the present and in the past. The lessons of spatiality derived from the cutlery industry are the first steps toward transforming relations of inequality that everywhere accompany industrial life.

NOTE

An earlier version of this paper was prepared for the Eighth Symposium of the George Meany Memorial Archives, "Building History and Labor History: Toward an Interdisciplinary Dialogue." We thank the conference organizers, Stuart Kaufman and Mary Corbin Sies, for their support of our work. The University of Massachusetts Archaeological Services under the direction of Mitchell Mulholland provided the opportunity to conduct investigations at the Russell Cutlery, which led to our understanding of the firm's local and national historical significance. Thanks to Thaddeus Kubis for providing the photograph of the Russell block in

Turners Falls. We appreciate the invitation of Jim Delle, Bob Paynter, and Steve Mrozowski to contribute to this volume. Their efforts to recognize the lines that divide come at a time when many find it psychologically easier to minimize or ignore societal divisions.

REFERENCES CITED

Abel, Marjorie. 1987. *Women, Labor Force Participation, and Economic Development: The Issue of Occupational Segregation.* Ph.D. Diss., Dept. of Anthropology, Univ. of Massachusetts, Amherst. Ann Arbor: University Microfilms.

————. 1990. Women's Work in the Western Massachusetts Rural Economy. In *Labor in Massachusetts: Selected Essays,* ed. K. Fones-Wolf and M. Kaufman, 30–52. Westfield, Mass.: Institute for Massachusetts Studies.

Banta, Martha. 1993. *Taylored Lives.* Chicago: Univ. of Chicago Press.

Bendix, Reinhard. 1956. *Work and Authority in Industry: Ideologies of Management in the Course of Industrialization.* New York: John Wiley & Sons.

Biggs, Lindy. 1996. *The Rational Factory.* Baltimore: Johns Hopkins Univ. Press.

Bishop, John Leander. 1868. *History of American Manufactures from 1608–1860.* Philadelphia.

Bond, Kathleen H. 1989. "That We May Purify Our Corporation by Discharging the Offenders": The Documentary Record of Social Control in the Boott Boardinghouses. In *Interdisciplinary Investigations of the Boott Mills, Lowell, Massachusetts.* Vol. 3, *The Boarding House System as a Way of Life,* ed. M. Beaudry and S. Mrozowski, 23–35. Cultural Resources Management Study No. 21. National Park Service, North Atlantic Regional Office, Boston, Mass.

Braverman, Harry. 1974. *Labor and Monopoly Capital.* New York: Monthly Review Press.

Brecher, Jeremy. 1972. *Strike!* Boston: South End Press.

Bucki, Cecilia. 1987. Dilution and Craft Tradition: Munitions Workers in Bridgeport, Connecticut, 1915–19. In *The New England Working Class and the New Labor History,* ed. H. Gutman and D. Bell, 137–56. Urbana: Univ. of Illinois Press.

Cameron, Adis. 1993. *Radicals of the Worst Sort: Laboring Women in Lawrence, Massachusetts, 1860–1912.* Urbana and Chicago: Univ. of Illinois Press.

Chandler, Alfred D. 1981. The American System and Modern Management. In *Yankee Enterprise: The Rise of the American System of Manufactures,* ed. O. Mayr and R. C. Post, 153–70. Washington, D.C.: Smithsonian Institution Press.

Clancey, Gregory K. 1989. The Origin of the Boott Boardinghouse Plan and Its Fate after 1836. In *Interdisciplinary Investigations of the Boott Mills, Lowell, Massachusetts.* Vol. 3, *The Boarding House System as a Way of Life,* ed. M. Beaudry and S. Mrozowski, 7–21. Cultural Resources Management Study No. 21. National Park Service, North Atlantic Regional Office, Boston, Mass.

Clawson, Dan. 1980. *Bureaucracy and the Labor Process.* New York: Monthly Review Press.

Cockburn, Cynthia. 1983. *Brothers: Male Dominance and Technological Change.* London: Pluto Press.

Comstock, William Philip. 1919. *The Housing Book.* New York: William T. Comstock Co.

Davin, Anna. 1978. Imperialism and Motherhood. *History Workshop* 5:9–66.

Demers, Paul, and Jerome Voss. 1995. "Social Space, Social Engineering, and Social Control in Nineteenth Century America." Symposium presented at the annual meeting of the Society for Historical Archaeology, Washington, D.C.

Ehrenreich, Barbara, and Deidre English. 1979. *For Her Own Good.* New York: Anchor Books.

Ferguson, Eugene S. 1968. *Bibliography of the History of Technology.* Cambridge: MIT Press.

———. 1981. History and Historiography. In *Yankee Enterprise: The Rise of the American System of Manufactures,* ed. O. Mayr and R. C. Post, 1–23. Washington, D.C.: Smithsonian Institution Press.

Foucault, Michel. 1979. *Discipline and Punish: The Birth of the Prison.* New York: Vintage Books.

———. 1980. *Power and Knowledge.* New York: Pantheon.

———. 1984. *The History of Sexuality.* Vol. 1, *An Introduction.* Trans. Robert Hurley. London: Penguin Books.

Frederick, Christine. 1913. *The New Housekeeping.* New York: Doubleday.

Gardiner, Jean. 1975. The Role of Domestic Labor. *New Left Review* 89:47–58.

Gordon, David, Richard Edwards, and Michael Reich. 1982. *Segmented Work, Divided Workers.* Cambridge: Cambridge Univ. Press.

Gordon, Robert B., and Patrick M. Malone. 1994. *The Texture of Industry: An Archaeological View of the Industrialization of North America.* New York: Oxford Univ. Press.

Gottman, Jean. 1980. Organizing and Reorganizing Space. In *Center and Periphery: Spatial Variation in Politics,* ed. J. Gottman, 217–24. Beverly Hills: Sage Publications.

Handsman, Russell G. 1987. Class Histories, Self-Doubt, and the Archaeology of Preserved Landscapes. Paper presented at the annual meeting of the Society for Historical Archaeology, Savannah, Ga.

Harvey, David, 1989. *The Condition of Postmodernity: An Enquiry into the Origins of Cultural Change.* Oxford: Basil Blackwell.

———. ed. 1973. *Social Justice and the City.* Baltimore: Johns Hopkins Univ.

Hayden, Delores. 1981. *The Grand Domestic Revolution.* Cambridge: MIT Press.

Hegmon, Michelle. 1989. The Styles of Integration: Ceramic Style and Pueblo I Integrative Architecture in Southwestern Colorado. In *The Architecture of Social Organization in Prehistoric Pueblos,* ed. W. D. Lipe and M. Hegmon, 125–42. Occasional Paper 1, Crow Canyon Archaeological Center, Cortez, Colorado.

Hofstadter, Richard. 1955. *The Age of Reform.* New York: Vintage Books.

Hounshell, David A. 1984. *From the American System to Mass Production, 1800–1932.* Baltimore: Johns Hopkins Univ. Press.

Humphries, Jane. 1977. The Working Class Family, Women's Liberation, and Class Struggle: The Case of Nineteenth Century British History. *The Review of Radical Political Economics* 9 (3): 25–41.

Hunter, Robert. 1904. *Poverty.* New York: Harper Torchbooks.

Jenkins, Paul. 1982. *The Conservative Rebel: A Social History of Greenfield, Massachusetts.* Greenfield, Mass.

Jones, Edgar. 1985. *Industrial Architecture in Britain, 1750–1939.* New York: Facts on File.

Kelley, Robin D. G. 1992. An Archaeology of Resistance. *American Quarterly* 44 (2): 292–98.

Kightlinger, Lisa. 1985. Cutlery as an Indicator of Change in the Connecticut River Valley. Manuscript on File, Dept. of Anthropology, Univ. of Massachusetts, Amherst.

Kulik, Gary, Roger Parks, and Theodore Z. Penn. 1982. Introduction. In *The New England Mill Village, 1790–1860,* ed. G. Kulik, R. Parks, and T. Z. Penn, xxii–xxxv. Cambridge: MIT Press.

Landes, David S., ed. 1966. *The Rise of Capitalism.* New York: Macmillan.

Lefebvre, Henri. 1976. Reflections on the Politics of Space. *Antipode* 8 (2): 30–37.

Leone, Mark P. 1984. Interpreting Ideology in Historical Archaeology: Using the Rules of Perspective in William Paca Garden in Annapolis, Maryland. In *Ideology, Power, and Prehistory,* ed. D. Miller and C. Tilley, 25–35. Cambridge: Cambridge Univ. Press.

Levin, Jed. 1985. Drinking on the Job: How Effective Was Capitalist Work Discipline? *American Archaeology* 5 (3): 195–201.

Lewis, Jane. 1980. *The Politics of Motherhood.* London: Groom Helm.

Lewis, Peirce F. 1979. Axioms for Reading the Landscape. In *The Interpretations of Ordinary Landscapes,* ed. D. W. Meinig, 11–32. New York: Oxford Univ. Press.

Linebaugh, Donald W., and Gary G. Robinson, eds. 1994. *Spatial Patterning in Historical Archaeology: Selected Studies of Settlement.* William and Mary Center for Archaeological Research, Dept. of Anthropology, Occasional Papers in Archaeology No. 2.

Lloyd, Godfrey I. H. 1913. *The Cutlery Trades.* New York: Longmans, Green and Co.

Marglin, Stephen A. 1974. "What Do Bosses Do? The Origins and Functions of Hierarchy in Capitalist Production." *Review of Radical Political Economy* 6:60–112.

McBride, Kim A. 1995. The Concept of Order at Pleasant Hill: A Shaker Approach to "Urban Planning" as Seen in the Built Environment. Paper presented in the Symposium "Social Space, Social Engineering, and Social Control in Nineteenth Century America." Organized by P. Demers and J. Voss at the annual meeting of the Society for Historical Archaeology, Washington, D.C.

McGuire, Randall H. 1991. Building Power in the Cultural Landscape of Broome County, New York, 1880–1940. In *The Archaeology of Inequality,* ed. R. H. McGuire and R. Paynter, 102–24. Oxford: Basil Blackwell.

McMurry, Sally. 1997. *Families and Farmhouses in Nineteenth-Century America: Vernacular Design and Social Change.* Knoxville: Univ. of Tennessee Press.

Merriam, Robert L., Richard A. Davis Jr., David S. Brown, and Michael E. Buerger. 1976. *The History of the John Russell Cutlery Company, 1833–1936.* Greenfield, Mass.: Bete Press.

Miles, Henry A. 1972 [1846]. *Lowell, As It Was, and As It Is.* New York: Arno Press.

Mill, John Stuart. 1848. *Principles of Political Economy.* Boston: Little and Brown.

Milroy, Beth M., and Susan Wisner. 1994. Communities, Work, and Public/Private Models. *Gender, Place, and Culture: A Journal of Feminist Geography* 1:71–90.

Mrozowski, Stephen A. 1991. Landscapes of Inequality. In *The Archaeology of Inequality,* ed. R. H. McGuire and R. Paynter, 79–101. Oxford: Basil Blackwell.

Mrozowski, Stephen A., Grace H. Ziesing, and Mary C. Beaudry. 1996. *Living on the Boott: Historical Archaeology at the Boott Mills Boardinghouses of Lowell, Massachusetts.* Amherst: Univ. of Massachusetts Press.

Nassaney, Michael S. 1992. *Experiments in Social Ranking in Prehistoric Central Arkansas.* Ann Arbor: University Microfilms.

Nassaney, Michael S., and Marjorie Abel. 1993. The Social and Political Contexts of Cutlery Production in the Connecticut Valley. *Dialectical Anthropology* 18:247–89.

Nassaney, Michael S., Uzi Baram, James C. Garman, and Michael F. Milewski. 1996. Guns and Roses: Time Capsules, Ritualism, and the Massachusetts Agricultural College. *Old-Time New England* 74 (262): 59–80.

Nassaney, Michael S., Nicole Kuemin, and Daniel Sayers. 1998. Landscape Reconstruction and Its Implications for Social Relations at the Shepard Site. In *Historical Archaeology in Battle Creek, Michigan: The 1996 Field Season at the Warren B. Shepard Site (20ca104),* ed. M. S. Nassaney, 111–34. Archaeological Report No. 20. Dept. of Anthropology, Western Michigan University, Kalamazoo, Mich.

Nassaney, Michael S., Alan McArdle, and Peter Stott. 1989. An Archaeological Locational Survey, Site Evaluation, and Data Recovery at the Russell-Harrington Cutlery Site, Turners Falls, Massachusetts. Univ. of Massachusetts Archaeological Services Report 68. On File at the Massachusetts Historical Commission, Office of the Secretary of State, Boston.

Nassaney, Michael S., and Robert Paynter. 1995. Spatiality and Social Relations. Paper presented in the symposium "Social Space, Social Engineering, and Social Control in Nineteenth-Century America." Organized by P. Demers and J. Voss at the annual meeting of the Society for Historical Archaeology, Washington, D.C.

Nassaney, Michael S., and Kenneth E. Sassaman, eds. 1995. *Native American Interactions: Multiscalar Analyses and Interpretations in the Eastern Woodlands.* Knoxville: Univ. of Tennessee Press.

Nelson, Daniel. 1981. The American System and the American Worker. In *Yankee Enterprise: The Rise of the American System of Manufactures,* ed. O. Mayr and R. C. Post, 171–87. Washington, D.C.: Smithsonian Institution Press.

Noble, David F. 1986. *Forces of Production: A Social History of Industrial Automation.* New York: Oxford Univ. Press.

Oliver, John W. 1956. *History of American Technology.* New York: Ronald Press.

Orser, Charles E., Jr. 1996. *A Historical Archaeology of the Modern World.* New York: Plenum.

Pattison, Mary. 1915. *Principles of Domestic Engineering.* New York: Trow Press.

Paynter, Robert. 1982. *Models of Spatial Inequality.* New York: Academic Press.

———. 1988. Steps to an Archaeology of Capitalism: Material Change and Class Analysis. In *The Recovery of Meaning: Historical Archaeology in the Eastern United States,* ed. M. Leone and P. Potter Jr., 407–33. Washington, D.C.: Smithsonian Institution Press.

Robert Paynter, and Randall H. McGuire. 1991. The Archaeology of Inequality: Material Culture, Domination, and Resistance. In *The Archaeology of Inequality,* ed. R. H. McGuire and R. Paynter, 1–27. Oxford: Basil Blackwell.

Reader, William. 1973. *Yankees, Immigrants, and Social Climbers: A Study of Social Mobility in Greenfield, Massachusetts, 1850–1970.* Ann Arbor: University Microfilms.

Rosenzweig, Roy. 1979. Middle-Class Parks and Working-Class Play: The Struggle over Recreational Space in Worcester, Massachusetts, 1870–1910. *Radical History Review* 21:31–45.

Ross, Edward A. 1914. *The Old World and the New.* New York: Century Co.

Rotman, Deborah L., and Michael S. Nassaney. 1997. Class, Gender, and the Built Environment: Deriving Social Relations from Cultural Landscapes in Southwest Michigan. *Historical Archaeology* 31 (3): 42–62.

Ruxton, George F. 1951. *Life in the Far West.* Norman: Univ. of Oklahoma Press.

Sanborn Fire Insurance Company. 1884. Sanborn Fire Insurance Map of Turners Falls, Massachusetts, 1884. Chadwyck-Healy. Microfilm on File at the W. E. B. DuBois Library, Univ. of Massachusetts, Amherst.

Sande, Theodore A. 1978. *Industrial Archeology: A New Look at the American Heritage.* New York: Penguin.

Scott, James. 1990. *Domination and the Arts of Resistance: Hidden Transcripts.* New Haven: Yale Univ. Press.

Shackel, Paul A. 1993. *Personal Discipline and Material Culture.* Knoxville: Univ. of Tennessee Press.

———. 1996. *Culture Change and the New Technology: An Archaeology of the Early American Industrial Era.* New York: Plenum.

Shaiken, Harley. 1985. *Work Transformed: Automation and Labor in the Computer Age.* New York: Holt, Rinehart and Winston.

Siskind, Janet. 1991. Class Discourse in an Early Nineteenth-Century New England Factory. *Dialectical Anthropology* 16:35–48.

Smith, Merrit Roe. 1985. Army Ordnance and the "American System" of Manufacturing, 1815–1861. In *Military Enterprise and Technological Change: Perspectives on the American Experience,* ed. M. R. Smith, 39–86. Cambridge: MIT Press.

Smithurst, Peter. 1987. *The Cutlery Industry.* England: Shire Publications Ltd.

Soja, Edward W. 1971. The Political Organization of Space. Association of American Geographers Resource Paper 8. Washington, D.C.

————. 1989. *Postmodern Geographies: The Reassertion of Space in Critical Social Theory.* London: Verso.

Spain, Daphne. 1992. *Gendered Spaces.* Chapel Hill: Univ. of North Carolina Press.

Stone, Orra. 1930. *History of Massachusetts Industries.* Boston: S. J. Clarke Publishing.

Taber, Martha Van Hoesen. 1955. *A History of the Cutlery Industry in the Connecticut Valley.* Vol. 41, *Smith College Studies in History.* Northampton, Mass., Department of History, Smith College.

Thompson, Edward P. 1967. Time, Work-Discipline, and Industrial Capitalism. *Past and Present* 38:56–96.

Tilley, Christopher. 1990. Michel Foucault: Towards an Archaeology of Archaeology. In *Reading Material Culture: Structuralism, Hermeneutics, and Post-structuralism,* ed. C. Tilley, 281–347. Oxford: Basil Blackwell.

U.S. Commissioner of Labor. 1904. *Eighteenth Annual Report on the Cost of Living and Retail Prices of Food.* Washington, D.C.: Government Printing Office.

Welter, Barbara. 1966. The Cult of True Womanhood, 1820–1860. *American Quarterly* 18:151–74.

Wiebe, Robert H. 1967. *The Search for Order, 1877–1920.* New York: Hill and Wang.

Winner, Langdon. 1986. *The Whale and the Reactor.* Chicago: Univ. of Chicago Press.

Wobst, H. Martin. 1977. Stylistic Behavior and Information Exchange. In *For the Director: Research Essays in Honor of James B. Griffin,* ed. C. Cleland, 317–42. Museum of Anthropology, Univ. of Michigan, Anthropological Papers 61.

Yamin, Rebecca, and Karen B. Metheny, eds. 1996. *Landscape Archaeology: Reading and Interpreting the American Historical Landscape.* Knoxville: Univ. of Tennessee Press.

Zimiles, Martha, and Murray Zimiles. 1973. *Early American Mills.* New York: Bramhall House.

Zonderman, David A. 1992. *Aspirations and Anxieties: New England Workers and the Mechanized Factory System, 1815–1850.* New York: Oxford Univ. Press.

CHAPTER ELEVEN

The Growth of Managerial Capitalism and the Subtleties of Class Analysis in Historical Archaeology

Stephen A. Mrozowski

Historical archaeologists have made the study of class one of their most potent research topics (Paynter 1988; Beaudry and Mrozowski 1987a, 1987b, 1989; McGuire and Paynter 1991; Seifert 1991; Scott 1994; Shackel 1996; Wurst and Fitts 1999). Much of this work has focused on the sharpening of class distinctions and class consciousness during the nineteenth century as the growth of industrial capitalism reached its zenith. One element many of these studies have shared is the view that they see the material world as an active voice in social discourse (Beaudry et al. 1991; Little and Shackel 1992). As such, it serves as a medium for expressing cultural differences. This communication often takes subtle form. Usually when people of various classes saw each other in public spaces, their status was visible in the clothes they wore, their speech, and their material props. These images conveyed and sometimes proclaimed a person's or group's ethnicity, their gender, or their social class.

The purpose of this chapter is to examine the subtle character of material communication in the expression of class. I will argue that all too often archaeologists focus their attention on the largest classes of material culture in their interpretation. They should compliment this approach with a concern for specific items. Individual pieces of jewelry or a certain ceramic pattern may exhibit as much interpretive potential as a hundred undecorated ceramic sherds. This is particularly true when the aims of the analysis are expressions of personal or group identity.

To illustrate this point I will present a comparison of material culture from four distinct classes of workers living in Lowell, Massachusetts, during the nineteenth century. The groups of workers include the mill agents for the Massachusetts Mills, the operatives and skilled laborers working for the Boott Cotton Mills, and the overseers working for the Lawrence Manufacturing Company (fig. 11.1). Each group lived in company-supplied housing. The Massachusetts Mills agent and his family shared a duplex with the agent of the Boott Cotton Mills (fig. 11.2). This well-appointed building was two and one-half stories surrounded by front, side, and rear yards. The more economical, three-and-one-half story Boott blocks included four center units sandwiched between four end units. The middle units served as the boardinghouses for the operatives, most of whom were single women and men. The four end units were home to skilled laborers and their families. Yard space was limited to rear yards at the Boott blocks. The overseers for the Lawrence Manufacturing Company resided in a block the company constructed purposely for them and their families. The Lawrence block included ten two-and-one-half story units that had both front and rear yards.

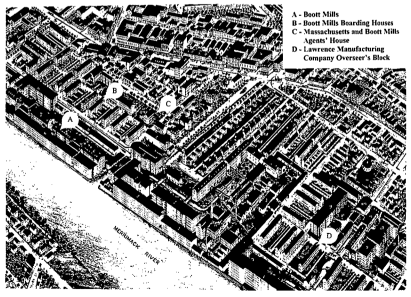

A - Boott Mills
B - Boott Mills Boarding Houses
C - Massachusetts and Boott Mills Agents' House
D - Lawrence Manufacturing Company Overseer's Block

Fig. 11.1. Bird's-eye view of housing units in Lowell, Massachusetts, 1876.

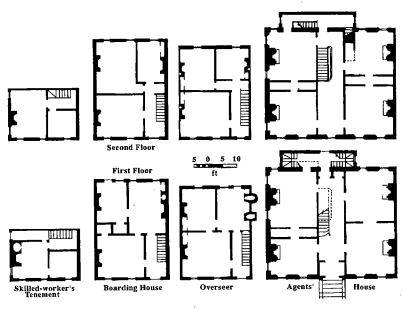

Second Floor

First Floor

5 0 5 10
ft

Skilled-worker's   Boarding House   Overseer   Agents'   House
Tenement

Fig. 11.2: Interior floor plans of four classes of company-supplied workers' housing.

The occupational differences that separated these four groups of mill employees probably went a long way toward distinguishing them socially. Yet, it would be a mistake to assume that analytical constructs like working class or middle classes tell the whole story. Class is fluid and subject to wide-scale variability (see below). Therefore questions remain concerning the manner in which the members of these different groups identified with one another and whether they saw themselves as part of a visible, culturally cohesive unit. One way to answer these questions and to explore the formation of cultural consciousness is through the examination of material culture. Yet before we can begin to examine the forces that contribute to the cultural consciousness of a particular class or classes, some conceptual ambiguities concerning both class and capitalism need to be considered.

THE GROWTH OF MANAGERIAL CAPITALISM

Over the past decade, the archaeology of capitalism has become a dominant theme in historical archaeology. Many have argued that historical archaeology is, by definition, the study of modern capitalism and the cultural consciousness it engendered (see Leone 1982, 1988, 1989, 1995; Paynter 1988; Beaudry and Mrozowski 1987a, 1987b, 1989; Mrozowski 1991; Mrozowski,

Ziesing, and Beaudry 1996; Johnson 1996; Shackel 1993, 1996). Historical archaeologists who have focused their efforts on capitalism have stressed the historical continuities that link contemporary society in the United States with its nineteenth-century cultural antecedents (for example, Leone 1989). As a result we have missed an opportunity to examine the changing character of capitalism and the manner in which it influenced class formation.

One such change that capitalism experienced was the growth of what business historian Alfred Chandler has described as managerial capitalism (1977, 1990). The essence of Chandler's argument is that the early partnerships that led to the establishment of large industrial cities like Lowell and Lawrence, Massachusetts, continued a pattern of mercantile enterprise that had appeared during the later eighteenth century (1977, 15–49). This stance is supported by Dalzell's (1987) work on the Boston Associates, who founded Lowell, a group whom Dalzell maintains were motivated chiefly by a desire to invest their inherited wealth in some new enterprise. Thus, although many see the establishment of Lowell as revolutionary (and in many senses it clearly was), Chandler stresses that it continued an old pattern. The key differences between the original partnerships that led to Lowell's development and the managerial capitalism that shaped its growth after 1840 were the tremendous expansion in the scale of operations and the growing importance of managers. Prior to 1840, growth among even the largest industrial enterprises was limited by scarce labor and reliance upon what still amounted to traditional technologies (Chandler 1977, 62–63). Improvements in machine technology and the development of railroads provided the conditions for rapid growth. In fact the increased scale of operations after 1840 owed much to company diversification into railroads and communications technology (Chandler 1977, 81–203). The result was a new highly structured, hierarchically organized enterprise that was the precursor of the modern industrial giants that we know today (Chandler 1990, 51–89).

A key element of this transformation was the growing need for a class of professional managers. Unlike the early agents and treasurers of the Lowell mills, these managers and overseers were seldom company stockholders. They were salaried employees whose success was based on their ability to improve profits by pushing workers they supervised to be more productive. These management positions were filled by a group whose very existence was linked to the development of managerial capitalism. Corporations thought enough of this new class of employee to construct housing units for their express use. The overseer's block constructed by the Lawrence Manufacturing Company appears to be an early example of housing built exclusively for the corporation's most prized workers. The same was true of the mechanics who worked in the machine shops. As railroads became increasingly important and the expansion of industry prompted the need for machinery, company owners shifted production accordingly. Lowell's machine shop, which had primarily produced power looms and the like, began producing locomotives in the late 1830s. When a new machine shop was constructed by the Essex Company in Lawrence, Massachusetts, in 1846, a new "mechanics' block" was established as well. This was a planned community expressly built for the skilled workers who built machines, tools, and turbines for the many Lawrence mills.

The construction of new housing units for overseers and mechanics marked a new phase in capitalism's evolution. Companies had always differentiated between skilled and unskilled workers in terms of wages; however, it is difficult to say whether the placement of skilled workers and their families in tenements rather than boardinghouses was a product of class or merely demographics. Most operatives were single, while most skilled workers appear to have been older and married. The only noticeable difference in the material culture of the two groups was the presence of slightly more tea and dinner wares in the yards of tenements. This distinction was attributed primarily to household composition and not to class or income differences (Beaudry et al 1991, 173–74). A company agent, by contrast, held a position of social prominence, a position that required all the material trappings of middle-class life. In this instance some of those trappings came with the job in the form of the well-appointed dwellings supplied by the corporation. In effect, this institutionalized class differences. By providing large dwellings constructed of superior materials and handsomely landscaped, Lowell's corporations consciously chose to emphasize the social distance between the agent and his employees (Mrozowski 1991, 96–97).

The overseers and mechanics who lived in separate blocks represent still another gradation in social hierarchy. The overseers in particular represented a new order just emerging in the 1840s. The question that remains unanswered is how the overseers and their families saw their own lives. Did they see themselves as middle class or were their sympathies with the workers? Another question concerns the manner in which these people constructed their material world. Did they accept new ideas about gentility within the home? Is there material evidence that suggests the overseers and their families adopted social behavior that was in keeping with the new social order that accompanied the continuing growth and reconfiguration of capitalism during the nineteenth century? Did gender effect the manner in which men and women participated in what amounted to a cultural dialog? And, finally, what was the true character of this new class of worker and can that character be read in the material record?

Several studies have pointed to the role that material culture was to play as an expression of this new cultural consciousness. The taking of tea, formal dining, and ornamental landscapes, for example, were all expressions of a cultural view that saw order as desirable (for example, Burley 1989; Mrozowski and Beaudry 1990; Wall 1991, 1994; De Cunzo 1995, 1996; Beaudry 1996; Mrozowski 1996). This was especially true of the middle class, where women appear to have increasingly viewed their roles as arbiters of the domestic domain (Wall 1994, 147–58; Shackel 1996, 143–45). Some have argued that these values first appeared among the urban elite of eighteenth-century colonial society (Leone 1984, 1988; Mrozowski 1988; Shackel 1996), an idea consistent with what Chandler (1977) and Dalzell (1987) have suggested concerning the origins of the nineteenth-century industrialist class. Often these values are attributed to particular groups, most notably the elite merchant class or land-owning gentry of the seventeenth and eighteenth centuries or the newly emergent middle class in the nineteenth century. In contrast, little attention has been given to examining the cultural variability within these groups. Class is viewed as a rather uniform, somewhat static concept, when in fact it appears to have been more fluid (Beaudry et al. 1991).

THE FLUIDITY OF CLASS

In the same manner that anthropologists have come to understand the fluid character of culture (for example, Marcus and Fisher 1986; Rabinow and Sullivan 1987), students of class analysis have acknowledged a similar awareness (for example, Wright 1985, 1993). One of the most important facets of this new awareness is the recognition that class should no longer be accorded causal primacy (see Wright 1993, 26–28). Powerful though it may be, class is not the only factor that shapes the dynamics of social interaction. Age, gender, ethnicity, and race all converge in the social arena to shape the discourse (for example, Scott 1994, 7–9).

Another change involves the concept of class itself. Historical archaeologists have too often approached class as a rigid, objective social category rather than the discursive force it can be (Hunt 1989, 7–16; see also Wright 1993, 28–29; Revel 1995, 492–502). In his reappraisal of class as an analytical construct, Wright (1993) has argued that class formation and class consciousness need to be reconsidered in the face of postmodernist critiques and the collapse of world communism. Of specific interest here are his comments concerning the middle class. Wright concedes that the middle class poses problems for Marxist class analysis because "if the abstract concept of class structure is built around polarized classes, what does it mean to be in the 'middle'?" (29). Initially Wright pondered the possibility that certain class locations were inherently contradictory. This was based on the assumption that class structures being rigid, an individual could only be part of one class. The middle class was therefore either "part of the working class (a new working class), part of the petty bourgeoisie (a new petty bourgeoisie) or as an entirely new class in its own right (a professional-managerial class)" (29).

Although Chandler employs the term *managerial hierarchy* instead of *class* when referring to the new managers, he nevertheless leaves little doubt that over time they became a separate and significant group of employees: "Thus the existence of a managerial hierarchy is a defining characteristic of the modern business enterprise . . . once a managerial hierarchy had been formed . . . the hierarchy itself became a source of permanence, power and continued growth. Managers carrying out similar activities in different enterprises often had the same type of training and attended the same types of schools. They read the same journals and joined the same associations" (1977, 7–9).

Today we would refer to Chandler's characterization of the members of this management hierarchy as a class and a class that had its own culture. But is this characterization accurate for the early managers, people like the overseers for the Lawrence Manufacturing Company? Were they a separate class who shared a culture different from either the workers they supervised or the agents who directed them? Or were they, as Wright would argue, a group of individuals with one foot in each class, "simultaneously capitalists and workers-capitalists insofar as they dominated the labor of workers, workers insofar as they did not own the means of production and sold their labor-power to capitalists" (1993, 29). Answers to questions such as these hinge on the social relations that characterized the interaction of the various groups that comprised the company hierarchy. These are difficult to reconstruct without detailed information on social networks, however (see Cerutti 1995, 593–94). The problem is further complicated by the recognition that individual strategies are often more influential in shaping behavior than are pressures to conform and promote group solidarity.

Examining networks and individual behavior are earmarks of the new microanalysis pioneered by Italian and French historians (see Ginzburg 1980;

Cerutti 1995; Revel 1995). Predicated on the assumption that group identity is not necessarily the determinant force in shaping individual behavior, microanalysis seeks to "explore how individual rationality relates to collective identity" (Cerutti 1995, 595; see also Revel 1995, 499). In the same manner that E. P. Thompson (1963) emphasized that the English working class was constantly in the process of being made, produced and reproduced through both group and individual action, micro-historians have stressed the fluid character of the culture consciousness of social or occupational groups (Revel 1995). Therefore, the key to examining the cultural consciousness of a group like the Lawrence Company overseers is a combination of individual and comparative analysis. Unfortunately, isolating individual household assemblages in the archaeological record is extremely difficult in the urban context (see below). Although documentary research can aid in the identification of household-level assemblages, the challenge still remains recovering enough material from well-controlled archaeological contexts to allow both individual household and interhousehold comparisons to be carried out. One method to overcome these difficulties is to combine the broad-based comparative analysis of assemblages from large residential units like boarding-houses and tenements with the examination of individual artifacts that can, as argued above, be more interpretively evocative. Context, however, is the key to both approaches and for this we must turn to what is known from documentary sources concerning individual corporations like the Lawrence Manufacturing Company and the housing blocks they constructed.

THE LAWRENCE
MANUFACTURING COMPANY

The Lawrence Manufacturing Company was chartered by the Massachusetts General Court on June 7, 1831. In May of the same year, Amos A. Lawrence entered into an indenture with the Proprietors of Locks and Canals "for six mill seats and the Lower Level of the Western Canal . . . with about 203 acres . . . and water power" (Indenture between Locks and Canals and Amos A. Lawrence, May 5, 1831, hereafter L&C/LMC 1831). Authorized to raise $1.2 million in capital, LMC contracted with Locks and Canals for the latter to "supervise the erection of four mills including gearing and such appurtenances to the same" (L&C/LMC 1831). A total of 1,200 shares at $1,000 per share were quickly sold. The Tremont and Suffolk manufacturing companies were organized in the same year. These three companies were directed as a single unit under the watchful eye of one treasurer, Henry Hall.

Hall oversaw the financial operations of the mills from his Boston office and depended on the individual agents for each of three companies, who resided in Lowell (Vernon-Wortzel 1992, 9). Two years later, in 1833, the first mills were operating. At this time, LMC purchased lots for boardinghouses from the Proprietors of Locks and Canals.

The construction of the mills and company housing was a massive undertaking that involved moving millions of square yards of earth. During the first two decades of the company's operation, LMC sustained 1,300 employees, with five mills in use. Between 1846 and 1853, employment remained steady at 1,200 female and 200 male operatives. This number increased to a total of 1,600 workers (1,300 females and 300 males) by 1857. Production and employment remained at this level until the Civil War, when cotton shortages closed the mills in Lowell until 1864. After the end of the Civil War, LMC transformed one mill that originally processed cotton to woolen knit hosiery and underwear production. Production of these knitted goods was so successful that by 1884 employment increased to about 4,000 individuals. In 1896, a portion of the cloth mill yard was sold to the Tremont and Suffolk Manufacturing Company. LMC continued to focus more of its production on knitted merchandise. By the end of the nineteenth century and into the early twentieth century, with an estimated 4,200 employees, LMC became the "world's largest producer of cotton seamless hosiery and flat and ribbed underwear." Production declined in the 1920s, however, and in 1926 LMC was sold to C. Brooks Stevens. Stevens was president of the Ames Worsted Company and treasurer of the Middlesex Manufacturing Company. From 1927 to 1939 the majority of the mill yard was sold off in separate lots.

THE LAWRENCE COMPANY OVERSEERS' BLOCK

The Lawrence Company overseers' block was constructed between 1845 and 1850. Like other company housing constructed for mills in Lowell, its design evolved as part of the early "Waltham system" of architecture and company planning that found expression in the industrial towns and cities established throughout New England between 1820 and 1850 (Candee 1985, 17–43). The earliest corporate-owned boardinghouses constructed in Lowell were two-and-one-half–story duplexes erected in 1825 for the Merrimack Corporation and the Lowell Machine Shop. These early boardinghouse blocks were part of a phase of building and design that reached its apex with the Appleton Corporation's construction of three housing blocks around 1828 (Clancey

1989, 8). These large, three-and-one-half–story blocks then became the standard for Lowell and other New England mill towns for roughly the next decade. In Lowell, Locks and Canals began moving away from this design after 1840 (13). Instead they began using tenements that were originally designed as blocks of overseer housing. Although some of these early blocks retained characteristics of the Appleton-type boardinghouses—for example, three-and-one-half stories with kitchens and parlors of units abutting—they differed in that there were no end units, and rooms were generally larger (13). Their exterior design differed as well, reflecting the transition from Federal to Greek Revival style.

Unlike the large, three-and-one-half–story tenements that were constructed in Lowell after 1840, the LMC overseers' block was only two and one-half stories tall. In a report prepared for the National Park Service, Sheply, Bulfinch, Richardson, and Abbott (1980) raised questions concerning whether the Lawrence overseers' block actually housed mill overseers. Clancey (1989, 20–21) had similar concerns, but he was more interested in the source of the two-and-one-half-story plan of the block and its relationship to the mechanics' block in Lawrence, Massachusetts, discussed above. The latter was designed as the residence for skilled craftsmen and overseers exclusively. In fact, when the block was sold in 1859 the deed contained expressed instructions that the unit was to be used for skilled workers only.

In an effort to address questions concerning who actually resided in the Lawrence block, Lowell city directories for 1851, 1855, 1861, 1870, 1880, and 1890, as well as the federal census of 1870, were consulted. These sources revealed that the Lawrence block, the focus of our examination, contained units 19 through 28 along Tremont Street. The possibility that unit numbers changed was checked by comparing the 1879 city directory with the earliest map of the site showing street numbers dating to the same year. The same was done with the 1924 city directory and the 1924 city atlas, which is the last atlas that illustrates the block. These comparisons confirmed that Lawrence Company units 19 through 28 were consistently associated with this block between 1879 and 1924. Fortunately, some of the overseers and other mill workers listed as living in the Tremont block had also lived in the same units from as early as 1851. This is fairly strong evidence that the street addresses seen in the City Directories remained consistent over the life of the LMC's overseers' block.

A review of the city directories and the 1870 census revealed a pattern of occupation that suggests that cases did occur when LMC overseers and operatives lived intermingled in the same company-owned housing block, rather than separated into different residential areas. In the 1851 directory, for example, only three of the ten units were home to overseers. These were units 24, 25, and 26, home to overseers Horace Parmenter, Charles Abbott, and Daniel Wheeler, respectively (map 11.1). These same three were again listed in the 1855 directory. By 1861, three additional units now housed overseers, units 21, 22, and 23. By 1870, units 20, 27, and 28 were also homes to overseers (including Daniel Wheeler, in

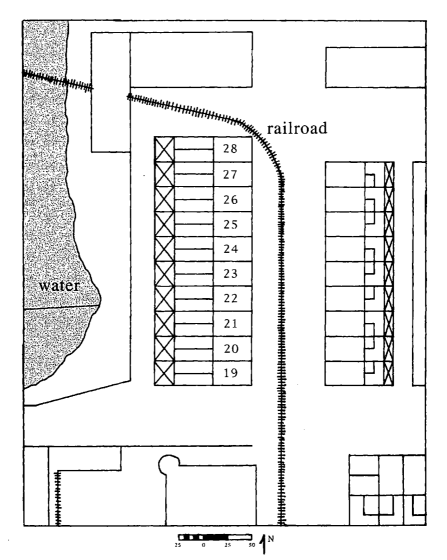

Map 11.1. Housing unit numbers of Lawrence Company
overseers' block, Lowell, Massachusetts.

Stephen A. Mrozowski

unit 20, having moved from unit 26 sometime after 1855), establishing a trend that would continue in the 1880 and 1890 directories. Although the documentary sources clearly show that over time the overseers' block increasingly housed overseers, the sources also show that movement from unit to unit as well as between other company housing blocks was common.

The continuous movement of families from unit to unit represents the kinds of activities that are quite common in the urban context and which have a tremendous impact on the character of the archaeological record. In New England the link between frequent household shifts and an archaeological record shaped by those changes has been well established (Mrozowski 1984, 1991; Beaudry 1984). Because of the rapid turnover in households and the intensity of land use, it is sometimes impossible to identify discrete assemblages that can be linked to individual households. In some instances it is possible (for example, Mrozowski 1984; Beaudry 1984; Beaudry and Mrozowski 1987b, 1989; Wall 1994; Yentsch 1994), but this often requires a rigorous analysis of archaeological formation processes, a long, single-family occupation, luck, or some combination of these factors. Others have argued that household analysis is not only difficult, but possibly misguided because of the question of representativeness (see Cheek and Seifert 1994, 268–69). For many, the more appropriate analytical unit is the neighborhood (Cressey 1983; Brown 1987; Rothschild 1987, 1990). This overcomes the issue of representation and allows analysis to focus more on the issue of class. Because of the movement of overseers' households from unit to unit and in and out of the block, it was decided to focus our attention primarily on units which were overseers' residents for the majority of their occupational history. For the purposes of this chapter, material culture from units 20, 21, 23, 24, 25 (map 11.1) was approached as a single group representative of its class. Despite its limitations, this approach seemed the most appropriate for comparative purposes.

THE MATERIAL EXPRESSIONS OF CLASS

Ceramics

Like the yards and yards of cloth produced in Lowell, ceramics and glassware were a mainstay of the industrial order. By the mid-nineteenth century the ceramic and glass industries had reached a point where they could offer an overwhelming variety of types and styles affordable for wealthy and poor alike. Historical archaeologists working with nineteenth-century sites have stressed the need to employ typologies based on decoration rather than ware type in conducting social analysis (Miller 1980; Majewski and O'Brien 1987). This emphasis on the use of decoration in the analysis of ceramics was also used to examine the ceramics from the Boott Mills' boardinghouses and tenements (Dutton 1989; Beaudry et al. 1991; Mrozowski et al. 1996). It was decided to approach the analysis of ceramics from the overseers' block in the same manner, using the Boot Mills' material for comparative purposes.

A second consideration in the ceramics analysis was the vessel types present and what they suggest concerning dining habits. Two important questions stem from this issue. The first is the degree of dining formality as indicated by ware and vessel types. In most instances formal dining can be measured by the degree of vessel diversity—whether there are several classes of vessels, or whether they are more standardized. The second is the presence of ceramics for entertainment purposes. This is usually measured by the overall percentage of tea wares, cups, and saucers, but especially by those made of porcelain or that are finely decorated. In order to measure the overall social position of the household, it is also helpful to compare the percentages of both table wares and tea wares in contrast to food-preparation or food-storage vessels.

The ceramic analysis focused only on vessels. In quantifying the results of the ceramic analysis, efforts were made to make the data comparable to those presented in the Boott Mills' report (see Dutton 1989). In order to generate tables that incorporated the Boott Mills' ceramic data, it was necessary to use the same categories. In most instances this presented little problem, although the ironstone ware type that was used in the analysis of overseers' block material was not employed during the Boott Mills' analysis. Another problem was the lack of comparable data from the Kirk Street agents' house. Only the ceramics recovered from the utility trench excavations were quantified according to vessel type (see Rodenhiser and Dutton 1987, 91), and even here, no tables were generated concerning decoration or functional categories.

A summary of ceramic vessels by ware type is presented in table 11.1. The assemblage has an interesting mix of pearlware, whiteware, ironstones, and redware. Combined, the pearlware and whiteware dominate the assemblage, representing a little more than 65 percent of the total vessels recovered. These consisted primarily of green, brown, mulberry, and black transfer-printed pearlware and whiteware. Several examples of embossed, blue-shell edged pearlware were also recovered. These date to the period 1830 to 1860 and represent some of the most popular ceramics of the period (Hunter and Miller 1994). The large percentage of pearlware and the presence of ten redware vessels is interesting, especially in contrast to the small number of stoneware vessels. Stoneware was often a ware of choice for storage vessels, but in this instance only two such vessels were recovered. The large number of redware vessels is also somewhat misleading, in that seven of the ten recovered were from flowerpots (table 11.2). The presence of these flowerpots is significant, however, because they suggest that plants were used extensively for ornamentation. The larger percentage of pearlware could be the result of the temporal differences between the overseers' block and the Boott housing units. Although the Boott block was constructed before the overseers' block, it contained fewer early deposits of cultural material. It is also possible that the larger percentage of pearlware could signal a status difference.

In terms of functional categories it appears that the overwhelming majority of ceramics recovered can be categorized as either tea- or tablewares (table 11.3). In fact, if the number of plates, cups, and saucers is combined, as a group they represent close to 65 percent of the assemblage. Add to this the eleven bowls and two serving dishes found on the site, and almost 84 percent of assemblage is made up of food consumption or serving vessels

TABLE 11.1

Summary of Ceramics by Ware Type

| | Tenement Block | | Boardinghouse | | Overseers' Block | |
	n	%	n	%	n	%
Ware Type						
Bennington	0	0.00	1	0.52	0	0.00
Creamware	1	1.16	5	2.61	0	0.00
Earthenware	0	0.00	1	0.52	0	0.00
Ironstone	0	0.00	0	0.00	10	13.69
Lusterware	0	0.00	0	0.00	1	1.37
Pearlware	2	2.32	1	0.52	21	28.77
Porcelain	11	12.79	8	4.18	1	1.37
Redware	12	13.95	12	6.28	10	13.70
Stoneware	3	3.48	11	5.75	1	1.37
Whiteware	56	65.11	149	78.01	28	38.36
Yellow ware	1	1.16	3	1.57	1	1.37
Total	86	100.00	191	100.00	73	100.00

TABLE 11.2

Summary of Ceramics by Vessel Type

	Tenement Block		Boardinghouse		Overseers' Block	
	n	%	n	%	n	%
Vessel Type						
Ale bottle	1	1.15	0	0.00	0	0.00
Bowl	18	20.65	50	26.50	11	15.50
Chamber pot	1	1.15	0	0.00	0	0.00
Crock	1	1.15	2	1.05	0	0.00
Cup	13	15.00	22	11.65	12	17.00
Flowerpot	3	3.50	5	2.65	7	10.00
Gravy boat	0	0.00	1	0.53	0	0.00
Jar	4	4.60	4	2.12	0	0.00
Pan	0	0.00	0	0.00	1	1.37
Plate	10	11.50	30	15.85	20	28.00
Platter	3	3.50	10	5.30	1	1.40
Pot	4	4.60	1	0.53	2	2.80
Saucer	18	20.65	36	19.00	16	22.50
Serving dish	0	0.00	0	0.00	1	1.40
Teapot	0	0.00	1	0.53	0	0.00
Washbasin	0	0.00	1	0.53	0	0.00
Unidentified	11	12.55	26	13.76	NA	
Total	87	100.00	189	100.00	71	100.00

(see tables 11.2 and 11.3). This stands in stark contrast to the small number of food preparation vessels represented by only three vessels, or a little more than 4 percent of the assemblage (see table 11.3). This pattern is similar to that seen at both the Boott tenements and boardinghouses. There is, however, a more noticeable difference in the number of bowls with percentages found at both Boott housing types as compared to the overseers' block. This could be a subtle but important distinction suggesting that fewer stews were being consumed by the overseers and their families in comparison to either the skilled workers' households or the operatives residing in the boardinghouses. This pattern also seems to correspond with the larger number of platters at the boardinghouses, exactly what one might expect where communal eating was the practice.

The question of assemblage diversity is difficult to address given the limited number of reconstructible vessels recovered from the block. As a result it is difficult to determine whether there is tremendous range in the size of plates, for example. Assemblages comprising entire sets of dinnerware often exhibit the kind of vessel diversity needed to speak to the issue of dining formality. In this case the preponderance of secondary refuse in the yards limits our ability to address this issue with a level of satisfaction. What the results do indicate is that a degree of formality was brought to the table by the presence of platters, a serving dish, and several sizes of bowls, cups, and saucers. Based on this, it appears the overseers possessed ceramic collections diverse enough to offer their guests formal dinnerware. This pattern is also evident when comparing the percentages of table- and teaware between the three household types (table 11.3). In this case, there is a considerably larger percentage of tableware appearing in the overseer households than at either the tenement or boardinghouses. A comparison of teaware, however, once again points to important but more subtle distinctions between the three housing types.

The functional character of the assemblage indicates one of the reasons why decoration has been used more widely as a means of determining its social personality. In this instance it proved equally if not more valuable when

TABLE 11.3

Table, Storage, Serving, Tea, and Coffee Ware

	Tenement Block		Boardinghouse		Overseers' Block	
	n	%	n	%	n	%
Functional type						
Tableware	19	24.05	71	36.59	33	50.00
Storage ware	9	11.39	11	5.67	2	3.00
Tea and coffee ware	28	35.44	56	28.86	28	42.50
Serving flatware	13	16.45	40	20.61	2	3.00
Serving bowls	10	12.65	16	8.24	1 pos	1.50
Total	79	100.00	194	100.00	66	100.00

conducting comparisons on the basis of ware type and function alone. Table 11.4 contains a summary of the site assemblage grouped according to decoration. As it illustrates, much of the assemblage comprises undecorated whiteware. The two other notable decorative treatments are transfer printing, 19.18 percent, and hand-painted vessels, 16.44 percent of the assemblage. The percentage of transfer-printed vessels at the overseers block is relatively comparable, though still higher, than those from the Boott Mills' boardinghouse and tenement (see table 11.4). The number of hand-painted vessels at the overseers' block, although slightly larger than that recovered from the Boott tenement, represent a much larger percentage of the assemblage as compared with the Boott boardinghouses.

Overall the ceramic assemblage from the overseers' block seems to reflect the higher status of the overseers when compared with the results from the Boott Mills' boardinghouses and tenements. The slightly higher percentages of hand-painted and transfer-printed ware is evidence of the greater buying power of the overseers' households. Overseers' salaries were usually twice to three times

TABLE 11.4

Summary of Ceramics by Decoration

	Tenement Block		Boardinghouse		Overseers' Block	
	n	%	n	%	n	%
Decoration						
Decal	1	1.16	4	2.09	1	1.37
Dipped	0	0.00	3	1.57	0	0.00
Edged	6	6.97	11	5.75	4	5.48
Gilded	9	10.46	8	4.18	2	2.74
Hand painted	9	10.46	8	4.18	12	16.44
Lead glazed	6	6.97	10	5.23	0	0.00
Molded	9	10.46	29	15.18	4	15.48
Overglazed	1	1.16	0	0.00	0	0.00
Salt glazed	1	1.16	5	2.61	1	1.37
Sponge	3	3.48	6	3.14	0	0.00
Transfer print	12	13.95	32	16.75	14	19.18
Undecorated	28	32.55	74	38.74	35	47.94
Wash	1	1.16	1	0.52	0	0.00
Total	86	100.00	191	100.00	73	100.00

what a mill operative was paid. Although the differences between the three assemblages are less stark than might be expected, it seems safe to assume that they are best explained as reflecting differences in disposable income.

As noted earlier, ceramics recovered from the yard of the Massachusetts Mills agents' house were not quantified in the same fashion as those from either the Boott tenement or boardinghouse. Clearly this inhibits certain kinds of comparative analysis. It does not, however, make the assemblage useless for comparative purposes. An excellent example of this comes from a small deposit of ceramic sherds recovered from a small trash deposit along the property line between units 20 and 21, which had a long history serving as housing for Lawrence overseers. The assemblage from this trash deposit contained a large number of green and black transfer-printed pearlware similar to those recovered from the yard of the Massachusetts Mills agents' house (see Rodenhiser and Dutton 1987). Among these were fragments of a small plate decorated with the Texian Campaign pattern (see Laidecker 1954, 34). This discovery was important for two reasons. First, it is a pattern that was manufactured during the mid-nineteenth century (circa 1850), which, along with the other material dating to this period, provides information on the material culture in use during the initial phases of the block's history. The plate fragment is also important because it represents a decorative pattern that also graced the table of Massachusetts Mills agent Homer Bartlett based on its association with a large assemblage that was attributed to the Bartlett household (Rodenhiser and Dutton 1987, 75; Beaudry and Mrozowski 1987b, 144). Bartlett, along with his wife, Mary Starkweather Bartlett, and three servants lived at the Kirk Street agents' house between 1846 and 1858, when Mary Bartlett died (Bell 1987, 19–20). Bartlett remained in the house, where he was joined until 1861 by his daughter and her husband.

This is but one example of how a single artifact can grow in significance when it draws a connection between different households. In this case, it suggests a similarity in tastes that can be interpreted as one attempt to define social position. It is, however, only one example. Fortunately it is not an isolated instance, as we shall see.

Smoking Pipes

The collection of pipe fragments recovered during the investigations of the overseers' block was quite small, comprising only thirteen stem and bowl fragments. All but one of these pipe fragments was made of white clay. The lone exception was a plastic stem recovered from the yard of unit 21. This dark black plastic stem seems more like the one found at the Massachusetts Mills agents' house (Rodenhiser and Dutton 1987, 83) than the bent-shaped examples that Cook (1989, 205) describes from the Boott Mills's boarding-houses. None of the white clay pipes recovered from the overseers' block exhibit any decoration or markings that would lend themselves to interpretive discussion. The only exception to this is a curious stem fragment that was whittled at both ends. Examples of pipe stems that were purposely modified were found at the Boott Mills' boardinghouses (see Cook 1989, 196–98). These modifications have been attributed to workers shortening the stems of pipes so that they could smoke while at work. These "workers cutties" were highly symbolic of working-class culture. To smoke and work at the same time was considered to be indicative of someone who worked with their hands and was proud of their working-class status (see Beaudry et al. 1991). The example from the overseers' block does not appear to represent a pipe that was whittled so that it could be smoked, although this remains a possibility. Instead it seems to have served as a bead or some other form of decoration. Whether this represents something that a child would have created or whether it could have been used by an adult is impossible to say.

On the surface it would seem that the small size of the collection of smoking pipes limits its interpretive value. Yet, as was the case with the Texian Campaign pattern, the pipe collection contains subtle hints of more meaningful patterns. The presence of a plastic stem and small sample of white pipes is comparable to the smoking equipment from the agents' house and therefore may provide further evidence of a cultural link between its occupants and those of the overseers' block. This observation is based more on the other classes of material culture (see below) recovered than the smoking equipment alone; however, it once again demonstrates the interpretive advantages of looking at individual artifacts.

Personal Items

The assemblage of personal items from the overseers' block is substantial and diverse enough to make up for some of the more limited classes of material culture. The personal items examined here are clothing (including buttons and fasteners) and jewelry. In many respects these items are the most evocative because of the assumed class connection with individual identity. Obviously this is truer of some artifacts than others, but in most cases personal items provide that important human element to the final picture.

The assemblage of buttons recovered from the overseers' block is similar to that found at the Boott Mills's boardinghouse (Ziesing 1989). The assemblage comprises buttons manufactured from a variety of material, including bone, shell, metal, porcelain glass, plastic, and jet. The latter was a black glass used to imitate real jet—made popular by Queen Victoria, who wore black after the death of Prince Albert (Ziesing 1989, 144). The overseers' block button collection, like that from the Boott Mills, reflect the changing technology of the nineteenth century that resulted in an explosion of material production. Materials like glass, shell, bone, horn, and ivory were quickly replaced by plastics. Much of this did not take place until the last quarter of the nineteenth century. When it did happen, however, it altered the purchasing patterns of the middle and lower classes, who could afford the lower cost, mass-produced items. Jet is an excellent example of this because it could be substituted for the real materials, in buttons and jewelry, providing the costume jewelry still popular today.

The shell and bone buttons recovered from the site fall into the category of two- and four-hole types, most of which would have been cloth covered. Dating these artifacts is difficult because the design remained unchanged for centuries. They served a variety of purposes in dresses, waistcoats, and shirts. These bone

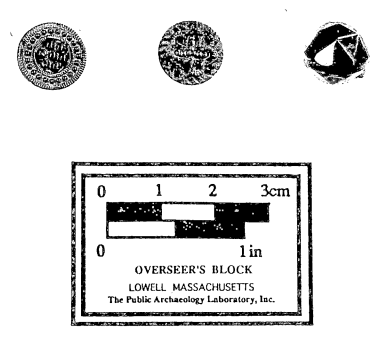

Fig. 11.3. Black glass buttons from overseers' block, Lowell, Massachusetts.
Courtesy of the Public Archaeology Laboratory, Pawtucket, Rhode Island.

and shell buttons were replaced by white porcelain buttons that were durable and attractive enough to be used plain. In some instances they could be decorated with pie-crust edging. These porcelain buttons were often larger than their bone or shell counterparts and served a variety of purposes. They could also be used for both utilitarian, everyday clothing or fancier items for special occasions.

The metal buttons recovered from the overseers' block included a small cache of metal alloy and iron examples. These appear to have been associated with a single garment, possibly a sweater or waistcoat. A single small brass button was also recovered that appears to have come from a man's coat.

The majority of the collection were buttons made of either porcelain or glass. Of these the jet examples were the most interesting. Included among these were several dress buttons similar to some of those recovered from the Boott Mills's boardinghouses (fig. 11.3). One of these was a hobnail example. An identical button made of porcelain was recovered from the Boott Mills's boardinghouse (Ziesing 1989, 149). Another jet button is a molded, faceted ball button similar to one illustrated in the 1895 Montgomery Ward catalog (1895, 84).

These jet buttons all appear to have served as fasteners for women's clothing. This is some of the clearest evidence of women's status and consumer choices recovered from the overseers' block. In her discussion of personal effects from the Boott Mills boardinghouses, Ziesing (1989) argues that jet items are best interpreted as inexpensive substitutes for real jet pieces. The same argument can be made for the women who resided at the overseers' block.

In addition to the assemblage of buttons from the overseers' block, there was also a small but interesting collection of jewelry. The entire collection consisted of four beads: one glass, two porcelain, and one ceramic. One other possible bead was the whittled pipe stem noted earlier. It is difficult to confirm that this pipe stem did indeed serve as a bead, but that may represent the most likely interpretation. All five beads were cylindrical in design. None exhibited any additional decoration. They all appear to have served as either necklace or bracelet links. It is possible that some could have been used to decorate clothing, but this is less likely than their use as items for personal adornment.

Although it would be a rarity to find truly expensive jewelry on an archaeological site unless it were lost or buried with someone, the jet items do suggest another point of cultural similarity with the workers who lived at the Boott Mills boardinghouses. Jet beads were found at the Massachusetts Mills agents' house, but included in this assemblage was at least one example of a gold gilded jewelry piece. Although only one artifact, it nevertheless represents an article of material culture that measures the social distance between the company agents and the overseers they managed. Two gold-plated rings were recovered at the boardinghouses, but like the jet glass items, these represent inexpensive imitations of more expensive pieces.

Summary

The assemblage of personal items recovered from the overseers' block represents some of the most interesting material found at the site. Although the assemblage is small, it offers excellent interpretive information and most importantly, it provides a sensitive measure of class consciousness and consumption patterns. Like the ceramics and smoking equipment described above, these personal items speak to the status of their owners. The buttons and jewelry, for example, are similar to those recovered from the boarding-house and tenement at Boott Mills. One notable exception to this was the small number of jewelry pieces. This is comparable to the assemblage from the Massachusetts Mills agents' house, which shared a similar lack of jewelry. This is perhaps best interpreted as more typical than the Boott Mills boardinghouses and may speak most directly to the larger proportion of women present at the site. The similarity in buttons, however, seems to indicate that the women living at the overseers' block may have worn clothes similar to those worn by working-class women. It is also possible that the buttons belonged to servants. This pattern differs from the ceramic and pipe evidence, which seems to suggest closer cultural links with the mill agent's household.

Taken as a whole the material assemblage from the overseers' block lends support to Wright's (1993) observations concerning the middle class being located in two classes. Yet the evidence also indicates that there was considerable social distance between the overseers and the mill agents. In this sense the overseers appear to be more representative of the kind of middle-class population Wright had in mind. As a group, the overseers appear to have straddled the working class and middle class. Their company-owned housing was slightly larger, with more yard space and, in particular, a front yard. Arguing as Lefebvre (1991) does that space is produced, it would seem that the overseers' block provides an excellent example of a space created expressly for a distinct class of employee. This social distance did not find expression in other classes of material culture, however. Although individual artifacts illustrate points of cultural similarity between the overseers and agents, the same evidence points to connections with the boardinghouse and tenement populations of the Boott. Therefore it seems the overseers were part of a new class of employee that had not yet discovered a degree of cultural cohesion. It also seems that men and women may have been adopting a new cultural identity at varying rates. This observation is based primarily on the black glass buttons that imitate more expensive jet. This same pattern was seen at the boardinghouses and tenements and suggests that the wives of the overseers were dressing in like style. Conversely, the presence of a plastic pipe stem and the Texian Campaign pattern, in conjunction with the ceramics as a whole, seems to indicate greater cultural affinity with the agents.

CONCLUSIONS

As historical archaeologists refine their abilities to examine the evolution of capitalism, they will need to be sensitive to the subtleties of social discourse. In so doing we can begin to redefine notions of class consciousness through the study of its material expression. The evidence from the Lawrence Manufacturing Company's overseers' block suggests a group of employees who had not yet cast themselves as a separate class. In this sense, they had not yet matched Chandler's expectations as a self-sustaining, self-perpetuating cultural group. This would come, but as the nineteenth century progressed, perceptions of work and the social relations of production were still changing. Managers were a new kind of employee who had certain expectations concerning their work and behavior imposed from the top. The additional front yard space that the Lawrence Company afforded their overseers is one material expression of these new expectations. The symbolic importance of this extra space should not be overlooked. It was, after all, an abstract space produced by the companies, not the result of some historical evolution (see Lefebvre 1991, 46–53). The small front yards of the overseers' block, like the front and side yards of the Kirk Street agents' house, were abstract expressions of a new social order that gave texture to the urban industrial landscape. What the overseers and their families chose to do with that space is another question. And it is perhaps the most important questions we can ask, because embedded in this question is the key to extracting the most from the material record. In this instance, the landscape evidence suggests that front and rear yards were used primarily as ornamental spaces. This observation, which is more fully developed in another work (Mrozowski 1999) is based on a combination of landscape and archaeobotanical data. Complimentary information is provided by the material culture recovered from the overseers' block. As noted above, it suggests that the overseers and their families were actively engaged in negotiating their new status. Although the evidence takes subtle form, it is present nonetheless. It can be read in the embossed, shell-edged, and trans-fer-printed pearlware plates recovered from the site. This new status can also be read in the plastic pipe stem found on the site. Together these fragments of material life indicate the negotiation of a new cultural position, situated comfortably between the company agents and the skilled and unskilled laborers the overseers supervised. At the same time, the presence of clay pipes and black glass buttons from women's dresses evoke a consciousness more in keeping with the working-class members of Lowell's population. Ambiguities like this are to be expected, however, as individuals mediate their positions in a rapidly changing social environment.

When the founders of Lowell set their experiment in motion they knew they needed to attract workers. The strategy they chose to accomplish this goal was to offer workers weekly wages and a company-supplied home. In return they demanded a good day's work and behavior in keeping with their own ideals of what was proper. For the first generation of mill operatives and skilled laborers, this covenant was kept. By the 1840s, however, the nature of industry was changing. New technologies and expanding markets presented new opportunities for industrialists to expand their economic power. Large operations like those in Lowell and Lawrence, Massachusetts, were less flexible than smaller mills in experimenting with new technology. Unlike the smaller mills in Rhode Island, for example, that continued to be run by owners who played an active role in daily operations, the larger mill cities experimented with a new generation of personnel, managers like those who resided in the Lawrence Company overseers' block. Eventually this group would, as Chandler (1977) suggests, become a fairly cohesive cultural group that shared similar values. As the nineteenth century unfolded, the material trappings of this new cultural consciousness came more clearly into focus. This process took time and was far from uniform, however. For many it was a struggle for identity in a world that was feeling the weight of momentous change. With the end of the twentieth century, this process, started 160 years ago, has reached a curious juncture, with many middle managers, as they are now known, seeing their positions eliminated as part of downsizing. The cultural dislocation many of these unemployed workers feel today is the same as that felt by generation after generation of mill workers who saw their lives fall prey to the never-ending quest for greater profits. In the end we are left with the stark reality that, after a few generations, the commitment of Lowell's corporations to their workers was as ephemeral as the cloth they produced.

NOTE

Several organizations helped to support the research discussed in this chapter. I would like to thank Diana Prideaux-Brune of the Division of Planning and Development of the City of Lowell, who funded investigations of the Lawrence block. I would also like to thank Deborah Cox, president of the Public Archaeology Laboratory of Pawtucket, Rhode Island, for supporting the preparation of tables and photographs for use in this publication. My thanks also go to Donna Raymond and Kirk Van Dyke for the preparation of tables and photographs. David Brown of the University of Massachusetts Boston is responsible for the preparation of the graphics used in this publication. Thanks also to Martha Mayo of the Center for Lowell History at the University of Massachusetts, Lowell; Richard Candee of Boston University; Daniel Walsh of the National Park Service; Mark Bograd, former curator at the Lowell National Historical Park; and Albert Bartovics, curator, Historical Manuscripts Division of the Baker Library, Harvard University. Some of the information used in this paper was generated as part of the Lowell Archaeological Survey, a five-year collaborative effort between the Division of Cultural Resources of the North Atlantic Regional Office of the National Park Service and the Center for Archaeological Studies at Boston University. Mary C. Beaudry and I served as co-directors of the project. Finally, I would like to thank James Delle, Robert Paynter, and Charles Orser for their help and ideas concerning the manuscript.

REFERENCES CITED

Beaudry, Mary C. 1984. Archaeology and the Historical Household. *Man in the Northeast* 28:27–38.

———. 1996. Reinventing Historical Archaeology. In *Historical Archaeology and the Study of American Culture,* ed. L. A. De Cunzo and B. L. Herman, 473–97. Knoxville: Univ. of Tennessee Press and The Henry Francis du Pont Winterthur Museum.

Beaudry, Mary C., and Stephen A. Mrozowski, eds. 1987a. *Interdisciplinary Investigations of the Boott Mills, Lowell, Massachusetts.* Vol. 1, *Life at the Boardinghouses.* Cultural Resources Management Study No.18. Division of Cultural Resources, North Atlantic Regional Office, National Park Service, U.S. Dept. of the Interior, Boston.

———. 1987b. *Interdisciplinary Investigations of the Boott Mills, Lowell, Massachusetts.* Vol. 2, *The Kirk Street Agents' House.* Cultural Resources Management Study No. 19. Division of Cultural Resources, North Atlantic Regional Office, National Park Service, U.S. Dept. of the Interior, Boston.

———. 1989. *Interdisciplinary Investigations of the Boott Mills, Lowell, Massachusetts.* Vol. 3, *The Boardinghouses System as a Way of Life.* Cultural Resources Management Study No. 21. Division of Cultural Resources, North Atlantic Regional Office, National Park Service, U.S. Dept. of the Interior, Boston.

Beaudry, Mary C., Lauren J. Cook, and Stephen A. Mrozowski. 1991. Artifacts and Active Voices:

Material Culture as Social Discourse. In *The Archaeology of Inequality,* ed. Randall H. McGuire and Robert Paynter, 150–91. Oxford: Basil Blackwell.

Bell, Edward L. 1987. "So Much Like Home": The Historical Context of the Kirk Street Agents' House. In *Interdisciplinary Investigations of the Boott Mills, Lowell, Massachusetts.* Vol. 2, *The Kirk Street Agents' House,* ed. M. C. Beaudry and S. A. Mrozowski, 5–27. Cultural Resources Management Study No. 19. Division of Cultural Resources, North Atlantic Regional Office, National Park Service, U.S. Dept. of the Interior, Boston.

Bond, Kathleen H. 1989. That We May Purify Our Corporation by Discharging the Offenders: The Documentary Record of Social Control in the Boott Boardinghouses. In *Interdisciplinary Investigations of the Boott Mills, Lowell, Massachusetts.* Vol. 2, *The Kirk Street Agents' House,* ed. M. C. Beaudry and S. A. Mrozowski, 23–36. Cultural Resources Management Study No. 19. Division of Cultural Resources, North Atlantic Regional Office, National Park Service, U.S. Dept. of the Interior, Boston.

Brown, Marley R., III. 1987. "Among Weighty Friends": The Archaeology and Social History of the Jacob Mott Family, Portsmouth, Rhode Island, 1640–1800. Ph.D. Diss., Dept. of Anthropology, Brown University, Providence, R.I.

Burley, David V. 1989. Function, Meaning, and Context: Ambiguities in Ceramic Use by the Hivernant Métis of the Northwestern Plains. *Historical Archaeology* 23 (1): 97–106.

Candee, Richard M. 1982. New Towns of the Early New England Textile Industry. In *Perspectives in Vernacular Architecture,* ed. C. Wells, 31–50. Vernacular Architecture Forum.

———. 1985. Architecture and Corporate Planning in the Early Waltham System. In *Essays from the Lowell Conference on Industrial History 1983: The Industrial City,* ed. R. Weible, 17–43. North Andover, Mass.: Museum of American Textile History.

Chandler, Alfred D. 1977. *The Visible Hand: The Managerial Revolution in American Business.* Cambridge, Mass.: Belknap Press.

———. 1990. *Scale and Scope: The Dynamics of Industrial Capitalism.* Cambridge, Mass.: Belknap Press.

Cheek, Charles D., and Donna J. Seifert. 1994. Neighborhoods and Household Types in Nineteenth-Century Washington, D.C.: Fannie Hill and Mary McNamara in Hooker's Division. In *Historical Archaeology of the Chesapeake,* ed. P. A. Shackel and B. J. Little, 267–81. Washington, D.C.: Smithsonian Institution Press.

Cerutti, S. 1995. The City and the Trades. In *Histories: French Constructions of the Past, Postwar French Thought.* Vol. 1. Ed. J. Revel and L. Hunt, 588–595. New York: The New Press.

Clancey, Gregory K. 1987. An Architectural Study of the Kirk Street Agents' House. In *Interdisciplinary Investigations of the Boott Mills, Lowell, Massachusetts.* Vol. 2, *The Kirk Street Agents' House,* ed. Mary C. Beaudry and Stephen A. Mrozowski, 29–42. Cultural Resources Management Study No. 19. Division of Cultural Resources, North Atlantic Regional Office, National Park Service, U.S. Dept. of the Interior, Boston.

———. 1989. The Origin of the Boott Boardinghouse Plan and Its Fate after 1836. In *Interdisciplinary Investigations of the Boott Mills, Lowell, Massachusetts.* Vol. 3, *The Boarding House System as a Way of Life,* ed. Mary C. Beaudry and Stephen A. Mrozowski, 7–22. Cultural Resources Management Study No. 21. Division of Cultural Resources, North Atlantic Regional Office, National Park Service, U.S. Dept. of the Interior, Boston.

Cook, Lauren J. 1989. Tobacco-Related Material and the Construction of Working-Class Culture. In *Interdisciplinary Investigations of the Boott Mills, Lowell, Massachusetts.* Vol. 3, *The Boarding House System as a Way of Life,* ed. Mary C. Beaudry and Stephen A. Mrozowski, 209–30. Cultural Resources Management Study No. 21. Division of Cultural Resources, North Atlantic Regional Office, National Park Service, U.S. Dept. of the Interior, Boston.

Cressey, Pamela J. 1983. Sharing the Ivory Tower. In *Approaches to Preserving a City's Past.* Alexandria, Va.: Alexandria Urban Archaeology Program.

Dalzell, R. F., Jr. 1987. *Enterprising Elite: The Boston Associates and the World They Made.* New York: W. W. Norton & Co.

De Cunzo, Lu Ann. 1995. Reform, Respite, Ritual: The Archaeology of Institutions; The Magdalen Society of Philadelphia, 1800–1850. *Historical Archaeology* 29 (3).

———. 1996. Introduction: People, Material Culture, Context, and Culture in Historical Archaeology. In *Historical Archaeology and the Study of American Culture,* ed. Lu Ann De Cunzo and Bernard L. Herman, 1–17. Knoxville: Univ. of Tennessee Press and The Henry Francis du Pont Winterthur Museum.

Dutton, David H. 1989. Thrasher's China or Colored Porcelain: Ceramics from a Boott Mills Boardinghouse and Tenement. In *Interdisciplinary Investigations of the Boott Mills, Lowell, Massachusetts.* Vol. 3, *The Boarding House System as a Way of Life,* ed. Mary C. Beaudry and Stephen A. Mrozowski, 83–120. Cultural Resources Management Study No. 21. Division of Cultural Resources, North Atlantic Regional Office, National Park Service, U.S. Dept. of the Interior, Boston.

Ginzburg, Carlo. 1980. *The Cheese and the Worms: The Cosmos of a Sixteenth Century Miller.* Baltimore: Johns Hopkins Univ. Press.

Gross, Lawrence F. 1993. *The Course of Industrial Decline: The Boott Cotton Mills of Lowell, Massachusetts, 1835–1955.* Baltimore: Johns Hopkins Univ. Press.

Hunt, Lynn. 1989. Introduction: History, Culture, and Text. In *The New Cultural History,* ed. L. Hunt, 1–22. Berkeley: California Univ. Press.

Hunter, Robert, and George L. Miller. 1994. English Shell-Edged Earthenwares. *Antiques* (Mar.): 432–43.

Johnson, Matthew. 1996. *An Archaeology of Capitalism.* Oxford: Blackwell.

Lawrence Manufacturing Company. 1830–31. Miscellaneous Records. Vol. 1. Historical Manuscripts Division, Baker Library, Harvard Business School, Boston.

Laidecker, Samuel. 1954. *Anglo-American China Part 1.* Bloomsburg, Pa.: Keystone Printed Specialties Co.

Lefebvre, Henri. 1991. *The Production of Space.* Oxford: Basil Blackwell.

Leone, Mark P. 1982. Some Opinions about Recovering Mind. *American Antiquity* 47:742–60.

———. 1984. Interpreting Ideology in Historical Archaeology: The William Paca Garden in Annapolis, Maryland. In *Ideology, Power, and Prehistory,* ed. Daniel Miller and Christopher Tilley, 25–35. Cambridge: Cambridge Univ. Press.

———. 1988. The Georgian Order as the Order of Merchant Capitalism in Annapolis, Maryland. In *The Recovery of Meaning: Historical Archaeology in the Eastern United States,* ed. Mark P. Leone and Parker B. Potter, Jr., 235–61. Washington, D.C.: Smithsonian Institution Press.

———. 1989. Issues in Historic Landscapes and Gardens. *Historical Archaeology* 23 (1): 45–47.

———. 1995. A Historical Archaeology of Capitalism. *American Anthropologist* 97:251–68.

Little, Barbara J., and Paul A. Shackel, eds. 1992. Meanings and Uses of Material Culture. *Historical Archaeology* 26 (3).

Majewski, Teresita, and Michael O'Brien. 1987. The Use and Misuse of Nineteenth-Century English and American Ceramics in Archaeological Analysis. In *Advances in Archaeological Method and Theory,* vol. 11., ed. M. Schiffer, 97–209. Orlando: Academic Press.

Marcus, George E., and M. J. Fisher. 1986. *Anthropology as Cultural Critique: An Experimental Moment in the Human Sciences.* Chicago: Univ. of Chicago Press.

McGuire, Randall H., and Robert Paynter, eds. 1991. *The Archaeology of Inequality.* Oxford: Basil Blackwell.

Miller, George L. 1980. Classification and Economic Scaling of Nineteenth Century Ceramics. *Historical Archaeology* 14:1–40.

Montgomery Ward & Co. 1895. *Montgomery Ward & Co. Catalogue and Buyers Guide* 57 (spring and summer). Reprint ed. New York: Dover Publications

Mrozowski, Stephen A. 1984. Prospects and Perspectives on an Archaeology of the Household. *Man in the Northeast* 27: 31–49.

———. 1988. For Gentlemen of Capacity and Leisure: The Archaeology of Colonial Newspapers. In *Documentary Archaeology in the New World,* ed. Mary C. Beaudry, 184–91. New York: Cambridge Univ. Press.

———. 1991. Landscapes of Inequality. In *The Archaeology of Inequality,* ed. Randall H. McGuire and Robert Paynter, 79–101. Oxford: Basil Blackwell.

———. 1996. Nature, Society, and Culture: Theoretical Considerations in Historical Archaeology. In *Historical Archaeology and the Study of American Culture,* ed. Lu Ann DeCunzo and Bernard L. Herman, 447–72. Knoxville: Univ. of Tennessee Press and The Henry Francis du Pont Winterthur Museum.

————. 1999. The Commodilocation of Nature. *International Journal of Historical Archaeology* 3 (3): 153–66.

Mrozowski, Stephen A., and M. C. Beaudry. 1990. Archaeology and Landscape of Corporate Ideology. In *Earth Patterns: Essays in Landscape Archaeology*, ed. W. M. Kelso and R. Most, 190–208. Charlottesville: Univ. Press of Virginia.

Mrozowski, Stephen A., Grace H. Ziesing, and Mary C. Beaudry. 1996. *Living on the Boott: Historical Archaeology at the Boott Cotton Mills, Lowell, Massachusetts*. Amherst: Univ. of Massachusetts Press.

Orser, Charles E. 1988. Toward a Theory of Power for Historical Archaeology: Plantations and Space. In *The Recovery of Meaning: Historical Archaeology in the Eastern United States*, ed. Mark P. Leone and Parker B. Potter, Jr., 313–43. Washington, D.C.: Smithsonian Institution Press.

————. 1996. *A Historical Archaeology of the Modern World*. New York: Plenum.

Paynter, Robert. 1988. Steps to an Archaeology of Capitalism: Material Culture and Class Analysis. In *The Recovery of Meaning: Historical Archaeology in the Eastern United States*, ed. Mark P. Leone and Parker B. Potter Jr., 407–33. Washington, D.C.: Smithsonian Institution Press.

Rabinow, Paul, and W. M. Sullivan. 1987. *Interpretive Social Science: A Second Look*. Berkeley: Univ. of California Press.

Revel, Jacques. 1995. Microanalysis and the Construction of the Social. In *Histories: French Constructions of the Past, Postwar French Thought*. Vol. 1. Ed. J. Revel and L. Hunt, 492–502. New York: The New Press.

Rodenhiser, Lorinda B., and David H. Dutton. 1987. Material Culture from The Kirk Street Agents' House Site. In *Interdisciplinary Investigations of the Boott Mills, Lowell, Massachusetts*. Vol. 2, *The Kirk Street Agents' House*, ed. Mary C. Beaudry and Stephen A. Mrozowski, 73–95. Cultural Resources Management Study No. 19. Division of Cultural Resources, North Atlantic Regional Office, National Park Service, U.S. Dept. of the Interior, Boston.

Rothschild, Nan A. 1987. On the Existence of Neighborhoods in Eighteenth-Century New York: Maps, Markets, and Churches. In *Living in Cities: Current Research in Urban Archaeology*, ed. E. Staski, 29–30. Special Publication No. 5. Society for Historical Archaeology.

————. 1990. *New York City Neighborhoods: The Eighteenth Century*. San Diego, Calif.: Academic Press.

Scott, Elizabeth M. 1994. Through the Lens of Gender: Archaeology, Inequality, and Those "of Little Note." In *Those of Little Note: Gender, Race, and Class in Historical Archaeology*, ed. Elizabeth M. Scott, 3–24. Tucson: Univ. of Arizona Press.

————, ed. 1994 *Those of Little Note: Gender, Race, and Class In Historical Archaeology*. Tucson: Univ. of Arizona Press.

Seifert, Donna J., ed. 1991. Gender in Historical Archaeology. *Historical Archaeology* 25 (4).

Shackel, Paul A. 1993. *Personal Discipline and Material Culture: An Archaeology of Annapolis.* Knoxville: Univ. of Tennessee Press.

———. 1996. *Culture Change and the New Technology.* New York: Plenum.

Thompson, E. P. 1963. *The Making of English Working Class.* New York: Vintage.

Vernon-Wortzel L. 1992. *Lowell: The Corporations and the City.* New York: Garland Publishing.

Wall, Diana diZerega. 1991. Sacred Dinners and Secular Teas: Constructing Domesticity in Mid-Nineteenth-Century New York. *Historical Archaeology* 25 (4): 69–81.

———. 1994. *The Archaeology of Gender: Separating the Spheres in Urban America.* New York: Plenum.

Wright, Eric O. 1985. *Classes.* London: Verso Publishers.

———. 1993. Class Analysis, History, and Emancipation. *New Left Review* 202:15–35.

Wurst, LouAnn, and Robert K. Fitts, eds. 1999. Confronting Class. *Historical Archaeology* 33 (1).

Yentsch, Anne E. 1994. *A Chesapeake Family and Their Slaves: A Study in Historical Archaeology.* Cambridge: Cambridge Univ. Press.

Ziesing, Grace H. 1989. Analysis of Personal Effects from Excavations of the Boott Mills Boardinghouse Backlots in Lowell. In *Interdisciplinary Investigations of the Boott Mills, Lowell, Massachusetts.* Vol. 3, *The Boarding House System as a Way of Life,* ed. Mary C. Beaudry and Stephen A. Mrozowski, 141–68. Cultural Resources Management Study No. 21. Division of Cultural Resources, North Atlantic Regional Office, National Park Service, Boston.

EPILOGUE

The Rise of Capitalist Civilization and the Archaeology of Class, Gender, and Race

Thomas C. Patterson

The authors of the chapters in this volume are concerned with class, race, and gender. They argue that these are socially constructed and culturally constituted categories that leave footprints in the archaeological and historical records. The categories themselves express social relations between groups of people that are distinguished from one another. That the diversity they express is constructed means that categories were produced by the peoples whose activities bolstered and sustained those relations rather than by the archaeologists and historians who study them.

The rise of civilization—that is, the formation of social class structures and state institutions—is one important circumstance in which social and cultural hierarchies manifesting class, ethnic, racial, and gender divisions have been constructed, reproduced, and contested. The totality of the relations that exist constitute the social relations of production of each society and endow it with its distinctive character and peculiarities (Marx 1977, 212). The episodes examined here are moments in a large story—one that began five hundred years ago and involved the interconnected rise of capitalism, imperialism, and colonial settlement. Each of the societies discussed in this volume occupied a particular place in the development of that story.

That story has complex beginnings in the fifteenth century. On the one hand, it included the creation of a landless class in northwestern Europe whose members were separated from land and other means of production by the enclosure acts and the simultaneous formation of a domestic market for agricultural produce and other commodities (Brenner 1985). On the other, it involved the dissolution of important Mediterranean trade networks connecting northwestern Europe with those of lands whose shores were washed by the Atlantic, Indian, and Pacific Oceans (Tracy 1990). Gold and silver plundered from the Americas, peoples enslaved in Africa, and colonists from Europe all moved along these routes. Theft, slave raiding, and colonial settlement brought civilization and the hierarchies invented by its beneficiaries for their own purposes to new peoples and places (Patterson 1997, 9–27, 87–116). The inhabitants of the Andes, for instance, were already enmeshed in tributary class and state relations and social hierarchies that bore striking similarities to those of Europe (Patterson 1991, 129–56; Haldon 1993). Other peoples, like the Tupi-Guarani of Brazil, had successfully avoided the civilizing experience (Clastres 1987, 198–217).

The warrior elites of the Andean and Spanish states of the fifteenth century lived on goods and labor they appropriated from direct producers. When the two clashed in the 1530s, each recognized the script used by the other. As Karen Spalding (1998) observed, they saw each other as members of a dominant class, with whom they had more in common than they did with the direct producers of their own societies, and they shared a contempt for non-elites, whether they be Indian or Spanish peasant. By 1600, members of the colonial bureaucracy, whose fortunes were tied to those of the Crown, successfully fractured this Andean-Spanish dominant class along ethnic lines and laid the foundations for a colonial society that was imagined as two separate societies and ruled by a European elite. At the same time, many of the direct producers of Andean society fled from their natal communities to avoid tribute and labor obligations imposed by the state. Some migrated toward the mines of Potosí to engage in wage labor. Some were recruited by local *caciques* (members of the native elite) to fill labor shortages in their own districts. Others migrated to the cities to become artisans, servants, or retainers in Spanish homes (Powers 1995, 45–46).

Doña Luisa Maldonado de San Juan, as Ross Jamieson reports, lived in highland Ecuador in the mid-seventeenth century. She was a member of the provincial Creole elite, whose father had been an official in the municipal government. She was a twice-widowed merchant who inherited property from her deceased husbands as well as social, political, and economic networks they had forged together. She built a house on the plaza in Cuenca and owned four African slaves, a cloth shop in the mining town of Zaruma, and four farms, where four Indian *mitayos* (tributary laborers) raised grain, sheep, and oxen, some of which may have been sold as far away as Lima. While she imported cloth from Panama, she probably also acquired cloth made locally in *obrajes* (textile manufactories) by native women. In all likelihood, she had access to the local cloth and to *mitayo* labor as a result of contractual relationships with local *caciques* (Spalding 1973). The inventory of her possessions showed a mixture of European and Andean objects: gold and silver tableware, Indian-style jewelry, and coconuts, probably inlaid with precious gems or metals, for drinking chocolate. The personal possessions and items found in her urban residence resembled those of other elite families, both Creole and Andean, of the time (Spalding 1984, 199).

There was nothing exceptional about the amount or the sources of Doña Luisa's wealth or the control she exercised over her economic affairs. The only thing that distinguished her from the male members of the Creole elite was that she could not hold political office. However, given her wealth and social connections, manifested partly by her house on the plaza and partly by the political networks she had known from childhood as a result of her father's position, I would suspect that Creole elite men were both respectful and deferential in their face-to-face meetings with her. She was a woman with considerable economic and interpersonal resources at her disposal who could certainly call in favors from both the colonial and church officials if she were inclined to do so.

In 1701, the Catalan aristocracy and guilds, long sympathetic to regional and cultural autonomy, aligned themselves with a faction that, thirteen years later, would ultimately lose a dispute over succession to the Spanish throne. The aristocrats were replaced by bureaucrats loyal to the Crown; the guilds were dismantled; and Catalan language and culture were repressed by the Spanish state. Nonetheless, the region thrived economically during the eighteenth century. The rural population, three quarters of the region's inhabitants, shifted increasingly to capitalist viticulture and the production of wine and brandy for both domestic and foreign markets. Catalan merchants, rivaled only by the Basques, controlled the Mediterranean trade in printed cotton cloth and sugar from the Antilles. By mid-century, Catalan textile workers in the towns and cities were producing calico cotton cloth for sale at home and abroad. Eighteenth-century capital accumulation in the region was underpinned initially and primarily by agriculture and foreign trade. This involved class differentiation and the development of capitalist agriculture in the countryside; the formation of a landless proletariat, some of whom sought continued employment in the agricultural sector and others of whom moved to the cities in search of waged work; and the expansion of monopolistic trading companies (Vicens Vives 1969, 471–605).

Aspects of the economic transformation of Catalonia in the eighteenth century, as Patricia Mangan describes, are manifest in the domestic architecture of Montblanc. Two features are especially evident. One was associated with the growing number of people who were moving to the cities in search of employment; the other involved new construction outside the walls of the old medieval city. Owners of second- and third-class residential structures—but not the aristocrats, professionals, and merchants who owned first-class houses around the plaza—subdivided the interiors of their homes in order to acquire rental income from members of the emerging working class. Public buildings—like the wall towers—were also made inhabitable with a few inexpensive renovations and converted into fourth-class houses by the municipality. The municipality gained income from renting these units and from fines that were levied on residents who violated ordinances that prohibited the construction of window or doors in the town wall. In addition, new houses were built outside in less expensive neighborhoods outside the town wall. One, the shop and residence built by Andreau Bilella i Obradó in 1793, combined features found in first-, second-, and third-class houses in the old city: a first-floor shop opening on the street and a two-room apartment on the second floor with a separate entrance. The apartment was presumably rented to a domestic unit that reproduced itself through wage work.

The eighteenth century witnessed the consolidation of slave-based plantation agriculture in the British and French Caribbean and in the American South. The economic systems that developed in these areas had several distinctive features. First, they were based on labor of slaves imported originally from Africa and then bred in the Americas; for example, more than 900,000 African slaves were brought to Barbados and Jamaica alone between 1701 and 1807 to toil on the plantations. Second, the economies were based on monocrop agriculture, and the commodities produced—cotton, sugar, tobacco, and coffee, for instance—were destined for an expanding world market whose existence depended on the availability and consumption of wage workers living elsewhere. Third, the self-sufficiency of yeoman farmers, particularly in the American South, restricted the development of its domestic market.

This new market differed from the earlier long-distance trade in luxury goods that were consumed by the ruling classes. Merchant capital, as Elizabeth Fox-Genovese and Eugene Genovese (1983, 3–25) have shown, has the capacity to link together different economic systems. Unlike latifundia, which consumed what they produced, the modern plantation system depended on the existence of an industrial capitalist class whose members transformed raw materials, like cotton, into commodities and of a landless proletariat, whose members were forced to purchase the goods they consumed. The Genoveses argue that the wealthiest and most powerful members of the slaveholding class in the Caribbean were, in fact, English capitalists; they were absentee landlords who resided in England and derived income from their plantations; and they had a large stake in the development of English commerce and industry. However, the resident slaveholders in the Old South, who were driven to produce for the world market, sought to forge a culture that simultaneously manifested the dialectic of the master-slave relation and inhibited the development of a social system in which the institutions and mentality of capitalism were predominant. In other words, while the members of the slaveholding class of the Old South were in the capitalist world, they were not of it; this was true of those slaveholders who resided in the Caribbean.

The rise of plantation slavery in the New World during the later half of the seventeenth century underpinned the social construction of racial difference and the rise of racism. As Terrence Epperson (1991, 126–236; 1994) showed elsewhere, the constitution of race as a meaningful analytical category began in the 1680s with the first static classifications of racial differences based on allegedly neutral, empirical criteria, the most important of which was skin color. The construction of racial difference was part of the process of spatial segregation (Epperson 1998, 2). These classifications of the races appeared at the same time that plantations were being reorganized in the Chesapeake. By the late 1680s, these plantations resembled small villages in which the residential structures housing master and worker had become spatially separated. This physical separation of master and worker also manifested dichotomies within the labor force between indentured laborers and slaves, on the one hand, and between Christian slaves and Negroes or nonbelievers, on the other.

Here Epperson develops observations he made earlier: Slaves were rendered increasingly invisible on eighteenth-century plantations and their associated landscapes in Virginia (Epperson 1990). In mid-century, planters like George Mason and Thomas Jefferson imposed unified spatial grids on the plantations. At Gunston Hall, the landscape Mason had constructed could be appreciated only by the owner or by a privileged guest standing in the center of the front doorway; the formal gardens were built for his private enjoyment. Jefferson acquired a nearby hill so that everything that could be seen from Monticello was owned, controlled, and contrived by the owner. The two slaveholders had a shared aesthetic understanding: The world could only be truly understood from a single viewpoint, that of the plantation owner. In their materialization of this perspective, they rendered the slave quarters invisible. This allowed a vibrant slave culture to crystallize on the plantations out of the owners' sight. This culture flourished in spite of repeated efforts by the owners to discipline and control their slaves.

The manuals on plantation management, examined by James Delle, were attempts to teach the plantation owners and their overseers how to behave in order to discipline their slaves. These were incredibly practical polemics written by individuals who sought to guide and advise the slaveholders on how to best conduct their affairs in the exercise of power. Several of them contained detailed instructions for controlling sexuality, not only that of the enslaved women but also of the male overseers. This was important, they acknowledged, because enslaved women reproduced the labor force—a fact that would become increasingly more pressing after the slave trade was abolished in 1807. Controlling sexuality was also, of course, a means of avoiding what the owners viewed as disruptive social practices—for example, induced abortions or infanticide—or what the slaves must surely have seen as acts of violence—for example, rape by male overseers or the breakup of families.

The industrialization of the United States after the War of 1812 was a complex process. In the North it was linked with the rise of industrial capitalism. The capitalists purchased raw materials, the implements of production, and human labor power. The workers created value when they used the tools to transform the raw materials into commodities that were appropriated and sold by the capitalists. The development of industrial capitalism was impeded in New England as long as the local population retained control of the means of production; these conditions dissolved with the collapse of agricultural production in the region during the first half of the 1800s. Many of the first factory workers were young women from the countryside who were eager to escape the constraints of patriarchal relations, and male artisans with access to farmland who had flexible work schedules in the factories. The proletariat was enlarged when capitalist agricultural production dissolved, and its composition changed as the women employed as unskilled workers were gradually replaced by immigrants who accepted lower wages for the same work (Prude 1993; Siskind 1991). The rise of industrial capitalism in New York City and Philadelphia during the early nineteenth century did not involve increased mechanization and large manufactories. Much of the production occurred in firms that grew steadily in size and that intensified the division of labor and the practice of out-of-shop contracting for goods that were produced in workshops by heavily supervised debased artisans, each of whom performed a particular semiskilled task in the production process (Wilentz 1984, 107–44).

Industrialization had a different trajectory in the South during the early nineteenth century, as Paul Shackel and David Larsen show. It was based on industrial slavery, and slaveholders rather than capitalist entrepreneurs owned the industrial enterprises. The slaveholders used their own industrial slaves as well as slaves rented from plantation owners and farmers to toil in the their ironworks, textile factories, and gristmills. The structural difficulty with industrial slavery, as far as capitalist entrepreneurs bent on maximizing profits were concerned, was that the costs of maintaining the industrial slaves when they were not working were born entirely by the slave owner; they argued wage labor—*wage slavery,* as the industrial slaveholders called it—was economically more efficient (cheaper), because the workers bore the costs of reproducing themselves and their families when they were not working. In reality, they were arguing that the social costs associated with the reproduction of wage labor were lower than those associated with the reproduction of slaves.

Some southern industries employed both slaves and freemen, both black and white, in the same factory. In southern cities, like New Orleans, more than 60 percent of the free blacks were artisans or skilled workers; however, fewer than 10 percent of the free blacks in the North were employed as skilled workers. Shackel and Larsen survey the legal restrictions that were placed on black freemen, especially at work sites. They were prohibited from selling food and drink in St. Louis, from transporting agricultural goods in Maryland, or from engaging in artisanal trades. In Harpers Ferry, the development of the racially segregated, industrial workforce in the middle of the century preceded the appearance of racially segregated neighborhoods and housing. At the time, black and white workers not only lived in the same neighborhoods but occasionally also in the same boardinghouses. The formation of a racially segregated and stratified proletariat at Harpers Ferry, in which African Americans had access to low-wage occupations, paralleled the formation of a stratified workforce in the North, where women, children, and Irish immigrants from rural areas—constituting a large reserve army of labor—were slotted into and removed from low-wage positions, as Yankee men, increasingly separated from their means of production, were forced to seek wage labor.

Class formation accompanied the development of industrial capitalism in the northern United States during the mid-nineteenth century. It involved the polarization of the capitalist and working classes, the appearance of gaps be-tween skilled and unskilled members of the proletariat, and the emergence of unstable intermediary or middle layers—the middle class—composed of the manager, shopkeepers, ministers, artisans, and professionals who served as a buffer between the two primary classes of capitalist society. The middle classes were often able to avoid the economic dependency of the proletariat on the capitalists, and they were not subjected to the complete separation of home and workplace that the proletariat experienced when its members were forced to toil in factories outside their homes. The middle-class work ethic, stressing the attributes required by the owners of small stores and white-collar workers, stood in opposition to the daring and possessive individualism of the entrepreneur or the spontaneity of traditional working-class culture. While middle-class par-ents subsidized the education of their sons in order to allow them access to the emerging white-collar sectors of the economy, the bourgeoisie sponsored cul-tural institutions to educate the middle classes, to ensure that they would adopt cultural tastes and practices—attending the opera or visiting museums rather than frequenting saloons, music halls, or boxing matches—that would further isolate them from their working-class neighbors (Coontz 1988, 185–96; DiMaggio 1982a, 1982b).

A new gendered division of labor emerged within the middle classes and intensified the interdependency of husbands and wives. It has been called the cult of domesticity (Hewitt 1994). While middle-class men worked for wages or fees in the labor market, their wives produced clothing and provided a range of services like washing, cooking, and laundry. Middle-class women focused their energies on nurturing and socializing their children in order to prevent them from associating with their working-class peers, and to educate their sons for white-collar careers and their daughters for roles as mothers and educators. The women also organized the family's home entertainment and consumption. Diana diZerega Wall shows that, when women from the more affluent layers of New York City's middle class entertained professional and business acquaintances in their homes, they used more elegant porcelain and glassware at their dinner parties than less affluent middle-class families.

Stephen Mrozowski relates the formation of a managerial, middle class to the transformation of U.S. industry in the mid-nineteenth century. Increases in the size of factories—combined with the appearance of joint stock companies, piecework, improved record keeping, and new kinds of machinery—led to new forms of supervision and management (Clawson 1980, 167–201). Factory own-ers no longer managed and supervised the work site; instead, they employed an increasingly complex hierarchy of salaried agents, managers, and overseers who were their representatives at work sites in factory towns like Lowell, Massachusetts. The members of these industrial bureaucracies resided in housing that the company built near the factories. The size of the houses, combined with the materials used in their construction, reflected the place of their residents in the hierarchy. The mill agents at the top of the hierarchy resided in the large, elaborately appointed dwellings; overseers whose positions were near the bottom of the industrial hierarchy lived in houses that were significantly less elaborate than those of the agents and only slightly more substantial than the tenements occupied by the skilled workers or the boardinghouses where the unskilled workers resided. The consumption patterns of the overseers were also more similar to those of the skilled and unskilled workers than they were to those of the agents.

The industrial bureaucracies composed of overseers and managers played central roles in transforming the conditions of work on the factory floor and in undermining the craft system of production. The overseers ensured that both skilled and unskilled workers maintained reasonable paces of work and levels of output. The managers and overseers provided the workers with detailed instructions about what needed to be done, by dividing the production process into a succession of jobs and specifying what needed to be done by the workers at work station; this involved deskilling the labor force, replacing skilled artisans with unskilled workers who were trained to perform a limited task in the overall production process. More detailed and accurate records were required as the division of labor increased, piecework became more important, and the labor force as a whole was steadily deskilled. The deskilling of the workers went hand in hand with the mechanization of the production process. The new machines controlled both the operations and speed of production. They reinforced the division of labor and increased productivity, which meant that the owners were able to extract more relative surplus value from the workers. The new machines were typically operated by semiskilled or unskilled workers who could perform only a step or two in the production of the finished good.

Nineteenth-century capitalists, as Michael Nassaney and Marjorie Abel show, were very concerned with controlling their workforce both inside and outside the factory. By installing machines and reorganizing the shop floors, they transformed the production process into a series of standardized, repetitive tasks performed by deskilled workers who were effectively interchangeable with one another. By hiring young boys to perform certain tasks, the managers made use of the reserve army of labor to depress wages and increase their own control over production. By locating factories in rural environments away from cities and by creating built environments outside the factory—employee housing, company-owned stores, and churches—the companies sought to isolate their workers and to exert some degree of control over their activities outside the workplace. Needless to say, the overseers, however close they may have been to their working-class kin and neighbors, did not share those aspects of working-class culture that opposed and resisted the introduction of these changes by factory owners.

It is an old adage among historians that the victors always write history. This is evident in William Fawcett and Walter Lewelling's exposition, which shows how the participation of Shoshoni in the development of capitalist agriculture in Utah in the late nineteenth and early twentieth centuries has largely been erased from accounts based on official records. Anthropologists and historians who have relied on public records have reconstructed the pristine cultural past of the Shoshoni as they believed it was before the arrival of Europeans; in the process, they have also ignored archival data and written accounts by Native Americans that supplement oral traditions about the homesteaders, which indicate that some Shoshoni were farmers who produced for the market. Such reconstructions make indigenous peoples like the Shoshoni far more homogenous than they actually were, thereby stripping them of large parts of their history and culture and of one role they played in the historical development of the contemporary social formation.

Warren Perry focused on popular and scholarly accounts that sought to explain social transformations and the rise of the Zulu state in southern Africa during the nineteenth century. This is another instance in which those accounts that are popular among European settlers and local African elites fail to consider critical pieces of information. The settler model, which underpins most current explanations, asserts (1) that South African society was composed of a number of discrete ethnic groups in the late eighteenth century; (2) that the systemic contact between them was poorly developed; and (3) that the political turmoil which erupted in the area that would become the Zulu heartland resulted from various internal conditions and processes—for example, the scarcity of grazing land and population pressure promoted warfare among the inhabitants of the area, led to the migration of weaker groups, and promoted trade. What these accounts either minimize or ignore altogether is European participation in the events of the nineteenth century—specifically, their involvement in the processes of primitive accumulation and slave raiding. White settlers are attracted to the settler model because it absolves them of any responsibility for the disruption that occurred in the nineteenth century; the Zulu elite appreciates the settler model because it freezes forever a single moment in what must have been a continually shifting, hierarchically organized set of social relations—a moment in which the Zulu state was the dominant polity in the region.

Theresa Singleton and Mark Bograd provide a third instance in which scholars, this time archaeologists working in roughly the last third of the twentieth century, have either overlooked or minimized the significance of a particular kind of information: colonoware pottery. At issue are two questions: Did the African slaves who were imported to eastern North America arrive with certain cultural traditions and practices—that is, pottery making—intact? Or, were these practices disrupted as a result of the crossing? For some archaeologists, colonoware was manufactured by slaves; it therefore provides evidence of plantation life and supports the view that African cultural practices were not completely dismantled by the crossing. For those who believe that colonoware was manufacture by Native Americans, the fragments recovered from plantations say little about whether or not African cultural traditions were disrupted by the crossing; however, they do point to exchange between native groups and plantation slaves. That colonoware was manufactured and used by both African slave and Native Americans allows one to pose new questions—for example, about the existence and significance of maroon communities in eastern North America during the eighteenth and nineteenth centuries—that could not have been raised as long as the evidence could only be viewed in dichotomous terms.

The essays in this volume reveal diverse moments in the rise of capitalist civilization, both in Western Europe and in settler colonies, like the United States. They imply a good deal about imperialism both as a process of colonial expansion which involved the formation of political and economic linkages with metropolitan countries, and as economic relations that involved overseas markets and investment opportunities in countries whose dominant modes of production were not capitalist. Consequently, they raise again the issue that was debated by John Hobson and Rudolf Hilferding, on the one hand, and Rosa Luxemburg, on the other. Was imperialism a particular form of capitalist society that transformed social relations both at home and abroad, as Hobson (1965, 81) and Hilferding (1981, 322) claimed? Or, was capitalism a social form that could only develop and *exist* in an environment where noncapitalist forms exist to serve its ends, as Luxemburg (1951, 368) claimed?

The essays should also force us to examine carefully the assertions of today's globalization theorists, who claim that, since the top-down dismantling of the USSR and the communist states in Eastern Europe, all of the world's peoples are becoming enmeshed in capitalist market relations, and that the world itself will soon be a capitalist one shaped increasingly by narrowly conceived neoliberal market practices and decreasingly by the policies and practices of nation states. The essays provide contradictory evidence—the kind traditionally ignored by groups that view themselves as being in the driver's seat—to such claims. The evidence examined by the authors suggests that the interconnected rise of capitalism, colonialism, and imperialism did not produce the king of cultural and political-economic homogeneity predicted and prophesied by the globalization theorists, but rather that these processes produced instead historically contingent diversity in which peoples living at different times in different places labored and even succeeded at times in making their own history in milieu shaped by preexisting sets of property relations and class circumstances that simultaneously constrained their actions and afforded them opportunities for charting new courses.

NOTE

The arguments outlined in this paper have profited from the insights of James Delle, Terrence Epperson, Colleen O'Neill, Robert Paynter, and Karen Spalding.

REFERENCES CITED

Brenner, Robert. 1985. The Agrarian Roots of European Capitalism. In *The Brenner Debate: Agrarian Class Structure and Economic Development in Pre-Industrial Europe,* ed. T. H. Aston and C. H. E. Philpin, 213–327. Cambridge: Cambridge Univ. Press.

Clastres, Pierre. 1987. *Society against the State.* Cambridge, Mass.: MIT Press.

Clawson, Dan. 1980. *Bureaucracy and the Labor Process: The Transformation of U.S. Industry, 1860–1920.* New York: Monthly Review Press.

Coontz, Stephanie. 1988. *The Social Origins of Private Life: A History of American Families, 1600–1900.* London: Verso.

DiMaggio, Paul. 1982a. Cultural Entrepreneurship in Nineteenth-Century Boston. Pt. 2, The Classification and Framing of American Art. *Media, Culture, and Society* 4 (4): 303–22.

———. 1982b. Cultural Entrepreneurship in Nineteenth-Century Boston: The Creation of an Organization Base for High Culture in America. *Media, Culture, and Society* 4 (1): 33–50.

Epperson, Terrence. 1990. Race and the Disciplines of the Plantation. *Historical Archaeology* 24 (4): 29–36.

———. 1991. "To Fix a Perpetual Brand": The Social Construction of Race in Virginia, 1675–1750. Ph.D. diss., Dept. of Anthropology, Temple University, Philadelphia, Pa.

———. 1994. The Politics of Empiricism and the Construction of Race as an Analytical Category. *Transforming Anthropology* 5 (1–2): 15–19.

————. 1998. Critical Race Theory and the Archaeology of the African Diaspora. Paper presented at the annual meeting of the Society for Historical Archaeology, Atlanta, Ga.

Fox-Genovese, Elizabeth, and Eugene D. Genovese. 1983. *Fruits of Merchant Capital: Slavery and Bourgeois Property in the Rise and Expansion of Capitalism*. New York: Oxford Univ. Press.

Haldon, John. 1993. *The State and the Tributary Mode of Production*. London: Verso.

Hewitt, Nancy. 1994. Beyond the Search for Sisterhood: American Women's History in the 1980s. In *Unequal Sisters: A Multicultural Reader in U.S. Women's History*, ed. V. L. Ruiz and E. C. DuBois, 1–19. New York: Routledge.

Hilferding, Rudolf. 1981 [1910]. *Finance Capital: A Study of the Latest Phase of Capitalist Development*. London: Routledge and Kegan Paul.

Hobson, John A. 1965 [1902]. *Imperialism: A Study*. Ann Arbor: Univ. of Michigan Press.

Luxemburg, Rosa. 1951 [1913]. *The Accumulation of Capital*. London: Routledge and Kegan Paul.

Marx, Karl. 1977 [1849]. Wage Labour and Capital. In *Karl Marx and Fredrick Engels, Collected Works*. Vol. 9. New York: International Publishers.

Patterson, Thomas C. 1991. *The Inca Empire: The Formation and Disintegration of a Precapitalist State*. Oxford: Berg.

————. 1997. *Inventing Western Civilization*. New York: Monthly Review Press.

Powers, Karen V. 1995. *Andean Journeys: Migration, Ethnogenesis, and the State in Colonial Quito*. Albuquerque: Univ. of New Mexico Press.

Prude, Jonathan. 1983. *The Coming of Industrial Order: Town and Factory Life in Rural Massachusetts, 1810–1860*. Cambridge: Cambridge Univ. Press.

Siskind, Janet. 1991. Class Discourse in an Early-Nineteenth-Century New England Factory. *Dialectical Anthropology* 16 (1): 35–50.

Spalding, Karen. 1973. *Kurakas* and Commerce: A Chapter in the Evolution of Andean Society. *Hispanic American Historical Review* 53 (4): 581–99.

————. 1984. *Huarochirí: An Andean Society under the Inca and Spanish Rule*. Stanford, Calif.: Stanford Univ. Press.

————. 1998. Constructing Indians. Yale Latin American Studies 1. New Haven, CT: Latin American Studies Center, Yale Univ.

Tracy, James D., ed. 1990. *The Rise of Merchant Empires: Long-Distance Trade in the Early Modern World, 1350–1750*. Cambridge: Cambridge Univ. Press.

Vinces Vives, Jaime. 1969. *An Economic History of Spain*. Princeton, N.J.: Princeton Univ. Press.

Wilentz, Sean. 1983. *Chants Democratic: New York City and the Rise of the American Working Class, 1788–1850*. New York: Oxford Univ. Press.

CONTRIBUTORS

MARJORIE R. ABEL teaches anthropology at the University of Massachusetts–Amherst.

MARK BOGRAD was formerly curator at Lowell National Historical Park in Lowell.

JAMES A. DELLE is assistant professor of anthropology at Franklin and Marshall College.

TERRENCE W. EPPERSON teaches anthropology at Temple University.

WILLIAM B. FAWCETT is assistant professor of anthropology in the Department of Sociology, Social Work and Anthropology at Utah State University.

ROSS W. JAMIESON teaches anthropology at Trent University in Peterborough, Ontario.

DAVID L. LARSEN is a training specialist for both the National Park Service and the U.S. Fish and Wildlife Service.

WALTER ROBERT LEWELLING is a graduate student in the American Studies Department at Utah State University in Logan.

PATRICIA HART MANGAN teaches anthropology at Mount Holyoke College in South Hadley, Massachusetts.

STEPHEN A. MROZOWSKI is associate professor at the University of Massachusetts–Boston and director of the Andrew Fiske Memorial Center for Archaeological Research.

MICHAEL S. NASSANEY is associate professor of anthropology at the University of Western Michigan.

THOMAS C. PATTERSON is professor of anthropology at Temple University.

ROBERT PAYNTER is professor of anthropology at the University of Massachusetts–Amherst.

WARREN PERRY is associate professor in the Anthropology Department of Central Connecticut State University, in New Britain, Connecticut.

PAUL A. SHACKEL is associate professor of anthropology at the University of Maryland–College Park.

THERESA A. SINGLETON is associate professor of anthropology at Syracuse University and curator at the Smithsonian Institute.

DIANA diZEREGA WALL is associate professor of anthropology at City College of New York.

INDEX

Abortion, 172, 175
Africa, southern, 78–99
African Americans: and
    colonoware, 6–8; disenfranchise-
    ment under industrialism, 26;
    exclusion from occupations, 26–
    27, 29, 31, 34, 35; as free laborers
    in Harpers Ferry, 32–33; and
    material culture, 9; relations
    with whites, 29–30, 34; and
    skilled work, 27–28
Appleton Corporation , 284–85
Austen, Jane, 109

Balcarres Plantation, Jamaica, 169,
    179, 181, 185–86
Bantu, 80
Bear River Massacre, 42–43
Bear River, Utah, 40, 44
Beecher, Catherine, 120, 265; advice
    on dishes, 23
Bentham, Jeremy, 58, 260
Blue Mountains, Jamaica, 169, 171
Bluff Plantation, S.C., 11
Boardinghouses, 266, 315; in Lowell,
    284; in Turners Falls, 262–67
Boott Cotton Mills, 277; ceramics
    from, 288, 290–92; personal
    items from, 297
Boston Associates, 279
Botetourt, Lord, 16
Bourbon dynasty, 213–14
Bourdieu, Pierre, 110, 135

Breakfast, material culture associ-
    ated with, 120–21

Cachaulo *estancia*, 148–53; archaeo-
    logical testing at, 152; described,
    149–53; rendering of, 149
Caciques, 308; women as, 145
Capitalism: Agrarian, 44; coexisting
    with Feudalism, 209; and
    colonialism, 307; and disciplinary
    institutions, 58; and discipline,
    262; emerging in Latin America,
    143; and exploitation of labor,
    208–9; and gendered division of
    labor, 144–45; and historical
    archaeology, xvi–xxii, 278–79,
    298–99; and the household, 266;
    and imperialism, 307; industrial,
    145, 258–59; managerial, 278–81;
    —, defined, 279; mercantile v.
    agricultural, xv–xvi; and planta-
    tion slavery, 310–13; as political
    economy, xiv–xv; and redefinition
    of spatial forms, 231–32; rise of,
    307; transition from Feudalism,
    208–10; as a type of civilization,
    317; and urbanization, 209
Carter, "King," 12
Catalonia, Spain, 309–10; and
    development of monocrop
    agriculture, 214–15; and rise of
    Capitalism, 215, 309–10
Catawbas, and colonoware, 15–16

Cattle, as social markers, 92–93
Cattle enclosures, 92–94
Ceramics, and class, 287–93; and
    gender, 120–30; uses of, 288–89
Charles II, King of Spain, 213
Charlottesville, Va., 73
Chocolate, 159
Class: and ceramics, 287–93; and
    fluidity, 281–83; formation of,
    313–14; and historical archaeol-
    ogy, xvii–xviii; and material
    culture, 276, 287–98; —, ceram-
    ics, 287–93; —, personal items,
    294–97; —, smoking pipes, 293–
    94; relations between, 278; and
    other social categories, 281
Class consciousness, 281–82
Class struggle, 259, 262
Clem, 64–65
Clydesdale Plantation, Jamaica, 195
Coconuts, 159, 309
Coffee plantations, 168–97; archaeo-
    logical testing of, 188–90; layout
    of, 190–93
Collins Axe Company, 259
Colonialism, 317–18; impact on
    southern Africa, 83–84; Spanish,
    161, 308–9
Colonoware, xxi–xxii, 3–19; and
    African Americans, 6–8, 11–15;
    defined, 4; and European
    Americans, 9; as intercultural
    artifact, 10–17; and Native
    Americans, 4–8, 15–16; use and
    manufacture, 317
Cuenca, Ecuador, 146–62, 309
Cultural resource management, xii
Cutlery industry, 239–69; artifacts
    of manufacturing process, 248–
    51; history of, 243–47; mechani-
    zation of, 240–41; processes of
    manufacture, 243–44

Deagan, Kathleen, 142, 161
Deetz, James, and colonoware, 6

Denmark Vessey Rebellion, 25
Dick, 64–65
Dinner, material culture associated
    with, 121
Discipline, 262
Domesticity, and material culture,
    120–21
Domination and resistance, 60
Drayton Hall Plantation, 5

English immigrants, 255, 256
European settlers: in the Great Basin,
    42; in southern Africa, 80–82; and
    violence, 84
European Trade Goods, 96–97

Factory design, 242, 259–60;
    accommodating agrarian
    culture, 261; and efficiency of
    production, 260; extended to
    domestic sphere, 262; in Harpers
    Ferry, 29; and labor discipline,
    253–54, 260–61; masking social
    relations, 261–62; and the
    panopticon, 58
Feudalism, 206–8
Foucault, Michele, 59–69
Frederick, Christine, 265
French-Canadian immigrants, 256

Gender: defined, xvii–xix, 168–69;
    and division of labor, 257, 314;
    and historical archaeology, xviii–
    xx; and material culture, 169; and
    occupation, 178–80; and planta-
    tion space, 193–97; and power,
    188–97; and sexuality, 169; as
    structuring principle, 169
German immigrants, 31, 114, 255, 256
Great Trek, 84
Gunston Hall Plantation, 58–74;
    described, 61–63; gardens at, 61;
    as landscape of power, 73; optical
    illusions created by landscape,
    62–63; and panopticism, 59–60

Managers, *cont.*
culture, 280; as new class, 279; place in social hierarchy, 282
Martins Hill Plantation, Jamaica, 169, 177–78, 179, 181, 186, 187
Mason, George, 59, 310; and Thomas Locke, 72–73
Mason, John, 61–63, 64–65
Material Culture: and class, 276–77, 287–98; —, personal items, 294–97; —, smoking pipes, 293–94; and domesticity, 120–21; and entertainment, 121–22; and gender, 169; and middle-class, 280; multivalent, 52; and power, 143; of Spanish colonial elites, 157–58
Mavis Bank Plantation, Jamaica, 193
McEwan, Bonnie, 142
Mechanization, 258
Merrimack Corporation, 284
Mfecane/Difaqane: archaeology of sites related to, 85–99; defined, 78; demography of, 87–90; explanations for cause, 79–85; as masking of European colonialism, 84; rank-size relation of sites related to, 94–96; as result of European colonialism, 83–84; and trade, 82–83; Zulucentric explanation for, 79
Middle-class: homes in Greenwich Village, 116–19; and ideology of domesticity, 120; material culture associated with, ceramics, 124–30; —, glassware, 131–34; spectrum of, 110–11; —, and material culture, 120, 134–36; urban, defined, 111; women, 281; —, and Gothic style, 112; women's roles, 111–12
Mita system, 147, 148
Montalto, purchased by Jefferson, 68
Montblanc, Catalonia, 205–32, 310; built environment of, 205–6, 215–31; extramural house forms, 224–

31; history of, 210–15; house classes defined, 215–17; and relations of inequality, 206; renovation of houses, 222–24; spatial uses in, 217–18; towers as domestic space, 218–22
Monticello, 58–74; construction of, 66–68; gardens at, 70; as landscape of power, 73; and modern development, 73–74; observation towers at, 68–60; and panopticism, 59–60, 66–68; slavery at, 70
Mormons, 41, 44; relations with Native Americans, 53–54; and settlement of Great Basin, 42; and Shoshoni converts, 44
Mount Vernon, Va.,10, 12, 13
Mulberry Row slave quarters, 70

Nat Turner's Rebellion, 25
National Park Service, 285
National Register of Historic Places, 52
Native Americans (*see also* Catawbas, Pamunkeys, Shoshoni): and colonoware, 4–8; destruction of resources by Euro-Americans, 42, 43; and Historical archaeology, 50; and Homestead Acts, 40, 46; and Mormonism (LDS), xxiii, 40–41; Pamunkeys, 15–16

Orser, Charles, and colonoware, 6
Ottogary, Willie, 46–49, 52–54; photo of, 48
Oudepost I, 86

Page, Mann I, 12
Page, Mann II, 12–13
Pamunkeys, and colonoware, 15–16
Panopticon, 260; defined, 58–59; and factory design, 58
Panopticon, or The Inspection House, 58

Slavery, *cont.*
—, and childbirth, 172, 174, 176, 184–87; —, and childrearing, 173–74; —, as contested term, 17–18; —, impact on southern Africa, 99; —, at Monticello, 70; —, resistance to, 64–65; —, slave raiding, 84; —, urban, 14; —, wage, 25
Smithsonian Institution, 10, 17
Society for Historical Archaeology, xi
Sotho-Tswana, 80
Springfield, Mass., 28, 243
St. Augustine, Fla., 142,161
Surveillance, by the Church, 144
Surveillance technologies, 22, 253
Swaziland, 85; archaeology of sites in, 87
Symington, Major John, 29

Tea, 281
Tea parties, material culture associated with, 121
Tetanus, 172
Thomas Jefferson Memorial Foundation, 73
Thompson, E .P., xvii, 283
Town designs, Spanish colonial, 155–57
Transnationalism, 239
Tremonton, Utah, 40, 44
Tumipampa, 155–56; appropriation by Spanish, 155–56

Turners Falls, Mass., 240, 246, 256, 262
Typologies, 3–4, 8

University of Cape Town, 85
Urbanization, 209

Vanderhost family, 14

Wallerstein, Immanuel, xv
Watt, 65
Wolf, Eric, xv–xvi
Women: and agency, 266–67; as caciques,145; and economic power as widows, 145; and labor in Turners Falls, 266–67; and material culture, 142, 109–11, 161; and middle-class, 281; and traditional Spanish restrictions, 145
Worcester, Mass., 262
Workers (*see also* labor): enslaved at Gunston Hall, 64–65; surveillance of, 28–29
Works Progress Administration, 8

Zaruma, Ecuador, 145, 309
Zulu state: effects on southern Africa, 80; and European imperialism, 316–17; rise of, 78, 79, 84–85; —, and archaeology, 86–87
The Zulu Aftermath, 82

Lines that Divide was designed and typeset on a Macintosh computer system using PageMaker software. The text is set in Minion and the chapter openings are set in Smaragd. This book was designed by Angela Stanton-Anderson, typeset by Kimberly Scarbrough, and manufactured by Thomson-Shore, Inc. The recycled paper used in this book is designed for an effective life of at least three hundred years.